All About Pressing in Soccer

Laco Borbély | Jaroslav Hřebík | Peter Ganczner | Andi Singer

ALL ABOUT PRESSING IN SOCCER

HISTORY. THEORY. PRACTICE.

Meyer & Meyer Sport

British Library Cataloguing in Publication Data
A catalogue record for this book is available from the British Library

Originally published as *All About Pressing in Football–On the axis: History, Theory, Practice* by Slovakian Football Coaches Association (UFTS), 2017

All About Pressing in Soccer
Maidenhead: Meyer & Meyer Sport (UK) Ltd., 2018
ISBN 978-1-78255-147-8

Auckland, Beirut, Dubai, Hägendorf, Hong Kong, Indianapolis, Cairo, Cape Town, Manila, Maidenhead, New Delhi, Singapore, Sydney, Teheran, Vienna
Member of the World Sport Publishers' Association (WSPA)
www.w-s-p-a.org

Printed by: Print Consult GmbH, Munich, Germany

ISBN 978-1-78255-147-8
Email: info@m-m-sports.com
www.m-m-sports.com

CONTENTS

PART 3

THE AUTHORS' OVERTURE

This monothematic elaboration on pressing in soccer is the result of team cooperation, with the plain ambition to provide the reader with not only an encyclopedic knowledge on this theme but also a historical context for the development of this frequently used defensive-game instrument up to the present day. Based on its genesis within the game, we have tried to illustrate the general and specific theoretical aspects of this defensive-game instrument. Since our ambition has reached all the way from the pitch and to the soccer match, we have also dealt with practical topics concerning practice, improvement, and the application of pressing in the game.

This publication is a collective work, and it follows up the series of publications oriented toward the tactical-play analyses of the basic phases of play. In particular, the books Defensive Modernism, Offensive Modernism, and Attacking of the Whole Team I and II served as a conceptual platform for us in order to profile pressing problems in modern soccer. In connection with this, we would like to point out mainly the publication Defensive Modernism (1998). Nineteen years ago, in the special chapter of this publication titled Pressing Theory and Pressing Practice, we illustrated many thematic groups concerning this issue. We decided to draw information from the forementioned publication, offer it in a new and revised form, and adapt it to contemporary requirements.

The outcome of this effort, by Slovakian and Czech authors, is the first Czechoslovakian trilogy of pressing, *All About Pressing in Soccer,* which, with its format as a "recipe book," enables its readers not only to dive deeply into the present issue but also to understand the basic principles of this modern defensive instrument. This publication will also help active coaches clarify this issues' historical continuity, basic theory, methodology, and practice for direct use in the team.

During the interpretation of the strategic and tactical aspects of the issue, we sometimes helped ourselves with the analogies from the Art of War. As it has been established for the military campaign, the same goes for the soccer match. There is a confrontation between two parties, two teams in time and space. The convergence of competitive motives is very similar, and the space for the confrontation is based on the same principles. Moreover, Sun Tzu understood his Art of War in a timeless and universal manner, meaning that the strategic-tactical consequence, concerning the confrontational model of two fighting parties, can be transmitted to the concept of two opposing parties. The one who acknowledges the tactical timelessness of the fight between two teams on the pitch would be inspired by this ancient Chinese Art of War, which, in connection with theoretical features of the game, can create an effective base for tactical-play timelessness. This does not apply only to soccer. If we compare it to other areas of the peoples' activities, it is hard to imagine a successful politician without the adoption of some fundamental Machiavelli rules and such things. A coach can't be successful in professional soccer if there is a lack of elemental strategic-tactical knowledge of the game.

Laco Borbély – Jaroslav Hrebík – Peter Ganczner – Andi Singer

PART 1

HOW IT ALL BEGAN—
HISTORICAL ROOTS OF PRESSING

FOREWORD TO PART 1

It was an autumn rainy day in London on November 25, 1953. The Wembley Stadium was packed by 105,000 spectators. England was hosting Hungary in an international match, which had already been referred by the British press as "the match of the century." Nobody had been able to even guess how shaken the cradle of the soccer would be and how much would one match change the conception of soccer and release more significant evolution of the tactic.

You are getting in your hand a book that will not be describing the course of the match that took place in Wembley in 1953 but will be a guidance in the element, which we can't imagine soccer without. Pressing has become an element of soccer game. It has also become soccer's exceptional activation symbol, a mark of the team's quality and harmony, and a strong sign of collectivism, which doesn't represent an enforcement of any ideology, however, without which it's impossible to achieve any success.

The meaning of pressing was strengthened during the period of total soccer in the Netherlands when Kubrick's *Clockwork Orange* got from film to soccer awareness because Michelson characterized in the most explicit way the sophisticated system of blending the differences between defense and attack. It was a sketch that was transferred from Cruyff's soccer canvas to next generations into his own Barcelona Dream Team from early '90s all the way to majestic team of his protégé Pep Guardiola in 2008–2012.

You can scroll through history the way it was written by pressing itself and its big visionaries. These visionaries were and are not only coaches whose showcases are packed with trophies but also coaches whose work is still reflected after years and whose experiments with nonorthodox methods moved the game forward. There probably wouldn't be great Lobanovskyi without less famous Maslov; there wouldn't be many great coaches in Italy without magicians such as Rocco, Herrera, or later Sacchi, and we wouldn't experience a deluge of excellent Argentinian contemporary coaches without Marcelo Bielsa.

We don't recognize soccer philosophy as an exact science; it doesn't have its Plato, from whose work we could derive everything. Soccer has plenty shades and philosophers.

Marcel Merčiak at the soccer temple in Brazilian Maracana during World Cup 2014

There are many people who consider the team of Brazil at the World Championship in 1970 in Mexico as the best team in history. The Brazilian team brought to the top the classical soccer era, which was dominated by attack and improvisation. One of the most famous players "White Pele" Tostao said about the huge triumph: "People think that jogo bonito is only about creativity, improvisation, dribbling, and tricks. In the year 1970, we were good because we were sure we have nothing to lose if we improvise. We didn't create problems to each other with this. In order to have a beautiful game, you need appropriate players and team." It has always been and always will be this way. "In fact, soccer is an easy game; the most complicated part of it is to play it in a simple manner," said once Johan Cruyff. The ones who were looking for simplicity in the most various executions were moving pressing as a part of the soccer strategy to the borders of today's soccer form. This book is dedicated to those who carried their visions beyond the borders of their times and were able to assemble a perfect team from perfect players.

–*Marcel Merčiak*
Sports commentator R1VS

1.1 DIAGNOSIS OF PRESSING, OR WHY, HOW, AND WHEN TO APPLY PRESSING IN SOCCER

Why Pressing?

Modern-day soccer is a game that takes about ninety to hundred minutes to play. The players attempt to keep the ball or gain possession of the ball through sophisticated tactical game concepts for the two basic phases of play (attacking and defending) and for the two transitional phases (transition to attack and transition to defense). These phases follow each other at a certain pace, on the border of actual physiological options of the organism. It seems that nowadays most of the soccer teams with the highest level of defensive performance have achieved the level where the implementation of a supra active form of defense (the use of different forms of pressing) is a more or less automatic, unstudied (natural) process and possibly a necessary prerequisite for achieving successful results in modern soccer. From a historical approach, the fact that pressing has developed into its contemporary form can be attributed to the evolutionary changes in the game itself. Soccer has gradually moved (within the framework of the use of defensive concepts such as the zone defense) to the highest limit of defensive intensity, which is consistent with the principle of proactive defense (the internal driving force or "engine" of a proactive defense). This means that the defensive team does not wait for their opponent's offensive activity. Immediately after losing the ball, the defensive team decidedly limits the spatial aspect (the spatial limits set by active defensive positioning that will influence the direction and progress of the opponent's offensive action) of their opponents' offensive game, through the use of directed resistance (pressuring the ball) with the immediate effect of reducing the quality of offensive play. If we want to define this boost in the development of defensive play, we can say that there has been a transition from a reactive mode of defense to a proactive one and from defensive reaction to defensive proaction. Over the last fifty years, the features of proactive defense have appeared repeatedly but not in such a systematic form as we can see nowadays in major soccer teams.

In addition to spatial movement strategies, when using a spatial defense, the special group-tactical approach to active defense, known as pressing, is used. In the context of spatial defense, pressing can be considered the most active, and the most aggressive (as accepted by the rules), form of defensive activity that can be used in any part of the game area. For this reason, pressing represents the highest level of defensive activity that is demonstrated through a proactive defense, which is based on the proactive defensive principle.

Statistical analysis of soccer confirms the increasing number of ball repossessions in the offensive zone; this takes into account that nowadays more than half of the scored goals are achieved by teams in the aforementioned "Offensive restart" (the regaining of ball possession in the offensive zone). The success of scoring goals using the previously mentioned tactics is seven times higher than in the defensive zone. This confirms the justification of using pressing in the defensive aspect of soccer tactics. The resulting statistics, as stated above, show that pressing can be a distinctive part of the progress of game quality.

The Evolution of Soccer

In fair play, as should be the case in soccer, the natural rule, according to which only the best will succeed, is valid. Darwin's theory of evolution can be applied to soccer. In this case, as a reflection of the natural adaptation of human existence to its conditions for survival, only the strongest and fastest and especially those who can adapt to their environment—the soccer environment—will survive. Although the soccer environment is constantly changing, the game itself is changing as well; this becomes a natural part of evolutionary progress. A quick "retro-analysis" of the soccer environment should start when soccer came into existence as a ball game. Soccer, as with any type of entertainment, game, or competition, has its rules, goals, plot, and game objectives but also limitations that provide some "fair" competitive rules for its participants. When it was originated, soccer had these mentioned attributes as well. The hidden and relatively stable parts of soccer are the game rules that can only be changed by consent; in order to help improve the environment of the game and to improve the performance of the game itself. The changes that soccer has gone through from its beginnings are key points for us. These changes can reveal the rules that soccer has followed over its history. We are persuaded that pressing is a natural part of the game, and this is the reason we are trying to outline (through this short historical reconstruction) the process of its formation up to its current form. We would also like to give the reader an idea of the chronological order of crucial elements, which has determined its development and tendency.

Pressing As an "Innate Diagnosis" of Soccer (Coded by the Confrontational "Gene" in Its DNA)

The point of a soccer game lies in its interactive character and confrontational principle. The fact that there are two teams simultaneously occupying the field of play (one offensive unit, one defensive unit, and only one ball) enables the use of team-oriented tactics in order to regain the object of the game (the ball); this represents the expression of defensive team synergy. The spontaneous presence of the signs of pressing and its different isolated features, forms, and elements can be added to its interactive and confrontational character. These attributes (confrontation, coordination, and teamwork) are present in all of these games, from their origin, and they are integral to them. We can say that the confrontation aspect of the game stimulated the use of different spontaneous forms of pressure (at first, unrestrainedpressure) to be exerted on the opponent with possession of the subject of the game. Pressure is the general manifestation of the desire to regain possession of the ball and possessing the ball (ball magnetism). Pressure, as the "child" of confrontation, naturally occurred in all developmental stages of soccer, independently of the stages of time frame. At first, different forms of soccer were established sporadically, then more often and more thoughtfully. Soccer was even forbidden for some time, because pressuring was very aggressive, and it exceeded the limits of acceptability. Soccer literally became a dangerous game.

When formulating the objectives of the game, the "authors" of soccer tried to generate direct pressure on the ball. This fact started and accelerated confrontation: first through the determination of the variable parameters of the game (the players, ball, field of play, game area

where the goals are placed) and afterward by creating the organizational framework of the game, including the objectives of the game (the game rules). Reaching the objective of the game (to score by putting the ball into the opponent's goal) is possible only by the subject of play—the ball. Confrontation, fighting for the ball (pressuring and different forms of pressuring the player with the ball) were encrypted into the game by the "founders," respectively the authors who agreed on the initial rules of the game. Soccer came into the world with the immanent "gene," the innate "diagnosis," pressuring. Pressuring is the "natural" form of pressing in its most general sense.

Pressing As the Need for Pressure

Pressure is the natural form that enables the achievement of the goal of the game—victory. The enforcement of the partial intention and the global aim of effectively breaking the resistance of the opponent are possible only through the use of a certain form of pressure and force. Soccer has been endowed with competitiveness. The one who "pushes" harder, more persistently, more actively, more intensively, more systematically, with more organization, and with the enforcement of his will and intention to win, will finally achieve victory.

Pressing and Putting the Offense and Defense on Equal Footing

In soccer, since a long time ago, the natural form of offense has dominated. A strong proportion of offense over defense will disrupt the offensive-defensive balance of the game in favor of the offense. In a historical context, as the pyramid of the basic formation changed (the 1:9 system changed to the 9:1 system), the opinions for the roles of the players in these basic formations changed. At first, there were highly specialized defensive players on one side and players who concentrated mostly the offensive on the other side. At the beginning of its development, soccer "entered" into this era; a division of the players, based on close cooperation, dominated (defensive players and important, highly valued offensive players). This meant that in the initial "game concept," there were players responsible for preventing their opponents from scoring, and, vice versa, there were other players (offensive players) whose main task was to score goals. The reason for the implementation of this narrow specialization of players was the fact that the playing area was "too long." What's more, soccer was influenced by the concept that it was impossible for the defender to shoot goals and the left or right wing prevented the opponents from scoring except at their own goal line. Defensive and offensive players were simply too far away from each other and far away from the opposite goal. It seemed that such a strict functional differentiation of the players was the only and the best solution. Everybody did his intended "job" on the pitch. This style of play was done with the highest possible ratio of effort, activity, and enthusiasm. All-out attacks "tolerated" the failures of offensive players when they were playing defense. After losing the ball, the exhausted offensive players didn't apply a comparable level of play when playing defense. Their aim was to make a goal whereas after losing the ball, they recovered their energy for the next offensive play.

At that time, the active play area was extended between the penalty boxes. Till now, the slang expression, "between soccer boxes," was used for the evaluation of this sterile way of play. At the time when the WM formation originated, its primary strategic goal was to reach an equal balance in player function, on the basis of defender-offender.

In the basic formation, the letter "W" represented five mostly offensive players, and the letter "M" represented players who were specialized for defense. Initially, crossing the thin center spot was like a knife through butter. The fate of matches was often decided by an overwhelming number of offensive players not defensive players. Today we witness the opposite, which goals are scored, almost on the principle of an underwhelming number of offensive players. In the past, this phenomenon was also reflected in the results. At that time, there was often a two-digit combined score, such as 8:5. (In the match of the century, England—Hungary, both matches combined resulted in seventeen goals scored, combining the results, 6:3 and 7:1, in favor of the brilliant Hungarian players).

Diagnosis of pressing and its confrontational "mycelium" (two teams, one ball, confrontation, pressure, urging, pressing):

1. Intentional organized pressing

2. Spontaneous unrestrained pressing

3. Active pressure as the unique and effective form exerted on the opponent who owns the subject of the game

4. Confrontation, the continual fight for the ball during the game

5. Experimenting by means of confrontation

Universalism and the "Totalization" of the Game

Universalism and game "totalization" meant that both of the basic phases of all the players began to move from the existing division of player activity to a system where defensive players took on an offensive role while gradually increasing their defensive repertoire. The intersection of universalism with the existing game concepts led to increasing demands on the players. They couldn't "take a rest" in the course of the "reversed" phase of the game. The "equalization" of the players resulted in vigorous universalism, with its "Mount Everest" being Total Soccer. Universalism changed soccer forever.

It pulled down the inviolable tactical myths of this time. It overcame the barriers of traditional and conservative prejudice in soccer tactics. Spreading the mantel of the player's activity enabled the players to hit the maximum of their universality in a biunique, offensive-defensive understanding of their roles in the game. It enabled the inventive and emotional "growth" of the players; although, at the beginning, they could see universalism as an extra duty. In fact, it was about the broadening of the "self-realization" space for all eleven players of the team. Because of the "equalization" of the players, followed by the vigorous penetration of universalism into the game concepts of soccer, the imaginary bonds of the players were broken. These bonds limited their real potential, possibilities, and abilities. Why, because until that time, the traditionally applied and preferred tactical models of the game contained limits and restrictions, which slowed down, repressed, and "hid" the potentially higher, but "deep-lying" powerful offensive assertiveness of the individual players for a long time. For "tactical" reasons, the players often weren't able to use the aforementioned active mode of play together with a high level of "involvement" and activity in both phases of the game. This was true not only for the individual players but also for the whole team, and, what's more, this was also true in terms of synergy.

The "Liberalization" of Soccer

This refers to the transitional form leading to the predominant zone defense with a strong orientation toward the ball. Universalism liberalized soccer at an unprecedented level, and it brought a new space-time perception, the exchange of player functions, zone shifting, and rotational maneuvers between formations. And most importantly, the players were able to direct themselves at the ball. This change in how defense was approached partially repressed elements of one to one defense and for the first time it opened the door to the gradual transition to zonal defense. The training process was focused on the continuous increase of fitness parameters that resulted directly from the more universal perception of the division of labor between the players. All this can be considered a big step in the formation of the intentional forms of pressing on the soccer pitch. All the players began playing defense and offense—maybe not at the same time, but in total soccer, this was joined to total offense and defense. The slogan was, "We all do everything." This slogan is still used in soccer.

Defensive Reaction Is Replaced by "Action"

The analogical "defensive term" collocating with "offensive action" is still missing from the professional literature. The answer to the question of why the term "offensive action" still hasn't been used is quite simple. In soccer, the misguided view that there was no need for well-thought out action directed toward regaining the ball originally prevailed. Loss of the ball was viewed more or less as the fault or failure of the opponent. This "tradition" (the conventional understanding of ball confrontation) still hasn't been overcome. However, defensive "action" is the semantic equivalent of offensive action; the action of the group of players or the whole team of players implemented toward a well-thought out and interactive basis.

In the historical development of soccer, the equalization of the offense and defense was the catapult for pressing. This was reflected not only in the fact that the defense and offense were both considered as the equal and important

activities but also in the fact that the intensity of playing activity after losing the ball increased. Proactive features markedly "interlaced" with defensive reaction. More organizational features dealing with pressure, enforcement, and defensive proactivity appeared in the defense. The Brazilian ball jugglers (of the 1970s and 1980s) quickly found out that besides excellent technique, they needed the physical condition that was necessary for regaining the ball after its loss. However, they often lacked this physical conditioning at the time when the offense was being developed. There were losses (within the context of a transformed Darwinian theory) connected with "adaptive" countermeasures. Thanks to the accelerative and systematic adaptations of the Brazilians to new trends, these "ball jugglers" were able to endure and dominate in the soccer arena.

The form of offense of one team and the intensity of defense of the other team predetermines the spontaneous presence of certain game features in the defensive team. The intensity of defensive activity can be defined as a ratio between the reactive and proactive features within the defensive activity of the team. A reactive defense is a type of defense that is always in a time sequence with the result arising from immediate defensive reaction on the offensive activity of the opponent.

In contrast, proactive defense, a higher and more difficult level of defense (either from conditioning, space-time, or cooperation of the defensive team), enables the highest possible rate of defensive activity. It is based on persisting (if it is used immediately after losing the ball) or initially (again) used offense of the team (pressing initiation) at the time when the team doesn't possess the ball.

Proactive Defense, More Effective Offense

Soccer reached a positive progressive "reaction" to the proactive forms of defense in its next developmental stage. Even in the period when total soccer flourished, teams tried to increase the offensive effectiveness of their play through strong and direct support of the offense. It was impossible to keep increasing the striking power of the team through extensive or intensive forms because of a more concentrated resistance by defensive players (number of players, space limitations, etc.). For example, anyone who vehemently attacked Lobanovkyi's team, Dynamo Kiev, probably lost after Blochin's contras. One fast player was enough for "naïve offensive dreamers" who thought that they would score the first goal against Dynamo. Paradoxically, knowledge obtained in this way presumed that for an effective offense, it was necessary to support the defensive phase through proactive defense, and this reaction could be reflected directly by the offense. Defensive proactivity, an increase in physical effort and the total improvement of game activity and

organization, in the defensive phase, led to a change in the proportion of used game resources in the offensive and defensive phases of play. This ratio was increased in favor of the defensive phase of play, and gradually there was a more balanced use of the team's game resources.

Pressing Elements Before Chapman and After

Application of the natural evolutionary principle confirms the genesis of pressing in the game. This means that new elements of the game (such as the pressing elements) often appear in isolation within the others in order to profile themselves to some form of specific game principle, game-play, style, or system. So, in historical context, some features of pressing appeared long before it appeared in a more concentrated and explicit form in the game of a specific team and accompanied by exact terminology. The genesis of the game finally led to the point where these isolated elements connected to the integrated pressing form. For example, Estudiantes aggressively pursued the ball after losing it, and Bielsa made this more rational and organized. In the game of the century, support of the defensive team provided by the offenders is another "pulled out" fragment of pressing from an earlier period of time. Graham Taylor's form of searching for the ball is a significant feature of the graded emphasis on the ball through the zonal elements of defense with a clear orientation on the ball and its active pursuit. The "small islands" of pressing possibly appeared independently. Gradually they transformed into a "continent" across, which the teams currently walk in this period of globalized pressing. This continent is starting to fragment again because teams have learned how to "exist" among different forms of pressing, which they consider to be forms of a mutated "virus." As the time goes on, everything will mutate, and this is good, otherwise the development of soccer would stop.

The tendency of the evolutionary "vector" of pressing had already been "defined" at a time before Herbert Chapman and continued in the period after Chapman through the same course. Pressing in soccer "overcame" a developmental journey from spontaneous pressing to intentional pressing, from natural pressing to organized pressing and from individual pressing to collective pressing.

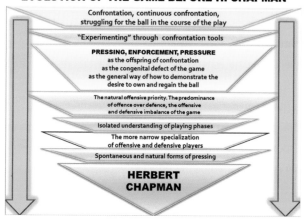

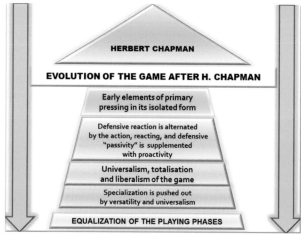

Fig. 1.1-1 Evolutionary scheme of soccer

It can be presumed that on the basis of the above defined elementary confrontational characteristics of the soccer game itself, pressing and especially some its elements occurred before Chapman in a form typical for that time and without being exactly defined. But how did intentionally organized pressing become a part of soccer? This is the answer: through tactics and everything related to it.

The "Father" of the modern soccer coaching is Herbert Chapman. He created the WM system and pointed out the importance of pregame technical and tactical preparation for the match. Herbert Chapman introduced a magnetic board to explain his game-tactical intent. By means of these aids, he definitely started to organize and manage the movement of players round the pitch, their formation, and the organizing and directing of the game through tactics. We can consider this as a turning point not only for the development of the game but also for the use of intentional play behavior within the player model.

The reason we have decided to use this bold analogy is the fact that soccer has often gained a form of contemporary sports religion, thanks to its socio-cultural, economic, and value parameters. It speaks to such a great number of people, that this analogy is not only bold but also logical.

After Herbert Chapman, a new period of cultivation was very slowly approaching. This period is significant for the preference of organization and for a highly developed interaction between the team players. At this time, a strong use of interactive play-potential, a higher emphasis on the organization of the play, and a player cooperation that provides synergistic effects on the effort made during the game is setting in.

A new era of the gradual enforcement of a more rationalized game-tactical model of play is coming. However, from the point of view of the diagnosis of a "congenital defect" in soccer, pressing has become an effective therapy for play. In modern soccer, players try to intentionally "implant" pressing onto the game. The beneficial "virus" or "infection" called pressing is still developing in the same way as variable offensive play; its resistance to pressuring causes intentional mutations in the form of different varieties of pressing. The breeding ground for the latent and spontaneous period of pressing up to its "boom" period within the historical development of soccer is represented by the principal modifications in tactics and strategy of the game as well as the game rules. A new era of organizing pressing in association with the situational tactical-play model has begun.

This question can only be answered within the context of the history of soccer. History offers us particular game elements, which didn't use exact pressing terminology, but these elements significantly contributed to

Fig. 1.1-2 Synergic effect of the team organizing play, team interation

PART 1

an intuitive link within the game. The proactive form of defense started to form that led to the modern globalized form of pressing. Throughout the history of soccer, the different elements of pressing started to interlock with each other; this interlocking gradually profiled the contemporary highly sophisticated, physically intensive and effective form of pressing. We will try to outline some of the pressing elements that contributed to the contemporary form of this highly aggressive defense:

1. Shifting of the defensive team toward the ball (Hungarians—Aranycsapat) on the opponent's half of the field; after losing possession of the ball on the opponent's half of the field, the players immediately attempt to quickly orient themselves toward the ball and immediately attack the player with the ball.

2. The concept of the defensive tactics in pressing (Viktor Maslov) required the permanent movement of all defenders, primarily the midfield players, into a temporary and reciprocal interchangeability of player positions; reciprocal protection; top physical fitness; preparedness and a professional soccer background. Besides a sophisticated and detailed approach directed toward tactics, it also includes sports nourishment that helps the players reach the higher physical demands that are necessary when using pressing tactics.

3. Maximization of direct pressure on the player with the ball in relation to an increase in the often uncon-

trolled and aggressive concept of defense (Estudiantes de la Plata) that focuses on formation and space.

4. The engagement of all players around the center area for defense (game tantalization, Dutch, Ajax, Michels, Cruyff, Barcelona Dream Team I and II) Space, as a unique defined element within Dutch soccer, helps give us a new game-perspective and, thanks to its conceptual flexibility, enables working within its elementary dimensions that are related to the basic phases of the game and the specific forms of applied pressing.

5. Style of play based on area-wide pressing involving the constant pursuit of the ball and a high tempo game-play (Graham Taylor, Watford).

6. Sophisticated defensive maneuvers by a large number of players, or the whole team, based on game organization (Sacchi, AC Milan). The basic idea of the Sacchi concept is the need to compress the play area, between the defensive and offensive line, to 25 m. Thanks to this compression, it is possible to apply an offside trap effectively, conserve energy, decrease the tiredness of the players, and provide for the output of the entire team. This is followed by authentic pressing within zonal access to defensive tactics.

7. Bielsaism is representative of the Argentinian school of soccer, which stresses pressing as the typical defensive tactic with the aim of regaining the ball as close as possible to the opponent's goal and the transition to an immediate counterattack after a fast

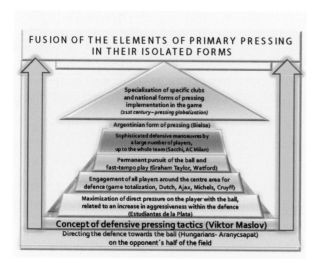

Fig. 1.1-3 The evolutionary pressing scheme

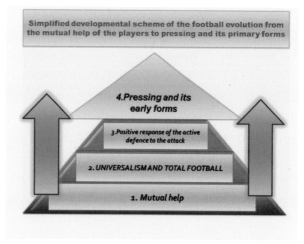

Fig. 1.1-4 Simplified developmental scheme of the soccer evolution from the mutual help to early pressing

shift from defense to attack. The main representative of this tactic is Bielsa. Martino, Pochettino, and Sampaoli are his successors, and they represent a Bielsa-style stream in modern soccer.

8. Gradual movement toward complex team pressing behavior at the point of ball-loss and the profiling of specific club and national forms of applied pressing tactics within the game (twenty-first century—van Gaal, Wenger, Guardiola, Mourinho, Klopp, Simeone, Conte, etc.)

The gradual exploration of pressing elements clearly shows that the final form of pressing as a standard defensive instrument utilized by most of the top teams in modern soccer was an evolutionary process, which is a typical feature of soccer game development.

1.2 ONE FLEW OVER THE SOCCER PRESSING NEST, OR THE BEGINNING OF PRESSING

How It All Began

The first documented references about the origins of soccer date back to Chinese civilization. The oldest documents about the beginnings of the game are dated to 1697 BC, when the Chinese emperor Huang-Ti officially codified a game called Tsu-Chu in which "a leather ball was set in motion by foot." In Central America, the Mayan and Aztec civilizations played a ball game that appeared around the year 1500 BC, which contributed to the development of ball games that directly preceded soccer. Around the year 1200 BC, these civilizations contributed to the formation of the first play-areas for soccer. In Europe, the first documented references about soccer date back to the year 350 BC. It was a game called "harpastum," later it was renamed "il calcio." During the Roman Empire, this game was played with a crude ball. It was played with the hands, and the object of the game was to keep the soldiers in good physical condition.

The expansion of the Roman Empire contributed to the expansion of "Roman soccer" to Roman provinces throughout Europe. Its most relevant appearance was in Southern England around the year 800 AD. Another reference concerning this game is a document called "cuju" from the 200 BC Han dynasty of China that involved juggling the ball and keeping it in the air as long as possible. The Japanese game called "kemari," from around 600 AD, had a similar system. The game closest to modern soccer was played in England, where "harpastan" evolved into "street" or "folk" soccer. Folk soccer was played on a delimited area outside the town. It was something between soccer and rugby, with a specified number of players. Street soccer was a festive game; it would be played between two neighboring towns or villages involving an unlimited number of players on opposing teams who would clash in a heaving mass of people struggling to drag the ball from one end to the other, similar to modern rugby. This event or match took many hours or even days.

This brutal form of the game had very strict rules, and it could sometimes lead to death. In 1313, King Edward II issued a decree prohibiting of this brutish game. Soccer was at risk of disappearing until the beginning of nineteenth century when public schools in England took charge of this game and used it, in a modified form, as an instrument to instill the following in young people: physical conditioning, team cooperation, courage, and fairness. The first form of soccer rules, the so-called Cambridge rules, were instituted by Cambridge University in 1848. This was the beginning of contemporary soccer. On October 26, 1863, the deputy directors of twelve schools and soccer club deputies met in Freemason's Tavern, in Lincoln's Inn Field, London, to codify the first version of the rules and to establish the Soccer Managing Body (Football Association—FA). So, we have a precisely defined birth certificate for soccer, with its day of birth and place. The soccer cradle was filled up with viable content that still persists. It is evident, that the ball-games of the so-called presoccer period were miles away from modern soccer; however, in the frame of a historical approach, many people would like to usurp, but often wrongfully, preferred positions at the genesis of this game. Historical sources are often ambiguous in interpretation of the facts. So there is often new space for historical misinterpretations and unjustified local patriotic approaches that often make it impossible to authentically reveal the historical reality and find the answer to the question; "Who exactly started it?" But this isn't important. Whether soccer originated in China or by the Aztec's in Mexico or anybody else, we can only claim, that it didn't originate in Slovakia; most of us would agree on this. Despite this fact, through retrospective analysis of the game development, system of play and tactics, we will try to discover some origins of this phenomenon called pressing, which didn't appear accidentally but was the logical result of the development of the game and its basic phases. Mainly isolated, pressing elements had previously appeared in many forms. We will try to outline these elements in this historical analysis of the evolution of the game-system and the game tactics. The evolution of the playing principles and systems contributed to the establishment of pressing in its modern, more concentrated form. The evolution of tactics and playing styles run in parallel to the evolution of the system. In the frame of historical extras aimed at the relevant factors of system evolution and playing principles, as well as the crucial soccer schools, are those playing elements that participated in the development of pressing in modern soccer.

In connection with the game's evolution, it is necessary to say that the main historical and developmental stream had spread from the British Isles by way of English soccer propagators such as **Jimmy Hogan** (the greatest teacher of the old Scottish game). This Englishman, of Irish origin, who introduced the theoretical preparation of players and tactics by the use of blackboard and chalk, came up with the concept of training and became the founder of coaching and the father of soccer methodology. He helped develop soccer in the Netherlands, Austria, Hungary, and Germany. **Jack Reynolds** used ball-work during training; he introduced the same game-style for all age levels for the club (Ajax), and he contributed to the development of the offensive game in the Netherlands, which was reflected by his quotation "Offense remains the best form of defense." In the Netherlands, another great man, **Vic Buckingham,** laid down the fundamentals of playing style "pass and move" with a high number of passes and holding the ball. With the assistance of Michels and

Cruyff, he contributed to the outline of "tiki-taka." As we can see, most of these relevant impulses for innovation from that period came from the same direction, from England and the British Isles. It seems that the cradle of soccer has been already defined by itself and without any additional searching with GPS.

The non-English missionary followers of soccer include the following: **Emerico Hirschi,** who brought the classic Danube pyramid to Argentina; **Dori Kürschner,** who brought the WM system to Brazil; and **Béla Guttmann,** who created the manager cult, which was applied in Brazil, Uruguay, the USA, and Portugal, as well as the playing style of fast passes, the so-called **tak-tak-tak** and **ping-pang-pong.** Possibly, thanks to them, continental Europe and Southern America became the citadels of soccer. Of course, the national uniqueness of individual countries later combined with this developmental stream, which was often manifested by not only the individual mentality of a given country but also by its socio-cultural and economic conditions. This is why the playing styles of individual countries and soccer schools maintain their individuality. Thanks to this individuality, their contribution to the developmental spiral of the game is irreplaceable, either in the sense of game evolution or the playing systems that markedly determines playing expression.

For us, the historical point for the birth of "modern soccer" was 1863. Eleven English clubs met in London to establish the Football Association of England (FA). The aim of this historical excursion is not to produce a system chronology, but mainly to notice some game-tactical elements in the frame of game evolution, which, at this time, had already hid the preconditions for a change from defensive reaction to a higher form of defense, defensive productivity. The development of this system confirms that the basic developmental impulse for new tendencies in the game was the mutual interaction of the basic playing phases (defense–offense), when, in the context of the game, mutual influence causes a new movement of trends in the frame of the individual phases that actually generates the very development of the game. Let's not forget that system evolution always creates new playing principles that are typical for the individual playing systems developmental period. A new playing rule appeared from the English cradle: the **"kick and run"**; thanks to spontaneity and a chaotic spontaneity that attracted many viewers, who were tired of traditional rugby; they were looking for a new option.

By withdrawing some players from the offensive line and forming a defensive formation, and later middle formation, Scotland (between 1870–1880) and England (1880–Nottingham Forest 2:3:5) added tactical features based on the principles of team cooperation and the creation of a relative balance between the gradually forming phases of defense and offense. Here we can find the beginnings of team organization, in which the concepts of the game were very important. However, the individual conception of play-action prevailed over the team-game system, resulting in the "pyramid" concept that can possibly be considered the turning point for the beginning phase of system evolution.

While Scotland developed tactics for ground passes to get around the opponent, the English preferred long passes through the air using athletic dominance and a dynamic way of playing. In connection, we cannot forget the offside rule (at that time called offside of three players) that influenced the tactics of the game and became a significant evolutionary impulse for further development of the game in both basic phases. Thanks to this rule, the defenders effectively applied a mutual vertical formation, which enabled them to keep the attackers as far away as possible from their own goal.

Soccer came to the European continent at the end of the nineteenth century (Italy 1896 and other European countries). It brought other national influences that contributed to the initiation of a continental system of evolution and new playing principles, which had a great impact on the game.

In 1907, another modification to the offside rule enabled its application at only the opponent's part of the pitch; this led to a new arrangement of the players on the playing pitch. The curved formation was the most preferred formation besides the linear formation. Through this formation, the playing surface was occupied more effectively. This led to the four-layered depth formation with a more variable game system (2-3-2-3) that produces greater involvement by the attacking players in the center of the field.

The Sun Rises Over Pressing

The year 1925 was the next significant milestone for game evolution, at which time, the offside rule was again modified (the two-player rule). This rule reduced the need for defending players (including the goalkeeper) behind the last offender to position 2/number 2. This rule affected not only the development of new playing systems but also markedly influenced the content of the game in both basic phases. The tactics of the game acquired a new shape. The increase in goals improved the attractiveness of the game, which led to an extraordinary increase in popularity. The integration of more players into the defensive game-phase and the width of the defensive line was covered well enough so that it led to the changes of the attacker's tactics. This contributed to an increase in offensive speed while also using offensive depth. The three center midfielder formation started to be applied, which used the triangulated formation (Rapid 1-3-1-2-3). Man-to-man defense started to prevail over a zonal defense, which will be changed, but within a different developmental context of the game. In terms of the occurrence and development of pressing features, the emergence of **Herbert Chapman's WM system** (3-2-2-3) was successfully applied in Arsenal (1925–1934).

The rectangular formation in the midfield zone created organizational conditions for a more compact defense in the middle of the field and also for the fast change to the attack after gaining the ball while producing the engagement of seven offensive players. Soccer started to develop vertically; thanks to this, both basic phases of play reached a significant in-depth playing dimension. At the start of the **Swiss Riegel** system (1-3-1-2-3), not only did the position of the sweeper appear but also the predecessor of the modern "6" that ensured the offensive M formation.

In moving toward profiled pressing, another preparatory play system appeared that presented a clear defensive philosophy for the game. It contributed to the formation of a more concentrated block form of defense. This was the **Verron system,** developed by **Rappan** (2-3-2-3), which allowed a very compact defense with two sweepers, a winger and movable strikers, who change their positions **(Tourbillion-spiral effect in attack).**

Bit of Chili Pepper to Spice Up the Game and Initiate Forms of the Hungarian Golden Team's Pressing

In 1950, the Hungarians developed their own system modification (3-2-3-2), the pentagon in the middle of the field. With the significant help of the meaningful teamplay concept the **"Aranycsapat" (the Golden Team),** this system offered the first pressing elements that were often connected to compact pressing sequences (offensive and midfield pressing). This was obvious mostly after losing the ball in front of the opponent's penalty area. There was an immediate switch from offense to defense, which contributed to the effective defensive application on the opponent's part of the pitch. While visual historical records are very limited, we can say, on the basis of the available archival records, that the first elementary forms of pressing appeared during the match, the "Aranycsapat."

However, this appearance was in the slower tempo typical for that period but with a clear tactical concept of formation and well-dealt special playing roles for the defense (withdrawing the wings and the midfield attacker, two defensive midfielders as the first players of the defensive shield), which introduced the application of pressing during the entire match without being explicitly termed in their tactical repertory. Of course, the frequency and intensity of application corresponded with the then physical-conditioning standard. The same could be said for the game-tactical and spatial aspects, which used different types of pressing during the match. Except for these issues, the coach, **Gusztáv Sebes,** evidently didn't have any idea that, with respect to the terminology, it is pressing—extra help by the attackers who defend the players. This tactical intention was also reflected through changing the basic WM formation, by using the M formation for attacking in the middle of the field.

Fig 1.2-1 From the classic WM system to the MM system that made the application of the attack and regaining the ball on the opponent's part of the play area easier

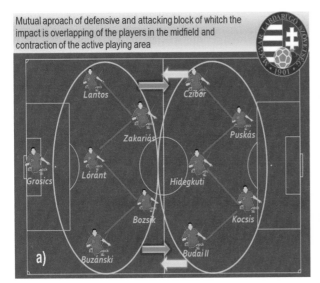

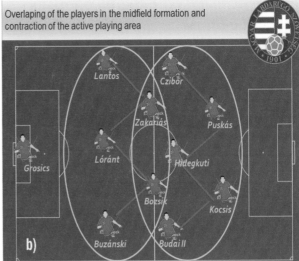

Fig. 1.2-2a,b Mutual approach and overlapping of the formations, which allows the active playing area contraction

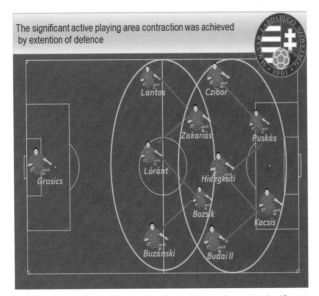

Fig. 1.2-3 Extension of defense line, which allows a significant compression of the active playing area

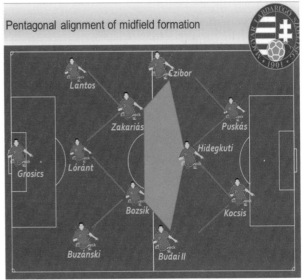

Fig. 1.2-4 Pentagon in the center of the pitch

Pressing features that had already occurred at that time in defense of the Hungarian team:

a. Priority of the game center with players' orientation preference toward the ball

b. Increase of movement intensity after losing the possession of the ball, which means intensification is the activity and effort after losing the possession of the ball, mainly in the area where it's possible to retake the ball control. Its evidence was the quick start of offensive players leading to successful passes and an advantageous battle for the ball. The players also showed a successful high rate regaining the neutral and the rebound balls.

c. Reducing of space for the attacking defenders by tackling from above with the collaboration of all the offensive players.

d. The initial defensive players are the forwarders (offensive players).

e. The continuous quest of numerical superiority in the center after losing the ball as well as at the time when the opponent executes the attacks from his own half of the pitch. Statistical comparison of recaptured balls occurring on the opponent's half of the pitch is certainly in favor of the pressing team.

f. Effective driving of the ball in the offensive half of the 120

g. followed by frequent and continuous short counterattacks toward the open, unstable, and unstructured defense of the opponent.

h. In the battle, the Hungarian offensive succeeded many times using centric and offensive formation and targeting attacks toward the opponent players immediately after the beginning of the offensive action. That definitely resulted in a worse structural formation of the opponent.

i. It was obvious that the shortening of the pitch by moving the center players and the offensive formation from the depth toward the center.

The Hungarians defended and played at that time in the same way exhibited by many other soccer teams in present times, showing a significant superiority in the use of the depth offensive principle as well as other analogies of the basic tactic principles and strategies. The Hungarian defensive clearly fulfilled all aspects of the offensive pressing, which extended over the entire opponent's defensive zone. The objective was to regain the control of the ball immediately after losing it, which was possible due to a flexible switching from attack to defense formation and vice versa. As a result, pressing is the phenomenon of the team. Pressing doesn't tolerate any withdrawal of individual players into any comfortable zone, and that's a heavy price to pay for the whole team. Therefore, the presented form of pressing was a surprise for the Hungarian team. The unity of the team spirit and the so-called team synergy are not possible to achieve without tactical discipline. Hungarians have surpassed their opponents in this discipline many times. In the 1950s, they built an unbeatable team at an international scale.

We will try to outline the relevant factors, which enabled the "Aranycsapat" team to influence the historical direction of soccer in a very noticeable way regarding tactic evolution or the playing systems. Excluding the individualities in the offensive stage, the team also offered new forms of defensive tactics mainly consisting of pressing principles. The factors representing the progress related to the philosophy of the game, the system, and tactical principles applied in the game are shown in the following formulations:

1. **Philosophy changes, different from the traditional concept of that period, relied on keeping the verti-**

cality of the offensive. The result was, logically, an enhancement of the movement parameters, mainly from the running point of view (especially the midfielder, withdrawn forwarders, and wingers).

2. **The concept of attacker's withdrawal to the center zone resulted in their supremacy in the center zone** and the formation of numerical advantages, not only for attacking but also for the **introduction of proactive defensive tactics (defensive algorithm) in the opponent's half of the pitch immediately after losing the possession of the ball.** Withdrawal of the attackers also offered more possibilities for offense due to a better circulation of the ball, more combinational options, and an increase in the attractiveness of the play (less readability of the offensive play). Withdrawal of the players was an expression of the positional flexibility. It enabled permanent outnumbering in the center zone, and it also brought conditions for active defense. Moreover, it built a pressure on the player with the ball, which was the preparation for pressing, not only in the center zone but also on the opponent's half of the pitch. On the other hand, the construction of the offensive offered significant variable alternatives in the offensive stage.

3. In the late twenties and in the early thirties, Herbert Chapman initiated for the first time the withdrawal of the forwarders in his WM system (3-2-2-3) since the beginning of soccer. Later, in the 1940s, the Argentinean team "La Máquina" continued using it. This team formed a link between the Middle European soccer and the South American's. Similarly, Vasco de Gama team used the features of the Middle European soccer in a 2-3-2-3 formation as well as the asymmetric variant of the 2-3-3-2 system. And thus, **the beginning of pressing started with the withdrawal of the center-forward attackers and wingers from their positions to a lower zone in order to achieve more efficient connection between midfield and attacking formation. This connection is not created only for the purpose of attacking but also for the needs of the whole team defense.**

4. **Asymmetry of formation (3-2-3-2, 3-2-4-1) depended on pointing up the defensive tasks for**

the left midfield (Zakarias), who was a pioneer of the position "6" in the way we know it today. He represented the modern conception of defensive midfielder. Situational withdrawal of Zakarias to the level of DF was a sign of four-defense system formation. Later, the Brazilians structured the 4-2-4 and 4-3-3 formation (featuring Zagallo). An innovative feature within the system was the concept provided by dropping off the attacker (Hidegkuti). His main task was to join the attack from a deep position and finalize the attacking runs. He built an outnumbering in the defense in a very interesting and effective way. In this withdrawal position, he was free to pass the ball and to build the formation of the play, but he was much occupied taking the penalty kick. In the playing system, the fixed connection of the traditional center-forward positions is lost. Extended positions in the offensive were flexible depending on the situation as performed by Kocsis and Puskás. Another factor, which contributed to the systems evolution, was the position and performance of the wingers (Budai and Czibor). They offered a new concept of winger performance, thanks to their withdrawal to the center zone. **The changes of the tasks of these vertical players**

significantly contributed to change the traditional WM system and to build basic preconditions for the pressing application immediately after losing the ball.

5. Players receiving and passing the ball were the more characteristic of positional defense rather than individual defense. They could build defensive outnumbering by skillful movements in the area. **Fast switching from offense to defense after losing the ball and withdrawing many offensive players to the center zone built the basic situation for pressing defense application in the way that was typical for that time.**

6. **The attacking stage was characterized by dynamical circulation of the ball, less contact, fast passes to the "corridor," and significant vertical movement of the players when building up the offense.** Asymmetric formations enabled the application of diagonal runs in the prefinal stage as well as the application of diagonal passes to center position. **Typical feature of the attacks was depth offense, which consisted only of four to five passes.**

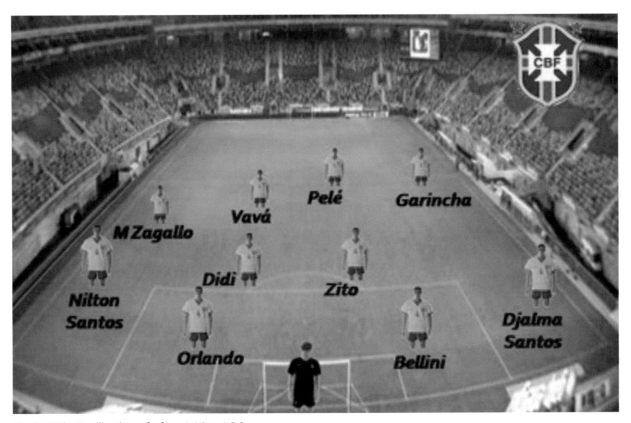

Fig. 1.2-5 The Brazilians' transfer from 4-4-2 to 4-3-3.

These factors represented a revolutionary potential of soccer, thanks to which we can consider the historical contribution of the Hungarian "Golden team" as one of the key points in the development of soccer tactics. From the point of view of the influence exerted by other soccer schools, through direct monitoring of the performance or the replication of its elements, we can consider this contribution to be respected.

And Others Are Coming...

Historically, another return to a zonal defense was used by the Brazilians in 1958. That year they presented their new 4-2-4 system with a transition to 4-3-3 in the defensive phase. From the pressing point of view, their double teaming is the most significant element, which will play an important role in the later development of pressing. This is also similar to the case of "taca la bala" (attacking the ball) where a strict man-to-man defense and defensive ball orientation was preferred by Milano International in 1962.

Alf Ramsey and his English team stressed this type of "seeker" of the ball position in their playing system, which

Fig 1.2-6 The 4-1-3-2 formation helped the English team to win the World Championship in 1966.

was embodied in the 4-1-3-2 Stiles formation. This player played in front of the defensive line and controlled offensive approaches by the opponent. This was another sign of the midfielder who actively defended, resp. a defensive shield without wing attackers.

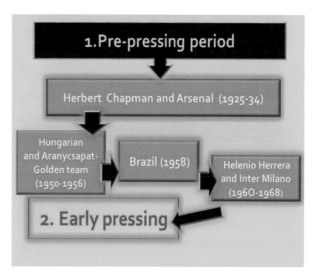

Fig. 1.2-7 Prepressing period

In some Italian clubs, one of the nice examples of the two playing-phase concept was the role of **the offensive "sweeper."** Besides providing for the defense, active participation of the player in the offense was expected, in a similar fashion to Cera from Cagliari, coached by **Scopigna.**

Early Pressing

In connection with pressing, we shouldn't forget about the Soviet school, which established its tactical concept in soccer in 1946 when Arkadyev published his bible for soccer coaches for Eastern Bloc countries called, "Tactics of Soccer." Under the Basque influence, Soviet soccer started its journey toward pressing; it is quite paradoxical that the Soviets identified playing tactics with the ideology of their country. This led to the preference for a collective game as the basic principle of Soviet soccer. Individualism was repressed in the tactical concepts, so the enforcement of "collective" forms of the game, either in defense or offense, logically resulted in a preference for team-tactical approaches. This ideologization of playing tactics might have enabled the early emergence of a collective form of defense using a type of pressing as presented by **Viktor Maslov, the "father" of modern tactics.** Through the 4-4-2 formation (resp. the 4-1-3-2 formation; the creativity and defensive force of the midfielders was increased by withdrawing both wings), a good play-strategy and spatial-defense, performed by outnumbering the defensive players in all parts of the pitch, was applied that enabled the use of pressing. He was the first coach behind the iron curtain to apply the position of defensive shield (Turyanchyk), which enabled the wing defense to engage in the offense. The period of traditional wings ended by their being withdrawn. Acting under his authority, Dynamo Kiev won its first title in 1966. It was based on the application of team attacks on the player with the ball, spatial blocking of the opponent, and the application of game activity in unusual areas of the pitch. It was very surprising that the Soviets refused to use pressing for ideological reasons, and they considered the team attack on the player with the ball as unacceptable. Of course, this attitude toward a pressing form of defense sounds very funny and incoherent nowadays. However, this attitude characterized the mentally suppressive environment of the Soviet Union and the unjustified ideologization of the sport itself. When applying pressing, except for sophisticated and detailed approaches to the preparation of tactics, Maslov required the constant movement of all defending players, primarily the midfielders, the temporary and mutual interchangeability of playing positions, top physical conditioning, and a professional soccer attitude, thus enabling in catering

to the sport so as to help the greater load on the players, which is necessary for using pressing tactics. When the two offensive formations were introduced, Maslov (Wilson 2008) predicated the possibility of playing with one striker. "Soccer is like an aeroplane. As its speed increases, air resistance increases as well. So you must hold your head aerodynamically." We can mark his concept as a prototype of total soccer, which developed its evolutionary line in the Dutch soccer environment.

This obviously resulted from insufficient communication between Soviet soccer and Western European soccer. In terms of the initial application of pressing tactics, Maslov can be categorized as one of the most influential coaches. He contributed the professionalization of soccer by his revolutionary application of proactive defense, tactical innovation in the formation of the players, and his visionary management. He used psychological approaches enabling him to apply principles of team building, and he motivated his players. In his application of these methods, he was ahead of his time. The launching of zonal defensive principles, and the application of pressing on the opponent's part of the field, brought important features into defensive strategy, through which he markedly affected tactics up until the present period. **Maslov (Wilson, 2008) says, "Man-to man defense degrades, insults and even ethically oppresses the players, who fall back to it."**

At the beginning of the seventies, through the game conception of Ajax, Rinus Michels took over Maslov's tactics of pressing, which became one of the building blocks of modern tactical thinking. By the end of the seventies, Arigo Sacchi brought this concept to perfection during the match of AC Milano.

We shouldn't forget about the fact that, besides Europe, South America is another soccer citadel. In addition to the Brazilians, it offers developmental impulses through Argentina. This country, in relation to its mentally and physical conception, created ideal conditions for the application of pressing forms of defense. **Osvaldo Zubeldia** was the expert regarding this concept. In the midsixties (1965), he took over the sinking club, **Estudiantes La Plata**. The cornerstones of his philosophy were formation and space. First, he taught his players tactical theory by using a chalk-board and then practical application on the pitch. He improved handling in

Fig. 1.2-8 Dynamo Kiev Viktor Maslov used pressing in the 4-4-2/4-1-3-2 formation.

all standard situations (penalty kicks, corner kicks, and outs). He used secret signs and language directly during play, and he taught his players to foresee playing situations. During the game, he often applied game traps. Thanks to his characteristically defensive way of the play, his team was called an ultradefensive and destructively biting team, which was logically achieved through the use of pressing. In Argentina, and in the whole of South America, defensive aggressiveness, defensive pressure on the opponent, fighting spirit, collective thinking, precise game organization, elimination of improvisation, and the use of offside traps in a 4-3-3 formation was seen as a curiosity. How did Zubeldia get down to it? He studied training units from all over the world, but mostly through watching visual recordings of Dynamo Kiev under Maslov's supervision, which was one of the very few clubs at that time that knew pressing tactics. This fact also confirmed Maslov's astonishing global influence, not only on soccer methodology in general but in particular the methodology of pressing. Zubeldia's form of pressing and highly shifted offside line were rightfully accepted innovations in defensive tactics. However, a side effect of this game strategy was inappropriate aggressiveness accompanied by a negative psychology that utilized various dirty tricks, pretending to fall and verbal

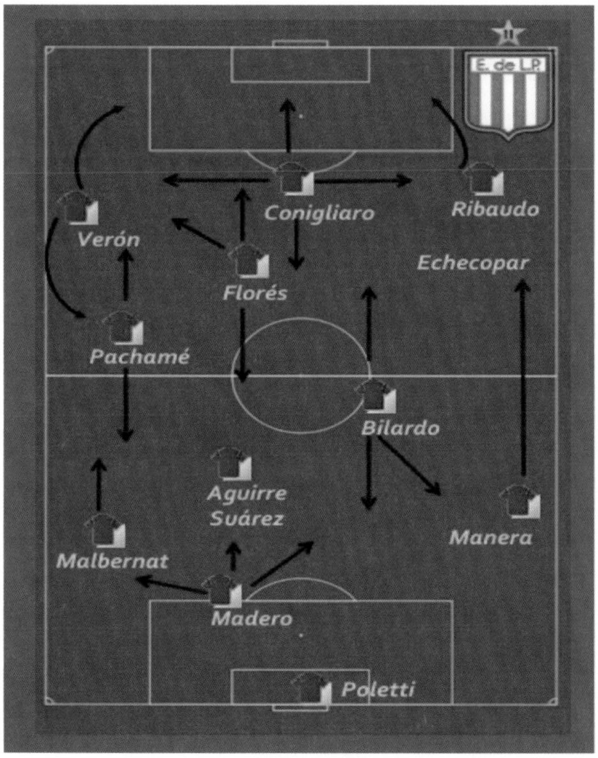

Fig. 1.2-9 Osvaldo Zubeldia and his 4-3-3 alignment for active defense

provocations during the game. Zubeldia's comment on this was that the key to success is not a path paved with roses. Finally, thanks to this method game-play and despite high success rate of scoring, as El Grafico stated in an editorial, their game became a "soccer parody" of themselves, and a demonstration of their play was defined by the derogatory term "antisoccer." Basically the progressive way of defense was coated with loads of antisoccer tactical elements, which, in this context, led to its destruction. Luckily, the evolution of tactics headed toward somewhere else, so abusive pressing didn't result in soccer's self-destruction.

We can observe the fundamental beginning of zonal defense accompanied by doubling in the **Brazilian team of 1970,** when they changed their system from 4-3-3 to 4-4-2. Similarly, the Italians began using this formation, however with a noticeable man-to-man defense. This contrasting conflict between diametrically opposed defending methods contributed to the commencement of game tantalization and resulted in an early form of pressing, which was wonderfully formulated by the Dutch in "total soccer."

After the World championship in 1966, the center of evolution for playing systems and tactical organization started to move gradually toward Europe and its characteristic continental game features, such as the pace of offensive leading, tactical player movement, even without the ball, change of game tempo and rhythm, and the combination of short and long passes. These features contributed to the significant dominance of European soccer in comparison to South American soccer. It sparked off the beginning of a new style of game, presented mostly by the **Dutch soccer school of "total soccer."**

To better identify pressing elements in the frame of the Dutch soccer school, we present those, which had a relevant effect on game evolution. The maturity of the individual players connected to team strategy resulted in mutual support and a doubling of defensive play, which began to be similar to pressing; the form as we already know it. The offensive base of this game method contributed to the immediate shifting of defensive players toward the ball after its loss, which was followed by a fast change from offense to defense and vice versa. Shifting, changing, and pressuring the ball, achieved by outnumbering at the center of play, were clearly visible signs of pressing in Dutch total soccer. Furthermore, after gaining the ball, the whole team engaged offensively, which represented the features of progressive postpressing playing behavior. But we think that in the seventies, from a systemic and tactical aspect, the Dutch soccer school was, for contemporary concepts, one of the main sources of evolutionary inspiration.

Orange Pressing in the Soccer Garden of Tulips

An important historical stage of the pressing evolution is represented by Dutch total soccer, which already offered clear contours of this assertive way of defense; however, it still wasn't the distinct and authentic form of pressing, which we are globally starting to notice at Sacchi. The form of the total soccer, which was formed in Netherlands, was based on the characteristics of the soccer and wider environment of this country. The foundational soccer influence came right from the cradle of this game through English soccer missionaries Jack Reynolds and, later, Vic Buckingham. By coincidence, both of them influenced the shaping of modern Dutch soccer form precisely through their work in the natural center point, which was Ajax Amsterdam. Dutch soccer started significantly changing by introducing professionalism in 1954. The evolution WM phase was skipped, and also, thanks to English soccer missionaries' philosophy, Dutch soccer started radically changing its form from the 2-3-5 system. Reynolds, by his perception, obviously contributed to the birth of Dutch soccer form that spread worldwide and gained respect and appreciation in the package of "total soccer." His theory of attack being and remaining to be the best form of defense is still considered as a valid postulate of soccer tactics. And precisely this ethos of attacking became the fundamental characteristic of the "total" version of the game, which profiled itself under the influence of the English soccer missionaries. The prediction value of **Willy Meisl's** prognosis has completely come true. In 1956, he claimed in his "Soccer revolution" **that the future of soccer will be built on defenders who are able to attack and attackers who are able to defend in the areas of the formations in which players will keep constantly changing their positions.**

The basic dimension of total soccer was its proactivity that was based on mutual exchange and rotation of positions especially in continuous pressing on opponent's half of the pitch. Fast counterattacks only completed the picture of the universal repertoire of the game. Moreover, if we add fast circulation of the ball, free flow of players' movement within tactical schemes intentions, and an effective positional game resulting from this, we get clear border lines of total soccer in its example form.

The strict discipline of the game, that is supported by the technique gained in training with a ball, was the stepping stones for shaping today's soccer form in the country of wind mills, clogs, tulips, and cocoa. Similarly, the Vic Buckingham's influence in the late '50s and early '60s brought the play orientation based on the "pass and move!" principle that pushed out the traditional "kick and rush!" principle. This is exactly the emergence moment of the idea that has persisted until today as the support and justification of "tiki-taka," which was formed precisely by **Buckingham: "Long passes soccer is too risky. If you have the ball, keep it! The other side can't score" (Winner, 2000).** This is where we have to search for the foundation of "tiki-taking" of which the roots go all the way to Scotland (R. S. McColl Queen's Park); however, the more attractive form was acquired after the Dutch wind mills blew the tiki-taking seeds into the soccer tulip gardens.

Adding these two fundamental influences to the specific atmosphere of the '60s Amsterdam, which was surrealistic and anarchist with significant orientation against the official establishment, the result of the cultural social revolution could also be soccer revolution based on connecting such elements of the game that hadn't coexisted before in such a progressive form. All these things together created the intellectual spirit characteristics of Amsterdam and the Netherlands of those times especially as a fertile soil for the emergence of the cult of the game, which significantly influenced the evolution of the game through total soccer and contributed to the pressing tactic profiling. The era of shaping the new form of soccer, so-called total soccer, began by arrival of Ajax coach **Rinus Michels** in 1965. Obviously, this type of play wasn't called "total soccer" right in the beginning. The official name "total soccer" was brought up in 1974 as a description of the play of the Dutch national team in the World Championship, which concluded from Ajax play and represented Ajax in orange color.

He introduced discipline not only in the game itself. Bobby Haarms (Wilson, 2008), the assistant coach of Ajax at that time, says, "The main issue then was discipline; he treated even his assistants as an animal trainer." By the change of the team spirit and the tactical focus, he gradually formed the variation of the game. Michels changed the essence of training to the preference of work with the ball. The impact of focus on the ball in training was significant increase in technical skills of the players as the key feature of the Ajax play style. In the beginning, he preferred 4-2-4 alignment; however, later he found out that when applying the pressing tactics, especially in midfield zone, it's more suitable to play in 4-3-311-3-3-3 alignment mainly due to better opportunity for regaining the possession of the ball. In addition, for the purpose of achieving more effective defense, libero extended to midfield zone as an additional midfield player operating in the transfer alignment 3-4-3 in front of the defense line. This system created excellent conditions for pressing application, which became an effective weapon of the tactical arsenal of Ajax and part of the progressive play concept.

Fig. 1.2-10 Typical alignment of Ajax during their biggest fame: 4-3-3

Pressing was mostly started by Neeskens who focused on opponent's playmaker and didn't hesitate to frequently attack him deeply in the opponent's half of the pitch. Part of the pressing tactic was also an offside trap, which they prepared by extending an offside line by one zone thanks to risky performance of libero Vasovic. Another spatial condition for the pressing application was playing area compression and an alignment of more defending players in this space. Pressing wasn't only frustrating for an opponent with the ball, but it was also about manipulation with the ball. Winner (2000) explains that the Dutch players' tendency to apply manipulation with the ball concludes mainly from the fact, considering the flat landscape of their country, they frequently had to deal with floods that forced them to manipulate with space in everyday life.

Buckingham (Wilson, 2008) says that the Ajax players were able to instinctively comprehend the space relations and mutual connections of their positions, and they created an intelligent team that was able to play the so-called learned soccer. Part of this type of play was also fast mutual position exchange, which became defining feature of Ajax. The 4-3-3 alignment allowed players to apply vertical positions exchange and form player's position group suitable for performing pressing. The players of those times said that they were able to perform pressing for even sixty minutes straight, which wasn't possible to achieve by any other team in that era. Apart from exceptional physical readiness, the players sometimes helped themselves by so-called chocolate energizers combined with pills (Hulshoff, 1973). Later analysis showed that these pills contained pain-suppressing and muscle-relief component and mind-calming agent. The use of scientific knowledge was applied in conditional training as well as in training schemes creation. Their nutritional regime was enriched also by pharmaceutical supportive products. It was an impact of the complex intensification of sports preparation in soccer, which was reflected in physical, technical-tactical, and mental level. From this point of view, especially pressing was relevant because it significantly contributed to increased demand on the players' performance. In connection with pressing, Michels (2001) preferred creating pressing on opponent's half of the playing area. Michels himself considered this type of play as a form of pressing soccer, also called **"opponent**

hunting." In this type of play, the first player, who is creating pressure on the opponent with the ball, can hardly get the ball. The second player, who is also attacking, is usually late too despite the fact that the opponent player applies perpendicular or back pass. The third player has the biggest chance to attack the ball.

Michels thinks it's necessary for the first and second player to take different positions depending on the situations created by the third player. In these situation, the players follow **"the ball hunting" strategy.** Michels points out that creating pressure on the opponent on his half of the pitch doesn't only increase mental and physical demand on the payers but also requires mainly comprehension of the play situation in close team and tactical coherence. The main condition for pressing the opponent can be considered the team and the team's three formations, which must play close to one another and "together" as well as restrict the opponent's operating area between the lines. During total soccer profiling, they realized that a player of any position is without the ball up to 95 percent of playing time. Also, they learned that the imperative of the correct alignment of adequate positions must become a part of the play comprehension of the player at the time of having the possession of the ball but mainly at the time of regaining the possession for his team.

In relation with pressing, it's important to bring to attention another important characteristic of total soccer, which is connected to the Dutch space concept. Space, as a uniquely defined Dutch soccer element, helps to have the new perception of the game. The flexible perception of space allows players to specifically operate with the main dimensions of space in relation to basic stages of the game and specific forms that are applied in pressing. This is reflected in all characteristics of total soccer, which are connected to space (offside trap, special position play, position exchange, movement of players, and the ball through clock mechanism and circulation of the ball). The main space attack algorithm requires "the pitch enlargement" as much as possible and filling it out by reasonable movement in order to achieve offensive cooperation. On the contrary, defense the algorithm requires "the pitch contraction" as much as possible or to the necessary size in order to ensure more efficient coordination of the team. The pressing algorithm demands maximum number of players in a minimal space for the purpose of reducing playing options of the team that has the possession of the ball at that time. The concept of total soccer requires players to keep the opponent deep in his half of the pitch and not let him cross the midfield line.

This architecture of space, in connection with pressing, brought new view at the game marked with geometrical alignment, which is currently gradually changing to geometry of diamond or pentagonal alignment at the time of preparation for or application of pressing tactics. **Cruyff** (Michler, 2008) talks about space in connection with this very pertinently: **"If you give weaker players enough space let's say 5 m, they can do anything with the ball. You have time to think, you don't have to play fast, you don't have to make fast decisions, and you don't easily panic. If the player, who can do anything in a 5-m space, loses the ball, and you give him only 2 m, panics easily."** This is where we can search for impacts of pressing geometry and its effects. An increased attention to space, which the Dutch pay with all play-tactical impacts, probably concludes from their mentality. Michler (2008) characterizes this mentality as a space neuroticism forcing the players to perceive space in an inventive manner in all the areas of their lives and create new relations within. The value of space is also transferred to their perception of space and space management in soccer.

Michler explicitly adds that the Dutch perceive space in soccer in a creative and abstract way because they had to think about space inventively for a long time in all the aspects of their lives, and they are a nation of space neurotics. One of the characteristic features of Dutch soccer is defense and attacking opponent far from the their own goal and creating an outnumber in midfield zone, This creates essential conditions for application of active defense forms, which often conclude to a pressing form. Based on these factors and facts, we can undoubtedly consider total soccer as an absolute basis of today's perception of the game, especially pressing. The purposeful position exchange and permanent movement, mainly without the ball, gave the tone and directed the evolution of the game to physical totalization and noncompromising pressing tactics, which are enriched by a high level of technical offense solutions executed either immediately after successful pressing or during the course of the game. From historical continuation point of view, the total soccer position is depicted in figure 1.2-11. Early pressing as a prediction of shaping into its authentic form. This figure also confirms its meaning together with other representatives of early pressing in the process of pressing's authentic form conception.

In the seventies, another relevant club contribution by Dynamo Kiev appeared, with the authorization of **Valeriy Lobanovskyi.** His soccer concept emphasized team play, resp. the team complied with collective playing ideas. While Maslov was rather intuitive and taught the players how to play soccer, Lobanovskyi preferred process control, the evaluation of the physiological parameters, condition of the players, and the implementation of systematic pressing into team play. Active defense and the changes in the size of the play-area (narrowing, shortening) forced the opponent to make mistakes. In basic soccer strategy, he tried to answer, how, when, and where to attack, resp. defend. His defensive system was based on fourteen tasks for the defensive phase of the game, which, except for the requirement of possessing the ball as much as possible (midfield resp. offensive line), included the immediate switching to an attacking and offensive formation. The requirements for

the offenders included the playing behavior of an attacker around the pressing line and trying to regain the ball, resp. through their own movement, the enforced pushing of the ball out of the area occupied by the opposing team. These were clear signs of institutionalized pressing in the defensive concept of the team, which hadn't appeared in such a revised form. It was an evident outline of defensive strategy for the whole team, which described how to move effectively in the play-space to regain the ball as quickly as possible. It required universalism of the players for both basic phases of the game; applied not in relation to the player's role, but in relation to the balls position on the playing area. He required defense from the attackers, and he required his defenders to attack. Active reduction of the game area, attacking in the opponent's side of the pitch in an effort to outnumber the opponent in different parts of the playing area. It was necessary to create an all-star team rather than a team of stars to remain effective and successful. Repressing individuality led to the application of individual abilities in connection with the team.

According to Lobanovskyi (Wilson 2008), this tactic is not chosen to suit only the best players. The tactics has to fit to our play. First, the requirements of the coach must

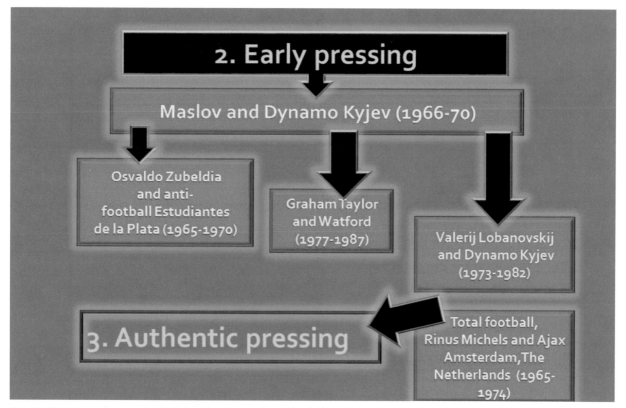

Fig. 1.2-11 Early pressing as a prediction of shaping into its authentic form

be fulfilled, which is followed by the individual skill of the player. Not only has the perception of the game and the application of pressing, in the frame of the defensive-tactical arsenal of the team, changed, but the content of the training process has also changed. New scientific methods (the use of statistical data from game-play, determination of the player's physical stress, etc.), the modification of training orientation (speed, special tenacity), different approaches to the game-tactical preparation of the team, as well as the formation of match situations, started to be applied as a result of the revolutionizing of the game. The revolutionizing of the game strictly influenced the evolution of the training process in respect to the application of pressing. Lobanovskyi stressed the need for gametactical training by modeling a three-level system that included the coaching of individual techniques, specific tactics for individual players, and the team strategy. Due to the requirements of the total soccer system, the unsustainability of half-amateurism was evident.

The beginnings of pressing on "The Islands," especially in England, goes back to the late seventies. **Graham Taylor** started to apply pressing at a club in Watford, which was owned by Elton John. At this time, Taylor was the most radical coach in the country. After accepting the requirements of the club owner to break into the First Division and into the international soccer scene, and after reading a series of specialized articles by Viktor Maslov, he decided to develop a playing style that was based on general pressing, consisting of continuous pursuit of the ball and a high tempo game.

This demanding playing style helped the club to advance to the first division and to reach the international soccer scene within period of five years. His straight forward approach to the game pushed him into second place of the first division and into the finals of the FA Cup.

Italian Soccer Orchestra Conducted by Jockey Sacchi, or Spaghetti Pressing a'la Sacchi

During the eighties, an increase in combinational playing speed began; the technical ability of the players got better and, at the same time, the total physical condition of the players also increased. As a result of these efforts, the aggressiveness of the zonal defense increased, which in

turn resulted in the application of pressing. Even though German teams applied generally high-pressure soccer, it cannot be claimed that they applied pressing. Through this method of play, the whole team was required to maintain a compact shift and a compact defensive formation. The **"Sacchi era"** came at the end of the 1980s. This period was connected to AC Milano and a group of Dutch players (Gullit, Rijkaard, Van Basten), who enriched and improved the original Dutch model with typically Italian defensive features and overall development of the play in both phases.

In the '80s of the last century in European context, there was dusk over personal defense with libero and, at the same time, dawn over space defense. This important fact also ignited pressing tactics rediscovery in a completely new context of defending, which was probably its logical outcome. The elements of compactness, space coordination of defending players in the center of the game as well as out of the center and local outnumber in a defense stage, were exactly the elements that contributed to pressing tactic profiling. One of the first Italian attempts to introduce zonal defense can be considered Naples zonal variations of Luis Vinicio in 1974 as well as an effort of Nils Liedholm to introduce space defense in AS Roma in 1984. However, only after arrival of **Arrigo Sacchi AC Milan club in 1987, the story of authentic pressing within zonal approach to defense tactics began.**

The roots of his approach to the game came from admiration of Hungarian club Honvéd Budapest (the club's core were the players of Aranycsapat), Real Madrid (the '50s and '60s), Brazil's representation team (1970) but above all, Dutch soccer of the '70s (Michels, Ajax). Lobanovskyi came similarly to conclusion that the important element for development of the game and its context isn't only the player with the ball but equally important are also the players who are not directly close to the ball because all the players together create a dynamic system consisting of eleven individuals. That's precisely why Sacchi needed, for the game evaluation purpose, to observe the course of the game all over the pitch and not only the players in the center of the game. He needed to capture the whole pitch together with the rest of the team. Sacchi said that the roots of Italian defense culture, not only in soccer, come from the historical experience of Italian nation, which was being attacked for centuries. In addition, he was convinced that the Italian mentality is lazy and defensive (Wilson, 2008). "We lack hard work culture, and if you don't work hard, it's easier to play defensively that offensively," said Sacchi (Zauli, 2002). When conceiving his soccer concept, Sacchi was aware of the fact that apart from winning, he must also entertain and offer joy and pleasure from the game. He preferred players with similar mentality and emphasized to his players that if a coach wants to achieve a difference, he needs his team to support him and be patient, thanks to the players who gain confidence. The team is the reflection of the coach, who is like a scriptwriter and director. He was often taunted for his absence of professional soccer career, which can put his coaching success in doubt. In relation to this, he said his well-known classical pressing reaction:

"I never realized that to become a jockey, you needed to be a horse first. Even an orchestra conductor doesn't have to play all the instruments..."

Sacchi's philosophy is well-described in his idea; if you have a ball, you conduct the game, and if you defend, you control the space. The main point of his concept is the necessity to play "short," compress the playing area between defense and attacking line to 25 m due to which it's possible to apply the offside trap efficiently as well as save energy and limit overall players' tiredness. This concept also requires whole team's synchronized movement forward, backward, left, and right. The "short" play alignment enables all the players to participate in defense or attack stage of the game. **Sacchi (Zauli, 2002) says: "Our real formation is the movement relating to the ball, opponent, and the playing area."** The obsession by the movement of the players without the ball in both basic play stages was the fundamental element of his theory.

Another important aspect of the game is constantly **creating outnumber situations in the center of the game and around.** This is precisely where we can find the

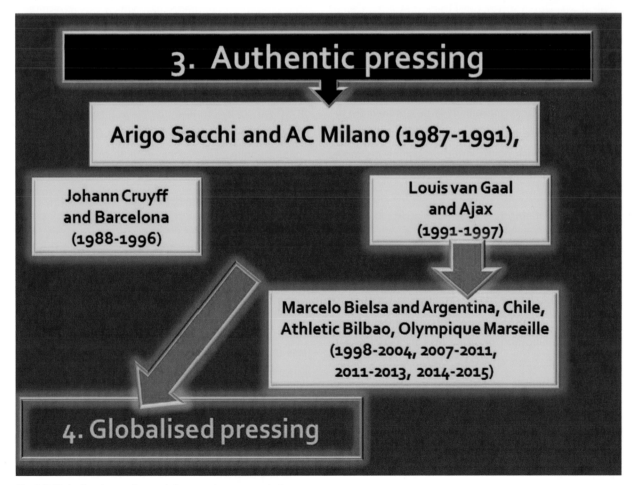

Fig. 1.2-12 Authentic pressing and the presseing representatives

essential preconditions for activation and application of the pressing tactics, which required the mentioned synchronized maneuvers of the defending team.

Sacchi considers the course of the game as the most important dynamic system of synergic formation of eleven players (similarly Lebanovskyi), which helps the team to follow the scenario with frequent personal interpretation of the players. The organization within the system was also confirmed in the training model where he proved that five organized players can neutralize ten disorganized ones and ten disorganized players can't beat five organized ones. Sacchi's organization of team's defense stage can be undoubtedly regarded as one of the best in soccer history.

The stated characteristics allowed Sacchi to profile the proactive defense model within space defense, which is characterized by four elements: the ball, space, team players, and opponents. In relation to pressing, **Sacchi says (Wilson, 2008): "I was influenced by many things. Most of all, it was Dutch soccer. But I think they are different from us, because their play was built on physical ability while our play is built on tactics. Every player has to be in the right place. In a defense stage, all our players focus on four points: the ball, space, an opponent, and a team player. Every movement is determined by the influence of these points. Every player had to decide, which one of these points could determine his movement."** Regarding this, Paolo Maldini (Wilson, 2008) says that before Sacchi's arrival to AC Milan, the key playing activities were fights between two players. After that, everything was about movement of players without the ball and that helped us to win matches. Not positions but players were important in both stages of the team's game. From Sacchi's point of view, pressing is not about running and hard work, but about controlling the space. By pressing application, he wants his players to feel confident and his opponents weak. The opponent team's confidence is broken by disrupting their usual way of playing. Apart from physical impact, pressing therefore acquires psychological impact, too. **Sacchi demands from his whole team to participate in pressing tactics, because all players in "active" positions influence the opponent with the ball. Every movement of the players**

performing pressing must also be synergic and in accordance with the team's intention.

Sacchi defines several types of pressing, which are variably applied throughout the game. Partial pressing is more about "tricking," total pressing is about gaining the possession of the ball, and false pressing is about faking pressure, which is used for getting more time for reposition of players. It's obvious that Sacchi, when putting his team together, didn't prefer solo players and stars but team players in order to form an orchestra. The biggest compliment he has achieved was (Wilson, 2008) when he was told that his soccer was like music.

In order to achieve these attributes of playing performance, Sacchi radically changed the content and focus of the training process and enriched it by several interesting elements. **His training speciality was so-called shadow play, which was based on the play of eleven players all over the pitch against no opponent and without the ball. The team was moving in a systematic alignment according to an imaginary ball, which was determined by Sacchi.** Besides this, he also applied numerous play-tactical exercises. For the purpose of an effective pressing application and positional play within zonal defense, these exercises were a necessary condition for an increase of tactical ability of individual players, space formations as well as the whole team. Sacchi adds (Zauli, 2002): "If I hadn't applied any tactical exercise for one week, the players such as Ancelotti, Baresi, or Donadoni came to me and asked for them, because they didn't want to lose their feeling for the play."

In training, Sacchi often applied a space drill. The drill was based on the principle of practicing the correct positional alignment of players in various functions for different playing situations and often without the use of the ball. By this, he achieved great team compactness in both basic playing stages in which they were better than any other team of the world. The mixture of conditional and tactical training, which fulfilled Sacchi's play scheme, was physically and mentally tiring and exhausting; therefore, Maldini stated (Il Calcio, 1996): "After few years, we wouldn't be able to continue at this pace."

Fig. 1.2-13 Sacchi's 4-4-2 alignment

The tactical revolution of Sacchi's AC Milan (1987–1990) worked on the principle of omitting personal defense and replacing it by an accurate zonal defense while focusing on pressing and also by enriching the play by defensive and offensive maneuvers, which reached the perfection never seen before.

Sacchi's indisputable contribution to soccer is the rediscovery of zonal defense especially training improvement but most of all, the use of pressing tactics in the evolution process of the soccer game tactics. Despite his effort to improve Italian soccer tactics, which were based on the improvement and enhancement of offense, it was paradoxically precisely the typical Italian "perfect" defense, which he reconstructed and built on new zonal principles in which he departed from personal defense and traditional use of libero function. **He enriched defense by proactivity principle in which he "rediscovered" the most aggressive and defense-destructive pressing tactic that had been unknown until then and has been developing is different variations until today.** His tactical visionariness was reflected by the fact that he offered defensive standard and direction of defense in the future. According to Ancelotti (Tribute to a Master: Don Arigo Sacchi, 2005), Sacchi changed the philosophy of Italian soccer, he put a bigger emphasis on attacking play, bigger pressure and organization on the pitch and changed the organization of work in the training process. Especially, by using modeling exercises, he contributed to the improvement of "match" movement schemes of individual players in specific positions but mainly movement coordination of the team as a whole in defense and attacking. He shifted offensive also to defensive stage where it became a part of proactive defense form in pressing tactics application. Even today, various well-respected coaches, who are protagonists of a soccer modern, identify themselves with Sacchi's message (e.g., Klopp).

The players had to adapt to Sacchi's scheme; however, he never adapted the scheme to the players. Sacchi's space perception of the game in 4-4-2 alignment allowed him to perform the play in a different style with significantly proactive type of defense applied already on the opponent's half of the pitch by the use of pressing tactics and work with space for the benefit of the defending team. The team's defensive approach was kept in the offensive stage too by which the team achieved a high level of defensive as well as offensive compactness and coherence in both basic stages; this coherence is based on mutual movement of the whole team regarding the position of the ball.

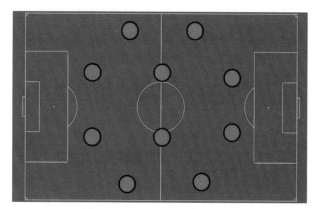

Fig. 1.2-14 Sacchi's compressive 4-4-2 alignment model, which allowed his team to apprise efficiently

We can state that Sacchi directed soccer to a new direction of which the result was an exciting game, and the essential tool was an efficient pressing connected with active spatial behavior of players in both stages of the game. Sacchi mostly stressed whole team play, and a significant feature of his playing concept was compactness in offense and defense. Sacchi stressed the application of the play to the offside, thanks to which he could shorten the playing area of the opponent (withdrawing the defensive line and forming offside traps). He also used doubling in defense and attacking the opponent on his part of the pitch. By involving the whole team in defensive action, he purposefully brought active defense into team play; ultrapressing strategies, connected to excellent physical readiness (through the introduction of the position of fitness trainer). Sacchi, as one of the first coaches, practiced pressing and formed pressing terminology, which significantly contributed to making pressing strategies in modern soccer more official. This period can be considered as the official beginning of pressing that has formed the principal defensive mode of play up until its present form, thanks to creative and evolutionary features in the field of playing systems.

Cruyff's Fluidum of Pressing Tactics

The proactive form of zonal defense started to be applied as defensive response by gradual enforcement of tiki-taka style, even though the name of this style wasn't known in the '90s. The proactive form of zonal defense was enriched by the highest possible (allowed or controlled) assertiveness in order to gain the possession of the ball especially in the center zone or to regain the ball after an unsuccessful or interrupted attack.

This part of the historical presentation is associated with the Barcelona period, which is the result of the Dutch transference of Total Soccer that is marked by specific interpretation of the Spanish soccer concept by **Johan Cruyff.** Double influence of the revolutionized play brought significant effects to the development of the FC Barcelona in 1988–1996. The influence was first seen directly on the pitch from the cult player point of view and later from the coach's point of view. Particularly, it affected in relevant way the development of the tactics for the following period.

It's obvious that not every top player must automatically become a successful coach. However, Cruyff had optimal dispositions to become successful as a coach. As a player he had excellent movement abilities. He was endowed with brilliant tactical understanding of the play, which wasn't only the result of his instinctive soccer brilliance, but it was also one of the cornerstone of his visionary success in designing the Barcelona's version of the tiki-taka style (of course the name of this style wasn't known at that time) in "Dream Team 1" (1992–1994).

Fig. 1.2-15 Typical Cruyff's diamond midfield formation of Ajax Amsterdam (3-4-3)

Fig. 1.2-16 Dream Team 1 FC Barcelona and typical diamond midfield formation 3-4-3 / 3-3-1-3

Within the self-reflection, Michler (2008) says: "In my opinion, in tactical field, I had more than most of the players...I could see things a bit earlier, and I could play the ball a fraction earlier where the ball should be." His ability of tactical X-ray perception of the team and the play itself was confirmed in his eight-year coaching period with FC Barcelona. The tactical power of the play was later proved when he held the position as Consigliere Club President in the era of Laport (2003–2008).

We are especially interested in his contribution to pressing application in defense or its application immediately after losing the ball. This launched the whole era of pressing defense. The above-mentioned pressing defense still persists in different mutations to present days. Cruyff's concept of pressing can be considered only as a small part of his global contribution to tactics, which deserves of historical attention. **As a coach (1988–1996) during the Barcelona era, Cruyff left his DNA in all soccer structures, especially in the whole philosophy of the game. His playing concepts still continue to influence soccer today.** Total soccer by Rinus Michels, indisputably inspired him, and it was typified by him personally.

The players had to understand the positional rules in the field. Its main concept was the comprehension of specific philosophy of space in the soccer field during the offensive stage, the principles of space manipulation after losing the ball in order to apply pressing immediately after. He changed the basic formula of manipulation with the ball. It's based on the principle of the game with one or two touches and an accurate pass. Apart from that, within the club activities, he also contributed to change the scouting method, the reconstruction of training process, as well as the introduction of a brand new youth model in La Masia Academy. According to this model, every youth category has to be trained according to the same concept and the 3-4-3 formation. It can be considered as a positive transfer from the conditions of the club Ajax Amsterdam.

Cruyff's soccer philosophy is defined in "S" line formation with spacing of 9 m max (Cruyff, 2012). The leitmotiv of Cruyff's philosophy is its simplicity. As he says: **"Playing soccer is very simple, but playing simple soccer is the hardest thing there is."** He prefers only the necessary number of passes. The extra passes are unnecessary and increase the chances of mistakes. It also reduces the performance and effectiveness of the performance. **"Having and keeping the ball is the best way of defense, and you don't have to defend if you have the ball, because there is only one ball"** (Cruyff in Flax, 2014).

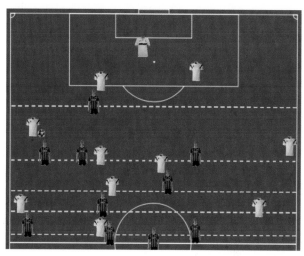

Fig. 1.2-17 Cruyff's model of occupying the space on the opponent's halt of the pitch in five vertical lines (Cruyff, 2012)

In total soccer, the space control and the control of keeping the ball depended on the following situation: when the players held the ball, the opponents closed the spaces, surrounded them, and occupied the space in the center zone. After gaining the ball, they tried to find space back and not to stay on the positions. **The attempt to regain the ball was as quick as possible, resulting in pressure on the opponent...hunting the ball seemed like a pack of hungry wolves** (Cruyff, 2014).

Cruyff's strange contribution to the evolution of pressing tactics was its use as a supporting instrument to enforce the total offense in the play. This aspect consisted of technical and positional mastering of the play with less ball touches in opening performance. Positional attacking is focused on movement "from the ball." It enables space manipulation and its opening to perform attacking sequences. Losing the ball was the signal for the whole team. Thanks to more line formation, the players could build an immediate pressure on the opponent. Shortening the area resulting from the basic alignment of the team enabled them to apply proactive elements in suitable quantities. These elements enabled regaining the ball and to save energy, which was necessary for further development of offensive play.

In his playing concept, after losing the ball, he switched his own way of offensive directly to the pressing tactics. By doing this, he built a remarkable continuity of basic playing stages, which became the matrix of the Spain's tiki-taka. He confirmed the double singularity of the fundamental playing phases in soccer. In addition, he established the offensive pressing as one of the decisive features of the team's defense. Later, this feature was applied and modernized by Guardiola in Barcelona's "Dream Team 2." Cruyff's style of pressing was, to a considerable extent, influenced by strictly holding the diamond midfield alignment 3-4-3. This system created the required conditions to involve the biggest amount of players in order to regain the ball during the initial attacking stage. The fast switching from offense to defense was part of the quick application of pressing tactics immediately after losing the ball, which later resulted in an important substage of the play. Thanks to the above-mentioned active switching after losing the ball, the pressing players didn't have to return to their own goal. It enabled them to save a lot of running and energy for the following playing activities. Another important pressing aspect was the fact that this action increased the intensity of pressure on the player with the ball. This pressure caused the opponents to lose the control over the ball weakening their performance and forcing them to get rid of the ball as soon as possible. In this context, the control represents the situation when the players are able to perform the objective through the application of actions from their own repertoire. The loss of control represents a state when a player with the ball, due to the opponent's defensive activity, is forced to execute only limited and less effective solution of the situation. It means that the limits of the actions are imposed on the opponent by the attacking player and not by the player who has the ball.

When applying pressing, Cruyff required approaching the attacking players as close as possible and not to let them enough space. This forced the opponent to performance erratically. The space and time deficit to perform vital re-actions caused the loss of control. Cruyff says (Michler, 2008): **"In small space, a player has to be capable of acting quickly. A good player who needs too much time can suddenly become poor player."**

The deficit of space and time parameters comes into focus. They were the decisive consequences of pressing tactics that started to change the character of the play toward a proactive defense and toward the dynamism of multipass interlude and overall structure of offense. There was also a shift in the consideration of tactics parameters. The technique was not about being able to juggle the ball, and the time overexposed when keeping the ball. The technique was about passing the ball with one to two touches at the right speed and to the right foot of the teammates (Cruyff, in Michler, 2008).

Specific requirement of Cruyff's philosophy, partially related to the pressing tactic, is presented in the rule. According to this rule, it's necessary to provide space to the teammate who is under an immediate pressure in a 1v1 situation. It's necessary to create sufficient space for the player to perform a pass by moving away from opponent (by opening the space) and by withdrawing the defending players from the center. The most remarkable rule of Cruyff's philosophy is the ban to use width or horizontal passes. It's closely connected to many lines in the players' alignment, which enable to the move of the ball forward. When the ball is lost after applying depth passes, a "safety net" of multiline depth alignment is formed behind the player. It makes the application of pressing easier. If there is an alignment of more players in one line, the application of pressing tactic is more problematical and almost impossible. As Cruyff (2013) says: "For the opponent, it's easier to enter the offense through the defense line performing a pass through a horizontal line." According to Cruyff, the attacker becomes the first important defender immediately after losing the possession of the ball. Other players, who enter the proactive defensive action, follow his movement.

There were more interesting thoughts from Cruyff's concept that referred to the evaluation of his difficult coaching carrier in connection with increasing requirements of the play: **"Every professional golfer has a separate coach for his drives, for approaches, for putting. In soccer, we have only one coach for fifteen players. This is absurd."**

Cruyff's style of play can be connected to the character of passes application, straightforward in-depth soccer, where the pass only represents the instrument to reach the victory of the match. Apart from it, the evolutionary flow directed the play toward the next modification of the playing style that was built up upon the concept of keeping the ball, which was represented by Pep Guardiola "Dream Team 2." He continued Cruyff's legacy enriched with some relevant elements of Bielsa's concept and some progressive features typical for that time. Thanks to those features, he shaped his own characteristic style of pressing that continue its evolutional trend.

Genealogy of the Pressing Evolution

At the end of this subchapter, we will try to form a following chronology of pressing through the time axis of pressing evolution, resp. a more simplified genealogy of pressing evolution:

1. Prepressing period

2. Early pressing

3. Authentic pressing

4. Globalized pressing

The first identified features of the intentional application of pressing elements occurred immediately after the implementation of tactical strategies using Chapman's method, at the turn of 1930s. This was at that time of the original application of the pyramid formation on the pitch (2-3-5). In order to create the real preconditions for the evolutionary beginning of pressing, this pyramid had to start to be inverted. The genesis of the inverted pyramid contributed to the formation of pressing elements, which were primary connected to changes in the players' alignment and possibilities and to the rearrangement of the players within and between formations.

The tactical evolution of game-play resulted in tension between game-experience and its result. The tension between soccer enjoyment and pragmatism is the driving force for the development of the game. When determining a personal style, there is an accent on individual preferences, which, by means of the coaches, directly moves the playing concepts, systems, and the game itself.

As an illustration, we have divided the historical continuum into four periods, where we thematically included teams, resp. coaches, who have significantly contributed to the evolutionary formation of this defensive instrument

in independent stages within the tactical development of the soccer game. **The developmental pressing sequences show that game evolution is not linear, it is rather spiral. In the genealogy of pressing, we have tried to illustrate the chronological sequence and the influence of individual representatives, streams, and schools on their successors.**

1. **Prepressing period**
   Herbert Chapman and Arsenal / 1925-34
   Hungarians and Aranycsapat / 1950-1956
   Brazil / 1958
   Helenio Herrera and Inter Milan / 1960-1968

2. **Profiling of early pressing**
   Maslov and Dynamo Kievl / 1966-70
   Total Soccer, Rinus Michels and Ajax Amsterdam, Netherlands / 1965-1974
   Osvaldo Zubeldía and Estudiantes de La Plata / 1965-1970
   Valeriy Lobanovskyi and Dynamo Kiev / 1973-1982
   Graham Taylor and Watford / 1977-1987

3. **Authentic pressing**
   Arigo Sacchi and AC Milano / 1987-91
   Johann Cruyff and Barcelona / 1988-1996
   Louis van Gaal and Ajax I / 1991-1997
   Marcelo Bielsa and Argentina, Chile, Athletic Bilbao, Olympique Marseille / 1998-2004, 2007-2011, 2011-2013, 2014-2015

4. **Globalized pressing**
   Arsène Wenger and Arsenal / 1996-2017
   Josep Guardiola and Barcelona, Bayern Manchester City / 2008-2012, 2013-2015, 2015-2017
   José Mourinho and FC Porto, Chelsea, Inter Milano, Real Madrid, Manchester, United Kingdom / 2002-2004, 2004- 2007, 2008-2010, 2010-2013, 2016-17
   Jürgen Klopp and Borussia Dortmund / 2008-2015 FC Liverpool / 2016-2017
   Gerardo Martino and Paraguay / 2006-2011
   Mauricio Pochettino and FC Southampton, Tottenham Hotspur / 2013-2014, 2014-2017
   Jorge Louis Sampaoli a Universitas de Chile, Chile / 2011-2012, 2012-2015
   FC Sevilla / 2016-2017

Diego Simeone and Atletico Madrid/2010-2017 Antonio Conte and Juventus, Italy national team, Chelsea/2011-2014, 2014-2016, 2016-17

NOTE: Information about the performance of the mentioned coaches for all their teams and their carrier is not included in this review. We state only those facts that are the most relevant from the aspect of pressing tactics.

In the historical part of the publication, we intentionally avoid the presentation of the giants of proactive defense in the so-called pressing globalization era. These personalities have enriched the model of defensive tactics. It's obvious that coaches, such as **Wenger, Mourinho, van Gaal, Bielsa,** have become living legends of coaching. The new generation that is taking over, such as **Guardiola, Klopp, Simeone, Sampaoli, Conte, Pochettino,**

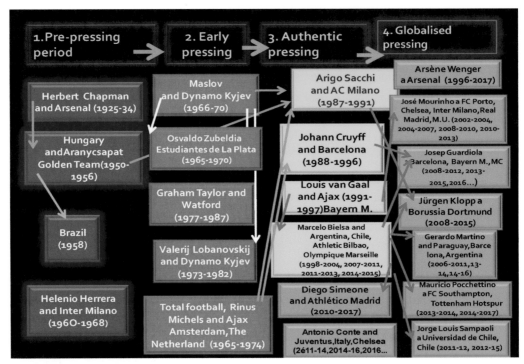

Fig. 1.2-18 Genealogy of pressing evolution

Fig. 1.2-19 Globalized pressing as a supreme period enforcing pressing defensive tactic

are surely going to engrave the history of the pressing tactics with their legacy and will undoubtedly ensure their place in the Hall of Fame. Their active coaching still opens more opportunities for further improvement and enrichment of their tactical repertoire; they are part of present soccer and to place them in the historical roots of pressing would be premature. In our opinion, at the end of their active carriers, their place in soccer tactic history will rightfully become a real fact.

Final Word on Part 1

The historical roots of pressing trilogy as detailed in this book try to reveal the evolutionary background of pressing, which gradually transformed into the most relevant defensive tactics of contemporary world soccer in the hierarchy of tactical instruments. Historical retrospective (part 1: "How it all began—Historical roots of pressing") offers a better understanding of the continuous development of the theoretical aspects of proactive defense and ways of rational assumptions for better understanding of the theoretical aspects of pressing theory effectiveness (part 2: "What is pressing and why, how and when to apply it—pressing theory") as well as the correct building of training tools (part 3: "How to do it—Practical manual for pressing") in order to master and ensure an effective method of pressing tactics performed by any specific team. In connection to this, we directly refer to its continuation in the second part of the pressing trilogy, which focuses on pressing theory and its practice.

The overall completion of the pressing problem is the third part of the pressing trilogy. It offers a broad range of exercises covering from the most basic ones (little pressing) to most complex methodical forms of practice (big pressing), thus mastering and improving the most up-to-date proactive defensive instruments of pressing. It offers a broad range of exercises from the elementary ones to the complex methodical forms of practice/drills, improving and mastering currently the trendiest proactive defensive instruments, which pressing definitely is.

WHAT IS PRESSING AND WHY, HOW, AND WHEN TO APPLY IT—PRESSING THEORY

PART 2

FOREWORD TO PART 2

Being successful in soccer means to win! That means permanently keeping track of developmental trends with an opportunity to respond to them as fast as possible and to try to put them into practice. The goal has always been to raise the level and quality of the game and to make it attractive for spectators. The contemporary form of modern soccer is characterized by a permanent effort to switch over the basic phases of the game, offensive and defensive as fast as possible. The effort to regain possession of the ball after it is lost by pressing is increasingly a more dominant part of the game concept of the soccer teams. From my own experience, I'm able to say that it is neither easy nor simple to change the deep-rooted tactical concepts and automated playing habits. During my coaching career, I took the opportunity to take part in a study visit in German Bundesliga in 1993 for a couple of weeks, during which I monitored tracking and the game play of the Bundesliga teams Bayern Munich, in 1860 Munich and Eintracht Frankfurt. These teams presented their active offensive play, engagement, and fight. However, I noticed that the emphasis in the training process and in the game itself was put on the fast reorientation from the offensive to the defensive activity and vice versa. In their tactical concept of play, after losing possession of the ball, the playersimprovement of the game-tactical version of offensive pressing in the training process and its subsequent implementation in the matches required a lot of effort, drive, and concentration not only from the players but also from us, the coaches. This demanding high-risk way of game-play expects engagement of all the players in the game, synchronous blocking activity and synchronous activity in blocks (shifting and switching of the players), the creation of pressure against the opponent by narrowing the active game area and restricting the playing time of the opponent with the aim disorienting him in the game and minimizing the quality of the playing activity. Application of this game method required systematic drill, simulations during training, and subsequent transmission into the warm-up matches. Except for the great condition training of the players, their basic assumptions were aggression, fearlessness, and fruitfulness

Coach Karol Pecze.

in the personal fight and the necessity of continually verbal regulation and reminding the coaches during the entire game. Our game became more offensive, dynamic, and more enjoyable for the viewers by minimizing the active game area in association with the integrated thinking and movement of the players. This was proved by a marked increase in the spectators' interest with an above-average gate (14000–24000). The spectator gradually became immediately concentrated on quickly regaining possession. Their intention one of the most important factors in our progress. This progressive way of game was to direct pressure (pressing) on the opponent with an immediate attack and reduction of the playing area to force him to make mistakes and loose the ball. From that point on, I was persuaded that the game-tactical version of the defensive activity of the team can become the base for spectator enjoyment despite our unfavorable conditions. Favorable conditions to implement this intention came along later, during 1994–1997 for the soccer team of Spartak Trnava. Pressing became the most important measure for our defensive tactic in regaining possession of the ball. Acquisition, drill, andplay impressed the spectator and made them interested in it so that they became the driving engine and the twelfth player on the pitch. I believe that this publication will offer coaches the detailed knowledge that is necessary for the effective management and understanding the pressing issues when creating effective defensive concepts of the trained team. Detailed facts and practical mastering of the pressing tactics drill are obviously the only way to teach your own team to apply this sophisticated way of defending in the game. One more note about this: I have personally implemented this technique.

–Karol Pecze
Soccer coach, board member of Slovakian
Football Coaches Association (UFTS)

2.0 PRESSING IN TEAM GAMES

In the first part of the pressing trilogy, chapter 1.1 Diagnosis of pressing, we indicated that integration of the confrontation principle into team games predetermines the discovery of pressing in a special form for all games (basketball, handball, hockey, rugby, futsal). For the purpose of an in-depth analysis of pressing tactics, we present their specific form in some areas, which are, by their movement, game-play and tactical structure, close to that of soccer. The basic motive for such a designed presentation of pressing is the effort for its complex impact in terms of a historical context, theoretical analysis, and practical learning for the soccer coach's needs.

Development of Rules in Team Games and Pressing

The partly specific but in many cases similar character of the course of playing confrontation in basketball, rugby, hockey, handball, futsal, or soccer is due to the rules of every single game that were obviously independently developed from the historical point of view. However, they followed the same goal. Their principle has been the support of open, pure, and permanent confrontation, and fair competitiveness that uses the highest rate of activity between the competing teams.

It has not been proven whether the experts on team games inspired each other when outlining the rule changes. However, their steps were led by an important mutual motive. It was the eminent interest to increase the level of the game, to prevent its developmental failure that could give rise to a game that is less interesting and less enjoyable to the viewers. Show business (sport in particular, mostly in time of the mass media boom) shouldn't be boring for the millions of viewers at the stadiums or for those in front of the TV. The "Litmus test" (indicator) of success at keeping, and increasing, the level of game quality in these related sports can be pressing and the level of its usage in these sports. Pressing equals confrontation. At the same time, pressing means enhanced game risk. Thereupon, it requires courage, self-satisfaction, more comfortable tactics, and calculated game responsibility refusal from coaches and players. Unless the systematic initialization and usage of direct fighting confrontation with the opponent brings long-term positive results for the team, a space for passive game tactics arises. That practically means avoidance of direct conflicts with the opponent. Tension, plot, drama but also variability, unpredictability, and surprise should dominate the confrontation sports arena. The basic function of the rules in team games is to create the most suitable conditions to build the game tension and at the same time, produce a fair outcome. Quickly changing the game phases (changing the possession of ball) is the source of unexpectedly unique and spontaneous game sequences. It is the essential flavor of a more vital, unpredictable, and dramatic game action. This is possible to achieve by designing rules that provide not only balanced spatial, but also other playing conditions, for possession of and regaining the ball, so that any activity can "guarantee" an equal and fair opportunity for a change in ball possession.

Confrontation (as an immanent source of game tension and design, which is typical for team games) can be more or less sanctioned or hindered by the rules. The more space-time that arises during the game, the more the game becomes visually boring which, due to the game rules, causes confrontation to be very restrained (however, we can express the reciprocal and logical statement that the game confrontation is not sufficiently supported in the game rules). The same goes for the case when the competitors adapt themselves to the existing rules so much, that they highlight their weaknesses to the extent that the ethics of the sport begin to bend. In team games, where the subject of the game is controlled by hand, it was necessary to eliminate the development of undesirable tends and rule deformations. These trends could arise from the possible misuse of certain ball-holding and ball-control actions during the game, which led to a team relatively long period of ball control. During dramatic match endings, game obstruction was used by the team, which had the score advantage. For the stated reason, gradual experimentation was accepted followed by the establishment of a wide range of restrictions and prohibitions. These rule changes significantly and directly affected the area of play and the frequency of changing between the offensive and defensive phases of the game. Some restrictions, which favored tactical game-space manipulation by the players became a part of the team-game rules (aimed at the easier creation of pressure on the players who control the ball or puck). These restrictions complicated the ability to increase pressure on the opponent with the ball and increased the resistance to his pressing. Moreover, currently valid sanctions for the passive game in handball and basketball, force the players into a final offense stance even in cases where the offensive players keep the ball under control, possibly until the end of the match, in order to sustain continuous play. In these games, the frequency of changing between game phases is increased by the innovative interference of the rules. The game will become more lively, more confrontational, and more offensive, which is more attractive and interesting for the viewers.

The historical assessment of team games would probably reveal weaknesses in their development. Each of these games was forced, relatively frequently, to deal with the "pathological" ills, which game-evolution brings about. During this evolution, the players developed the ability to "misuse" the free wording of some of the game rules, if the winning team was not the better team and misused the rules. Through cunning and a little luck, good sportsman's ship gets a slap in the face. Therefore, it is common that rule changes often bailed out the situation in the nick of time. (Dragging the time on, passively holding the ball, protracted change, long interruptions of the game and other frequently unfair obstructions were a part of the tactical-game arsenal of the most advanced teams and were the showcase team of their particular sport). Today, in many team sports (including soccer) where most of these previously mentioned "childish behavior" had been fairly common, the situation has improved. This increased professionalism is not only due to rule changes but also to the increasing attractiveness of these team sports, which is due to the logistics surrounding the development of the sport business, which in turn helps to keep team sports at an acceptable marketing level. The game rules are the first compelling reason why we (in connection with pressing in soccer) have plumbed the depths of the use of pressing in related team games. We are looking for the answer to whether soccer is a game where the rules sufficiently support the perspective penetration of proactive game forms, which includes pressing.

Game Rules, Game Area, and Pressing

A large "chapter" of the rules in team games is that which deals with defining the size of the play-area and the number of players in the game. When pressing is used, its success, as a proactive and proconfrontational method of game-play, is undoubtedly dependent on the spatial conditions (a small, limited area is advantageous to pressing). For example, basketball, with an area of 43 m2, handball, with 57 m2, and futsal, with 80 m2 of the total play-area for each player, satisfies the ideal spatial criteria. The initial or starting spatial "dependence" for the development of game confrontation is a directive in every team game, because the spatial parameters of the game are limited by the fixed, objectively given, rules. They affect the game scene outside the players' attention. The players systematically and extensively train for these required spatial conditions. They have learned automated tactical-game methods. Using these methods, they can implement their subjective, individual and team intentions in the game (purposeful "bending of" the active game area, preparation for the acceleration of active pressing). For instance, when implementing pressing, the defending team effectively works with the area, so the opponent can't get out of pressure. Active "formation of" the game area depends on the players themselves. It is about the subjective game activity of not only the individual but also the organized team. The rules for the given spatial limitation of the game, together with the appointed number of players, are the basic limits of game confrontation. The rules in every team game provide the starting point and the fixed spatial parameters. That is the basis for other, already mentioned possibilities for tactical-game manipulation of the game and active game area, which is performed by the players during the game-play. In all team games, pressing relates to the formation of pressure on the opponent who owns the ball. In accordance with physics, the reduction of area is directly proportional to the increase in pressure. In soccer and in other team games, pressure is also created in a smaller area. The rules of the game take this into consideration, and they are very precise in this way. A clear example of this occurs in basketball, and the rule, which is colloquially referred to as "through midcourt." This rule automatically decreases, in a marked and strict way, the active game area for the defending team after shifting the focus of the game across the midcourt line. On the contrary, the offensive team is pressured by the defending team through the spreading of the game all across the entire court. The game takes place only in the opponent's half of the court, and the time limit laid down for finalization, shooting the ball into the basket. In order not to take certain examples out of context, we will present a brief but systematic survey of the ratio between the area of game-play and the number of players in selected team games. Moreover, we will focus on the important segments of the rules, which are applicable to these games. These rules have different meanings in relation to the spatial criteria of the games and affect different temporary restrictions during game-play in specific zones of the game-area in relation to the implementation of pressing tactics.

BASKETBALL

The size of the basketball court: 28.5 m x 15 m, surface of the game area: 427.5 m².

Fig. 2-1 Basketball

Number of players: 10

The size of potential game area in proportion to one player: **42.75 m²**

The objective of the game: The ball is controlled only by the player's hands. No outside rules apply.

Spatial restriction: The player who obtains control of the ball can't bring the ball back to his part of the court (passing from the opponent's side to his own part of the court is not allowed).

The ball will be awarded to the opposing team, to be thrown back into play, from the spot nearest to where the infringement took place.

Time limit 8 seconds: The opposing team obtains control of the ball in their part of the court. The ball must be moved to the opponent's half of the court within 8 seconds.

Time limit 24 seconds: Once the ball is brought into the opponent's side of the court, the team with possession has 24 seconds to score.

HANDBALL

The size of the handball court: 40 m × 20 m, surface of the game area: 800 m²

Fig. 2-2 Handball

Number of players: 14

The size of potential game area in proportion to one player: **57 m²**

The objective of the game: The ball is controlled only by the players' hands. No offside rule apply.

Penalties for passive game: The players' team is not allowed to hold the ball without an obvious attempt at offensive action or scoring. In case the team does not change from the passive game, the team will be punished by a free shot.

ICE HOCKEY

The size of the hockey ring: 60 m x 30 m, surface of the game area: 1800 m².

Fig. 2-3 Ice hockey

Number of players: 12

The size of potential game area in proportion to one player: 150 m²

The objective of the game: The puck is controlled by the players' hands and the hockey stick. The movement of the players is sped up by skating, which allows the players to reach a higher speed of movement than running and the use of sliding inertia at certain speeds. A blue line, offside rules apply.

Spatial restriction: Icing

RUGBY

The size of the rugby pitch: 100 m x 70 m, surface of the game area: 7000 m^2.

Fig. 2-4 Rugby

Number of players: 30

The size of potential game area in proportion to one player: **233 m^2**

The objective of the game: The rugby ball (quango) is an ellipsoidal ball, dribbling is not allowed by the rules. Offside rules apply.

Spatial restriction: The ball can only be passed backward. That's why the players can't be positioned in front of the ball. In-depth movement of the center of gravity is achieved through by the movement of the player who has ball in his hand or by kicking the ball.

FUTSAL

The size of the pitch: 40 m x 20 m, surface of the game area: 800 m²

Fig. 2-5 Futsal

Number of players: 10

The size of potential game area in proportion to one player: 80 m²

The objective of the game: The ball is controlled by the players' feet only. No offside rules apply.

Restriction of the goalkeeper; the ball in the frame of the offensive action by his own team.

SOCCER

The size of the pitch: 100 m–110 m × 64–75 m, surface of the game area: cca 8000 m²

Fig. 2-6 Soccer

PART 2

Number of players: 22

The size of potential game area in proportion to one player: **364 m²**

The objective of the game: The ball is controlled by the players feet only. Offside rules apply.

No other spatial restrictions are included.

In relation to the size of the game area in proportion to the number of players and restrictions on the use of certain parts of the playing area, soccer is the most space extensive game. Despite the fact that soccer has the largest area for one player (364 m², by the way of illustration, this is an area of 35 m × 10 m), there is a high degree of freedom for reaching partial or strategic goals through the choice of tactical game variants; how to use or misuse the playing area. Before the soccer match starts, it is difficult to predict its progress. The teams can play either an open game or they can adopt a wait-and-see attitude. They can play a passive game or a super-active one. During the game, the players can react or they can determinate the course of the games progress (proactive defense). They can "hide" the opponent's ball, keep it, and patiently wait for the opponent's mistakes. Contrarily, the players can use defensive blocks, without controlling the ball for a long time, and win after sporadic counterattacks. Perhaps this outlined free hand makes soccer an attractive team game. During a World Cup, the viewers often have to sweat out a match, especially in cases where the opponents avoid physical contact with each other so as not to threaten themselves with a fault (Argentina–Netherlands, World Cup Final, Brazil, 2014, 0:0). It has been said that there was a lot at stake. One thing is for sure, the rules of soccer enable such disillusion of the soccer match, but the viewers know that the game can compensate for this type of game with a significant experience, perhaps in the near future (Brazil–Germany, World Cup Final, Brazil, 2014, 1:7).

For success with pressing, it is very important and necessary to reduce and close the playing area of the offensive team by eliminating the overlapping passing corridors and any means of escape by the ball in all possible ways. In soccer (which belongs to the "oligarchs" as we have proved before), the players cannot use rules available to other sports (as explained above), except for the offside rule. The movement of the ball is not restricted as it is in basketball or ice hockey (icing). There are many ways of escaping from the applied pressure in pressing. For example, when there is offensive pressing in the offensive zone, it is necessary to prevent:

1. reversal passes, including infringement of the constructive game by the opposing goalkeeper

2. transmission of the game across the width of the playing area to the opposite sideline

3. transmission of the center of gravity in depth, behind its own defense.

Fig. 2-7 When the active defensive team supports pressing by keeping a safe game—tactical policy and respecting the principles of defensive security—they wait for a favorable opportunity to use active pressing through defensive blocks.

Moreover (as circumstances allow), it is necessary to outnumber the opponent in the center of the game zone. These facts can be applied to any method of proactive defense and are important to pressing in particular. Even though, in soccer, the ball is handled by foot, and the technical error rate is, of course, higher in comparison to handball or basketball, where the ball is handled by hand, in the case of pressing, it is extraordinary difficult and complicated to handle the area and to achieve success in pressing traps.

While the opponent possess the ball, usually at the start of play, pressing tactics often accommodates the transition into patiently waiting for an opportunity through the application of continuously moving, elastic defensive blocks.

There are no limits to an alternative game progress in soccer. There is only one exception—the offside rule. This rule only applies to the player who is behind the defensive line of the opponent at the time of the pass that is directed toward him. This player becomes an offside player immediately after he contacts the ball. In its offensive phase, the previously mentioned large-scale spatial alternativeness of the game enables the player to hold the ball for a certain time frame (as allowed by the rules) to keep possession from the opposing player, namely, the game-tactical abuse of the width and the depth of the game area (secondary regressive passes to the goalkeeper). It needs to be emphasized that this mode of play is not prohibited nor limited by the rules.

The introduction of the offside rule was a necessity, especially in the team games where the playing field is larger in proportion to the number of players (soccer, rugby, ice hockey), in order to position the players for close contact. **Unless the rules help to "push" the players close together, spatial manipulation by all players will be ineffective, and the players will be deployed throughout the large field at large distances from each other.**

Physical contact, fights, confrontation as well as pressing tactics would disappear from soccer, rugby, and ice hockey. We could forget about the active game area in soccer, which currently compresses until it is 25–30 m in depth (thanks to the offside rule). In team sports where the field

is smaller in proportion to the number of players, there are rules concerning spatial and time limits, because the ball is more confidently controlled by the hand (handball and basketball). In these types of sports, it is possible to hold the ball at a "dead" point, and the opponent wouldn't have a clear chance of gaining control of the ball without committing a foul. Through strict, relatively tough and balanced game practice, and a proven time limit, these rules push the offensive players toward risk taking, physical attacks, and generally to a faster game outcome.

In all team sports, the rules purposefully restrict game conditions not only for the regular progress of the confrontation but also for the reason, that before the fight for the object of play (ball or puck) as such, there is a fight for space, in which the opponents try to get to the target area as best as possible (using every square meter of the playing area). In addition, the player can execute this point effectively and defeat the opponent if he remains in control of the ball. When attempting to move a ball into the depth of the game area, and also in the area of the sidelines, there is often a physical confrontation and an animated fight. Fighting in these situations and areas has a good chance of success (this topic is mentioned with regards to soccer in chapter 3).

In finalizing our speculations, with a brief look at the history of soccer, it has been shown that there is a plausible link between the rules of the game and the game's qualitative level. The confrontation often finished with a mutually satisfactory point spread: two points credited for a victory and one point credited for a draw. The teams passively waited for the end of the match without risking a loss. In the case where this did not happen, it would not have been necessary to reevaluate the assignment of points and credit three points for a victory. This rule applies to the present as well, and it is evident that this "operation" was successful.

"The patient" feels good, and his fragility and motivational balance is not disrupted. However, a victory in soccer became more valuable after fundamental rule changes. We can see pressing and other more risky elements in game with the result of an increase in the proportion of interesting matches.

PART 2

Team Games That Are Very Similar to Soccer

In trying to find an analogy to pressing in other team games, it is necessary to point out that contrary to other team games (basketball, handball, ice hockey, rugby); soccer is dependent on the preferred management of the object of the game (ball) with the feet. This is much more difficult than in other ball games, where the players use their hands.

The most inspiring soccer "consanguinities" are its "brothers," such as futsal and ice hockey. Icing and offside on the "blue line" makes hockey wilder, but luckily it is a winter sport rival of soccer. Hockey is familiar with an ultraoffensive form of pressing, forechecking. In hockey, forechecking is most often used as a tactical game option, because it is partially protected by the icing rule. The offside rule on the blue line is activated when the offensive side loses the puck in the offensive third of the ice rink, and it leads to forechecking.

Futsal offers special analogous movements and spatial parallels to soccer pressing, which most closely approximates the intentionally reduced active play area, which is achieved by pressing. **Currently, soccer is played on small areas of the pitch, which dynamically move around the whole playing area. The difference is that these "small areas of play" roam round the entire soccer pitch in a variable and sometimes unpredictable way.** Soccer players must overcome the distance between them at a high intensity level and without changing formation. The defensive trend in contemporary soccer requires maximally decreasing the active defensive play area. This decrease in size approaches the size of the playing surface in futsal. However, in comparison with soccer, the rules of futsal are the most dynamically developing rules in team games.

The "sliding tackle" rule, which hampered the effectiveness of pressing activities to certain extent in the past, is no longer prohibited. As a consequence of this change, experience has shown that the number of injuries and accidents in futsal has not increased.

A fundamental rule, which supports the pressing rule and which is contemporarily valid in futsal, is the limitation of the goalkeeper. The goalkeeper can't take an auxiliary back pass from his team players who have possession of the ball and are under the pressing pressure at the same time. The art of the game versus pressing tenacity and agility meet each other in this small area and sometimes during the entire match.

However, in close contrast with futsal, the most popular and safest antipressing measure in soccer is the auxiliary back pass to the goalkeeper who, with his active moving, creates an increase in the number of players with the ball with respect to the attacking opponents. If the goalkeeper is attacked by a pressing opponent, aftergaining control of the ball, he recenters the game through a long kick to the opponent's back field. The fight for the ball in the dangerous zone is postponed. And what about the viewer and the expert?

Examples from selected team games should lead to deeper and more inspiring comparisons. They should point out positive and proven trends, which should be an example for soccer. Despite the fact that many people consider soccer a "Mecca of conservatism," this most popular game in the world can gain knowledge and experience from other, similar games. Let's finish with the rhetorical question: Can we be satisfied with the current situation in soccer? Would it be possible, suitable, or necessary to support pressing tactics in soccer with a gentle push? Or is soccer such a cleverly conceived game that it does not need any fundamental development impulses from outside, and it can manage with its own inertia through proven tactics? The deciding factor is the viewer, who is satisfied with contemporary soccer. But for how long will this state be unchangeable—the future will show us. Perspectives on the development of soccer are described in chapter 4.5 Prognosis for pressing.

We can summarize, that pressing becomes a universal defensive tool for defensive tactics in many team games that enable and require using proactivity for the effective regaining of the subject of the game, the ball.

3.0 PRESSING PHENOMENON

As day changes night and most of the entities of our reality have bipolar and complementary character, the course of the game in soccer also consists of changing the basic attacking and defending stages of the game. Their complementarity is so natural that two teams are standing against each other on the pitch, and the one which is not attacking is defending and vice versa. However, the way the team attacks also limits the way the team defends, because the opportunities for attack are determined by the type of defense the team performs.

In the current modern defensive conditions, the defensive stage also becomes a kind of modification of an attack without a ball where the team, which is not in the possession of the ball, is trying to perform proactive defense instead of a traditional defense reaction. The main aim is to gain back the possession of the ball and to make an attempt to attack with it. It's the proactivity principal that is implicitly included in the modern defensive systems based on the space defense principle, which is enriched in some stages of the game by pressing in all its modifications as a proactive defensive tool of the team, which is performing active defensive and defensive proactivity.

An answer to the cardinal question "why exactly pressing?" is the fact that today the pressing tactic in combination with a block defense has become the most effective way of solving a defensive stage. The pressing is a tool that allows to gain a ball in predetermined area.

Of course, only in case that it is correctly performed in relation to time, space, and the players on the pitch. The safety restrictions of its application in the game are related exactly to the optimization of the mentioned game factors.

As a part of the pressing methodology, we offer "the knowledge system," which will make it easier to make decision when forming the game concept, applying the specific tools in the practice process, and pressing tactics improvement as well as in the analysis of the play in order to include it into the match by so-called coach's intervention.

In this part of the publication, we are focusing on the basic theoretical questions of pressing phenomenon. They are supposed to help understand this topic more deeply and get down to the core of the pressing tactics. We spoke about the pressing tactics evolution in detail in the first volume of the trilogy. The comprehension of the historical continuation of the pressing is important not only from the point of view of understanding its current form but also from the point of view of predicting its future direction in the evolution spiral of soccer and creating an effective training technology for its practical handling in match conditions. The transfer between the history and the practice, which this trilogy presents, could be an optimal model for handling the soccer topic of the pressing.

PART 2

3.1 PHENOMENOLOGY OF PRESSING AND GEOMETRY OF ITS SPACE

Phenomenology of the pressing, which focuses on the basic appearance of the pressing tactics, gives us a comprehensive definition of the elementary events that relate to this topic. By stating the place of the pressing in the strategy hierarchy, the game tactic, and detailed analysis of the space geometry for the pressing tactics, we are defining the interpretation model for the analysis of the pressing phenomenon in current soccer. The special application of the concept, "The hunting territory," for pressing, we are offering coaches a methodological tool, which allows them to understand the space relation more practically on the principal of the play theories and more effective interpretation of the positional principles when practicing and improving the pressing tactics.

3.1.1 Is Soccer a Science?

The character of the soccer knowledge parallels often bring us to the dilemma in which we are divided even in answering the cardinal question whether soccer is or isn't a science. The statement that soccer is not a science loses its substantiation the moment it's necessary by conscious coordination of more players to break through a compact defense block 20–25 m deep in a sophisticated manner in time-space pressure conditions.

But if soccer is a science, then we should consistently respect its scientism. Clear definition of the expressions and professional terms should be the core of the soccer theory, also for the purpose of not brining confusion into soccer methodology and practice (part of this publication is also the summary of basic terms definitions, which are commonly used in soccer but always in a clear meaning). The importance of a scientific approach to soccer is also proved by the fact that today we use lot of professional terms and expressions in soccer. Soccer was influenced by many scientific areas, which has enormously enriched the soccer theory. The truth is that soccer would hardly develop today without wide-specter knowledge of science itself. Soccer is gradually becoming a specific hybrid

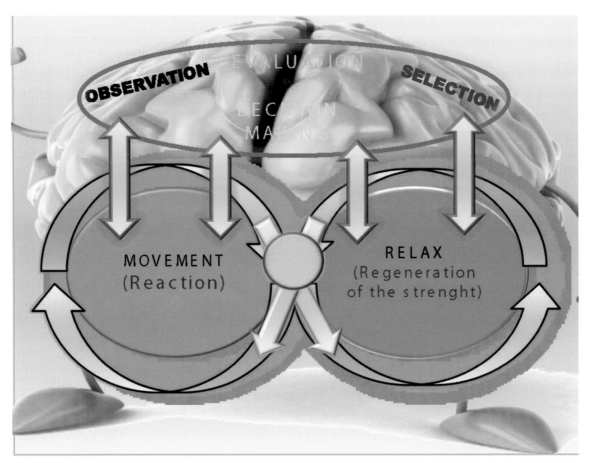

Fig. 3.1-1 Sensomotoric "knot" is an example scheme of traversing impulses, which stimulate the complex sensomotoric adaptation of the players during the preparatory as well as matches.

applied science. The complex use of this science results in systematic profiling of dynamically developed character of a soccer player who is able to solve play tasks in changing conditions slowly increasing in difficulty. The mentioned penetration of science into the methodology of soccer training doesn't relate only to individual sensomotoric adaptation of the player to soccer itself (fig. 3.1-1) but also to a controlled transfer of his individual potential to effective team compatibility (tactic and strategy of the play). This all happens in an environment marked by current civilization and commercial trends. The penetration of science into soccer ensures the influence of development impulses, which are entrenched in confrontational core of soccer as its immanent part.

Many scientists from various areas would envy soccer for the financial budget and finances that flow into soccer. Therefore, we think it's important for soccer to connect to the applied theoretical knowledge by precisely defined soccer terminology. In other words, soccer theory and practice should be more clear, precise, and exact. Specialized soccer "terminology" presented in the publication "The whole team attack or how the attacking is done today" (Borbely et al., 2006) is an attempt to clarify the terminology "confusion" in the soccer theory and enrich the soccer terminology.

For example the term "play sequence" (which is not used maybe because for expressing its meaning are necessary four words "defined time section of the game") or the definition of the brain-compatible training adapted from general pedagogy and didactics.

For the soccer practice, it's important to define the pressing in such a way that players, coaches, and gradually the whole nonprofessional public know what they are supposed to do on the pitch in order to call it the pressing. It's obvious that any initial pressure applied in a play looks like pressing. Our aim is to determine the clear boundaries, which define the term of the pressing because we are aware of the fact that vast majority of confrontational pressure actions in soccer can and must be a pressure and a certain type of enforcement. Whatever movement activity of a defending player, group of defending players, or a whole team is an obstacle for the opponent, which pressures and forces the opponent to overcome the obstacle in an attempt to score a goal. In certain conditions, only the presence of the defending players aligned in a net pushes the opponent with a ball into unsolvable situations while offensively attacking the opponent's goal, especially in time stress (if the team is losing just before the end of the match). In the presented theoretical pressing analysis, we are going to try to explain the readers what are the signs of the actions of the defending players in order to be able to consider these actions as some form of pressing.

3.1.2 Pressing and Its Place in the Tactics Hierarchy and the Strategy of the Game

In the following part of the chapter, we are trying to organize the pressing into a tactical register and tactical soccer database and also we are defining its place in the portfolio of the soccer strategy and tactic. We are focusing on the specification of the pressing in relation to the strategy and the game tactic, the game concept, system of the game as well as the basis alignment. Figure 3.1-2 depicts the order of the relevant terms (relating to the area and the game tactic within the structure of sports performance) in the form, content, and importance sequence.

The presented hierarchy will enable us to answer the question on which tactical level of the tactical pyramid we place the pressing. Consequently, we can focus our attention on defining the relation of the pressing to the game philosophy, strategy and tactic of the game, the game concepts, the game system, and the basic alignment.

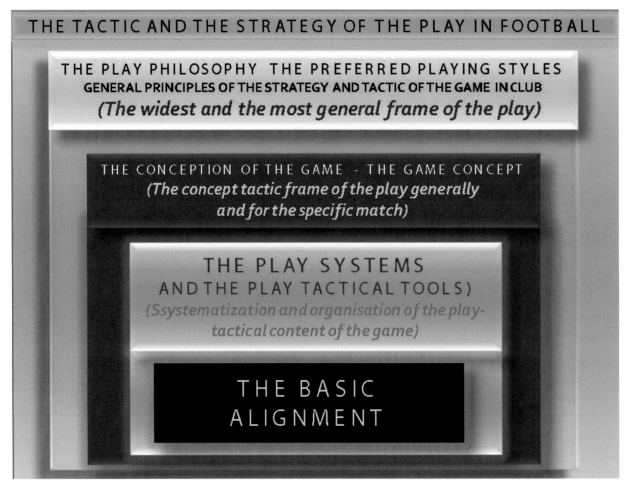

Fig. 3.1-2 The order of the terms relating to the topic of the strategy and the game tactic from the point of view to the content and the importance sequence.

PRESSING IN THE GAME AND PLAY CONCEPTS

The concept of the game is a part of general solution of the play strategy, which is built on the determined soccer philosophy, preferred playing style, and playing strategy in the specific club and the soccer environment. It reflects certain soccer culture, soccer traditions, and, most of all, it brings soccer value preferences into reality. The complex solution of the game tactic, on the theoretical level, determines the direction of the player's preparatory. The theoretical conception of the game is also a guideline for the preparatory conception, and it's not only a purposeless closed document. A long-term conceptual planning of the players' preparatory in a club concludes for the prognosis of the future development direction of soccer. It contains futuristic methodological processes, which are, however, approved by the expert analysis. The conception of the preparatory is so-called the club's "program declaration," which unites the preparatory on all its levels. For example, in children and youth preparatory, the concentration on the ball after losing the possession is the most natural and spontaneous pattern of the players' behavior, which lacks organized order, coordination of the players based on the designation of tasks, and so on. These aren't sophisticatedteam and group algorithms (which can be acquired by the players in higher an strictly defined age categories), but it's a true and sincere interest of the players to gain the possession of the ball based on the ball's magnetism. However, if these natural, unspoiled, and nondeformed predispositions are not suppressed by introducing careful tactics in the preparatory stage in the form of a play, they can become a foundation for deep and permanent habits that are a part of the player's future proactive behavior after losing the possession of the ball.

Pressing is also an alternative part of the game concept for a match with a specific opponent. The pressing has its purpose in the game concept in predetermined time and space stages or in a situational context, which is mostly

- connected to **the team's own game plan** and forcing the team's own playing style on the opponent,

- connected to **the current development of the match** according to the consecutive score,

- as a reaction to **the opponent's style of play,**

- in "play with the pace" of the match,

- in a rational regulation of using the playing, mostly physical and **conditional potential of individuals and team,** connected to the pressing situations and their intentional creation within an active manipulation with space.

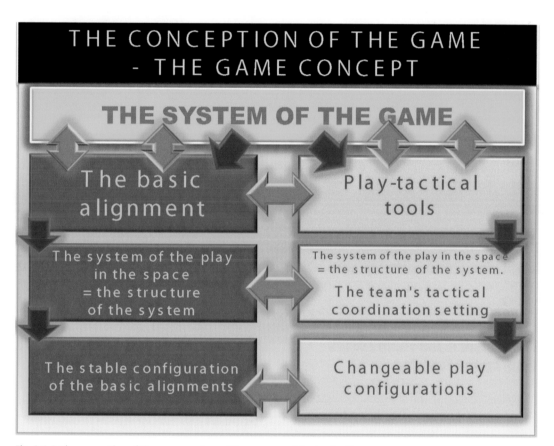

Fig. 3.1-3 The conception of the game, system of the game, and the basic alignment

PRESSING IN THE GAME SYSTEM

Can we speak about a system in connection with the pressing? When talking about a system, we presume it's a compilation of mutually connected and related elements that behave as a whole. **The game system in soccer represents such a connection between the players that** **allows them to act in the game context as a whole,** which is called a team. Even if the pressing itself is not a game system, it can be its part. The pressing's got a wider scope on the game tactic than the more narrowly defined specific play-tactical element (e.g., doubling the opponent with the ball).

Fig. 3.1-4 The position of pressing in the strategy and the tactical-play mosaic of the game plan are determined by a coach.

3.1.3 Introduction to the Theory of the Space for the Pressing

The most relevant factor of the pressing application is the comprehension of the space parameters that limit the possibilities of an effective pressing application and safe use in the game context. This is precisely why we focused especially on the space geometry and its specific characteristics that allow a safe and effective application of all types of the pressing tactics. The holy grail of the pressing are the time, space, and pressure. Their sophisticated implementation into the movement scheme of the ball-oriented team allows the team to fulfill the proactive and defensive model of the team's play behavior. Moreover, it's also because the ball undoubtedly radiates natural magnetism thus causes the play disorder, which can be only prevented by an intentional and tactical positioning of the team players through the play system or the play concept that is significantly complemented by a meaningful basic play alignment.

3.1.3.1 PRESSING, SPACE, AND TIME-SPACE

The term "time-space" often appears in this publication. By the use of this expression, we are trying to highlight "the progressive," sequential and not only situational fundamental of the course of the play in soccer. **The changeable parameters of the game** are the following:

1. **The space** even if restricted but with possibility to define its active zones during the game.

2. **The players** of both rival team in the number of twenty-two.

3. One **ball.**

Fig. 3.1-5 The changeable parameters of the game

From the figure, we can define the depth of the active play space, "rigid" position of the ball and every player. The space between them is unchanged, and they are measurable by the player's mutual spacing. The analyzed attributes of the play situation (PSt) are also called the characteristics of the play situation, because in the play situation, we only perceive the static space parameters of the game.

Fig. 3.1-6 The parameters of the game: space, players, and a ball, which are changeable, but they remain still in a play situation.

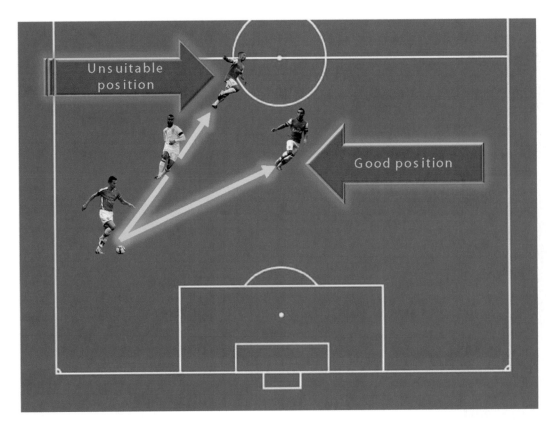

Fig. 3.1-7 The characteristics of PSt

The characteristics of the game, as well as its parameters, are becoming changeable only when the time "enters" the game, because the time makes them move and creates the continuity of the play process. The game can develop in the time-space in an endless variability of its alternative course, however, in only one specific direction. Is it possible to predict the course of the play and to manage it? If yes, how far and how?

The task of the coaches, specialists, and all the people involved is to reveal and find in the "endlessness" of the play situations "the time-space" logic of the connection between the play situations. Despite the "endlessness" of the play situations and sequences, many of them have similar or even identical characteristics. They appear in the game repeatedly maybe only with irrelevant differences. We can, therefore, call them "typical." **Therefore, there is a purpose in systematic standardization of the approved and affective alternative solutions of the**

play tasks that are connected with the typical play situations and sequences. Also it's important to drill them or even automatize them in the training process with the significant focus on the play details. This also applies to the standard situations (sequences) of which none of them is identical. Despite this, one of the most probable, statistically "mostly used," and even notoriously well-known alternatives of the opponent's reaction is expected. Therefore, in the training, it's suitable to master some solutions of **the standards situations** either individually or in coordinated group schemes, also called "signals." The debacle of Brazil with Germany in the World Cup in Brazil was significantly influenced by the first-scored goal by the Germans after a comer kick. The scorer Muller became a free player after his personal guard was "removed" by futsal block in the penalty area by one of his team players.

Fig. 3.1-8 The time and space—THE TIME-SPACE as a limiting factor of the play

Moreover, there was a parallel movement of the scorer intentionally directed into the area where the ball was supposed to get after the brilliantly performed kick from the corner. When Muller looked at his watch, the ball landed exactly according to the timetable to the place where he wanted, which was his leg. We might think it was a coincidence; however, **"the time-space synchronization"** of the individual stages of the mentioned corner-kick scenario was performed the best possible way. The successful realization of the play intentions isn't a coincidence, but it's the result of a systematic and persistent practice of the specific scheme. It should also contain the expected and may be traditional reaction of the players in defense. This reaction was probably discovered by German experts in video recordings from the previous matches. The Brazilians

hadn't played the personal defense in a corner kick for the first time. Thus, the Germans succeeded in performing one of the most remarkable planned and practiced tricks in the soccer history. Moreover, it happened in a major event like World Championship in Brazil and against the hosting Brazil right in Maracana. The German team may have succeeded also because they perfectly manipulated their opponent by their planned coordination **concluding from the time-space analysis of the play sequence and the corner kick. Therefore, the expression of time-space is a priority also in the application of proactive forms of defense. Without the time-space synchronization of all team players actions, it's not possible to expect a higher level of their success.** On the contrary, there can be huge energy loss of the team's potential.

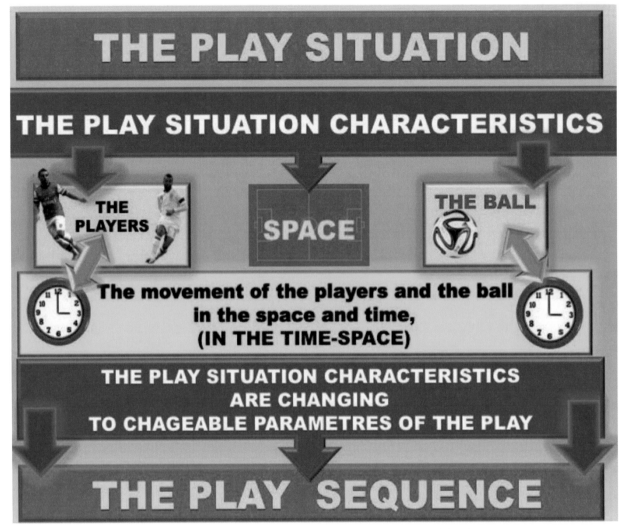

Fig. 3.1-9 The structure and the processes, the space and the time-space, or the play situation and the play sequence

3.1.3.2 THE TIME-SPACE LOGIC OF THE GAME AND ANTICIPATION OF POSSIBLE ALTERNATIVES DURING THE COURSE OF THE GAME

Is it possible to prove that the course of the game is actually a chain of logically linked play situations and play sequences? We'll try to achieve this by a simple speculation. In a closed space of the playing area, the ball can get into the current game center from the area, which we call "precentral" area. Let's connect theoretically the game center with the lines that link precentral areas, which relate directly to the play sequence. Then, according to the further positional and space characteristics of the game and according to the behavior of the changeable game

parameters, we can anticipate up to a certain level which way the course of the game will develop and where the new game center will be located (postcentral area, Fig. 3.1-10). Precentral area (where the ball came from) can be defined as a part of the playing area from which the ball came into the game center. The game center area (the current position of the ball) is the part of the playing area that is directly near the ball. Postcentral area (where the ball is heading) is the part of the playing area into which the game center is consequently relocated during the course of the play sequence.

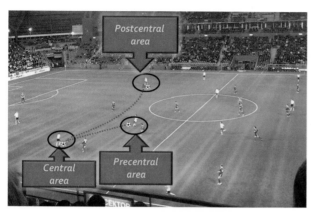

Fig. 3.1-10 Precentral, central, and postcentral area.

Fig. 3.1-11 Postcenter area is alternative because it's a future fiction.

Various postcentral alternatives, which happen during the course of the game, are characterized by different purpose of the ball's direction.

1. Auxiliary back pass—security.

2. Width pass—opening the space by a wide transfer of the play.

3. Depth pass—deep direction with relatively higher risk of losing the possession of the ball.

Different aimed focus of the mentioned alternatives of the postcentral play development (ranging between maximum preferred security and the acceptance of the maximum level of the play risk) concludes from the course of the match confrontation itself (e.g., the current score of the match, the usual style of the opponent's play, the environment in which the match is taking place, and other well known facts about the common play-tactical attributes of the opponent's play).

In relation to this, it's also necessary to take into consideration the possibility of the pressing failure, which the outnumber of the attacking team brings. It's one of the contra-productive moments of the pressing application. On the other hand, a successful pressing application brings this effect to the defending team the moment they gain the possession of the ball. The important stage of the game is so-called postpressing stage because the successful pressing result, consisting in gaining the possession of the ball, is the point of this defensive effort. Effective dealing with this stage after the pressing completion lies in maintaining the playing continuity. In other words, it's necessary to keep the offensive effective in order to give a tactical meaning to

the defensive action. However, it's important to teach the team play not only after a successful but also after an unsuccessful pressing.

Anticipation of the game, based on its time-space (but play-tactical too) logic, allows the players to enter the course of the game in a more proactive way. If in active defense we eliminate the applicability of some of the opponent's play solutions, and we reduce their number, we increase the probability of the correct prediction of further development of the game, and we also increase our own team's proactivity effect level. Erikson (2001) called it "closing the opponent into a performance cage"; however, in this case it's not only in psychological sense but especially in time-space sense.

The activity of the defending player, in figure 3.1-12, lies in attacking the opponent with the ball by parallel approach of the team player by the sideline. An active defense, which is connected this way, eliminates or increases the risk level of some of the opponent's play solutions (in this case, it's the offensive alternative of the play sequence continuation). The defending team enforces the opponent the direction of their own action. The defending team regulates the game development in the time-space the way that is predictable or expected. The conclusion of the presented play sequence in a real match (fig. 3.1-13a) was a width pass.

Another play reaction could happen in a faster and more flexible course of the game. The importance of the game reading is depicted in the figure where all the defending players are turning toward the game center in the direction of the width movement, which can also be a preparatory stage for an eventual pressing tactics application in the opposite side vertical line. (fig. 3.1-13b).

If the game center is moved by the continuation of the play sequence all the way to the sideline and the side defender, the players in blue shirts can intensify their width movement in order to create a right and asymmetrical "small" pitch. The aim of this is to stop the opponent's depth movement, to push the opponent out, and eventually to accelerate the pressure by defensive outnumber of the new game center or application of a proactive defense activity (fig. 3.1-14).

The mentioned situation is connected to a movement realization as well as to a sensory activity, which means active and operational exchange of the players' information in the space and time environment (observation, evaluation, selection, decision making, and choosing one solution or the other from more alternatives). Perception element of the game relies on the logic of the game's development, which is described in the presented figure.

The logic of the postcentral development of the play is a rational core of the prediction and its probable immediate direction. The logic of the game is based on a continuous course of events with meaningfully connected time-space characteristics, which enable and support the comprehension of the game. The "reading" of the game will then not be any charlatanism or fortune-telling from a glass ball. Quite opposite, it is and **always will be the reflection of "the perception ability" of the players to perceive, recognize, and understand the time-space logic of the game.**

According to the players' and the ball's position and according to the game canter that are in figure 3.1-15, one of the expected play alternatives is a long pass behind the back of the opponent's defense. In a situation, when the player with the ball has the ball under control, he is not under pressure and his team players from the other line are in a dynamic movement prepared to break the line of the offside. The mentioned characteristics of the play sequence are "a challenge" for the defense line to show an adequate play reaction despite the fact that the game may not develop according to the described scenario, but

there'll be an alternative and completely different course of the game. Therefore, we call it an **alternative logic of the game.** It's a game that is partially restricted by its "explicit logic" despite its variability (the game rules, the aim of the game, the tactical intention, the current score, and the play sequence characteristics).

Fig. 3.1-12 Tile activity of the defending players in the center of the game

Fig. 3.1-13a Width pass—opening the space by the transfer of tile play

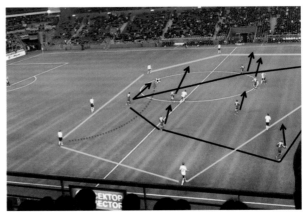

Fig. 3.1-13b The players in blue shirts in a time-space reaction are following the width pass by a parallel width movement and by creating a new, in this case, a right asymmetrical block.

Fig. 3.1-14 The movement of the game center all the way to the sideline

Fig. 3.1-15 An alternative logic of the game

3.1.3.3 GEOMETRY OF THE SPACE AND MANIPULATION OF SPACE

Every player's got his own team's game plan in his head. He's got imaginary plan how to solve the "Rubik's Cube" space puzzle in order to find the solution before his opponent does.

Every tactical plan includes a definition of a rational and the most optimal way of the space use that is available to the players. **"Manipulation of space"** is a term that could briefly and concisely express **the summary of play-tactical elements,** which the players can use in a permanent fight for every meter of the pitch. **By the expression manipulation of space, we understand an intentional reshaping of the conclusion active playing area into the target playing area (e.g., target pressing zone)** in a sense of play-tactical concept of the game or play intention. The mentioned space manipulation isn't considered as a single-sided act of will enforcement from one of the rival teams. The players of both teams equally take part in the final outcome of the time-space confrontation by which the active playing area is currently formed in the particular play sequence.

The active playing area can be defined as a section of the playing area that is bordered by the side positions of both rival team players. As the players and the ball move during the game, **the active playing area will also be a moving formation,** which elastically changes its position, borders, and shape. Manipulation with space usually happens continuously in a continual play sequences

and positional movements of the players. This consists of more or less continuous but permanent and elastic space bordering in which the players can perform their playing activities more efficiently. That means this is the type of the time-space action where its effect is determined by time and the speed by which the players can complete their mission when moving in the play space. The rivals create obstacles to each other in the space confrontation in order to be closer to meet their own intentions than the opponent.

The active playing area that is mark in figure 3.1-16 in blue color is the space for the team, which has the possession of the ball. The area marked with red lines inside the blue formation is smaller because the defending team is closing the gaps between the players and the team also reduces the space for their defensive activities (reducing the pitch).

Fig. 3.1-16 Schematic definition of the active playing areas

Fig. 3.1-17 The active playing area in the past

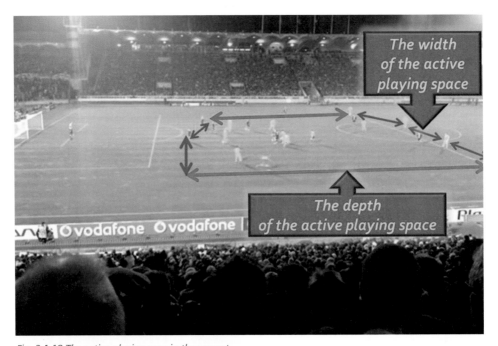

Fig. 3.1-18 The active playing area in the present

3.1.3.4 AN INSPIRATION OR A PRECIOUS EXPERIENCE FOR THE SOCCER SPACE FIGHT

An ancient Chinese Master Sun Tzu considered as the significant matter the landscape and the terrain where the armies were supposed to clash. The size and the physiognomy of the battlefield not only determines the strategy and the tactic of the battle but also determines when and where we must avoid direct confrontation with the enemy. Sun Tzu says: "Although the biggest ally of the commander is the physiognomy of the land, the ability to figure the rival out, promptly evaluate the difficulties and risks, and at the same time calculate the distances are the Characteristics, which the real commander cannot do without." Sun Tzu recognizes nine types of terrain:

1. Scattered that requires long distance movements.

2. Accessible.

3. Complicated, problematic.

4. Open, crossable.

Fig. 3.1-19 Crossable and open "terrain" on soccer

5. Crossroads.

6. Dangerous.

7. Demanding.

8. Closed.

9. Inconclusive.

The analogy of the Sun Tzu open "battlefield" in soccer can be a play situation presented in figure 3.1-19. The active playing area bordered by the players, shows that this space is **open and, therefore, it's easily crossable** due to its irregular scatter with few uncontrolled vertical zones. Moreover, the significantly big depth of the active playing area approx. 60 m results in incompactness of the passively defending players in yellow shirts. Sun Tzu would in this case probably withdraw his soldiers into their barracks.

"Each one of the nine terrains requires a specific approach, an appropriate use of defensive or attacking tactic and comprehension of human character. It's not possible to succeed without this knowledge." The first four types of the Sun Tzu landscape are the opposite of the other five types. What is their main difference?

In the theory of the pressing, we were inspired by the Sun Tzu theory about the fighting style in a closed terrain: "In the closed terrain, you must use trickery and block

all the escape ways. In the inconclusive terrain, you must fight; it's when the soldiers are surrounded, they create the biggest resistance." Open, scattered, and crossable terrain that requires long movements is generally complicated and problematic for the battle strategy and situations. The same applies to soccer where the open battle confrontation is epitomized by the pressing. Sun Tzu saw a huge advantage for leading the war campaign in the landscape types of "closed, demanding, and inconclusive." The same space rules dominate the soccer pressing today. The space closure and complicating the opponent's space activity (space "cage") precede the active pressing application. All this leads to the last type of the space. Inconclusive terrain and inconclusive playing area are the result of closing the space in the pressing. The intention of the team performing the pressing is to get the opponent team players constantly into inconclusive situations.

The Sun Tzu idea of blocking all the escape ways in a closed space is very educational for the pressing today. For the time-space theory, it represents the confirmation of the meaning and the importance of a gradual or even parallel application of proactive elements. It's not sufficient enough to close the targeted pressing zone, but at the same time, it's important to "block the escape ways." Sun Tzu theory goes even further, also it takes into consideration the rival's reaction that is squeezed in a small space.

Because the opponent is in an inconclusive terrain (space), they will create a great resistance. They'll act like fish in a small fish-tank, if you are trying to catch them with your hand. In life-threatening situations, they are looking for and often find escape ways. **Therefore, the pressing must always take into account the opponent's pressing resistance who is "squeezed" in a continuously reducing "living" area in which the opponent feels threatened (speeding up the opponent's play under pressing in a natural alternative, which we are actually enforcing).**

Any type of soccer activity concludes from the fact that there are two teams playing against each other with only one ball. The opposite intentions of the play, on one hand to gain the possession of the ball and on the other hand not to lose the ball, force the players to literally fight for the ball in order to defeat their opponent. Compared to the war campaign, the battle for gaining the possession of the ball in soccer happens in a well-known environment called a playing area, which is restricted by the rules.

Fig. 3.1-20 Twenty players are perseveringly fighting for the space. They tolerate nothing from one another, and they are mutually restricting the space conditions for the offensive.

The mentioned space or more precisely time-space "war" is a natural conclusion of the play in which there are two diametrically different aims against each other: to score a goal and to prevent scoring a goal. However, it's possible to score a goal only if you have the ball in your possession. The ball's magnetism (the desire to own the ball, to create and entertain the spectators with it, to permanently get closer to the ball, and to constantly look for it) is a natural "sight" in soccer, and it's manifested by the players making a big effort to gain the possession of the ball. The principle of the effective fight for the ball is a permanent creation

of time-space conditions for its keeping or gaining. But the "trick" is that these conditions are diametrically different for each one of the mentioned intentions.

3.1.3.5 THE CHARACTERISTICS OF THE SUITABLE SPACE CONDITIONS FOR KEEPING THE BALL

It could seem as a waste of time, if we focus our attention to the analysis of suitable space conditions for keeping the ball in connection to the pressing. However, if we want the pressing to be successful, we should also know our opponent, the range of his playing elements, which also have their own time-space specification.

In order to keep the ball safe, it's suitable to limit its possible contact with the opponent. That means to avoid a direct confrontation with the opponent (fight). The effort of the players owning the ball to open the playing area is maximally justifiable from the point of view of creating space conditions not only for keeping the ball but also for the purpose of the game center movement toward the opponent's goal. In the offensive depth or in the direction of the attacking action, the limiting restriction for opening (deepening) the active playing space is the offside rule in which the maximum width for opening the active playing space is determined by the sidelines.

The playing area and the playing space.

Fig. 3.1-21 The playing area and space

a) Opening the depth of the active playing space by the attacking team toward their goal.

In figure 3.1-22, the players in white shirt bravely opened the width of the central area space. The depth position of the middle defender is convenient for an alternative of a safe auxiliary back pass application, which would significantly deepen the active playing space.

When performing the more suitable offensive play-tactical alternative, the important element of an active formation of the playing space is the vertical movement of the middle defender by positioning himself in the line bordering the active playing space from the bottom (red arrow, fig. 3.1-25). This means that excessively stretched playing "field" isn't suitable for a potential loss of the ball, but especially for compact depth movement of the team forward in the direction of attacking action.

b) Deepening the active playing space by the attacking team toward the opponent's goal

The enforcement of the defending chain-depth withdrawal by moving the center of the game to the opponent's goal is the logical follow-up element of forming the active playing space by the attacking team. The defenders in blue are going to apply reverse move of so-called "pump," which is used when moving forward to the center of the game in an attack. On the contrary, after losing the ball in a situation when the ball is approaching the line of the defending chain, the tactically safe solution is to withdraw back to the optimal depth even when losing the "area" is at stake. By this, the attacking team doesn't only achieve the active playing space deepening in the direction of the attack but also the depth penetration of the offensive closer to the opponent's goal (figs. 3.1-26, 27). One of the mostly applied play-tactical tools for opening the active playing area depth by the attacking team toward the opponent's goal is:

1. Transfer of the game center as close as possible to the defending team's defensive chain line by quickened diagonal or depth circulation of the ball (fig. 3.1-26).

2. Transfer of the game center as close as possible to the defending team's defensive chain line by performing tempo dribbling and individual depth direction of the ball.

3. "Breaking" the offside line by long transfer of the game from the depth of the team's own defense together with the parallel movement of the offensive players behind the defenders' back or by other forms of time coordination of the players on the opponent's defensive chain line; in other words, on the offside line (fig. 3.1-27).

Fig. 3.1-22 Opening the depth of the active playing space by the attacking team toward their goal

Fig. 3.1-23 "A small pitch," apart from the attacking compactness, which is followed by the defensive compactness, it also saves energy

Fig. 3.1-24 Transfer of the game center as close as possible to the defensive chain line

Fig. 3.1-25 This picture shows how both rival teams promptly and flexibly work the depth of the active playing space.

Fig. 3.1-26 The white "pump" is pressing the team forward, the blue "pump" is sucking the air in and withdrawing, so the defense can primarily monitor the dangerous area closer to their own goal.

Fig. 3.1-27 A blind space behind the attacking players' backs

Fig. 3.1-28 The active playing space shortening over the middle line

A mutual effort to shorten the pitch automatically creates free areas behind the defenses, which are used by the depth offensive for the purpose of space compensation of the game in an extremely compressed area. Offensive deepening is possible by transferring the game center behind the extended defense's back (fig. 3.1-27).

c) Shortening and closing the active playing area depth by the attacking team toward the opponent's goal

If the defenders and midfielders didn't react to the successful vertical depth penetration of their team players by additional action and extension, the team wouldn't be able to maintain the purposeful and optimal depth for the offensive continuation (or after losing the possession of the ball) and for an effective continuation of the game in the defensive stage. Therefore, the extension of the defending formation into the depth toward the targeted offensive zone (closer to the opponent's goal) is the basic element of the additional, purposeful, and necessary space manipulation related mainly to the depth attacking and also proactive defense in the attacking zone (fig. 3.1-28).

This active "pump" works situationally both ways. It doesn't only work in defensive but also in attacking stage of the game during the whole course of the game.

The offside rule is advantageous to an attacking team when shortening the active playing space. The players can tactically extend all the way to the middle line level, the way that the rule II "covers their back" in case of losing the ball (even unexpectedly). This way they are closing half of the playing area, and they are intentionally leaving behind them temporarily **"blind" unoccupied and unmonitored area.** However, this doesn't mean that exceeding the density of the center of the game is a nontactical element. Quite opposite, if the team has the ball under their control with an appropriate playing confidence, the blind area behind the defensive chain is practically irrelevant. The team creates blind areas intentionally while these areas are elastically and situationally changing and adjusting. In order to achieve a sufficient control of these areas, the team has prepared compensational playing elements. At the same time, the strength ratio of each area and each predictable situation is well-respected. Attacking (gradual attack against the aligned defense) without shrinking and closing the active playing area depth has no chance to succeed. Now we know that the "pump" has two contradicting effects: on one hand, it creates an overpressure, and on other hand, it leaves an empty space (fig. 3.1-29). The crucial problem of an uncontrolled blind space arises after losing the possession of the ball and the ball approaching the defensive chain. In this situation, the "pump" will also start fulfilling different functions when reversing.

Fig. 3.1-29 So-called "pump" is one of the basic tactical elements of the defensive player's chain by which we achieve the pushing of our team and closing the space from the bottom.

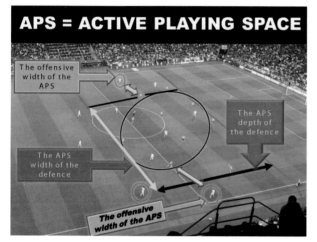

Fig. 3.1-30 Widening the active playing space by the attacking player

The extension of the defensive chain toward an attacking action is a significant element for shortening the active playing area depth, especially if the center of the game is located in the attacking zone or near the opponent team's penalty area. The tactical purposes of this play-tactical element are four basic intentions:

1. An active playing space shrinking that is more common for the defensive activity. The reason for this is the preparatory for switching after losing the ball. The loss of the ball is more than expected during the attacking action culmination; therefore, this is a logical alternative. The defense extension working as "a pump" creates suitable conditions for an immediate pressing application. This way it's possible to form more continuous pressure on the opponent.

2. The support for the offensive. The attacking team players would be incompact without extending the defending and middle formation. By extending the

defensive chain, we at the same time enable the participation of the midfielders and the defensive formation players in finalization preparatory, in other words we enable them to participate directly in finalizing the attacking actions.

3. The defensive and midfield formation behaves alternatively in order to efficiently support the attacking action or continuation of the attack after losing the possession of the ball by proactive forms of a defense.

4. In the case of losing the ball and the center of the game coming closer, the pump works in the reverse. The empty area is getting smaller by the withdrawal and takes the position on the level that is appropriate to the team's own defense safety.

The offside rule loses its "validity" on the opponent's half of the playing space. Therefore, when shortening the active playing space over the middle line, the players in blue, in figure 3.1-29, can't count on the protective effect of the offside rule. In this case, however, they are closing the active playing space more significantly and, at the same time, they are leaving a large and uncontrolled area behind their backs, which is "blind" from their point of view.

(d) Opening the active playing space depth by the attacking team

The tendency of the attacking players is to widen the active playing space depth (fig. 3.1-32). This is the proof of the attacking players' effort to occupy the positions that are out of the closed active playing space of the defending players. The side player in the periphery space is "the end" player in the left vertical that is opening the active playing space width. By taking this position, he is closing the area in front of him at the same time.

3.1.3.6 THE CHARACTERISTICS OF THE SUITABLE SPACE CONDITIONS FOR GAINING POSSESSION OF THE BALL

In order to gain the possession of the ball, it's suitable to limit the possibilities of the ball's circulation by the positional interruption of the possible passes line. For this task, it's necessary to reach the dominance of the players in the center of the game, which means to outnumber the opponent. The consequence of this is an excessive density in the center of the game. This state is possible to achieve only by shrinking and closing the active playing space.

a) The depth compressing of the active playing space in the defending stage of the game

The offside rule 11 significantly contributes to shortening the active playing space. Significant shortening of the active playing space happens by the movement of the "offside" lines of both rival teams. In some stages of a match, it can even be the distance of 25–30 m (fig. 3.1-33).

b) The width compressing of the active playing area in defense

If the center of the game is positioned in the area of one of the side verticals directly near the sideline, the closure of the active playing area width is possible only in asymmetrical playing shape of the defending team. The symmetry of basic alignment allows alternating, according to the position of the ball, an endless range of compressing and asymmetrical playing positions of the players and playing configurations of the whole team. These asymmetrically positioned small pitches can be actively shaped by a coordinated movement of the players where the active playing area depth is closed by the width movement and the side player's position. One of the sidelines is

a good helper; however, an uncontrolled and free vertical space is consequently created on the opposite side.

In figure 3.1-31, we are showing an example of the width manipulation with space. Together with the depth reduction, the players come to the peak of their effort to compress the active playing space by closing its depth.

The consequence of narrowing the active playing space is the fact that the players form an asymmetrical playing configuration almost always when the ball is in the area near any sideline (figs. 3.1-36, 37). Therefore, we can see seemingly extreme situations with clear and contrasting alignment of the players in the playing space.

The depth movement doesn't happen by crossing the positional configuration of the players, which strictly responds to their basic alignment. Despite this, the symmetry of the basic alignment is justifiable because the basic alignment is a structure, which connects hardly predictable and irregularly changing space positional asymmetry. Thus, the basic alignment secures the "order" and equally balanced positional game even in its asymmetrical variety.

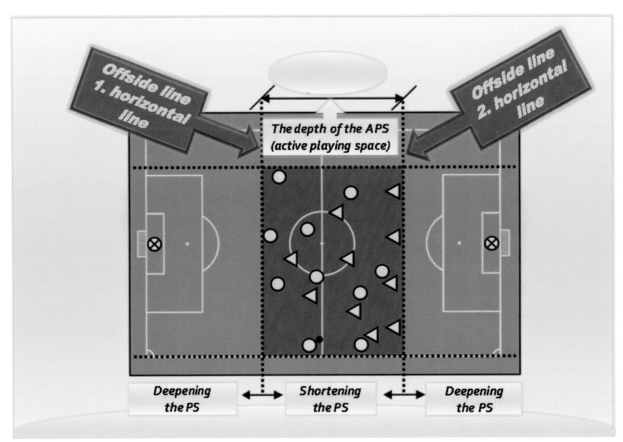

Fig. 3.1-31 Possibilities of the intentional tactical "manipulation" of the playing space depth

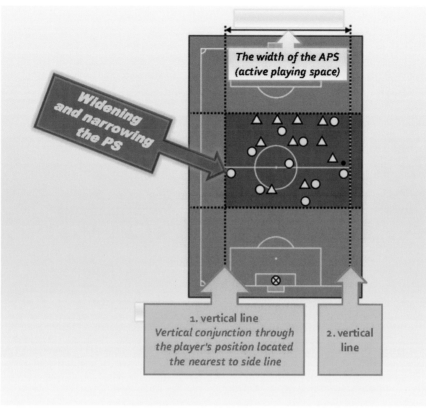

Fig. 3.1-32 An effort of the defending players is to narrow the width of the active playing area.

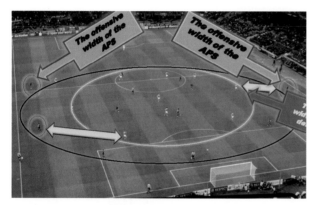

Fig. 3.1-33 The size and position of the active playing space is achieved, apart from manipulation with the depth, by closing or opening its width. An effort of the defending players is to narrow the active playing space.

Fig. 3.1-34 Left asymmetrical playing alignment

Fig. 3.1-35 Right asymmetrical playing alignment

Fig. 3.1-36 Symmetrically narrowed playing alignment shows that it's suitable to be flexibly changing the right and left asymmetrical configuration in the compact playing shape that also crosses the middle vertical.

3.1.3.7 THE "BLIND" SPACE

Let's try to define the expression "blind" metaphorically by an ancient philosophical analogy from the strategist Sun Tzu. We're taking into account the two-thousand-year-old space logic that relates to an asymmetrical alignment of soldiers in a battlefield (in our case, they're soccer players in a pitch). According to this, the logical reflection of the positional asymmetry is a positional space imbalance and contrast. The result of this is the fact that **if we overcrowd a specific part of the area, consequently we have to free or empty another part of the area.** Let's call the described time-space effect "full versus empty." Sun Tzu explained the practical consequences of his space philosophy on the example of an eggshell. If an eggshell is hit by a fist, it will have much harder devastating effect in comparison with the same blow on a stone. There is a simple conclusion from this, which is significantly important knowledge for the pressing. If we outnumber the center of the game, we'll create venerable areas in which we'll be temporarily positionally "thin." We'll call them "blind" areas if only because they are mostly located out of the players' horizon, which is behind their backs or by their sides.

The teams that we classify as the most progressive, from the point of view defensive proactivity application, can manage and positionally control the playing space by continuous reduction of the active playing space width almost to the half, and they alternatively significantly outnumber the opposite verticals. The most difficult task of the proactive defensive tactics is to run around the width in the compact block while frequently transferring the game alternatively to the opposite verticals all the way to the sidelines in order to allow the players to be within effective reach of the opponent (also in the depth of the active playing space). The effect of this asymmetrical play time-space option also depends on the depth of the defensive form. Having a four or five-member chain, the formations in one horizontal layer of one basic alignment are able to play proactively alternatively by both sidelines. However, in two or three-member formations, it's also necessary to include in the game the depth zone compensational movement of the defending players. By these maneuvers, we can achieve in proactive defense an effective application of the team's playing potential in the center of the game.

The opposite of the width activity is passivity, of which the consequence is a scattered and quite easily penetrable defense. Although, the blind spaces don't seem to be created, it's opposite. The cracks between the players could also be considered as uncontrolled areas (fig. 3.1-21). In the picture above, we can analyze in detail the playing situation from the defensive team's alignment point of view. The center of the game is situated by the sideline. In spite of this, the asymmetry of the defending team's alignment isn't visible. It's dominated by a significant passivity in manipulation with the depth and with of the active playing space. The result of this is unusually and comfortably open area of the game center to a big advantage of the attacking team. The active playing space is scattered and also the space between the players of both teams are big. All this is to an advantage of the attacking team as well as to a proactive defense. The described situation can be demonstrated as an example of defensive time-space passivity. The mice have a big "ball" in the huge spacious cage! The rule of "empty versus full" doesn't finds its use in the soccer "time-space" strategy only in an extreme form. According to the Sun Tzu rule, the spaces between the players in a defined active playing space are getting bigger proportionally to the growing distance of the players from the ball. The result of this is an effort of both teams to outnumber the center of the game, which logically leads to an excessive density of the area. The excessive density of the game center and its surrounding is gradually being reduced, and it's being dispersed more significantly in the periphery. The consequence of the application of the depth and width asymmetrical proactive defensive playing alignment is the fact that the opponent will try to take an advantage of the weak points of these time-space play schemes, maybe even the most unexpected situations.

Fig. 3.1-37 The blind space behind the players' backs. They might feel it; however, they can't see it because they are facing the center of the game.

Fig. 3.1-38 Even six players in red shirts weren't able to prevent the significantly free position of the player in white shirt that uninterruptedly centers blocked and covered by nobody. The width maneuver didn't work out and even if these situations are common in matches, there can be goals scored.

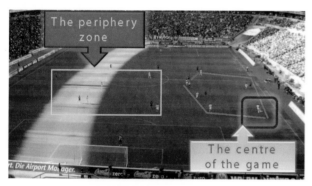

Fig. 3.1-39 The center of the game and the periphery playing areas and zones. The number of the players is increasing proportionally to the players' approach to the game center.

Fig. 3.1-40 Sun Tzu and his space axiom in the soccer practice of "full versus empty."

3.1.3.8 ATTACK–DEFENSE AND TIME–SPACE BALANCE, STAGE SWITCHING, AND SPACE

The basic strategic conclusion, in order to apply an effective playing (either attacking or defensive) activity in the time-space, is the set-up of the universal designation of the players' potential to perform during the game. This means to secure the organizational conditions that are suitable for the players' operational development in any part of the playing area during a constant attempt to solve attack-defense tasks as well as in unexpected changes during the course of the game. Therefore, from the space and time-space organization point of view, the most important step is to allow continuous and effective stage transfer and stage switch after losing or gaining the ball. The continuous cycle of switching from defense to attack or from opening and to closing the active space is the main problem of the play tactic in soccer. What happens in the so-called switching is the "overlapping" of the stages, especially the contrasting alignment of the players' positions.

The difference of the suitable conditions for gaining the position of the ball and for keeping the ball shows in full contrast at the moment of the ball ownership change. The transfer from the closed alignment of the players to the open alignment, while the opponent is performing a re-verse movement during the closure of the open positions, requires a certain time. The ideal solution is to shorten the transfer to the minimum, if possible with an immediate pressing that shortens the transfer time to almost a zero. The mentioned time lap is a transfer sub-stage, and its length depends on the players themselves, the flexibility of their reactions, and their movement ability by which they can realize the positional changes on the stages borders. The conclusion alignment and the transfer of the players in the time-space have its strategic and tactical rules, which determine the most rational way of the players' movement. One of them is also the space strategy using the alignment of a specific number of players in alternative positions in play sequences. As an example, we can state the maintenance of the sensitive attack-defense balance in the game by correct designation of the number of the players **over the ball line (the players that are attack oriented)** and **under the ball line (the players that are prepared to start immediately the stage for gaining back the possession of the ball).** The relation of the overall number of the players to the play space isn't possible to solve for the specific stages individually but only as an interconnected piece, because both stages are related to each other. What is effective for an attack might be contra-productive from the defense point of view and vice versa.

Today we can see more clearly that the part of the game on the stages border (the moment of the loss of the ball

PART 2

and the moment of the gaining the possession of the ball) makes difference the matches results. By applying the pressing, the teams significantly contribute to the fact that the ball ownership change happens more frequently during the pressing than during passive defense. If both rival teams apply some form of pressing, the frequency of the loss or gaining the possession of the ball increases. The issue of stage switching, from the tactic point of view, is one of the most relevant topics.

3.1.3.9 PRESSING AND PRESSING RESISTANCE

If one wants to be successful in pressing, one must not only win personal battles but also battles for the space by a conscious manipulation with space. If the team is inconsistent in the space confrontation, and it can't preplan good conditions for an advantage in personal fights, the team's more likely to lose. As a consequence of the play-tactical adaptation of the top teams, the resistance toward the pressing is being formed. This type of resistance enables the teams to play efficiently against pressing tactics of the defending players too. The players, who are performing the pressing, must be aware of the fact that the opponent, who they want to apply the pressing against, will be resistant toward this proactive defensive tactic because:

1. the team is prepared **to deal with the pressure effectively;**

2. the team's got prepared **purposeful escape alternatives,** and it'll be always looking for **ways to be released from pressing;**

3. the team intentionally directs the ball into an area in which **it will try to apply their own pressing.**

The players who are applying the pressing make big effort to reach the dominance over the opponent in the area where the ball is located. In order to create the pressure on the opponent, it's necessary to increase the density in the area with the ball. The opponent with the ball will naturally try to speed up the movement and the circulation of the ball in order to make it difficult for the defending players to density the area. Thus the confrontational spiral, which is specific for soccer, starts spinning. The players in matches operationally apply specific elements in order to eliminate the opponent. If the opponent speeds up the movement of the ball, the players of the pressing team are forced to increase the intensity of their movement. The more efficient, sensible, and faster the opponent is when moving the ball, the more difficult it is for the players to apply the pressing. Is it possible to be endlessly increasing the successful pressing movement after the ball? Will the ball or the players, who are literally hunting the ball, be consequently faster? When we think about the pressing, we mustn't pull it out of the mentioned confrontational spiral because what can happen is that we may never catch the rabbit (the ball). It's obvious that if the good organizational coordination of the players was absent in the pressing, the chances for the success would be thinner. **By the pressing organization, the players bring the order into their movement while the opponent's disorder is being increased by speeding up the movement of the ball. The order versus the disorder and the pressing versus the pressing resistance are two sides of the same coin. Therefore, we can accept the general knowledge that always when applying in the training the playing forms that focus on the pressing practice and improvement, one way or the other, we will also develop the ability of the players to resist the pressing.** This should be the point of every training session. It's like when you buy "two in one" in a shop; in this case it's playing "unisex."

3.1.3.10 SPACE AMONG LINES AND FREE SPACES BETWEEN PLAYERS

By creating the pressing space cage, into which we close the opponent, we significantly improve the conditions for the contra-triangular activities of the players who apply pressing, for example, in the finishing pressing zone, which we intentionally reduced and bordered before activating our own pressing (fig. 3.1-44).

The bigger the space cage is, the longer the sides of the triangle are; therefore, it's more difficult for the attacking players to get to the contact with the ball. The length of any sides of "the geometrical forms" (line, triangle, square, diamond...) create spaces among lines and spaces between the players relating to the team players but also to the opponent players. We will call the mentioned spaces the free spaces.

The analyzed space and tactical game axioms, which are related to attack and defense, have their purpose because

Fig. 3.1-41a Examples of free spaces

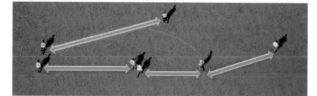

Fig. 3.1-41b Examples of free spaces

we can deduce the width and depth of so-called free spaces according to them. They are distances that are created, and they elastically change during the course of the game according to the size (width and depth) of the active playing space in other words, the space in which both teams actively play. On a specific example, we'll analyze in detail directly proportional relation of the active playing space and the size of the free spaces in a matching play sequence (fig. 3.1-46).

The mastery of working with the ball in small geometrical forms, by transferring the center of the game almost perfectly and precisely even bigger distances, is characteristic for the current Spanish school. The ability to keep the possession of the ball under an increasing pressure, even in a small area with flexible transfer of the game center, is a serious competition for proactive defensive forms of the game, which have generated it up to a certain level. What elements are used to create suitable space conditions for the pressing inside the defined playing form?

A. **Contra-triangulation** (which we talk about in detail in the chapter 3.2 that deals with the defensive principles) is an integrating expression, which defines the range of the specific defensive playing tools: tight occupation, attacking another player at the leg length, closing the passes corridors by a spiral movement in the final zone area, entering the passes, doubling, jumping in front of the opponent whom the ball is approaching, and body to body fights on the ground and in the air. Offensive alignment of the players based on the triangulation requires

from the players, who are attacking and gaining the possession of the ball, to close theoretically enormously high number of potential communication tracks in continuously created and dissolved combinational alternatives. This is the main issue and task in the application of the proactive forms of defense and various forms of the pressing. The effect of "the contra-triangulation" disturbing effort of the pressing players increases proportionally to an increased number of the players who are close to the game center (space cage).

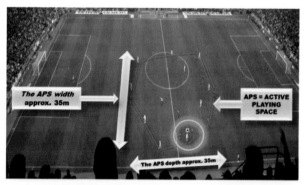

Fig. 3.1-42 The center of the game is after the interruption of the game after the arbiter in the right vertical in the middle zone. The active playing space, its depth and width are significantly reduced.

Fig. 3.1-43 Free spaces

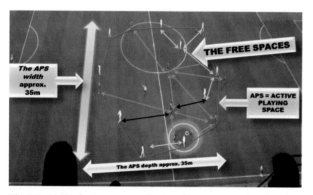

Fig. 3.1-44 The free spaces are shortened in compressed active playing space. The players are positioned closer to one another and to the center of the game.

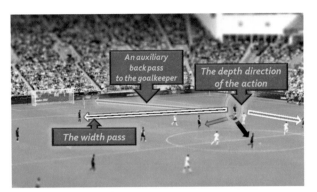

Fig. 3.1-45 Triangulation alternatives of setting up an attacking action in the defensive zone.

B. Another (just as important) tool for the elimination of the escape ways is cutting the player with ball off from the possibilities to use an auxiliary back pass to the goalkeeper. If we include in the triangular play scheme, the goalkeeper of the attacking team too, the defending players will have more work in order to eliminate the attacking or "escape" combinational game (fig. 3.1-47).

The point of the reduction of the playing space in the final pressing zone with the parallel closure of the escape ways is to push the opponent into the mentioned **space cage** (by the construction of creative attacking activity). The mentioned contra-triangular tools have a higher effect in the space cage, because at the same time, they close the opponent into the so-called **"performance" cage,** which is defined not only by the playing but also mainly psychological factors. The mental aspects of the pressing are analyzed in the specific chapter 3.4 in detail.

The attacking players, who are closed in the space cage, aren't able to solve the attacking play tasks according to their own plans and aspirations. Their playing performance is being decreased, and we can say that the space cage is becoming the main reason why the attacking players are trapped in the performance cage. The proactive pressing space defense is the area of the beginning and more frequent occurrence of territorial conflicts, which deepen the impact of the playing collapses on the opponent players' psychic. The frequent frustration caused by the failure in micro situations (in multiple overlapped personal zones of individual players in an over dense reduced active playing space) is the consequence of the territorial space conflicts (between team players but also between the opponent players who

are trying to use the free space of the playing area for their aims).

István Görgényi (Olympic winner, World Champion and European Champion), a Hungarian author living in Australia with his rich experience in playing and coaching, deals in his theoretical work with the issue of the narrow connection of space and psychological aspects of the game.

In the final part of the time-space phenomenology of soccer, we are presenting a special application of **Görgényi's "Hunting territory" theory** in the pressing with the focus on space. Taking into consideration, a big emphasis on the contemporary soccer space parameters, which are based on the zone principles, we have tried to **take territorial approach to the playing space.**

Apart from the territorial aspects of the positional game, the "Hunting territory" concept has also got **specific social-psychological aspects of the team dynamics.** Their soccer modification is dealt within the chapter 3.4 called "Mental aspects of the pressing."

3.1.4 The Hunting Territory Theory in Soccer and Its Special Use in Pressing

THE CHARACTERISTICS OF GÖRGÉNYI'S "HUNTING TERRITORY" THEORY

The main expressions, on which **Görgényi's "Hunting territory" theory** is based, are: **hunting territory** (hunting territory = playing area, action zone), **overlapping conflict zone** or **coordination zone** (space closure), **interregnum zone** (unoccupied area), **functional hierarchy** (playing positions, players' positions), **decision-making autonomy, privileged competencies** (special play tasks). In the text, we'll try to stick to the original terminology of the hunting territory concept and for better visualization of the interpretation model for soccer, we've presented the synonyms of soccer theory.

Görgényi assumes that if there's insufficient coordination or harmony in cooperation between the players, there can be conflict situations, which are stopping the team from achieving the required team performance. These conflicts, according to Görgényi, have a territorial background. The trigger for this might be a territorial dispute, territorial competition, or conflicts between the team players.

THE HUNTING TERRITORY

The conclusion of Görgényi's analysis is the fact that the players don't have equal space demands during the game, which they require neither personally nor as a part of the team in work, competencies, or functions designation. The space demands and also different load on the players (taking into consideration their individual potential, typology, readiness, and overall quality and also taking into account the team's play concept and the specific focus of individual players in the game system) is possible to regulate by differentiated specification of their action zones in the basic alignment. The functional differentiation of the players, which is specified by the players' positions, originates from the space "partition."

a. The first level of the hunting territory theory

Görgényi recognizes two levels of hunting territories: in the first level, he characterizes the personal (individual playing space), subjective relationship of the player to the area directly in his surroundings. Archimedes's phrase: "Don't touch my circles!" is a metaphor that explains the principle of the hunting territory theory function in the first level. The player is located in "the space bubble," which moves around the pitch with him and with every individual player (fig. 3.1-49).

The personal hunting territory of a player (individual playing area) is a territory, which is perceived by the players as a zone of an autonomy self-governance that is constantly under their control and in which they want to demonstrate their unshakeable dominance or sovereignty. The personal hunting territory is a living space, which the players need for a successful solution of play tasks in the game context. If another player enters the territory, he disturbs the territory, which is considered by the players as naturally privileged. It's important to differentiate whether this space is entered by an opponent, whose presence is an impulse for a responsive playing reaction of the particular player, or by a team player. If a team player enters the space, the player must

evaluate if it's a tactical intention (e.g., common corridor closure in order to block the opponent's passes) or a territorial overlapping, which appears as a space disturbance. As the players need relatively safe free space around them in order to realize their playing activities, any intruder, who enters this space, creates stress. According to Cruyff (in Michler, 2008): "If we give even to a weaker player enough space, for example, 5 m, he can do with the ball everything, because he's got enough play time. However, if we give him only 2 m, he loses the ball, panics, and he'll become even a weaker player."

Fig. 3.1-46 The hunting territory (the playing space) of the player, which is appropriate to his position and functional hierarchy in the basic alignment (left attacker).

Fig. 3.1-47 The personal hunting territory of a player

The personal individual play zone gives the player benefits and makes the player responsible for everything that happens in this area. A failure in solving tasks in the personal hunting territory is more or less considered as an individual failure of the player. The size of the personal zones of individual players is changeable according to the players' quality and their typology. A higher quality player uses his privileged position in this area more efficiently (determined by the level of his abilities and skills). A better player gradually gains bigger privileges, thus he is in charge of constantly larger personal hunting territory. It's also related to the assertiveness level of an each player. A player with a bigger courage and better playing skills (the general motivation rule applies here too: "It's not enough only to want, but it's also necessary to be able and it's not enough only to be able, but it's also necessary to want!") has got around him a larger "untouchable zone" while serving the team. But the opposite applies too. A technical player needs a smaller personal hunting territory in order to control the ball compared to a dynamical player who excels in a vertical draw and needs a bigger personal space. A good quality player doesn't need to be in charge of as big space as possible in order to play with the ball. On the other hand, a defender is valuable in defensive zone whose personal territory is wider. This means that he's got a bigger area under his control.

If the player wins in his own personal territory, he widens his territory similarly to a predator in the nature. There are players who were able to build respect, and their opponents don't like to enter fights in the space that they are in charge of. Assertiveness and confidence in fights strengthen the player not only in his action area and his action hunting territory but also the player's mental strength is boosted. Görgényi's hunting territory theory application enables to bring the mentioned knowledge into tactical consequences valid in soccer too.

PRESSING CONCLUSION 1

It's more suitable to perform the pressing with the players who have higher personal territorial demands and ambitions than to present team proactivity with individuals who run around the pitch with "their tails between their legs" and avoid fights in which they can neither defend their territorial position (playing position too) nor enforce their own assertiveness.

b. The second level of the hunting territory theory

On this level, the hunting territory theory deals with the issues of the territorial link, but also it solves the problems of **the competent coordination of all the team players in the space chain.** The aim is to have the whole area of the pitch equally, purposefully, and as reasonably as possible covered by an efficient performance of the whole team. The emphasis is put also on a safe and nonconflictive functioning of the territorial net of the team players in a coordinated activity. We usually talk about the basic alignment (almost out of bad habit) only by using numbers (for example 4-4-2) and not in a form of a space areal model (fig. 3.1-49). When Görgényi defined the expression of the hunting territory, at the same time, he widened the identification of the basic alignment (consisting of abstract numbers) by realistically existing territorial areas. His space analysis allows us to identify not only the size and the location of the hunting territories but also their intersection and just as important is the ability to identify free zones (unoccupied space), which he named interregnum zones.

Fig. 3.1-48 The scheme of the hunting territories and their mutual relation (intersections) in the specific basic alignment 4-4-2.

THE HUNTING TERRITORIES — INTERSECTING AND OVERLAPPING

The scheme of the hunting territories in the specific basic alignment is a simple zone structure in which a mutual overlapping takes place. There's also a geometrical intersection of the areas, which form the functional zones of the players who are positioned in the basic alignment directly close to one another. Only this way can the whole area of the pitch be equally, and in some parts even multiply, covered. **The conflict zones are created in the hunting territories intersections in which the players can't cooperate in a play-tactical coordination during**

the course of the game. In the formal scheme, we can show the difference in the comprehension of the overlapping of two players' hunting territory:

a. Potential overlapping is possible to present in a formal scheme of a geometrical hunting territories intersection in the basic alignment according to the players' positions (fig. 3 1-51).

b. Overlapping of the hunting territories happens during the course of the game in the time-space and consequently it creates temporarily uncontrolled interregnum zones.

The territorial alignment of the space parameters (the players and ball) in the time-space is more complicated.

This means that we won't be solving the territorial relationships of statically structured zone elements, but instead we'll focus on moving the players and the ball in the play space in a live mutual confrontation of the twenty-two players. The hunting territories, which are characterized in the second level, don't move with the player as a whole, because they're changeable in size, shape, and location. The player's got in his hunting territory designated privileged position; however, by his movement, he controls only the part that is directly within his reach (figs. 3.1-50, -51, and -52) The rest of his hunting territory is temporarily free and has become a zone of interregnum.

Fig. 3.1-49 Potential overlapping of the hunting territories of the middle attacker and left wing attacker in the attacking triple-tandem in the basic alignment 4:3:3.

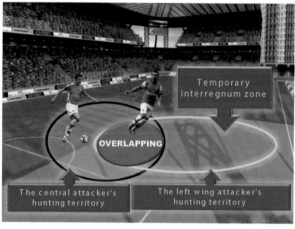

Fig. 3.1-50 The interregnum zones are located in the hunting territory of the player who is operating in the play sequence in his opponent's territorial area in territory overlapping.

Fig. 3.1-51 The player who is moving around the playing area is creating temporarily uncontrolled interregnum zones in his own hunting territory.

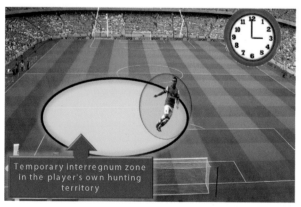

Fig. 3.1-52 The player intentionally repeatedly opens and occupies the interregnum zones in his hunting territory. He operates in the territory according to the tactical rules of the team's play concept and at the same time he is adapting to the real context of the game.

Fig. 3.1-53 The hunting territory intersection is a foundation for tactical play tools in manipulation with the space in the pressing.

Fig. 3.1-54 The positional chain of the players who form a block is based on an intentional overlapping of the hunting territories.

OVERLAPPING AND CONFLICT ZONES

Overlapping isn't automatically a source of tension and conflicts, because it also symbolizes an intentional and tactical closure of a chain or a block of players (figs. 3.1-55, 56). If it is realized in a controlled coordination, it doesn't represent a potential threat of a territorial conflict. If the overlapping is created due to a failed coordination, it can be the cause of a severe playing mistake or a wrong alignment (e.g., wrong doubling of a less important area and at the same time creating a free goal zone or, in other words, a relevant playing zone).

PRESSING CONCLUSION 2

If the players use the hunting territories overlapping in a coordinated way, they are able to mutually overlap their opponents' hunting territories in order not to offer the opponent any free important zones. The interregnum zones are for this specific situation irrelevant. This is valid, for example, **for a block of players' hunting zones chain in the pressing (overlapping of the potential corridor for the passes).** It wouldn't be possible to create blocks of

defending players without gaps and cracks, which disrupt their compactness, without a planned system of intentional and flexible (changing elastically) overlapping of the pressing players' hunting territories. **The intentional tactical overlapping of the block of players creates a space asymmetry in which the antipole (logical reflection) of the overlapped spaces on the opposite side is a free zone (e.g., a weak side, a blind space, intentionally opened and unoccupied space that is irrelevant from the current tactical intention point of view)** according to the concept of the hunting territory interregnum zone.

THE INTERREGNUM ZONES

We can schematically and formally idealize the interregnum zones in the basic alignment so we don't have these zones between the planned hunting territories of the players (fig. 3.1-57). From the action areas designation point of view, we can achieve theoretically trouble free state by their systematic overlapping (space definition of the players' positions in the basic alignment). However, this is only a theoretical and significantly optimistic illusion that can be broken into tiny pieces in the midst of the match paying confrontation.

Figure 3.1-55 offers a practical tool for coaches who can, as a part of their tactical preparatory, enrich a long-term, considerably simplex and arithmetical cliché 4-4-2 by a demonstrative and formal space animation of the basic alignment. According to this animation, the players can acquire the specific idea about their own operational areas in the basic alignment, space relationships with their team players who are directly near them as well as about the space alignment of all the team players.

Compared to the formal structure of mainly symmetrical basic alignment, there are also, in a comparable proportion, asymmetrical alignments with the layout of the action area of each player's competence, which is much more difficult "to class" and which is constantly and dynamically changing during the game. The interregnum zones are created by the moving ball and the players who react to their mutual and the ball's movement. As the time goes and watch-hands change their position during the game, the players' hunting territories also change their configuration taking into consideration the movement of the ball, the opponent, and the team players. The free zones during the game disappear and the new ones open while in time-space, they constantly and elastically change their form and the operational area. The intersections of individual players' hunting territories act in a similar variable way. The mentioned changes are often a consequence of the well-known intentional tactical coordination of the players (intentional intersections with the aim to achieve the compactness and unity of the team or a block). The territorial intersections also happen by enforcement from the opponent's side. The part of failed and faulty space maneuvers can, however, lead to territorial conflicts. The consequence would be misunderstandings of the players in the mentioned territorial intersections (space interference) that can cause the loss of the control over the free areas—interregnum zones.

The name **"interregnum zone"** results from the fact that none of the team players controls the particular zone. This means the opponent can enter this zone and gradually reach territorial dominance in order to realize his own intentions (fig. 3.1-58). This problem generates the occurrence of territorial conflicts between the players who are together responsible for faulty coverage of the areas.

If the player is located on the specific spot in his hunting territory, it's obvious that in the area where he isn't positioned, there'll be a temporarily free interregnum zone, because the players can't have their whole territory under their control all at once. By this statement, we have defined the relation of the personal hunting territory (which is defined in the first level of the hunting territory theory) to the team hunting territory and also to the temporary interregnum zones.

Every player generally controls by his purposeful movement (connected movement of the team players, the opponent players, and the ball) only the part of the hunting territory, which is within his reach in his personal hunting territory. The complexity of the systematic manipulation with space of all the team players emphasizes the fact that personal as well as team hunting territories are constantly moving during the game.

The outcome of all this is that Görgényi's interregnum zones isn't possible to plan in the basic alignment. It's

important in the game system **to model the mutual movement of the players so the interregnum zones are not uncovered (from the tactical point of view) in relevant play areas. On the other hand, the system of the intentional regrouping of the hunting territories in the target pressing zone is modeled in order to create space overlapping by the couple or a group of players who are participating in the pressing sequence.** The target pressing zone that is bordered by the players by permanent space "manipulation" (opening, closing, reduction, compressing, and outnumbering) can be compared to the space cage in which the players are located directly close to the ball in minimized space. The tactical overlapping of the hunting territories of the players who are performing the pressing consequently happens in the pressing zone. Therefore, it's important, in the training process, to model in detail their coordination, which can prevent the territorial conflicts that happen between the players due to their spontaneous, noncontrolled, and uncoordinated playing activity.

Fig. 3.1-55 It's not possible to define, identify, or plan the interregnum zones in the basic alignment.

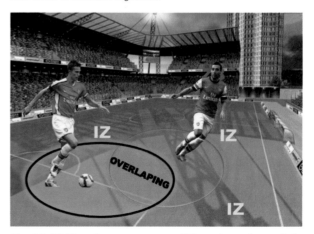

Fig. 3.1-56 These interregnum zones (IZ) are located out of the hunting territories of both players.

Changeability of the temporarily free interregnum zones in the player's hunting territory reflecting the player's movement

Fig. 3.1-57 The positional chain of the players who form a block is based on an intentional overlapping of the hunting territories.

PRESSING CONCLUSION 3

The intentional overlapping of the hunting territories in the pressing is the prevention from the possible space cracks being created. These cracks could be used by the opponent for increasing the pressure. The conclusions of the presented knowledge for the pressing is enhancing the meaning of **the precisely modeled timespace coordination of the players,** which is the route to the perfect pressing and, at the same time, it's the prevention from the occurrence of the territorial conflicts with unwanted impacts on the unity and mental strength of the team. The rule that is valid for the training method is **that the modeling exercises that are focused on the pressing must have a sequential character (sequence and intensity of acquiring the pressing elements).** The activity of the players can at first **happen in the training situationally according to the specific position of the ball in the pressing situation.** The practice and improvement of the pressing scheme should result into the expected **model of the game according to the ball's movement and the probable behavior of the players who are under the opponent's pressure (defensive anticipation).**

PRESSING CONCLUSION 4

Despite the time-space variability of the game, it's possible to define the zone of the most frequent contacts of two players or groups of players and the zone of the most frequent conflicts occurrence. The team players definitely must "get on," and the statistical analysis of the game will show that they are the agents of the main stream of

the game. This means that they are the players who are communicating with the passes the most frequently. According to this type of the statistic, it's possible to predict the conflict zones or the situations, which can threaten the team or the group coordination and cooperation from which the whole team's play depends on. The same applies to the defensive blocks maneuvers. **Two players who are performing the pressing on the principle of "swing and pump" and who are working as two swings usually have the task to carry out the transfers as one player in an identical or close area.** Moreover, **they must connect the coordination of the two swings with "a pump"** mostly in a typical area (more details about swing pressing in the chapter 3.6). **The hunting territory theory has a great importance and practical benefit, which is based on more practical comprehension of the zone principles of the game of soccer** that are necessary for the pressing modeling in the training and the game itself.

Coordination of the players in the potential, predicted, and conflict overlapping of the hunting territories can lead to the dominance of an intentional cooperation in these zones, in other words, there's **the coordination indicating synergy effect.** This coordination can be achieved by preplanning an individual's activity so that it fits into the whole piece. This plan, scheme, and algorithm (logically connected and purposeful sequence of the players chain) are creating in the pressing the way that individuals mutually complete each other by their action. How? By the practice, modeling, and improvement of the group and team attacking and defensive play schemes. By doing the modeling exercises and preparatory exercises, we will perfect and specify the individual's tasks in the time-space sequence. By multiple repetition and replay of these modeling schemes, we will also get into the player's minds the clear limits of their tasks in each one of the schemes.

The task of the coach is to give the players enough practical evidence in matches that his designation of competencies and hierarchy (expressed not only verbally but also by specific group play schemes or even automatisms, which are consensually approved, respected, and acquired in the training) doesn't only lead to order and an effective cooperation but mainly to avoiding unnecessary territorial and competition functions conflicts.

TERRITORIAL CONFLICTS AND COORDINATION OF THE PLAYERS

The hunting territories will overlap in individual play sequences in a different measure. This is reflected in the schematic expression of the overlapped area size (figs. 3.1-60, 61). The planned and practiced cooperation in the match realization (confrontational) can't be completely without any difficulties in the hunting territories intersection. These difficulties can lead to conflicts in spite of the fact that we spend a lot of time and make a big effort in the training process to model and practice the play coordination in a persistent, detailed, and precise way.

The center of the possible conflicts in a real game are the overlaps of the hunting zones in which the players don't have allocated the coordination algorithms (sequence in fig. 3.1-60a) or the coordination is restricted by the opponent (sequence in fig. 3.1-60d). It's possible to avoid the territorial and hierarchical conflicts (sequence in fig. 3.1-60b,c) by the play schemes (coordination practice and tactical intention). This means that despite the fact that the game is dominated by the situations, in which we can apply the practiced and stable play solutions, **the same positional alignment can represent a conflict in relation to the tactical concept or when play coordination is limited by the play situation (based on the practiced intentional coordination).**

The stated approach requires redoing the coordination rules not only between the neighboring territories but also between the seemingly unrelated territories. **For example, the center of the extended swing and the line of the defensive chain, that provides the pump function in the swing and pump pressing, are territorially divided, however, they create a functional coordinated body.** If one of the main requirements of this pressing, either a swing or pump, doesn't mutually complete each other in the strict time-space sequence according to the ball's position, **there can be a conflict between the groups of players that territorially don't overlap each other, but they are functionally related** (more detailed explanation is in the chapter 3.6). The mutual functional relation of the players and the territorial relation are equal when defining the sources of the possible conflicts.

The hunting territory theory discussion are bringing us to the conclusion that the presented theory can be generalized down to mainly unregulated and non-premodeled play situations and sequences. However, we are recommending accepting the theory's preventive formulated warnings from territorial conflicts in a team in the situations in which the players have more free hands. Taking into consideration the fact that the soccer play can't be formed into premodeled story (therefore, the scenario of whatever soccer match isn't possible to practice into details in the training and interpret it accurately like for example in the parallel bars in gymnastics), there's a big space opening in the soccer practice for the practical use of the hunting territory theory.

THE HUNTING TERRITORY, THE INTERREGNUM ZONES, AND THE PRESSING RESISTANCE

In the soccer circles, we can now often hear the opinion that FC Barcelona players move during the game according to a very liberal game model. It's demonstrated by the style of the play where individual players freely but more effectively change their positions in the space so that all of them happen to be everywhere. It's wrong approach to think that one system gives the players freedom another system doesn't. This approach doesn't reveal what requirements the specific system has to fulfill in order to offer the higher level of freedom. Isn't it only a camouflage from Barcelona while in reality it's all about strict order? What foundations do the Barcelona's players have their play built on, the foundation that is reminiscent of the free rough sea? Apart from the mentioned basic alignment, it's also the general attack scheme (fig. 3.1-63). On its base, it's possible to organize the play unbelievably accurately without any significant organizational complications and schematic restrictions. Besides this, every team player can understand the attacking, that is based on its generally acceptable logic, due to its simplicity and simplex logic and also because this type of play organization is connected directly to the game (its course) by exact copying. If we add to the general attack scheme, Görgényi's hunting territory theory and his interregnum zones, the mosaic of the game, that is based on the symbiosis of these time-space schemes (the general attack scheme and the hunting territory theory), starts showing in a clearer picture (fig. 3.1-62).

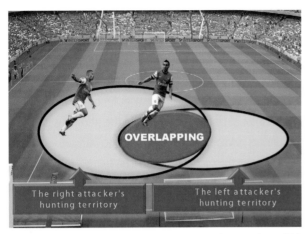

Fig. 3.1-58 *The hunting territories and zones of an overlap, which require the cooperation in the "A" sequence.*

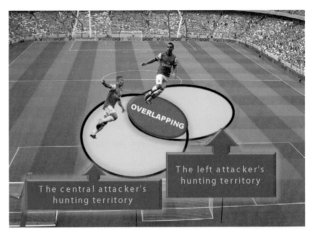

Fig. 3.1-59 *The hunting territories and zones of an overlap that require the cooperation in the "B" sequence*

Fig. 3.1-60a,b,c,d *The coordination is alternated by the territorial conflicts of the center attackers in the alignment 4:4:2 in the "A" and "B" play sequences.*

The continuous elastic alternation of the size and shape of the free interregnum zones is a practical impact of the permanent use of the general attack scheme by the players during the course of the game. For example, the Barcelona's players are able to be more assertive during the fights for the interregnum zones than their opponent. The "scattering" of the game gives the impression of an absolute freedom and "unbound" playing performance. In reality, they have adapted their playing performance

to the game itself. Therefore, it's possible that the players feel freer than they would in more complicated play-tactical structural game concepts. By introducing the expression of **"the interregnum zones" (IZ),** Görgényi didn't invent anything that was unseen before. He is only trying to focus our attention to the fact that there are more free areas in the pitch than it's necessary. This is the reason why it's important, from the tactical point of view, continuously assess and differentiate the important areas from the less important (also from the pragmatic and overall result point of view). The free territories in the playing pitch are the following:

1. Unoccupied areas, interregnum zones (IZ).

2. The areas, which are occupied; however, it's possible to free them by the movement (the general attack scheme).

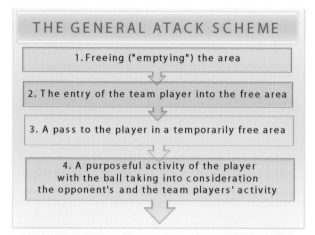

Fig. 3.1-61 The general attack scheme in soccer (theoretical model)

The fight for the space starts by the first referee's whistle. On the contrary, the mentioned fight for the space doesn't end by its occupation, but it continues by constant, intentional, and purposeful freeing and reoccupying. The point of these space "maneuvers" is to set a trap for the opponent on the chess board of the soccer pitch with the aim to give the opponent mate. Görgényi indicated by his theory that soccer is a strategic-situational game; however, in the symbiosis with the general attack scheme, it's possible to demonstrate it clearly and trustworthily.

If something is to be considered a scheme, it must explicitly show the characteristics of a scheme and organization.

We may not necessarily see sense, even with Brown's molecule under the microscope but scientists found it (Albert Einstein). Similarly, the general attack scheme fulfills the attributes of the time-space sense and logic. Together with fixed designation of the players' competencies in limited area (in the hunting privileged territory), they help to keep order and organization.

When we get to the final part of Görgényi's hunting zones theory, we can comprehend better the logic and the organizational background of the described liberal play concept of FC Barcelona. When the ball starts moving in a match, unplanned, and unpredictable space intersections and interregnum zones (IZ) are being created. The interregnum zones are areas, which the players use by their movement to enforce their aims. They enforce by trying to widen their own hunting territories on behalf of the interregnum zones without taking into consideration, which team is interested in them. If the team has big interregnum zones in their team, play, and territorial structure, it's obvious the team is offering them to the opponent who can use them in necessarily see sense even Brown's molecule movement under order to reach their goals. The hunting territory versus uncontrolled space will be the center of the interest of both team players. When the players of both teams are permanently making an effort focusing on widening their own hunting territories, it's clear it'll be on behalf of the interregnum zones. These zones will become the center of the space war between both teams that can't defeat their opponent without controlling the space.

The play concept of FC Barcelona is based on a continuous effort to positionally fill their own and the opponent's interregnum zones on the general attack scheme principle. Maybe it's enough to move in the direction of the space that is free and then leave it fast in order to create free space for the team players. From this, we can conclude that the problem arises if the player or players are standing in one place. In the continuous spiral movement and parallel possession of the ball, the Barcelona's players have a bigger part of the playing area under their control than their opponent. They demonstrate a higher level of the pressing resistance and, therefore, they are harder to get caught in the traps prepared by their opponent. At the same time, it's

Fig. 3.1-62 The general scheme of attacking in soccer (the play sequence in the pitch)

easier for them to manage getting back the possession of the ball and carry on playing the game based on the pressing resistance of not only an individual but all the team players, too.

The facts mentioned above are convincing us that the movement of the players without the ball, continuous, and permanent choice and change of the place performed by twenty-two agents almost at the same time create such hidden time-space reserves, which can be used in endless alternatives by the more skilled and mainly more active players. This also represents a promise to future soccer that its evolutional perspectives will be taking the course of application and strong enforcement of a constructive and constantly sophisticated activity of the players who are able to open and close the interregnum zones using their creativity in many different ways. If we are talking about endless alternatives of a match plot, it's important to realize the complexity of the coordination of individual players' playing action that is also based on the general attack scheme. It takes only a small time delay in

connecting two actions and the game gets in better case to the starting "zero" point. A new attempt to open space can start. This sometimes requires detailed time-space conformity of not only the two players but many times the whole team, too.

To organize the game, which is based on the general attack scheme, can still be unreachable for some. It's as if we wanted a traditional folk band to play free jazz but on the other hand, jazz musicians wouldn't probably have problems playing traditional folk music.

The second conclusion is related to the development perspectives of soccer. The coordination within play tactic rationalization, for example, conditional area (if we are coming close to the absolute top limits of physiological abilities of a human body) has a bigger reserves from the improvement point of view.

PRESSING CONCLUSION 5

The free areas and interregnum zones are the main enemies of the pressing. Görgényi indicates what is visible right away and that's the fact that even on a high perfection level of the basic alignment and the system of the play and the players themselves **there will always be in the pitch free areas, temporary interregnum zones in a changeable format in a continuously changing layout, form, and configuration.** Temporarily uncontrolled areas don't have from their importance point of view the same level of importance (their most effective use). In the defensive stage of the play, the teams preferably protect and overlap their own defensive zone and mainly the penalty area because loss of control over these areas is a huge danger for the final development of the match. On the other hand, in the offensive stage of the play, there are free interregnum zones, which can be of a greater importance from the point of view of reaching the dominance in the possession of the ball.

In pressing that is applied against the team, which is keeping the ball with the intention to be in the safe control of the game (the priority is not to get a goal), it's necessary to overlap much bigger free area and interregnum zones in the whole width and depth of the pitch. If the opponent plays without authentic offensive intentions and doesn't extend with more players over the ball's level, the permanent disruption, reoccupation, and interregnum zone overlapping is the most difficult task that is ahead of the players who intend to perform the pressing. The opponent players who are in the possession of the ball will, in order to maintain the safe control over the game, use in the depth of their own defensive zone auxiliary back passes to their goal keeper who has at his disposal the freest interregnum zone in the whole pitch (and relatively the safest). It's only possible to sacrifice one defending player for elimination or at least the disruption of the opponent's goalkeeper by employing a huge physical potential of the players and with a quite high risk level. In this case, the opponent's antipressing activities are a big advantage, because the players don't have to play in the depth while keeping the ball, in other words they don't have to go into offensive risk.

In pressing, resistance is essential the fact that the security of the team, that is playing under the pressing pressure, is to escape the pressure in the team's own defensive zone by maneuvering the play into the interregnum

islands (in any areas of the pitch). **The team that is playing under pressure near their own goal will prefer the transfer of the game into more distant zones (away from their own goal) often for the price of losing the possession of the ball.** In these areas, they can safely reorganize their play and definitely disrupt the pressing pressure of the opponent in the most relevant playing areas.

In other words, the value of the interregnum zones changes according to the pragmatic play-tactical indicators. In the pressing, there's a rule (regarding any course or the type of play) that **the most important area of the pressing team remains the team's own defense zone and penalty area.** The pressing, due to which the pressing team offers the opponent team free zones in the relevant areas of the pitch, is only a Russian roulette.

However, if the team only wants to keep the ball in order not to let the opponent get hold of it and at the same time hide the ball from a successful search by the players of the defending team with the aim to start the pressing hunt on the ball, every corner of the pitch is valuable for these aims. Görgényi's territorial division reveals the core of the soccer game, which together with permanent and variable reoccupation of the interregnum zones on the principle of the general attack scheme (alternative freeing and occupying of the area), offers the team, that has the ball, a changeable (and mainly endless) source of space, which almost unlimitedly widens the team's antipressing alternatives.

The extension of the opponent as high to their own goal as possible by this tactical ball keeping in the depth of the team's own defensive zone can also be an intentional offensive option of the play that is based on long kicks to fast attackers who are operating on the central line or blind space behind the defensive chain of the pressing team.

FINAL WORD ON SPACE

The content of the space confrontation of two rival teams in soccer is a continuous shaping of the active playing space and formation and consequential closure of the communication ways in the triangulation. The fight that seems to be a fight for the ball is in reality a fight for the space or a battlefield in the middle of which is the ball.

PART 2

Fig. 3.1-63 Illustrations of the reduction of the active play space

However, the active playing area is reducing in size without mercy. Its compressing isn't only an impact of the pressing tactics applications but rather by natural trend of the game's direction development due to tactical approaches. The time until the trend of the active playing space reduction in soccer will continue; however, it still remains an open question of the prognosis.

3.2 THE DEFENSIVE PRINCIPLES FOR A SUCCESSFUL DEFENSE APPLICATION

An inseparable part of **the defense theory is the definition of such priorities of a conceptual establishment of a defensive stage of the game,** which significantly influence the training process as well as the team's performance. These priorities represent the generally valid rules for the defense by which the course of the defense is limited and the achievement of the team's defensive performance characteristics is enabled.

Based on a thorough theoretical analysis of the game, we "picked" the defensive principles right from the game. Therefore, it's not quite possible (nor common) to enforce "the chosen" principles in the game artificially. According to us, the defense principles are directly linked to the changeable parameters of the game: space, time, players, and the ball. The presented defense principles clearly reflect the trend requirements of the game, and they contribute to the creation of the game concept and the tactical team profiling in a significant way.

In the confrontational background of the soccer match events, when the rival teams reciprocally overcome the opponent's permanent resistance by application of their own play-tactical "recipe," the generally used "attempt and mistake" method is becoming the basic test of the of the effect the playing tools application (fig. 3.2-1). The presented "circulating" verification "knot," which works on the principle of feedback relationship, determines any progress in the evolution of the soccer tactic, and contributes to the profiling of the teams' effective game concepts that are based on the confrontational theory and the practice during soccer matches.

From the long-term point of view, the soccer tactic and strategy theory has come to the conclusions, which have a general axiomatic validity. They are becoming the essential and **generally accepted rules**. In one word, they are principles. Between the general form of the play philosophy and strategy on one hand and between specific playing tools on the other hand, the soccer theory

recognizes an important theoretical midlevel. By respecting this midlevel, the general conceptual ideas are transformed into the specific real form. The mentioned tactic and strategic midlevel is what we call **the play principles.** They can be defined as a summary of rules, axioms as well as the specific rules of rational and tactical behavior of the players during the game. They represent the principles of the correct space and positional behavior, which allow an effective defense. If there were only ten, we could call them the tactical "ten" of soccer. The mentioned summary of the tactical "rules" concludes not only from empirically verified knowledge of the game but currently it also results from the statistical observation and evaluation of the success and effect of the playing tools that are used in standard as well as in nonspecific conditions of soccer matches.

Taking into consideration the specific features of the game in the attacking and defensive stage, it's necessary to think of the attacking and defensive principles differently despite the fact that they form one contextually connected piece. In the pressing theory, we'll be

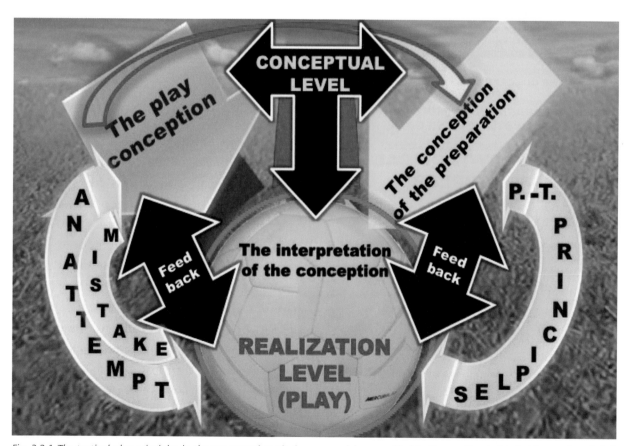

Fig. 3.2-1 The tactical play principles in the conceptual tactical game models are verified in the practice. A detailed innovation of their content happens continuously and according to the development of the game itself.

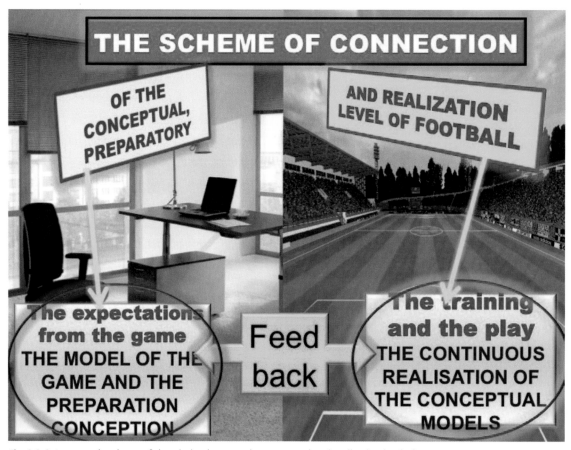

Fig. 3.2-2 An example scheme of the relation between the conceptual and realization level of soccer

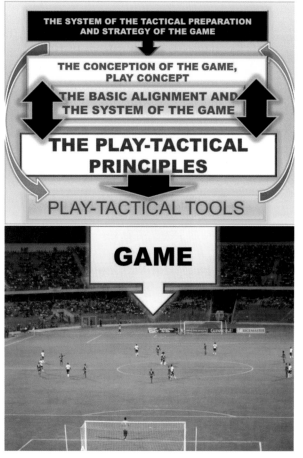

Fig. 3.2-3 The hierarchization scheme of the basic tactic categories

interested in the defensive game principles, which are closely connected to the attacking principles, but due to their specification, they are primarily connected to the defense.

While the play philosophy and strategy specifies rather the target categories (what we want to achieve: the playing performance, visualization, the play style, and pragmatic performance aims), the play principles determine up to a certain level the shortest and the most secure way leading to the realization of the team's own conception. The play principles and the play-tactical tools, which conclude from these principles, determine as effective way as possible for the achievement of the defined conceptual intentions. Moreover, the play principles can show the mutual incompatibility of some conceptual intentions. They can also show, still in the theoretical and preparatory stage of the conceptual planning, the impossibility to carry them out in the practice. The defensive principles are valid for any form of defense, from the passive block defense up to the ultraoffensive pressing. The same applies to the play tools where the defensive play principles are gaining directive character, if we purposefully connect the related defensive sequences. **The defensive principles**, on which the defensive play-tactical tools are based, **are the widest summary of the basic postulates of the conceptual defense.** By respecting the principal rules of the defensive tactic and strategy, the team's defense becomes a mutually connected, coordinated, united, compact, rational as well as creative activity (in addition, it's an activity that is "tailor made" and adjusted to the team itself and what's important, situationally appropriate and adequate to the game and development of the match). These are attributes of an effective, "bullet-proof" as well as "offensive" defense. In the following part, we are dealing with the analysis of these basic defensive play-tactical principles in detail:

1. The principle of the defensive coordination.

2. The principle of the defensive compactness.

3. The principle of the personal responsibility and the responsibility for the team.

4. The principle of the defense safety.

5. The principle of the logic of the play and the counter triangulation.

6. The principle of the defensive outnumber in the center of the game.

7. The principle of the positional advantage and stability in the defense.

8. The principle of the situational adequacy of the defensive aim.

9. The principle of the space dominances in the defense (the principle of primary defense of the goal area).

10. The principle of the activity and the defense dynamization (the changes of the rhythm and pace of the game in the defense).

11. The principle of the individual defense improvisation.

12. The principle of the stage response (mirror image of the game stages).

1. The Principle of the Defensive Coordination

The principle of the defensive coordination is a principle by the use of which the team's defense acquires the characteristics of a readable (clearly recognizable), coordinated, mutually connected, and coordinated tactical movement of individual players in the time-space. The term coordination means a managed cooperation of which the result is a purposeful coordination of the player in the game. The principle of the defensive coordination is transferred into the team's play by "an invisible" connection that unites "parts" of the defensive tactical concept, which doesn't allow the players to act contradictory. (It can be invisible because when you play in a concert, you don't have to read notes anymore, you've got them in your head.) Therefore, the intentional and planned steps of the movement maneuvers in the defense should be familiar to the players, and they should carry them out in an appropriately disciplined manner.

For example, it's not possible to realize the pressing as a defensive play-tactical concept in a match without respecting the principle of the defensive coordination. The signalization of the whole defense maneuver start happens in creating pressing situations. By the term signalization, we understand a number of movement challenges of the team players as well as the opponent players, which become in important information before the pressing activation. Based on this, we have a logical and rational coordination of individual players' activities in the game center and the players who are operating in the periphery of the game center according to the prearranged tactical defense alternative. Apart from the movement challenges, it's also suitable to use mutual coaching, which helps the players to correct the cracks and gaps in their defense "net" in time.

The logical and purposeful connection of individuals' activities (based on algorithms) enables the players to react to the opponent's action in time and especially in an appropriate time-space sequence Also, it allows the player to continuously correct the defensive reaction of their own team. In the pressing practice, it looks as if there was a locomotive pulling all the carriages the same direction (an example is "the pendulum and pump" pressing, which is characterized in detail in the chapter 3.6, fig. 3.2-4).

It looks similar to a lake surface when you throw a large stone in it. The waves spread in a regular amplitudes one pulling another but the opposite direction, away from the epicenter. In case of the pressing, the waves are directed toward the center of the game. By following this principle, we can also use another important principle in the defense and that is the principle of the defensive compactness.

2. The Principle of Defensive Compactness

The principle of the compactness can be demonstrated on the following example. You are trying to pick a bunch of grapes and if the bunch is meant to stay compact, it mustn't fall apart. However, if you separate the berries from the cluster, they uncontrollably roll away from the cluster to any direction. If you want to keep the berries on the table together, you will have to border the reduced space by boundaries in which the berries will be placed within the distance that can guarantee the necessary compactness. And that means that you are forced to manipulate with space and you are forced to restrict the movement freedom of the grape berries. The same thing happens in the pitch but instead of berries, we have intelligent players without visible boundaries. The pictures below can be used to demonstrate the absolute task equality of the players who "carry" the boundaries in the periphery of the playing area and the players who, thanks to them, also get success in the center of the game. The pictures confirm a crucial necessity to emphasize the importance of the expressions, such as "short pitch," width movement and space closure, and so on. The pictures also demonstrate an impact of the required space maneuvers without which would "the chasing the ball" by defending player be like looking for a needle in a stack of hay, especially at the times when keeping the possession of the ball and hiding it for an opponent is a significant tactical alternative of the game.

Fig. 3.2-4 The "pendulum and pump" pressing

Fig. 3.2-5 The scattered grape berries can only dream of compactness.

Fig. 3.2-6 The space that is reduced by the boundaries enables the berries to keep their compactness in a way that they can have the form of a cluster again. It only depends on the size of the space, which is restricted by the boundaries.

The principle of defensive compactness concludes from the optimization of the space parameters of the game in relation to the number of the players in an actively defined cutout of the playing area in a defensive stage of the game. This tactical space optimization is called a manipulation of with space in which the players use as much energy as possible for creating the active playing space during the game. They do it mainly because the mutual connection between the team players decreases proportionally by enlarging the distances between them during defense.

The principle of the defensive compactness is characterized by mutual space affinity and cooperation of the players who are connected together in a restricted reduced area more tightly than they would in an open area.

By the expression "defensive compactness," we understand a space, positional and action emergency, and the ability of the players, a block of players or the whole team to effectively enter the solution of variable play-tactical tasks in defense. By defining the rules of the space alignment, position, and regrouping of the defending players positions, we predetermine their potential abilities for solving defensive tasks from the space point of view. **The strength of the defensive pressure on the opponent with the ball is decided by the time-space and action compactness of the players.** If we have achieved the positional and consequently also the action compactness of the defensive players, we are on the best way to perform the proactive defense or the pressing.

Fig. 3.2-7 If you want to defend effectively, you must be as close to each other as possible. If you are positionally compact, you can help, secure and support each other when increasing pressure on the opponent. In fact, you can't be successful in the pressing or in other forms of defense, if you are "scattered" in space.

Fig. 3.2-8 In the red area, the ratio of the defending and attacking players in 4:4. The blue area is occupied by nine defending players who are keeping an eye on the six opponent players' play. The significant reduction of the pitch is nothing unusual today in most of the top teams, from the defense point of view.

Fig. 3.2-9 Extreme compactness in the center of the game

PART 2

Fig. 3.2-10 The compact defensive alignment of defending team (6:3)

The war strategist Sun Tzu already knew the expression "taboo" space. He says this about scattered defense: "Having an equal strength, a scattered defense doesn't allow to defend sufficiently all the necessary places, thus unnoticed attacker can choose the place of his attack. This is the place that is the worst defended. If I don't want to be lured into an attack, even if I drew a line on the ground and wanted to defend it, the enemy can't force me into a battle because I run his every move."

The compactness is the main condition for achieving the effect of the team synergy in defense, which was already wonderfully used by Hungarian players of "Aranycsapat" in Wembley in the match of the century. After the match, they said: "We were helping each other, defenders were helping the attackers, and the attackers were helping the defenders by our goal. In other words, mutual help of players can't be effective without their positional, space and action compactness (coordination). The compactness also gains importance from psychological point of view. To stick together, especially in bad times, isn't "automatic" attitude and character of majority of people in general. Naturally, this is also reflected up to a certain level in the soccer player's population. For transferring the compactness principle into the team's defense is typical that the defending players are positioned during the defense in the playing area in a way that they can influence not only the opponent's but also the team players' activity. Based on the principle of the defensive compactness, the defending players are creating a united and strong net and a defensive structure, which they can reinforce according to their needs, double, secure, and flexibly relocate in the playing area. The principle of the compactness is a bridge to the principle of the safety, because the defensive compactness allows the players to provide mutual help and support more effectively, especially in crucial playing situations.

If a riverbank breaks in a flood, one sand bag won't stop the water from bursting out.

The defensive compactness has its roots already in an attacking stage of the game because the transfer into compact defensive blocks after losing the possession of the ball get significantly harder due to an extremely open positional attack (This is, more or less the subject of the principle of the stage feedback). It's not possible to put scattered grape berries back into a cluster then let them roll away again and do all this repeatedly in a short space of time. It would be firstly tiring and partially also impossible (SPA-SVK 2015). This means that an excessive defensive compactness and space unity, which concludes from extremely small gaps between defending players in contracted and concentrated defense, leaves "tracks" in the form of limited possibilities for continuation of the play after gaining the possession of the ball.

3. The Principle of the Personal and Team Responsibility

Concluding from the principle of the defensive compactness, players reduce their active playing area when defending it; they close it and create a solid defensive net and block. However, this "geometrical" manipulation with space is only a structural operation, which ensures the size and form of the playing shape of the defending team. The content of the defensive play-tactical activity of players in this defensive space relates to another defensive principle, which is also, apart from the principle of the coordination, the principle of the personal responsibility and the responsibility for the team. This means joining together the defending players' personal responsibility for themselves and also for the whole team. This represents fulfilling two partial tasks in solving one specific problem. From the player's point of view, we could characterize this tactical feature in the concept of defense by a very simple rule: "I'm fulfilling my primary, individual, and personal partial task and, at the same time, I'm aware of the task, which the whole team faces." Being able to see the problems in a complex way as a whole and as the team's problem means to be prepared to help the team players in fulfilling their tasks too, however, my own task mustn't get out of my control. This is how strong connections between the players are created (otherwise they the players defend in isolated way); however, this is unacceptable in the pressing.

If the defending players rely on the principle of "multifunction," they are not connected only by personal responsibility but also by a team bond. By the term personal responsibility, we mean for example: not to lose personal fight on the ground, in the air, in a running confrontation and so on. Together with personal responsibility, of which success can be statistically evaluated individually, the necessary principle requirement in defense is also respecting the team bond of individual players. This represents the ability of the player to get involved into the functional space strategy of the whole ream's defense. **It's the ability to read and predict the logic of the events in the play** according to the development of the space parameters, the promptness, willingness, activeness in mutual securing, doubling, defensive outnumber, return, and other playing elements by which we "go out of our way" for the sake of our team. The principle of unity between the individual responsibility and the responsibility for team is reflected in the defensive tools, such as doubling the player with the ball, closing the space, transfer from the periphery to the center of the game, zone movements, defensive outnumber in the center of the game, mutual securing when attacking the opponent with the ball, and so on.

4. The Principle of Defense Safety

The basic evaluation criteria for justification of the playing elements application is (besides success and efficiency) also their safety level. The essential condition of the systematic access for the efficiency evaluation of the subject under review is respecting the principle of the safety. The application of the principle of the safety in the tactic and strategy of the game leads to sophistication of the play tactical details of the playing elements taking into consideration the elimination or minimization of mistakes in application. To say it in a simpler way, we can talk about safety optimization of the play tactical elements and the whole strategy of the game. The higher efficiency level of judged play tactical method doesn't necessarily mean also higher level of safety. **Therefore, when evaluating the successfulness, it's also necessary to evaluate the unsuccessfulness level, which means the**

level of unwanted side effect of the particular strategy of the game. If we also observe the counterproductive impact of the tactical alternative when evaluating the successfulness level, we can achieve acceptable results (overall success and efficiency). However, in evaluation, we should take into account the confrontational core of the game because the identical tactical alternative, which is applied to opponents of different quality, can have differ a level of success. On this basis, it's possible to compare, amend, innovate, and develop the play-tactical elements in the long term.

An extreme focus on the main target in building the tactic and strategy can lead extreme results especially occasional occurrence of extreme impacts. For example, although I shoot two goals after specific type of the pressing application, I get three goals. The presented knowledge directs the strategists to caution of which the result is an effort to create compensational security back-ups in every tactical game alternative in order to eliminate or weaken the opponent's strengths in a match.

A clear predominant positive effect of the game, which is up to a certain level related to the safety of the team's preferred play type, strengthens the confidence of the team players (and the coach himself too) in the correct application of the specific tactical play alternative. This can lead to the repetitive (even systematic) application in the team's game concepts.

5. The Principle of Play Logic and Counter Triangulation

The principle of the logic of the game is the proof of the existence of the logical characteristics and rules in the direction of the vents in the whole game. Despite the fact we have just mentioned, we don't want to get into the position of the experts who are able to scientifically explain even a coincidence in soccer. It's obvious that the occurrence of unplanned and hardly predictable events, which are connected to coincidence or so-called "sport luck," isn't a rare sight in the game.

The principle of the logic of the game together the principle of the offensive triangulation allow the defending players to predict the course of the game, anticipate probable play tasks, which they will have

Fig. 3.2-11 An example of the disruption the attack triangles and combinational play alternatives arranged by the players on the interface of the defending team's central and defensive zone (preferably in the direction of the attack depth of the opponent's attacking action)

to inevitably solve (without looking into a glass ball). The players might unconsciously, however, continuously think in the purview of the expressions of before-center and postcenter area. If we cut through the time line by these expressions, we are get again back to the expression the time-space. The game reading and consideration of its logic alternative are the conclusion based on which the players virtually "precede" the course of the game.

(The little defense game reading—the ability of the defending player to predict an immediate action of the player with the ball. The big game reading—the ability of the defending player to predict not only the action of the player with the ball but also the action of other attacking players who can participate in the play sequence.)

The principle of the triangulation is related to the attacking triangulation principles (the principle of the triangulation and maintaining the triangles for cooperation). The use of the principle of the triangulation for the defense means acceptance, application, and preference of the compensational principle. This is the principle of disruption of the offensive triangles, in other words, the principle of the triangulation. The logical outcome of the offensive triangulation in the confrontation of two teams is the activation of the defensive effort to disrupt the attack triangles by the annulment of as high number of offensive play and combinational alternatives as possible (preferably in the direction of the attack depth of the opponent's attacking action).

However, from the practical point of view, it would be suitable to talk about the uncovering and overlapping principle or blocking and unblocking principle in both stages of the game. For the game itself, it represents the fact that the attacking players are running in order to be free and the defending players are running in order not to let the attacking players be free.

The counter triangulation is more complicated to perform in the practice than to deal with it on the theoretical level. The overlapping of the possible alternatives in the offensive triangle is also complicated by the fact that the defending players can't definitely predict the triangles, which can be formed by a pass into free areas (a well-timed pass or a pass with the purpose to challenge the opponent to move). The conclusion of this is that the wide range of the attacking alternatives for the potential passes is neither theoretically nor practically possible to defensively overlap, block, or annul permanently. We'll try to demonstrate the play alternative (fig. 3.2-13).

Fig. 3.2-12 An example of uncovering and overlapping of the routes between the attacking players based on the principle of the offensive triangulation and the defensive counter triangulation. The sideline temporarily fulfills the function of another defending player because it limits further width movement of the player in yellow in the vertical position.

From the demonstrated play sequence, the overlapping of the currently existing triangles isn't sufficient for elimination of the biggest offensive threat (marked in fig. 3.2-13 with red arrows). The real threat of the fulfillment of the depicted fictive depth offensive alternative, that is based on a timed pass behind the defense's back, results from the logic of the game (the most dangerous postcenter area from the goal threat point of view). The conclusion of this is that the principle of the counter triangulation without the playing anticipation (defensive game reading), that is based on the logic of the game, isn't possible to use efficiently in the practice. Therefore, the success of the defense will be decided by a running race in which the defending player encounters a problem because he has to accelerate from the place, in addition to the danger of a penalty, which results from possible confrontation with the attacker in the penalty area.

The magnetism of the ball attracts unanimous attention of all defenders in figure 3.2-14. Only the defending player no. 17 can peripherally see and perceive not only the ball but also the acceleration of the player no. 10 in white shirt on the offside line who is creating by his movement ("L" shaped movement) a requirement for a timed depth pass from his team player. The running direction of the player even before the pass reveals his intention. However, this type of the intention signalization of the attacking player happens within tenths of seconds and due to a big distance of both defending player no. 6 and 2 from him, the function of their position can be compared to a position of a bowling figurine. The picture is the demonstration of an ideal time-space harmonization and coordination of the players in the prefinal attacking play sequence.

Currently, there's a big opinion exchange concerning the percentage of the ball possession, which is closely related to triangular attack-defense confrontation. The confrontation of two opinion streams is a battle of two soccer philosophies. The first one prefers the ball possession priority, which is related to a long-term adaptation of the payers to keep the ball under pressure already in the training process from the youth categories (e.g., Barcelona a La Masia). The second philosophy contradicts the first one by claiming that the ball possession isn't a crucial and qualitative indicator of the game according to which we can clearly determine the team that's going to win the match. Their theory relies on the players' willingness to play the most of the match without the ball, on other words in less attractive and defensive stage of the

game, while making an effort not to allow the opponent to threat the goal. In the more time restricted but on the other hand more vertical offensive (for which they are also prepared by typological structure of their team), they are trying to achieve a higher effect by a successful finalization of rare and fast confrontations that are performed by fewer players.

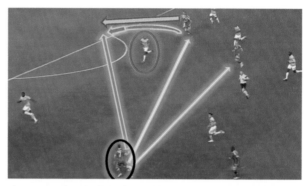

Fig. 3.2-13 The principle of the logic of the game helps the principle of the counter triangulation.

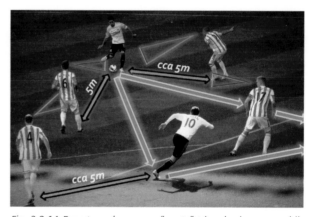

Fig. 3.2-14 Even two players can "create" triangles in soccer while even four players can't prevent their creative performance (although the performance is predictable according to the clear logic characteristics of the play situation in the picture).

The precise and well-aimed paraphrasing of these criteria was offered by the coach of the Chilean representation Jorge Sampaoli at one of his press conferences after the match. After the match in South American World Championship 2018 qualification, in which his team was defeated by the team of Uruguay 3:0, despite the fact that his team had in this match 73 percent ball possession, he said: "One day I went to a bar. I met there a beautiful lady, and we were talking all night. We were laughing, flirting, and I paid for several drinks. Around five o'clock, a guy came to us. He took her by hand and went with her to the toilets. He made love to her there, and then they went home together. But it doesn't matter because that night I had the bigger possession of the ball..." It seems that this statistic criterion expresses sterile numbers that doubt their value in relation to the real events in the paying area. The controversy is related to the negative impacts of the mentioned play-tactical conceptions or strategies especially in cases that involve their mutual match confrontations. Which one from the mentioned protagonists of the significantly extreme streams is more conductive to soccer and which one contributes more to a decrease of the soccer's quality? The magicians and entertainers with the ball, who are endlessly searching for "cracks" in the defensive trenches of deep, impenetrable, dense, and stable block defense, or tactical pragmatic opponent that are well organized gladiators and who sacrifice even the last bit of their inborn soccer playfulness for the sake of the victory?

The roots of the depicted rivalry are again in the confrontation (triangulation versus counter triangulation). Which approach is more appealing, more beneficial, and more acceptable? Let's leave the choice to the taste of each one of us. One thing is for sure and that is that both presented strategic alternatives are determined by each another, one can't in reality even exist without the other and, therefore, it's not possible to force them apart. They are part of the evolutional soccer development, which doesn't involve frequent changes of the rules of the game, which give advantage to either one side or the other. We could suppose that the primary cause of this polemic is withdrawn block defense. This probably generated the offensive alternatives based on an excessively long conquering the opponent's goal by using the fast circulation of the ball within many elastic micro or mini triangles. The battle of "pros" and "cons" will probably continue in future too, but maybe even in a smaller active playing area (mainly in the attacking zone) into which the attacking players will try squeeze functional offensive triangles. It'll always be bigger and bigger art to perform (not only technical) as well as to perform "a blind" coordination.

"The triangulation" principle is important for the attacking, because there are at least three "disturbers" (defending players) necessary for the elimination of the advantages of the game, which is based on a variable relocation and creative modeling of an endless choice of triangles.

Fig. 3.2-15 The third player, who focuses his attention on the ball, is missing.

The ratio between the attacking and defending players in an effort to eliminate two players is 2:1 and a trio of players is 3:3. The three defending players can make the three "lines" move. Obviously, it's beneficial for the attacking players to combine their play at least within the trio because by this number of players, they can increase the number of geometrical alternatives by "an endless" exchange of the lines, which form the sides of constantly new triangles. Even a relatively small area is sufficient for the attack maneuvering in a triangle (FC Barcelona).

If we gave the player a task to keep the ball in the ratio 3:2 in an unlimited area, the two defending player would not theoretically stand a chance to enforce a successful getting the possession of the ball, and they would more or less be able to get the possession after the opponent's mistake. For this reason, many preparatory and zone games ("bago," "rondo"...) are organized so that the playing area is not restricted. This way the defending players get the support of another four "team players" in the form of the four lines, which restrict the area. It really is true that the most reliable defender is the side or any line (the offside line), that limits the movement activity of the players who are in the possession of the ball (in this, we entirely agree with P. Guardiola: "The sideline is the best defender"). Therefore, in the training, the players adapt to the game in the area that is restricted by four invisible defenders (lines). Even if these players don't interfere in the game, they don't enter confrontations, they don't move and don't fight, by their presence, they limit the game with an absolute confidence and without any flaws (because without any movement they control the whole line of their position and they don't let the opponent cross the line in any play situation).

After describing the principle of the offensive triangulation, the principle of defensive counter triangulation seems as a conclusion, which indicates the necessity of mobilization of as many defending players as possible for any type of defense (fig. 3.2-18).

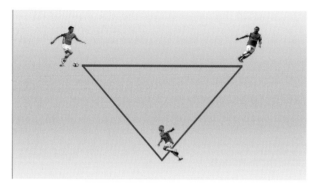

Fig. 3.2-16 The offensive triangle

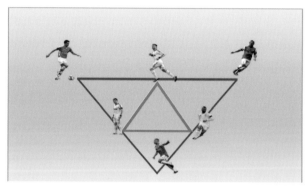

Fig. 3.2-17 The offensive triangle disrupted by three defending players

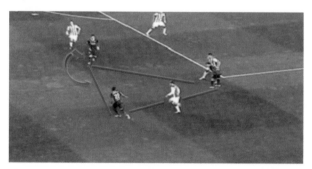

Fig. 3.2-18 The players, who are in the offensive triangle, are forcing the opponents in light blue shirt to mobilize their reserves and equalize the ratio of the defending and attacking players to 3:3. In this constellation they have an opportunity to force the opponent to fight at the ratio 1:1 and at the same time they'll be gradually pushing the opponent to the sideline (to the fourth defender).

The mentioned risk is related to the principle of the defensive out number of the game center and directly connected areas. The efficient elimination of the moving "multishapes" of the attacking players is very complicated, because the attacking players have got an advantage. The advantage is the fact that the defending players don't know their thoughts, intentions, automatisms and their swerve, sophisticated, masked, and tricky maneuvers.

The principle of the defensive counter triangulation is used for example in annulment of the most dangerous combinational alternatives of the attacking team and in doubling the player with the ball. The doubling happens parallel with overlapping the line of the possible pass while another player is approaching the pass. By using these tools, the attacking opponent is pushed out into less dangerous areas or into areas in which it's easier to create the defensive pressure (fig. 3.2-21).

Fig. 3.2-19 The elimination of the attacking players who are creating moving "multishapes," which are based on changeable triangles, is very complicated because the attacking players are not only moving but they are also more advanced in their thoughts (big rondo Barca).

Fig. 3.2-20 The dominance of the players who are in the possession of the ball is also multiplied by their positional dominance in the form of two defensive triangles (small rondo Barca).

Fig. 3.2-21 The defensive pressure of the four defending players pressing in the defensive zone is concentrated on pushing the center of the game to the sideline.

6. The Principle of the Defensive Outnumber in the Center of the Game

The principle of the defensive outnumber is reflected into play elements and specific activities of the players that are mutually connected. These focus on creating the dominance in the center of the game and the direct surrounding with the aim to increase the pressure on the player with the ball in the defensive stage of the game.

The higher number of players, who are involved in the defense in the center of the game, allows the players to disrupt the changeable "communication" net of the attacking players more efficiently (more effective "counter triangulation") and, at the same time, it gives them wider possibilities in doubling the player with the ball. His type of the space occupation give the attacking player less time. Thus it increases the team's overall playing and psychological pressure of the proactive defense on the attacking player (Cruyff in Michler, 2008): A good

player, who needs too much time, is suddenly becoming a weaker player."

If we evaluate the number of the defending and attacking players in the presented picture, it's obvious that the defense is in an overall outnumber 8:5. By the dominance in the defending zone and in the areas, which are situated near the penalty area, the defending players are also fulfilling the requirement of the principle of the space dominances. According to this principle, the security and confidence should dominate in the defensive zone and its close surroundings.

The confrontational core of the game in soccer (also in other team games in which the rival teams sometimes literally fight for the ownership of an object, e.g., a ball. puck and so on) is clearly demonstrated by a natural magnetism of the ball. The magnetism of the ball reflects a natural effort of the players to reach outnumber in the center of the game either in defending or in attacking.

Fig. 3.2-22 The natural magnetism of the ball is demonstrated by the fact that the players' eyes are following the ball during the game almost constantly. However, there are situations when this can lead to mistakes.

Fig. 3.2-23 The proactive tactical forms of the defense enhance the power of natural playing tendency in the players' behavior by precise organizational alignment.

Fig. 3.2-24 By the application of specifically adapted technique and their playing ability, the Spanish players can be located near the center of the game in a higher number also while possessing the ball.

Fig. 3.2-25 "A small" rondo directly in a match, five against two. The players can compensate the loss of the ball by an immediate pressing more successfully if they are located by and near the ball also during the attacking stage in spite of the fact that demands on the ball control are higher in this type of attacking.

Dominance in the defense makes it easier for the players to gain the possession of the ball and dominance in the offensive improves and widens the playing combinations as well as the alternatives for performing the attacking stage of the game. The outcome of this is the fact that the basic universal play-tactical principle of outnumber has natural roots in soccer. If we didn't correct the players' behavior by tactical impulses and tactical schemes resulting in tactical coordination, the effort of the players to achieve outnumber (resulting from a natural magnetism of the ball) would be one way or the other significantly visible but in an absolutely uncoordinated and disorganized form.

An interesting play-tactical phenomenon, which is currently demonstrated in the play style of the team FC Barcelona or by the playing behavior of the Spanish representation team, is based on the ability of the players to take an advantage of outnumber and dominance over the opponent in the center of the game and in an extremely reduced playing area in both stages of the game. Whether the players are in the possession of the ball or not, they are constantly trying to use the benefits of outnumber and the advantage of the position near the ball. But to squeeze close to one another when possessing the ball is against commonly preferred tactical theories (fig. 3.2-24).

The tactical aim, which keeps the Barcelona players directly near the center of the game while keeping the ball especially in the attacking zone, has its simple explanation. Despite the fact that a small space isn't an advantage for keeping the ball, the Spanish masters of the ball technique can present this type of possession of the ball with such an ease, overview, and relatively high level of confidence especially with a stoic peace.

The players of FC Barcelona are adapted to keeping the ball in an extreme shortage of time and space long-term by methodically, contextually, and specially managed technical and complex training (rondo and semicontact with the ball). While possessing the ball, they consequently gain more significant advantage from outnumber of the center of the game immediately after losing the possession of the ball because they are positionally closer to the ball. Therefore, they are able to apply an immediate individual and group pressing with a high and maybe the

highest level of a success. This way they managed to connect the attacking and defending stage of the game into one continual offensive piece in which the borders, that separate the attack and the defense, significantly disappear. There's a general rule that the positional alignment of the group of the players and all the team players with all the advantages and disadvantages (stage response) is transferred to the defensive stage at the moment of losing the possession of the ball. The positive response is when the attacking stage overlaps with the defensive stage so that the positional situation of the group of the players, at the moment of losing the ball, overlaps with the needs of the positional situation, which requires immediate and active defense and pressing. In this situation, the switching from the attacking to the defense happens in the blink of an eye. But not because the players would be thinking more quickly that it's possible (latent, mental, sensory, and perception part of the switching) or because they would act faster that it's possible. The realization of the performance and movement switch is significantly shortened because, in transfer to the defense (to an immediate pressing), the Spanish players don't have to transform their open attacking positions, which they had when possessing the ball, into the movement toward the ball that logically takes longer when the players have to move longer distances. The purposeful connection of the attacking and defensive alignment is nothing else but an alternative alignment. This type of alignment takes into consideration the requirements of the defensive stage already in the attacking stage and vice versa. However, the players must also be willing to play in attacking stage under a time-space stress because alternative positions (which create advantageous conditions for the transfer into an immediate pressing) are closed. The result is the fact that the players play under a time and space stress in both stages of the game. After losing the possession of the ball, they gain a big advantage for an instant pressing and consequently carry out an imaginary "Grand Tour" in the immediate pressing. Luis van Gaal (Tactical Philosophy, 2014) defines the stage response by this statement: "When you attack, you always take a risk because you've got a big space behind you because of which you have to think defensively even when you attack."

What did the Spanish soccer players do in order to have probably the best immediate pressing in the world? They adapted their attacking stage of the game to their pressing by which they have eliminated the negative response of the attacking when switching to the immediate pressing after losing the possession of the ball. However, they had "to learn" to keep the ball in a closed space in situations in which other players make mistakes, they give up beforehand and they kick the ball away or they solve the situations nonconstructively with mistakes. On the contrary, the increased effect of the immediate offensive pressing of the Spanish players (concluding from the principle of the center of the game outnumber even when possessing the ball) isn't only based on the successful management of the pressing sequence itself but also on the quality of their ball technique. This technique allows them to control the ball in a small dense area in which both rival teams fight for the dominance. By the use of the specifically adapted technique and the playing ability, the players can be located near the center of the game in an increased number. They can density the reduced space excessively also during their possession of the ball. This enables them to control the game in both stages. The percentage of the ball-keeping is significantly moved to their advantage. The can masterfully manage the ball even when playing under pressure in closed positions, which allows them to return the possession of the ball back under their control immediately in a more flexible and mainly more successful way after losing the possession. This perception of the play also brings a higher risk level. This is the reason why this type of confrontation intentionally takes place on the opponent's half of the pitch while the team's own half (all the way to the depth of the goalkeeper's position) is used by the team for calming the game down and for a safe transfer of the center of the game, but this time without higher risk level in open players' positions in the active playing space.

For the Spanish players, the circle (one cycle of losing and gaining the possession of the ball) is successfully closed in order to have another circle opened one after another. So two in one means, in this context, a double positive effect in one identical play-tactical activity (outnumber of the center of the game), which includes both game stages. This is the proof of the stage response, which we also deal with in more detailed way in the following sections of our publication.

7. The Principle of Positional Advantage and Stability in the Defense

Similarly to martial arts, the counteraction has a bigger success in soccer too. The counteraction is based on taking an advantage of the opponent's revelation of his initial intention. The player (fighter) reveals his intention by making his "first move" and his accelerated action and gets himself into a disadvantage in a 1:1 fight. A simple example: A defender decides to act first. An attacking player is, on the other hand, waiting for the defender's first move, which is directed toward the ball. At the moment of the defender's movement, the player with the ball is only moving the ball aside. The defender's move is therefore directed into "the vacuum." He usually loses the stability and isn't able to compensate his mistake, because the opponent is escaping the opposite direction. In many cases, even relatively "weaker" player can be more successful in the 1:1 fight. For the successful defending game in the 1:1 fight, the final position of the defending player before the fight is very important.

Similarly to martial arts, the basic approach of the player is also important. The player's stability is built on this approach. The positional advantage and stability of the defending player allows him to have a balanced reach in the area, especially to the right-left laterality. The opponent player uses the defender's "instability" for his escape, if the defending player, before taking the position prior to 1:1 fight, must run to the opponent with the ball in a maximum speed, and he first undertakes a deceleration at the place of the fight. Most of the time, the player applies the change of the direction with the ball in the opposite direction of the defender's move. Especially vertical players (Arjen Robben, Eden Hazard, or Lionel Messi) have built their extremely effective and successful offense on this principle. In spite of the fact that the defending players know that escapes of these attacking stars from the sideline toward the penalty area border, and with the ball on a stronger foot, they end up in dangerous shots, and they can't sufficiently ruin these individual actions, especially if they don't have the positional stability and security. It's important to gain some time for taking a good, stable, and final position in the expected area of 1:1 fight. However, this doesn't have to be fulfilled optimally in every play sequence. **The principle of the** positional advantage and stability in the defense is a tactical warning for the player that the space, and time are equally important in the game.

The fulfillment of the positional advantage and positional stability in the defense principle doesn't only offer a space positional advantage of the defending players but also the action advantage, which is in fact the time-space advantage. If we also add the ability of the defensive game reading, the result can be the positional promptness and readiness of the defending player for the situation, which is only going to happen. **The positional anticipation connects the defensive reading with the positional preparation for the expected movement activity** (the direction and speed of the ball or the players, the movement distance, the expected change of the direction, and the movement speed, twists, stopping, repeated acceleration). The mentioned, relatively complicated movements of the defending players require a high level of the motoric coordination. The fundament of the success in these defensive activities is the positional advantage, the positional readiness, the positional stability, and the positional balance.

The principle of the positional advantage isn't applied only in individual defense. It's also related to the defense of the formations or the whole team defense organization. In the pressing, the principle of the positional advantage and the positional stability in the defense is applied in forming the defense blocks. The positional advantage of the block of players, who are operating under the level of the ball, is indisputable. The active pressing can be applied from this type of stable structure according to prearranged triggers and pressing situations (pushing the game to the sideline, enforcement of long kicks, enforcement of auxiliary back passes, creation of situations uncontrolled by the opponent, and enforcement of technical mistakes). A stable, organized, and compact positional net of the defending players has got bigger demands on the time-space organization of the defense after losing the possession of the ball; however, it guarantees a higher security of the proactive defense. On the contrary, in an immediate pressing, we prefer a fast reaction or, in a lower level of the positional organization, the moment of surprise. We take an advantage of the opponent's temporary offensive positional disorganization right after gaining the possession of the ball. The

spontaneous and immediate pressing also represents a higher risk. The defending team consciously undertakes this risk due to the fact that a successful pressing creates suitable conditions for confrontations in the opponent's unformed defense. In this example, the principle of the positional stability is compensated by the positional stability, which the defending players achieve by performing a swift switch after losing the possession of the ball.

8. The Principle of Situational Adequacy of the Defensive Aim

The content of the defensive tactic are the alternatives of individual defensive activities and their variations, which the players apply in solving specific tasks that focus on the achievement of their aims.

The crucial parts are the defense activity itself, the right timing and space in which the players apply the defense and the intensity (level of the activity and physical effort), which is maintained in a bearable level of controlled aggression. The players' choice of the defensive activities is determined by the defensive aim. They use these chosen activities in solving particular defense problems so that they don't cross the acceptable level of play risk in order not to let their activity, even if it's active, become counterproductive.

Fig. 3.2-26 If the under numbered player runs toward the opponent in an attempt to take the ball from him at an unsuitable moment, he "contributes" by his increased activity to the success of his opponent's attacking action.

The adequacy of the applied defensive tools usually shows after finishing the action. However, it's objectively possible to prepare a situational hierarchical list of the defensive tools and activities that are, from the tactical point of view, suitable to apply in specific and typical play sequences. It's also possible to specify the situations in which, on the other hand, it's unsuitable to use these tools in defense, because they've got a counterproductive effects at an enormously high defense risk. From the playing activity point of view, we recognize two expressions of the opposite extreme poles; they are "irresponsibility" (if you take risk unacceptably) and albinism (if you don't risk even when you already should take risk). An adequate choice of effectively performed defense targets in defending is the most important for the success of the team's defense itself. The principle of the situational adequacy of the defense aims helps to rationally organize these aims. We are presenting the sequence of these aims in the simplified form according to the demandingness and the risk level:

a. approaching the players according to the arranged defense concept in the match;

b. slowing the player down and prevention of outnumber;

c. pushing out, stopping, blocking, or redirecting the opponent's movement;

d. blocking the shots;

e. attacking and putting pressure on the opponent and forcing the opponent to make mistakes;

f. preparation of the confrontational situations; g. entering the fights;

g. unconstructive removal of the ball in fights;

h. constructive removal of the ball in fights and switching to attacking.

Fig. 3.2-27 The scheme of the sequence of the defense aims according to the demandingness and the risk level

To the individual defense aims, we allocate the defense tools and playing actions, which enable the players to effectively achieve the chosen targets in the match practice. In relation to the principle of the situational adequacy of the defense aim, the mostly used word is "an adequacy," which is the synonym of the situational "appropriateness." An adequacy or a situational appropriateness in the choice of the tactical solution is the key to the successful defense, which is really pragmatic and suppresses the elements of irrationality or drama, which is focused on demonstration of sometimes pretended assertiveness, which in reality hides hopelessness, tactical naivety, and inability. The defense is done not only by legs but also by head.

9. The Principle of Space Dominances in the Defense

The principle of the space dominances in the defense guides the choice of the defense play-tactical tools and activities in relation to the situational playing area in which it's taking place; on one hand, from the dominance of the security (modesty, carefulness, and continence), on the other hand, to an increased level of the play risk in defense (activity, maximum output and intensity, emphasis, and controlled aggression). We are talking about the defense dominances in relation to the playing area, because the mentioned dominant attributes of the defense in diapason, from the security to a higher or high defense risk, are mostly connected to the depth of the playing area; however, we can also apply it in the width differentiation.

There's a simple axiomatic rule:

a. defending in the attacking zone allows or even requires an increased risk.

b. defending in the central zone counts on the balance of the defense successfulness.

c. defending in the defending zone expects the dominance of the security.

The high pressing in generally approved of and even appreciated by soccer fans, sport presenters, and experts too. It's attractive because it transfers the teams' confrontations into the areas from which it's possible to threaten the opponent's goal right after gaining the possession of the ball. The result of this is that the attacking zone is dominated by activity and output; however, it also involves a higher level of defensive risk. On the contrary, the defending zone is dominated, during the process of defending as well as setting attacking actions, by security. Moreover, the defense of the team's own penalty area multiplies the security or even carefulness dominance for two reasons:

a. after an unsuccessful defense (e.g., during escapes and lost fights), the opponent gains advantages in dangerous areas from which he can effectively threaten the goal and score goals,

b. after a foul in the penalty area, which is followed by a penalty or suspension.

Fig. 3.2-28 The defending team reassures its security dominance when defending in front of the penalty area by outnumber 5:3 and in the central zone 4:4.

The principle of the space dominances, from the defense point of view, isn't only related to the depth of the playing area but also to the width. In this case, we are talking about **the principle of the preferential defense of the goal area. The mentioned principle determines for the defending players the dominant focus of their attention, activity, and concentrated effort in order to preferentially defend of the goal area or the penalty area.** The players don't let themselves be "pulled" into the areas near the sidelines, if it represents the loss of the control over "the more relevant" goal area (fig. 3.2-29).

Figure 29 demonstrates the focus of the three players in red shirt on covering the opponent with the ball in the vertical area. The principle of the preferential defense of the goal area couldn't have been accomplished in this sequence because only two individual defenders (1:1) played in front of the penalty area; moreover, they played in an extremely open area far from each other without the possibility of a mutual back-up.

The natural magnetism of the ball is "an enemy" of the correct play-tactical behavior of the payers from the point of view of following the principle of the space dominances in defense.

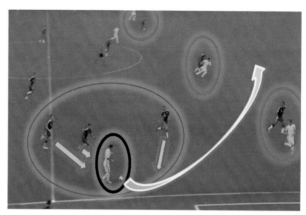

Fig. 3.2-29 Wrong distribution of the defending team's power

10. The Principle of Activity and the Defense Dynamization (The Changes of the Game's Rhythm and Pace in the Defense)

Soccer has come a long way during the process of a continuous effort to increase the overall capacity of the physiological, conditional, and technical potential of the players. There's quite frequent preference of the opinion, which ignores the fact that the additions in the conditional preparation of top players, that are reaching the absolute performance peak, are getting smaller. It seems as if we were knocking at the door that has already been open for a long time and in addition, "the treasury" is already half-empty. In order to increase the level of the players' readiness in this area, we can only use doping or "cosmetic" adjustments; however, they aren't insignificant either. In connection to the pressing, in our publication, we aren't avoiding the warning and frequent comments that emphasize the necessity of the flawless conditional readiness of teams, which use the whole-match pressing or proactive defense for longer stages in the game.

In order not to cross the border over to mysticism, charlatanism, or optimistic idealism (emerging from eagerness or in many cases from a pretended strictness of the participants in the conditional preparation of the soccer players), the topic of the rationalization of the game is becoming more and more discussed. We could compare it to the generally familiar situation in energy management, when quantitative expansion brings worldwide environmental damage or catastrophe. **Even the soccer players aren't an endless source of energy and, therefore, they can't run significantly more and faster. However, it's definitely possible to play wiser.** To play wiser (in relation to the physiological and conditional potential of the players) means to purposefully change the pace and intensity of the game and, at the same time, not to unnecessarily waste the energy sources. In order to use the energy of the players and the whole team economically, it's suitable to change the rhythm of the game so that it reaches the required tactical intention by a coordination of temporarily increased effort of individuals toward the team "explosion" (energy synergy). The periods of this maximum effort are changed over by the stages of the game in which the team compensates the loss of physical energy by "recharging their batteries." **The activity principle also contains its symbiotic antipole, which represents a continuous need for the renewal of the players' energy sources.** The coordinated switching between the impulses and calmer periods means to apply the cumulative effect of team activity or team synergy. In order to perform this, it's important for the players "not to shoot" their "energy munitions" recklessly, chaotically, and above all inefficiently.

A long-term physiological adaptation of soccer players is gained not only by practicing the training load but also by the competitions level of the matches in which the players competitively play long term. The calendar of club and representation event is so dense in top professional soccer that the cardinal issue of maintaining the conditional readiness of the players in the main soccer competition season (which is almost continuous for some players) is dealt with preferably by the correct setting of the regeneration process, which concentrates on the strength regeneration, bringing the body to "an emergency" mode between demanding stages, according to the expected "super-compensational" physiological curve of individual players. It's good if players complete the match reaching the upper limit of their conditional abilities. The conceptual tactical alternatives of the game are built on an imposition of the pace, which the opponent can hardly follow and relates to proactive defense forms in defense stage of the game. On the other hand, the proactive play in the defense stage of the game can increase the overall physiological load, which in return

very positively influences the exceptional condition of the players.

11. The Principle of Individual Defense Improvisation

It may seem that the defending players, who follow defense tactical rules, are bound by sticking to the arranged team rules of the defense coordination. The team tactical tasks in reality don't bind the players; quite opposite they widen the space for their individual presentation. The first part of the play schemes is usually realized according to a quite strict and restricting obligation to the team tactical game plan or algorithm. Despite this, even in this stage of the game, there's space for alternative play variations in which the players apply their own choice of solving the play sequence. The result of group or team defense patterns are, in most play schemes, the tasks, which the players solve by using a higher number of improvisational elements. We are talking about open tasks, which the players don't solve by a strictly imposed procedure. It's the opposite; they carry out individual decision-making in typical situations, which they also solve in the training process similarly. However, the defense that is based on differently restricting and binding coordination offers significantly more suitable conditions for individual improvisation. This means that the play schemes in conclusion also support an individual playing performance and efficiency. This relationship between team and individual pattern in soccer in general (not only in defense stage of the game) is the essential attribute of the play schemes functionality, even those which are part of various pressing forms.

Every defense conception (including the pressing even if it's a group or team coordination) also counts on an individual's own initial and improvisational potential. This is linked to bringing the individual's assertiveness into action, which would be a mistake to suppress.

Any player can dismiss the arranged scheme and planned defense alternative. It happens according to "a logic development of the game." The players who are a part of a long-term preparation and competition practice systematically gain experiences, which they apply in evaluation of the game during its course. This way they can anticipate the activity of the opponent with the ball or the whole opponent team. When they "leave" the schemes, by this action, they can determine not only the result of a personal fight but also the result of the whole match.

12. The Principle of the Stage Response (Mirror Image of the Game Stages)

The principle of the stage response is the principle of the reciprocal transfer of the play response "produced" in the opposite play stage during the change of the ownership of the ball. **The stage response transfers the situational characteristics from the last identified play situation before the ball ownership change into the play situation, which follows immediately after this change** (the number and space alignment of the players directly near the center of the game). We are talking about the border of the play stages. The course of the game in this period of time significantly determines not only the results of the matches. The feature that we can simply call "the stage response" is the fundamental reason why short play sequences, which are related to the loss or gain of the possession of the ball (stages border), significantly contribute to the match results. Although the play sequences are contextually different, they are connected by conditional causal relationship. **The attacking stage is a continuation of the defending stage on the sequence line and vice versa.** Therefore, it's not correct to perceive, analyze, and evaluate the effects of individual stages separately. Quite opposite, it's important to see the stages as a whole in which all the parts influence one another so that the content of one stage is reflected into another as consequence. Due to this, it's also more difficult to define the causes of mistakes (of the specific consequence); many times we are looking for them in wrong places (maybe even in the wrong play stage). Until recently, people couldn't explain some natural phenomenon, such as El Nino, of which influence on our planet is hidden, despite this it has an impact of huge proportions.

In soccer, we got used to quite frequent simplification of the relation between the attacking and defensive stage of the game by stating that the switching substage is to blame. A flexible, swift, or inflexible "switching" is simply comprehended as a universal medicine for compensation of mistakes resulting from disrespecting the stage sequence principle. Let's introduce the characteristic of the basic contradictory impacts of the relation and response between stages. This response can range from

significantly positive up to negative. In the practice, the players encounter and solve wide-range situations on the border line between the stages, which are in their essence placed between the extreme borders.

The task of the switching itself is to eliminate the negative influence or strengthening the positive influence of the stage response to the game. The movement realization of the switching, which, however happens in the following stage after losing or gaining the possession of the ball, can be identified as a specific playing activity of the players who participate in the play sequence. This is the reason why in general the switching is practically reduced only to its visible part (the specific play sequence that we describe as a switch after the loss or gain of the possession of the ball). However, the compensation of the stage response isn't possible to squeeze into a short space of time, when the switching is performed, because it's got much wider range (time course) let alone the consequences. The anticipation of the probable loss or gain of the possession of the ball happens on the mental level (latently) still during the period of time before the ball ownership change. The players constantly evaluate the play situations and if they "classify" it as a breaking-point situation (a threat of losing the ball or a possibility to gain the possession), they make decisions by which they tactically (in advance maybe even as a prevention) adapt their alignment and playing activities to the expected change of the ball ownership. Some players take alternative attack-defense and universal positions that allow them more effective transfer into the defense or attack. An experience eye of an expert can see on a tactically mature team when the players are aligning in the area so that there are visible and clear security elements and breaks in their alignment in the form of alternative playing positions of the chosen players.

The most significant supportive alternative of the game in relation to the stage response are the following:

(a) The attack in order to the defend

The most suitable conditions for the defense are created in the attacking stage of the game, if it's performed in a short space of time, by engaging as few attacking players as possible who are moving over the level of the ball. This is nothing else but the counterattack, which is desired by all the players and coaches too. The fast counterattack has got smaller demand on energy potential of the whole team. In the counteraction, the energy sources of several players are being used up while their activity that is being performed in maximum intensity lasts relatively short time. From the space point of view, there are much more suitable conditions for attacking created in fast counterattacks. These conditions are much more suitable for a fast penetration through the depth of the offensive playing area, compared to long and patient search for space cracks in a tight and concentrated defense of a compact opponent. From the tactical point of view, the counterattacks are carried out directly into the depth and heart of the opponent's defense without the width "bypass" and significant opening of the playing area width.

On the other hand, in order to conquer a tight and dense defense, the attacking players are required to perform positional opening of the whole width of the playing area in the attacking zone while extending the defensive formation to the central line.

Fig. 3.2-30 The finalization of the counterattack by one player who appeared behind the opponent's defense

Fig. 3.2-31 An extremely tight block defense of the players in white shirts (8 players in the penalty area) isn't an exceptional sight in matches against FC Barcelona. The yellow line demonstrates the positional opening of the whole width of the playing area by the attacking team.

Fig. 3.2-32 An extension of the defending formation to the central line in a gradual attack

If we add to this a high number of the players, who participate in the gradual offensive, and even higher number of passes in a small and dense area, the expected impact on the defense after each loss of the possession is more destructive than after losing the possession in any other fast counterattack. From the technical demandingness point of view, the counterattack can also be realized by more simple techniques. In a full attack, the players apply the highest level of the technical team creativity while the long ball circulation is accelerating in speed. In a small and dense playing area, the players are making technical mistakes more frequently. This type of attack is very difficult. Therefore, the attack response in the defending stage of the game, after losing the possession of the ball, can have, from the play-tactical point of view, more severely negative impact, especially, if they appear more often in the specific stage of the game. If the team finishes the fast counterattack, it continues defending in organized positions and chooses the type of defense that is the most suitable. From the further match development point of view, if the team scores a goal or more goals after counterattacks, it gains the biggest advantages not only for the defense. The attack stage, which takes long and causes a great loss of energy potential (individual attack without team players' cooperation), produces tired and exhausted individual players or whole team for the defending stage of the game.

If a high number of players take part in the attack, the team can get a positional advantage at the time of and after losing the possession of the ball. The players are forced to transfer into the defense in a disorganized way and, many times, they have to make a huge effort in order to compensate dangerous outnumber on which the opponent builds their counterattacks. In this case, the defending team can't choose from various alternatives of defensive solutions. The only option is to put the fire down, which was caused by the players themselves in the attacking stage of the game. The result of the stage response in soccer can also be this negative during overpowering an opponent's tight defense block.

Concerning the topic of the fast counterattack in relation to the stage response, we are presenting a logical debate. Why would every coach want to achieve a trouble free victory over an opponent by using simple tactics of performing fast counterattacks from a secure defense? In addition, coaches are able to contaminate, using their obsessive visualization of a perfect "Napoleon-style" strategy of fight by counterattacking, their teams in such a measure that even the players of top soccer, futsal, and hockey teams "quote" the mentioned more or less convincing cliché in interviews for the media like trained monkeys. Why? Because the counterattacks are, from the team's defense point of view, the safest and the most "convenient" form of performing an attacking stage of the game for the coach on the bench and for the players too. The counteractions don't have a negative reflection on the defending stage after losing the possession of the game. The players are plying the zone of relative security and comfort, and they don't feel threatened because in the suitable positions they are waiting for the opponent's next move. At the same time, they are not leaving their safe, multisecured, and tight block defense in large numbers. They don't break their block significantly in order to avoid problems when returning to the previous formation. These positive response and consequence of the fast counterattacks on the defense after losing the possession of the ball are the "reason" of the counterattack "popularity." It's relatively easier to shoot goals after them, and they "don't hurt" the defense. However, if there was a match of two equally "contaminated" teams, we would be witnesses of a long tactics-making, which was also paradoxically planned by the opponent who isn't able to get out of the defense trenches. So let's just wait because the biggest problem of the fast counterattacks is the fact that it's not possible and allowed to plan them in a rigid way, apart from the cases when the rival teams are significantly unequal.

The counteractions always were and will be, not only in soccer, the tactical weapon of the highest caliber due to

their moment of surprise. The only problematical part is the planning because soccer is a confrontational game. Therefore, it's necessary to have in the tactical repertoire the plan "B" too. Otherwise, we can brace ourselves with big load of patience and prepare ourselves for the long-awaited counteractions, which may not even come. The preference of the counterplay is also a sign of a certain type of tactical albinism of the team. These kinds of teams are suspicious of not being tactically well prepared and not being able to compensate the negative impact or responses of an attacking stage of the game in the frontal and gradual progress of the whole team's attack.

(b) The defense in order to attack

The most suitable conditions for an attack are created in the defensive stage of the game, if it's carried out shortly by engaging as few defending players as possible. And this is nothing else but an immediate pressing. **The pressing is becoming a form of "a counterdefense"** of the defending players (maybe that's why some authors use, in connection with the immediate pressing, expressions, such as "counterpressing" in Anglo-Saxon provenience or "gegenpressing" in German speaking countries). If the defensive action is carried out swiftly at the time of losing the possession of the ball, it can also be effective by employing fewer defending player in the center of the game. The essential part is that this type of defending reaction to the loss of the ball doesn't allow the attacking opponent to reorganize the team's power into open positions and widen the attacking active area. Thus, the chance of gaining the possession of the ball by the defending team is increasing significantly. The rule is: "The faster, more vigorous and active the defending activity of the group of the players is (also with the supportive activities of the defending players who are in periphery of the action), the more positive the conditions for the attack after the loss of the ball are." We are presenting the following alternatives for after gaining the possession of the ball:

1. The alternative of applying short counterattacks into disorganized defense of the opponent. This happened when Vittek scored the first goal at the World Championship in South Africa in 2010 in the match against Italy (the record of this sequence in on the enclosed DVD). The Italian midfield defenders didn't

consider Vittek to be a threat when they were preparing for an attack, because the Italian team was in the possession of the ball. Therefore, the defenders let themselves have a space crack between each other in which was Vittek. After losing the possession of the ball, the ball got to Vittek so fast that, due to lack of time, the Italians were not able to seal the positional gap between each other (because Vittek was shooting without preparation "straight way" in delay). In the stage of establishing their own attack, the Italians didn't have Vittek covered because the players were engaged in the attacking action by opening the space. The configuration of the Italian players before losing the ball directly affected the situation after the loss of the ball (it had an impact and immediate and direct response).

2. The simplified solutions for the offensive from the technical point of view too.

3. The saving in the energy and overall playing potential of the participating players as well as the whole team.

Final Word on Defense Principles

The fundamental tactical and strategic attributes of the defense organization include: **security and safety,**

Fig. 3.2-33 The unforced loss of the ball or similarly the loss of the ball after high immediate pressing can lead to short and direct counterattacks with the finalization by possibly only one touch, which also represents the final pass right after gaining the possession of the ball.

activity, space dominance, compactness, coordination, compatibility, position and stability, logic and creative improvisation, personal responsibility, and responsibility for the team (the team bond). The influence of the principles is simultaneous and **synergic**. Therefore, many of them mutually overlap in their functions and purpose. However, differentiated play-tactical tool can be used for their application. All this enhances the firmness of the team's own real defense. The play concepts, which are based on tactical defense principles, can bring a positive response in matches, if we respect them as a whole and not as individual fragments that are pulled out of the game context.

3.3 THEORY OF PRESSING AND THEORETICAL ASPECTS OF PRESSING TACTICS

When the team is defending the space, the players use special group-tactical system of active defense referred to as pressing, which can be considered as the most active and most aggressive defensive action applicable in any part of the game space. In its interpretation, we should clarify the answers to the five fundamental questions that identify the interpretation of the topic about the areas of pressing: What is pressing? Why is it used? How is it used? Where is it used? When is it used? Another important question that arises from this topic is: "What happens after pressing?"

3.3.1 The Terminology and Contextual Definition of Pressing

The contemporary soccer syncretism brought, within the mainstream, the elementary pressing forms and the play elements, which have become an inseparable part of most top team's playing performance in the form of pressing tactics. Nowadays, we talk very frequently about pressing but not always in the most adequate terminological context. It's appropriate, in connection with pressing, to think of it as a form of playing performance, a form of playing in a real-time defensive strategy applied in some strictly defined stages of the match, in a specific space, as well as in a specific time section of the match. Therefore, it's not appropriate, especially from the terminological point of view, to talk about any form of pressing as a defense system, as it's expressed in the English origin of the word; it's a sort of insistence and pressure on the opponent. **Pressing is a term taken from basketball terminology.** We think, in the Slovak terminology, that the closest term to "pressing" is ceiling active defense, which is a way of proactive protection applied to a predefined part of the play area. In soccer context, therefore, it's not recommended to talk about pressing as a playing system but as a way in which players use the space and time in a limited area of the playground when the team does not have the ball. Despite the fact that pressing is bound to a special playing systems, those in which the players shifting from formation to formation are particularly preferred when it does not interfere with the organization, but it's implied or contained in its essence (4-4-2, 4-3-3, 4-2-3-1, 3-5-2, 3-6-1, etc.).

We assume that the most common reason to think of pressing as a way of defensive playing is outside the similarity, in some of its characters, to a system of personal defense all over the playing area in which all the players of the attacking team, immediately after losing the ball, split the opponent players and, with the help of an active personal attack, try to reduce the playing area of the opponent as well as the playing time to regain the control of the ball. Therefore, it is necessary the connection of the space defense tactics to improve pressing as a defensive hybrid model, which combines elements of the hindrance zone enhanced in a limited space-time portion of the match for personal defense. However, there are several key strategic, tactical, and energetic-physiological differences that remark a sharp division line between the playing systems as such and the defensive style of playing in a particular time and space area of the match. So, what really is pressing in soccer? What does its micro-tactic and macro-tactic also specify? What do the special training and specific training mean to its development? **Pressing, in soccer, is to get the opponent under pressure to deploy active defense, which is, according to Hitzfeld (1992), "the offensive variant associated with aggressive defense."** Schaare (1993) describes pressing

as an offensive playing in which the main purpose is to get the opponent under pressure. Zeeb (1996) describes pressing as the tactical behavior of a team that has just lost the ball and now it's trying to regain its control as quickly as possible by forcing the opponent to get into a time and space distress.

According to Wilkinson (1996), defensive pressing is a form of defense in which the defenders force the attacking team to fall immediately under pressure. This can be achieved by expanding the defensive coverage of the playing area. Pereni and Di Cesare (1998) consider pressing as a specific tactical approach in which the players attack the opponent to gain the control of the ball and don't allow the opponent player to have enough time to easily and comfortably evaluate the situation. At the same time, they keep the opponent under constant pressure and forced them to think and act very quickly.

Lucchesi (2003) defines pressing as a tactical action involving more than one player, which is applied in situations where the team controls the ball in the defense stage. For Cecco-Sea (2003), pressing is an action performed by two or more players (within the same or different team formation) to reduce the playing space and time. Once the players apply pressing, the teammates who are away from the ball must take a position that will allow them to control the opponent.

Peter and Barez (2012) consider pressing as a teamwork form of prevention, in which the width and depth of the playing space is narrowed for all the players involved, even those who are further away from the ball.

We define pressing as the multiplayer defensive tactics involving the whole team, which currently represents the highest possible level of defensive activity to gain direct control of the ball. The dominant principle is a proactive defensive action applied when the team have lost the control of the ball. It is a natural part of the heme-tactical portfolio resulting from its confrontational nature. **The basic operational attributes of pressing are space and time, which define the dimension of space, the time, and pressure as relevant elements of the defensive tactics.** The purpose is to provide specific positional arrangement of the players in the right place and at the right time and to achieve rational shifting of the defenders to **the active pressing zone (APZ).**

Pressing is an element of the team defensive tactics, which generates an unlimited number of situations in the zone around the ball as well as an intensive use of panning in the defender techniques to limit the opponents to execute offensive movements in space and time due to pressure.

Multifactorial terminological definition of pressing affecting several basic levels that allows its comprehensive understanding. Pressing can be more widely defined as a purposefully structured set (algorithm) of tactical resources consisting of consciously connected or related maneuvers common to most players of a team. **The dominant objective of pressing is to recover the ball as quickly as possible,** usually applied immediately after losing it within any position of the playing area, as well as during the ensemble of individual offensive action of the opponent team. Pressing is often closed and enters into potential corridors in the opponent's offensive passage limiting the movement options and causing a systematic reduction in the midfield of the playing area. The characteristic features of pressing are proactivity, intense dynamics, extreme aggression, and concentrated effort, in other words, reactive defense. The result is a successful pressing, the space-time limitations of the opponent players, the favorable conditions for personal duels, the recovery of the ball and the subsequent vertical offensive. The development of each pressing stage determines the course of preparation defined in pressing together with the pressing performance. The safety measures that allow some level of tactical risks are part of the pressing scenario. Each time section of the match can vary substantially regarding the factors of the playing efficiency focused on its success (e.g., substituting a high pressing failure in the middle block, may be followed by pressing the center of the block again and repeating the block formation after the pressure on the opponent's performance can be used by the defending players on the opposing vertical pressing in the same defense actions consisting of a number of sequences). In the process of the pressing activities, it is possible to stabilize the situation of the tactic directives or to practice the selected automatism. For example, the instruction or the arrangement limiting the length of

time or the duration of the immediate intensive pressing allows the players to switch to a single obstructive block in at given time.

The pressing activities specifications, the playing combinations, and the tactical playing can be defined more accurately. This means that the player, if pressing is applied without the team collaboration, can lead to mistakes, bad timing, and inadequate pressing performance. The player can literally stab a dagger into the back of his own team. **Pressing can become counterproductive and dangerous for a team that can't effectively and safely apply it.**

In this context, we need to emphasize, once again, that pressing is not limited to any specific playing system. It is applied to cause the disruption of the opponent's performance, which often occurs in the opponent own half or at least in the middle of the playing area. It includes a systematic movement to disturb the opponent anticipating their psychological instability and, in case of a successful application, it will increase the incentive effect of the team. **Increasing the area is necessary not only on the tactical component of the performance and the performance conditions (i.e., pressuring the player with the ball, the local center of gravity rearranging the players, shifting within the formation, moving between formations, exiting the zone) but also the mental component of the performance (e.g., reading the situations, anticipating playing solutions, space coordination and cooperation with teammates, understanding nonverbal motor communication, understanding the value of the signal in space relationships, and feeling the zone).** The strategic space philosophy of pressing is targeted to manipulate the opponent into the desired area (e.g., extreme verticals), which presupposes the perception of the smallest resistance of the defenders, in other words, to perceive the most favorable conditions for the successful application of the pressing tactics. Paradoxically, the efforts in the application of pressing are concentrated in the areas where resistance can be at the maximum possible extent, because in terms of defensive efficiency, it is precisely this area the most preferred. In other words, pushing the opponent with the ball in areas where it is normally expected a concentrated defensive effort of the defending team and then creating gaps in the opponent's resistance within this space, which not only is a surprising rival action but at the same time, limits the effectiveness of the opponent's performance in the scope of the space.

The fundamental pressing rule in soccer is the creation of so-called pressing situations that are based on the permanent and local narrowing of the playing area for the opponent with the ball and the putting pressure on the opponent. The pressing situation is characterized by the following:

1. Horizontal and vertical shortening of the playing area

2. Creation of a temporary dominance near the player with the ball

3. An intentional creation of pressure on the player with the ball by one or often two players (the movement after the ball)

4. Tight cover of the opponent players toward "the ball" and closure of the potential corridors for passes in order to prevent the opponent to perform a micro combination or maneuvers for the purpose of getting form under the pressing

5. Slowing the opponent's rally down for the purpose of approaching the opponent players

6. An intentional creation of 1:1 situations in the crucial pressing areas

7. An attempt to create a temporary local isolation of the opponent's player with the ball

Apart from the suitable areas, there are also so-called **optimal areas for pressing**. They are the areas along the sidelines, which are exceptionally suitable due to the local pressure that is created on the player with the ball. The pressure on the sideline limits the space or play alternatives of the player with the ball to half because the operational area is reduced from 360° to 180°.

These facts should globally be reflected into **the soccer player's complex preparation**. Some specific supportive programs can be used in the area of the particular movement abilities. In the endurance development, we combine regular endurance run without the ball (pace-running that focuses on the pace creation from the accelerating and slowing the pace down point of view) with various

forms of the play in the large area with the minimum contact with the ball, In the end, we come to intensive ball programs **with the emphasis on the special playing endurance** and dynamic components of the movements that are used when applying the required playing activities. Besides the motoric speed and the speed of reaction and playing action, we are focusing on the flexibility of approach, passing, take-over, players' transfer, the opponent's game reading as well as prompt reaction of catching the movement, which is trained by various competition games with a ball. **The modeled block games** and different forms of defense movement waves enable us to improve the organization of move-spatial coordination, achieve a better movement coordination of the players who participate in pressing, and improve the switching from the attacking stage to the defensive stage and vice versa. **The defensive wave** represents the coordination of movement activity of the defending team toward the ball while performing a coordinated overlap of the defended area near but also further away from the ball.

The technical-tactical component is at the forefront of this training section. In maneuverability, we prefer the body contact and various alternatives of fight that are connected to coordination exercises, if possible everything with the ball.

In the technical-tactical area, we focus on the management of 1:1 situations, a play in outnumber or undernumber, a play of horizontal and vertical blocks by three or four players, and we intentionally stimulate the overall play-interactive focus of the players as well as the willingness of the players to search for and enter the 1:1, 1:2, or even 1:3 situations. The forms of play in a narrowed area, so-called pressing play, can be considered, from the pressing management point of view, as the dominant elements of the training process because they enable us to maximize the activeness of the playing perception, and they lead the players to the aggressiveness boundaries in fight "until the whistle" which depends on the sensitivity level of the specific referee toward aggressiveness, which is regulated according to the response received during the course of the match. We must adequately prepare the players for this from the mental preparation point of view too, because an effective solution of the pressing situations hasn't only got motoric but also specific psycho-social dimension that is demonstrated by the following:

- Continuous observation of the game while running too or during the transfer on the pitch

- The movement regulation by the means of verbal assistance with the team players and mutual coaching

- Being flexible for a temporary exchange of the players' functions or transfer into the opponent's space territory (alternating)

- Territorial variability of the playing behavior of the players who are performing pressing

- Group acting and thinking

- Play anticipation

- The ability to go "to the limit" at certain stages of the game

- The ability "not to lose" personal fights thanks to a maximum physical effort put into personal fights by players

- Tactical discipline

- Creativity and movement algorithmization that allows to carry out an effective space manipulation of an attacked opponent

- Permanent determination

- Space anticipation, space perception, and game reading

- Cognitive processing of the space relationship of the team players and opponents

Therefore, we can say that, when applying the pressing technique, together with motoric-playing skills on the movement abilities level(exceptional endurance, speed, maneuverability, body contact play, and affinity to 1:1 situations), we also have to dispose of a wide repertoire of psychological-social skills, which include the promptness to a permanent quality of the performance, boundary and regulated aggressiveness, cognitive adaptation, play adaptability, coordination of group, and individual thinking with the ability to reflect the coordination into the play compatibility, ability to stick to the concept of

the game or play according to the concept, controlled or stimulated emotiveness, determination, and permanent mobilization even after losing the possession of the game. For the purpose of the practice and improvement of the pressing tactics, we have prepared an 8-level model of a sequential process of the pressing elements development, which we are offering in the chapter 4.3.

The coordination of an individual and group thinking isn't possible to achieve any other way than by cognitive adaptation. What should the players, who perform pressing, adapt to? They should adapt to a steps sequence and team algorithm. In fact, they must recognize it and get familiar with it from the theoretical level up to the level of applying stable team automatisms. The cognitive adaptation of players (which can already start in tactical verbal-demonstrational presentation, animation schemes, or video recordings) is a concluding and, at the same time, necessary condition of the play adaptability. **When solving the play tasks, the players wouldn't be able to practically reflect the preplanned coordination into the play compatibility without the theoretical cognitive adaptation, which also includes motivational and wider psychological aspects of the players' relationship toward the pressing.**

By the term team algorithm we mean a preplanned tactical situational scenario used when solving typical play tasks or problems during the play sequences. Every situation and sequence in soccer has specific characteristics, which can be often logically predicted. They are becoming a challenge for all the team players with a high signal value (game reading). According to the prepared scenarios of the specific alternatives, the players this way not only adapt their thinking but mainly coordinate it into a team tactical sequence (algorithm). Every player is responsible for fulfilling his own mandatory and designated role where the result of this individual, sophisticated, and sequenced behavior is a synergic effect, which would Sun Tzu compare to an effect of an avalanche of rolling stones on the opponent. Synergy in this context means a multiplication of the player's playing potential according to the team's coordination, which gives the ability not only to exceed the limits of the player's performance but also to enhance the team's performance.

Sun Tzu said (2008): "An adroit commander expects the results according to the power coordination and he doesn't rely on an individual too much. Therefore, he can choose the right men and use the power in a complete collaboration. If he uses the power in a complete coordination, his soldiers are reminiscent of like rolling stones."

However, if only one stone in the algorithmic sequence chain of the pressing steps fails, the result can be even contra productive. Maybe this could be more expressive way to describe the pressing risks in which mistakes can occur more likely because the pressing is like a piece of work of an eleven-member orchestra and any failure of the orchestra can happen through a single member's failure. In the final part of this section, we will present an essential conclusion for the coaching methodical practice. Its aim is to work out and transmit the individual scenarios to players (cognitive adaptation), help the player to acquire the skills, and be able to improve and perfect them in the process of preparation (mentalization), with the ambition to apply them in the game safely and effectively (play adaptation).

If we get back to the theoretical summary of the requirements that are demanded by pressing, they form a group of skills that are gained by more or less genetic predisposition, natural players' tendency in their typology level and learnt, drilled, and practiced play-tactical solutions. From this point of view, the players' preparation for the pressing management runs continuously throughout the training process. It's mainly about general universal skills, which can be transferred by players into the pressing models. **The mentioned characteristics such as cognitive adaptation, play adaptation, coordination of group, or individual thinking with the ability to reflect the coordination into the play compatibility, the ability to stick to the concept and play according to the concept belong to the group of the specific skills that require particular attention.** We pay significant attention to these specific skills because shallow perception of this issue can lead to vagueness in the preparatory process of the whole team. The consequence of the shallow perception is mistakes of which the origin can be hardy identified. Whether it's the players' lack of knowledge of their role (insufficient cognitive adaptation) and then these players fail in the pressing or the cause of the mistakes is insufficient complex

playing ability to carry out difficult sequences (play adaptation). Therefore, it's suitable in the training process to divide the special preparation into the pressing section (the modeling itself) and the specific levels of the sequential practice procedure model (play adaptation and acquirement of the basic pressing elements), enhanced by cognitive adaptation through the theoretical preparation of the players for the specific pressing tactic.

Soccer has come a long way since the times when it was dominated by talented individuals, masculine defenders, and let's be honest, they sometimes disposed of a lower playing intelligence, but they could get by. In the contemporary soccer, everything is more about a team work, the play is more sophisticated, harmonized, synchronized into a synergy, and often it seems as if the players' freedom was restricted.

An individual's quality is today evaluated in various areas of life in the team context. Assertive, creative, and hardworking individuals can have their value if they are the pulling engine of the whole team. Today's priority is a team work; despite this we don't exclude the necessity and participation of an individual's activity and creativity, however still for the benefit of the whole team. Team coordination remains to be the highest level of players' coexistence in the game context, which is supported by a strong team spirit acquired through trendy strategy of teambuilding.

The creativity, of which the content is a creative solution of open tasks performed also in team coordination, always offers several alternatives. Not all the alternatives are always correct, and the choice is only one. The more tactical alternatives the team has in the repertoire, the bigger freedom and space is given to the team's players for putting their creativity into practice. The pressing can give the players wings, because it supports their natural desire to own the ball, participate in personal fights, and confrontations compared to passive standing around in front of the team's penalty area without the ball. The pressing also fulfils the confrontational-interactive core of the game itself.

The aims of the pressing can be divided according to the fact whether the pressing is supposed to support the team's own attacking technique or if it's only a part of the defending stage of the team that focuses on the space manipulation. In the first case, the domineering target is to gain the possession of the ball and, in the second case, the mentioned aim doesn't have to be dominant.

In this case, we use the pressing tactic for the achievement of the following **territorial-spatial aims:**

1. Pushing the opponent further away from their own goal

2. Pushing the opponent into the controlled areas from the defense point of view

3. Closing the playing area in order to build the opponent's offensive

4. Shortening and narrowing the active playing area and squeezing the opponent into a small area

5. Minimizing the possibilities to escape the pressure, therefore the opponent is playing under a permanent time-space pressure

6. Enforcement from the back

7. Slowing down the establishment and performance of the attacking activity

8. Prevention from a direct progress

Apart from these aims, the pressing technique can also be useful in the more **general tactical scale:**

1. **Disruption of the opponent's organization,** knocking the opponent players off their balance, restriction of the playing time and space necessary for the realization of attacking play schemes, breaking the opponent's coordination, enforcement of the opponent's mistakes or decreasing the quality of the opponent's playing solutions.

2. **Disruption of clear triangular positions of attacking layers** on the whole area of the pitch, ruining the attacking players' to carry out an attacking triangulation, which is necessary for continuous circulation of the ball when building the offensive. Attempts to perform auxiliary back passes are also ruined.

3. **Shortening the time the opponent is in the possession of the ball** in order to "see" and for the purpose of a visual contact with the "surrounding," which results in relative loss of the opponent's control when constructing an attack (preventing the opponent

from performing the game reading and exchanging information between the attacking players and their surrounding and creation of an overall time-space necessity for attacking). In other words, the bonds between the attacking players are being broken by performing the pressing technique. The opponent is forced to perform more risky, noneffective, and wrong solutions of play sequences.

4. **Weakening the opponent's offensive activity by constant attacks and slowing down the establishment of the attacking action.** The impact of this is often psychological discomfort, recklessness, noncoordination, dissatisfaction, and possible conflicts within the team.

Ruttensteiner (2010) presents, in relation to this, two cardinal principles in the pressing application:

1. When you perform pressing, the team is moving forward.

2. You must realize that unnecessary foul ends the pressing action.

He recommends several relevant principles for the technique of creating the pressing pressure:

1. Narrowing the area (in depth and width too)

2. Creation of dominance near the ball (time pressure)

3. Putting the opponent's team under pressure (psychological) and to force the players to make mistakes through aggressive play

4. Personal occupation of the players near the ball, provoking the opponent to perform wrong passes, and closing the passes corridors

5. After gaining the possession of the ball, avoidance to perform back passes to the goal keeper or defender

6. After gaining the possession of the ball, starting the attack or securing the ball while preparing for an attack.

Viviani (2003) indicates that good pressing can be performed when the opponent

1. makes mistake when taking over the ball;

2. looks down when kicking the ball away;

3. takes over the ball by the sideline;

4. takes over a high ball from the back;

5. takes over the ball with the back turned toward the opponent's goal; and

6. moves forward with the ball by his legs or he tries to perform an individual action.

According to him, the answer to the question of where to start the pressing depends on a few changeable factors, such as

1. the positions in the alignment;

2. the surrounding of the match (home team or visiting team);

3. the conditions at the pitch;

4. the score;

5. remaining time of the match; and

6. psychological-physiological state of the team.

Arias (2013) on the other hand, say it's unsuitable to apply the pressing technique in the following conditions:

1. If you are not convinced about what to do, if you don't act as a group

2. If you are not cautious and focused, if you are in under number

3. If you are in the state of mental or physiological exhaustion

Let's get back to the dominant offensive aim of the pressing, gaining the possession of the ball, which is generally approved to be qualitative evaluation criteria of the pressing application. **"The icing on the pressing cake" is gaining the possession of the ball by constructive means, so that the pressing itself is continuously followed by attacking action, which can be advantageous from spatial and wider play-tactical point of view.** Gaining the possession in the same area where the possession of the ball was lost immediately after the loss is the offensive extension of attacking and if we were to give points like in box, this type of pressing would keep winning matches.

The most valued aim of the pressing is **to gain the possession of the ball as soon as possible and preferably directly in the place where the loss of the possession in the attacking zone occurred** and to continue attacking in more suitable conditions when the opponent players are starting to take attacking positions, by their movement they are opening the area, and they aren't able to positionally reorganize themselves fast enough after the "surprising" loss of the ball. Visually, in good pressing we can observe that, after losing the ball, the team's swiftly gets the ball back under their control due to the team's extended defense, which "forces" the opponent to get rid of the ball in the risky areas.

Therefore, the play of two pressing teams "looks" as if they were not even defending due to a high level of offensive defense they perform that we may not even notice that they are "defending." According to the initiation, course of the game and the pressing application, the algorithm of individual logically connected pressing steps starts already in the attacking stage of the game, it continues after the loss of the ball in the defending stage and ends by retrieving the ball under the team's control or by fulfilling another additional aim, which we intend to achieve in the match. In order to achieve an effective pressing application, the most important stage of the game is often so-called the switching stage, which enables the team to optimize their positional alignment for the particular situation.

We think that not only switching is the most important part but mainly respecting the principle of the stage response. This shows a lot more about the tactics and strategy of the game. The switching itself isn't even that essential, if we prevent the opponent to switch from one stage to another efficiently by positional alignment of the players (by proportional designation of power already in the attacking and defense itself). By this, we directly mean the number of defending players who are positioned in authentic (they focus on the currently running stage) or alternative (they are prepared for an eventual change of the stage too) positions, in other words, over and below the ball.

All these theoretical aspects of the pressing confirm that the contemporary proactive soccer is played not only by legs but also by brain.

3.3.2 Pressing Typology

There are several theoretical pressing type classifications, which have been profiled in the space of last twenty-five years of evolution of this defense play-tactical tool. For demonstration, we are presenting some examples, which will help us to make a clearer picture of how the pressing developed.

Marziali-Mora (i 997) conceived pressing for **three different space depths;** they are:

1. The opponent's penalty area border

2. Three quarters of the playing area in the opponent's half

3. Midfield line and the team's own half

The most traditional pressing typology is **three-zone classification,** which is described by Peter and Barez (2012). The three basic pressing types were defined by the pressing zones specification:

1. Defensive pressing situated in the zone between the midfield line and the line, which is in the distance of 20 m from the team's goal, when all the players of the defending team withdraw to their half of the pitch.

2. Midfield pressing situated in the area of the midfield zone of 30–40 m deep; as soon as opponent with the ball appears in this zone, he should be stopped and pushed into a designated part of the playing area

3. Attacking pressing situated in the whole opponent's half of the playing area; midfield pressing frequently turns into attacking pressing.

Apart from this classification, Peter (2012) offers a classification of the **three forms of the pressing,** which prefers specific tactical intentions, compared to the traditional spatial classification. The first one represents **coordinated pressing,** which correlates with the zonal forms of the pressing tactics, from the point of view of the focus on the vertical or midfield space of the playing area. The second form is **situational pressing,** which represents the activation of the proactive defense. This defense is related to the specific play-situational configurations. The third form is so-called **pressing victims** in which the prechosen weaker opponent player becomes a victim of the pressing tactic

application. The analogy to this is so-called **challenge pressing,** which is characterized by Ceccomori (2003) as a pressing action, which isn't carried out in the specific part of the playing area, but it's aimed at an opponent player who, by the pressing team's judgement, could be having playing difficulties or may not be having "a good day." By performing specific maneuvers, the opponent is being offered seemingly suitable pass alternative, which in reality is "a trap." For this purpose, there are special techniques of the space manipulation, which allow an opponent player to get to the ball and immediately be attacked by the defending players.

An interesting classification of the pressing forms is offered by Mazzali (2001) who uses color differentiation to divide the playing area according to the typical pressing tactics. **The green zone (attacking zone)** is, in his opinion, potentially the most suitable area for the pressing application because it represents the highest play risk for the opponent. However, the big disadvantage is "a short" team, which allows the opponent to perform long ball play and counterattacks. **The yellow zone (midfield zone on the opponent's half)** considered to be the optimal area for starting the pressing technique application. Many teams start the pressing in **the orange zone (midfield zone on the team's half),** which is considered Mazzali to be unsuitable due to the big distance from the opponent's goal. The pressing application in the red zone is considered to be considerably instinctive as this area is the riskiest area for an application of this type of defense tactic.

After the traditional perception of the zone pressing, we can define three basic pressing types. The definition of these types depends on which part of the playing area (on the team's own half, midfield zone, or the opponent's haiD, the basic pressing alignment of the defending team is activated, and the active pressing zone (APZ) is formed.

In connection with the typology, we mustn't forget about the specific type of pressing, which has become a trend thanks to the efficient application by several top teams in the first decade of the new millennium (e.g., Arsenal, Barcelona). It's the most offensive alternative of pressing, which is applied right after losing the possession of the ball in any area but mostly on the opponent's half of the pitch. Taking into consideration, the overall attacking character of this alternative, which is built on defensive super-activity and the time dimension that demonstrates the promptness of the application moment connected to stage switching of the participating players after losing the ball, we can call it **immediate ultraoffensive pressing (IUP)**.

Figure 3.3-1 shows us the constellation when performing defensive pressing, figure 3.3-2 depicts the pressing situation in the midfield zone, figure 3.3-3 captures the situation that is typical for attacking pressing, and figure 3.3-4 demonstrates the situational form of the immediate ultraoffensive pressing.

We are intentionally presenting these types of pressing exactly in thins order because we think, that also from the practice and improvement chronology point of view, it would be suitable to start with the pressing first on the team's own half and then gradually move to the pressing in the midfield zone, which can continuously form into an attacking pressing by performing an extended that

active zone of the pressing to the opponent's half. An immediate pressing requires an individual type of practice because, apart from the positional reaction of the players involved, the most decisive factor for the pressing application is a prompt reaction to a negative stage switch, in other words from an attack to defense and an immediate switch from defense to attacking stage. The phenomenon of the stage switching is becoming an important factor that also relates to other types of pressing; however, the emphasis of this phenomenon in connection with an ultraoffensive pressing alternative is exceptionally important.

However, this doesn't mean that it's not possible to break the natural chronology of the pressing types practice and work, for example, only on attacking pressing, after dealing with defensive pressing. In other words, it's possible to keep in the team's repertoire only midfield zone pressing, so-called midfield pressing, or create a combination of the pressing tactics according to the basic play concept

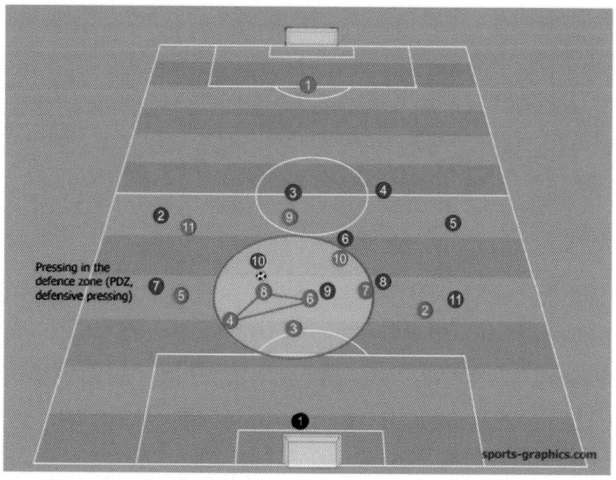

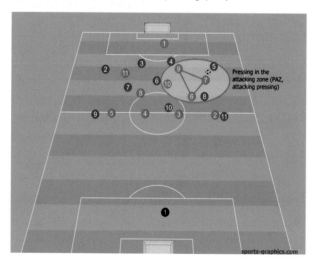

Fig. 3.3-1 An example of defensive pressing (PDZ)

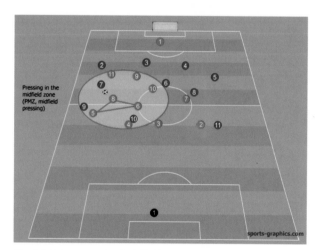

Fig. 3.3-2 An example of midfield pressing (PMZ)

Fig. 3.3-3 An example of attacking pressing (PAZ)

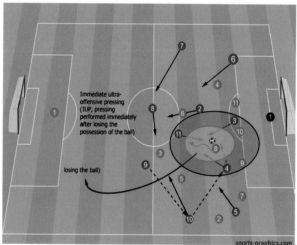

Fig. 3.3-4 An example of immediate ultraoffensive pressing (IUP)

PART 2

or the concept of the game for the specific match. Therefore, the alternating the pressing tactics is closely linked to specific play concepts and tactics for the particular match, team's typology, and the opponent's quality. We think that this depends very much on the specific tactical intentions of the team for the particular match and also on the typological structure of the team, which is the determining factor for the application of the specific type of play by the team. As in other type of games, the motoric schemes in the pressing also have a sequential character, which is represented by the following phases:

- **Creation of the basic pressing alignment,** position taking

- **Manipulation of space** for the purpose of pressing and creation of a pressing situation

- **Pressing activation,** maneuvering in a narrowed area, slowing a pass down, closure of potential pass corridors, configuration of a time-space pressure on the player with the ball

- **Pressing finalization** and active attack on the player with the ball

- **Direct removal of the ball from the opponent**

- **Effective playing reaction as an impact of the direct pressing activity result** that is directly connected to the continuity of the game's events (diametrically different in successful or unsuccessful pressing).

This classification has got mainly methodical meaning, because it provides us with the algorithmization of the practice and improvement of the pressing tactic in the training process taking into consideration the preservation of the psychomotor sequence of the training tools as well as increasing the effect of the element transfer into match conditions. In the following chapters, we are offering a detailed description of the basic forms of the zone pressing (PDZ, PMZ, PAZ) as well as in immediate ultraoffensive pressing (IUP).

3.3.3 Pressing in the Defense Zone (PDZ, Defensive Pressing)

The pressing application in the defense zone represents, within the zonal pressing tactics, the most

passive and the least proactive alternative of an active defense. Lucchesi(2003) talks more about covering the area and that ability to perform a tight occupation of an opponent rather than aggressive play and risky movement. **When applying this type of defensive tactics, all the players (including the attackers) must withdraw to their half of the pitch.** The defending formation (DF) is aligned 5–10 m in front of the penalty area (PA) and the highest positioned players of the pressing block operate right behind the midfield line on their half of the pitch so that the depth of the active playing zone (APZ) doesn't go over 30 m. When performing pressing in the defensive zone, the alignment of the defending players in their own defense zone is outnumbered. This allows the players to perform, at the right moment, an aggressive attacking on the player with the ball either by applying 1:1 situation or doubling the attacked player. The pressing in a defense zone is chronologically preceded by the correct alignment whereas the players of the team, which is performing pressing, must be correctly aligned before the opponent approaches them. Thanks to the defensive movements in the team's own defense zone and positional alignment, which allows the players to cover the active playing space in outnumber and advance, it's possible to activate the pressing tactic in the team's own defense zone.

An advantage of this defensive tactic is that there isn't usually an occurrence of outnumber of the opponent players in the defense line of the defending team, because the team is preoccupied by trying to break the defending team's defense alignment. In order to succeed, the team needs to have the number of the players high enough so reaching the outnumber of the defense line is quite impossible (however, if it happens, it's usually a consequence of an incorrect positional play of the defending players). Another advantage of pressing in the defense zone is the fact that thanks to deep position of the defense line, the number of the penetration passes is limited, because these passes already get into the defense territory of the spatially active playing goalkeeper. When applying the pressing in the defense zone, the location of the active playing space (APS) points at many space options for the offensive after the successful completion of the offensive stage. There is a choice of various alternatives of the depth offensive and fast counterattacks. Pressing in the defense zone creates a compact and closed defense form under the ball, which reacts more intensively to the opponent actions, and it's similar to a block defense in the defense zone due to its defensive character. When applying pressing in the defense zone, there are several interesting defense maneuvers available, which enable to defend effectively and apply this pressing tactic safely due to the correct positional alignment. T-position is used on the weak side of the team's defending form (fig. 3.3-6). This position shows the correct position of the defending player who intends to push the attacking player, whom the ball is approaching, into the area that is dangerous for the goal of the pressing team.

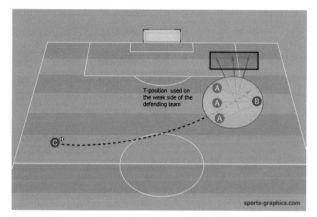

Fig. 3.3-5 T-position is used on the weak side of the team's defending form.

In this positional alignment, the defending player must be positioned vertically lower so that the line, which is positioned vertically to the line connecting the defending and occupied player is directed away from the team's goal; out of the dangerous area. An extreme situation arises, when both players (defending and attacking) are horizontally in one line. **From the goal's safety threat point of view, any position of the defending player, which is over the horizontal line, creates an advantage for the attacking player.** The only exception is the case of the offside tactic application, which allows the defending player to take this position.

Another positional defense maneuver used, when attacking the player who is under pressing, is **the position of the defending player in the imaginary triangle** in which the base is the goal line and the top vertex is the occupied attacking player (fig. 3.3-7). This position of the defending player, between the goal and the attacking player, allows the player to eliminate a depth alternative of the

attacking player's pass and keep him under control. This is also used in the technique called "sandwich," which is applied in the midfield area in front of the penalty area (doubling from up and down).

When occupying the player, apart from the spatial principle, the players also apply **the two-element principle of perceiving the occupied player and flying ball at the specific moment.** Lucchesi(2003) recommends concentrating on the player in situations where it's not possible to maintain the visual control of both elements at the same time. The problem arises, when the occupied player escapes into a so-called blind side, which lacks the defending player 's visual control. One of the pressing tactics is also so-called dirty defending. **The point of this type of defense is an extreme form of physical contact which, however, mustn't be punishable or judged by a referee as unpermitted play as this would ruin the whole purpose of the positional work of the defending team.**

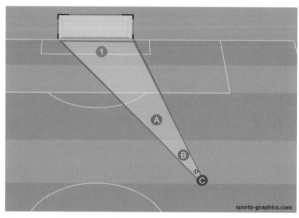

Fig. 3.3-6 The position of the defending player in the imaginary triangle when attacking a player

Apart from the correct position when occupying the playing area and opponents, the pressing tactic also includes several pressure levels applied in attacking opponents with the ball. The lowest level is represented by slowing the player with the ball down. This allows the team to find the most suitable playing situation and improve the defense organization for the purpose of performing the specific defense sequence. United attacking represents the medium intensity level for attacking, and it focuses on eliminating certain playing solutions (long kicks, ball balance, pace, dribbling, and so on) and the style and intensity of attacking is adapted to this. The highest level of

PART 2

the pressure in attacking is used by players, who perform pressing, when they directly remove the ball from the opponent or regain the possession of the ball.

The way the attacking is performed determines how much space and time we allow the opponent with the ball to have. Lucchesi (2003) recommends us to let the opponent have more space rather than allow him to pass by us, and he presents the following **rules for performing the pressing attack on the opponent:**

- Avoid fouls

- Approaching the attacking opponent as fast as possible

- Take a position while taking into consideration the line into which the ball is coming

- Follow the attacker's movement in the shortest possible space of time

- Take initiative

- Intervene only if the attacking player controls the ball insufficiently

- "go on the ground" only if it's necessary.

The attacking intensity is often determined by defense security provided by the nearest team player. This minimizes the risk of the organizational disruption of the team or the defense form in case of unsuccessful removal of the ball from the opponent.

An important defense technique in the pressing tactics application is so-called **provocative attack,** which represents a specific category of pressure. This works on the principle of directing the defensive movement activity toward the player with the ball and provoke him to perform the playing intention that had been preplanned by the defending team (e.g., long kick forward, back pass to the team player or goalkeeper, and risky pass to the tea player into unprepared position). **The main motive isn't directly to gain the possession of the ball but creating discomfort and stimulation of such a solution or the player's activity, which leads to the preplanned configuration of the playing situation that allows the team to prepare a safer defense alignment.** However, there's point in using this defense technique only if the defending

team is prepared to positionally react to this type of "liberating" playing activity of the occupied or "provoked" opponent (e.g., closure of pass corridors near the center of the game, effective distance of the defending players, correct position of the defending players from the point of view of the alignment, and optimal distance between them). If these essential tactical conditions aren't met, the application of the provocative attacking isn't justifiable. **This type of defense technique is mostly applied by attackers or offensive players who are involved in the preparation of the team pressing tactics.** One of the tactical intentions of the provocative attacking is, besides stimulation of the opponent's playing activities, also slowing the game down for the purpose of gaining time, which is necessary for creating the defending team's compactness or organizing an effective defensive form. In any case, we can consider this defense technique as a natural element of a proactively defending team's tactical portfolio. Having this technique in the portfolio, the team is able to actively influence the game even when the ball is under the opponent's control.

The doubling is the typical pressing technique when attacking an opponent with the ball. This is frequently applied in an immediate ultra-offensive pressing (I UP) but also in specific situations when applying zonal and coordinated pressing, especially the midfield zone.

Controlled doubling represents the situation in which the defending player, who is attacking the player with the ball, is secured directly near him by another team player who can, in case of unsuccessful removal of the ball from the opponent, immediately enter the active defense and secure the action of removing the ball by 2:1 situation. **The player who is farther away from the team's goal is supposed to be more active from these two attacking players. Authentic doubling** means the type of the defense technique in which the two defending players, by attacking the player with the ball simultaneously, focus on creating the attacked player's time and space deficit, which gives the attacking players an opportunity to gain the possession of the ball. When applying the doubling, the decisive factor is the position of the attacked player with the ball on the pitch (zone and vertical position) as well as his orientation on the pitch (direction toward the opponent's goal or the team's own goal, etc.). The doubling technique can be already included in the tactical defense tools in which the emphasis is put on the defending players' coordination. Apart from manipulating the player with the ball into entering the required area (sideline, preferred zone, vertical zone, and so on), it's necessary for one of the doubling players to close the direction toward the team's own goal and the other attacking player to flexibly react to the position and orientation of the player with the ball in the playing area. An important moment when bringing the doubling technique into practice is to approach the player with the ball at "leg length," which allows the player to get a direct contact with the ball.

Following these positional rules allows the team to achieve an effective doubling performance whereas the act of the ball removal itself is situationally determined and the player in the more advantageous position is bound to gain the position of the ball. The detailed tactical nuances of this defense tactic use, which is, according to van Gaal, the heart of pressing, are presented in the special chapter of part 3 in this book.

When applying pressing in the defense zone, the application is usually joined together with other forms of defense tactics. Currently, the most typical application is in connection with block defense, which is often also considered as depth block defense. The connection of defense block and pressing has it's logical point, which concludes from analogical and positional organization and the possibility to continuously transfer from the defensive into pressing form of defense and vice versa. The detailed analysis of this defense combination is presented in the chapter 3.5 of this volume.

3.3.4 Pressing in the Midfield Zone (PMZ, Midfield Pressing)

The main characteristic of this pressing type is the fact that after the loss of the possession of the ball all the players withdraw behind, in front of or directly on the midfield line and the attack on the opponent begins while in the midfield zone and around the center of the game, every defending player covers the nearest opponent player in the direction toward "the ball." When applying pressing in the midfield zone, from the playing resistance point

of view, the attacking zone is completely eliminated in which the player, who opens the play, isn't attacked.

The exact definition of the pressing activation line is the matter of arrangement between the coach and players, which results from the tactical intention of the team and has a practical purpose, especially from the point of view of some tactical nuances application. In fact, this type of play creates optimal conditions for performing counterattacks and in terminology sense, we could define it as preying on counter situations from the area of the active defense in the midfield area. The process of the basic play sequence of pressing in the midfield zone is

- Slowing the opponent's play down while reorganizing the team's own defense alignment according to the current situation

- Maneuvering the opponent to the sidelines in a synchronized manner while systematically narrowing the playing area (increasing the density)

- Creating a temporary dominance in the area near the ball

- Putting the opponent with the ball under time-space pressure by one or two players in order to provoke him to make mistake (technical mistake, wrong pass, unsuitable tactical solution, etc.)

- Tight covering of all the opponent players who are in the pressing situation and who are coming to assist and can receive a pass

- Finishing the pressing situation by performing an immediate and aggressive body to body attack and getting to the ball (squeezing between the player and the ball)

- After gaining the possession of the ball, switching to the attacking stage of the game, in other words counterattack (the way the attack is performed is situationally determined)

Compared to the attacking pressing, this form of pressing is more obligatory and generally it's used more frequently without any significant risk; although some typical pressing teams (e.g., Chile and Algeria) presented in the last World Championship the attractive form of the attacking pressing application. An important factor for this type of pressing application is also a flexible extension of the defensive line so that the active pressing zone isn't deeper than 20–25 m. **The disadvantage of this type of pressing is the fact that the attacking team has got, from the active pressing zone position point of view, quite a big maneuvering area, which allows the players to get out of pressing by performing back or auxiliary passes into their own defense zone.** Thus, the depth of the active pressing zone increases, and the efficiency of the defensive maneuvers of the pressing team are decreased.

3.3.5 Pressing in the Attacking Zone (PAZ, Attacking Pressing)

This form of pressing represents the most offensive form of defense, but most of all it maximizes the risk. In this type of pressing, we are trying to put the opponent team under pressure already in the very beginning of their attacking activity right on their half of the pitch usually 20–25 m from the goal. Compared to pressing in the midfield zone, in which we concentrate mainly on the situation on the sidelines, in the attacking pressing, we create pressure along the whole width of the opponent's defense zone.

It starts immediately after losing the possession of the ball by switching to defensive activity of the whole block of players who participate in the pressing situation. The attack on the opponent is performed with a significant effort to gain the possession of the ball still on the opponent's half of the pitch; this is preceded by slowing down stage as well as disruption of the opponent's pass development. **Activation of this form of pressing is started either by the attacker or midfielder entering the defined area** (the line of 20–25 m in front of the goal of the attacked opponent) whereas the movement patterns of the space maneuvers of the approaching player must be the subject of the special tactic training that uses modeling exercises. In relation to this, the most important element is the movement of more players forward while the consequence of this movement is the relocation of the other players into the empty areas in order to minimize the risk of these areas being opened. We mustn't forget that this movement and relocation must

happen in synchronized manner. It usually has a signal character, which means it starts by the entry of the first player (either the attacker or midfielder) who activates the situationally executed pressing. An **important fact also is that after activation of the attacking pressing, it's necessary to close the area vertically (vertical narrowing) in both directions,** which means from direction of the opponent's (allocated attacker) as well as the team's own goal (according to the positional location, it's either allocated player of the midfield or defense). For the pressing activation, it's essential in this situation to keep an eye on so-called the pressing triggers, which are the following: high pass, taking over the ball by high trajectory, taking over the ball with the back turned to the opponent's goal, slow and inaccurate pass, incorrect way of taking over the ball, absence of the control over the ball, a throw-in near the opponent's penalty area and so on.

The specific play-tactical tasks for attackers, midfielders as well as quadruple chain are presented in the manual for the practice and improvement of the pressing technique. The allocated attacker, after performing the maneuver for the purpose of pushing the play to the side verticals, closes the area from the top (from the opponent's goal direction) while the midfield defenders close the area in the defense area, which was created by the attacking defenders or the midfield formation players. They react situationally and activate their positional perception. By performing the transfer into the center of the game, the playing area is significantly narrowed, which gives the play under pressing a special character. The pressing is not likely to be used as a common style of play throughout the whole match. The use of pressing is only possible in relatively short periods of time and in specifically defined stages of the game when there's an opportunity for a successful application of the attacking pressing. These opportunities could appear according to the opponent's configuration, the team's alignment and an occurrence of the pressing triggers, which have a signal value for the defending team due to the simultaneous inclusion of the whole spatial blocks of players in the process. The basic movement sequences of the attacking pressing are carried out the following way:

- All the attackers and midfielders on the opponent's half **immediately switch to the defensive stage after losing the possession of the ball**

- **Entering the center of the game,** movement after the ball

- **Transfer of the players into the pressing situation area** and tight occupation of the opponent players and the player with the ball in order to limit their cooperation by performing a pass to the minimum

- **Closure of the area from the opponent's goal** in order to prevent the players of the team, that is in the possession of the ball, from moving in the direction of the attack (vertical closure)

- **Permanent visual observation of the playing situation (periphery vision)** together with verbal communication between the players when relocating and entering the pressing situations

- **Temporary narrowing and shortening the playing area (horizontal narrowing and vertical shortening)** is a signal for the players to begin the attack on the player with the ball

- **Doubling the attack** at the moment of attacking the player with the ball

- **Temporary exchange of the players' functions** is an obvious practice, which is determined by changed space relationships in the pressing situation

- **After gaining the possession of the ball, immediate switch to the attacking stage** and focus on the prefinal activities (individual penetration into the 16, depth crash into 16, penetration into the wing areas and shortened interlude).

However, it's vital to point out the fact that although the attacking pressing represents a high efficiency level of the play in critical areas from the score point of view (in front of the 16, around the penalty area, in the wings area, etc.), **this type of play also brings an unequal risk especially for top players who have already acquired pressing resistance,** they can easily deal with the 1:1 situations and area able to transfer the center of the game into an uncovered or relatively weakly covered area that is out of the pressing situation. The transfer of the game

to the opposite vertical or at least to the midfield vertical seems to be the most effective.

3.3.6 Immediate Ultraoffensive Pressing (IUP, Pressing Performed Immediately After Losing Possession of the Ball)

Together with the classical zonal pressing, which has its spatial specification, we also use a special type of the pressing tactic that is applied immediately after losing the possession of the ball. IUP represents an application of a proactive defense in the ball's territory at the moment of losing the possession, and it's accompanied by a synchronized movement of the whole team, which focuses on regaining the possession of the ball. The basic condition for application of IUP is losing the ball. This is followed by an immediate negative switch (from attack to defense) and application of IUP. The most relevant impact is its success (depth offensive pass and keeping the ball) or failure (reaction to the opponent's offensive). The main benefit of this pressing tactic is that it allows the players to make the use of the organizational and positional deficits of the team, which gained the possession of the ball, but still isn't in an optimal alignment to begin their own attacking action. Another benefit of the IUP is that smaller playing resistance to an immediate pressure, which is focused on regaining the possession of the ball, lowers the quality of the opponent's playing solutions and offers convenient alternatives for the defending team.

Contrary consequences of IUP are reflected on one hand by the fact that by creating outnumber in the center of the game and its direct surrounding, we limit the playing alternatives for constructive solutions and performing the offensive. On the other hand, it's precisely the time-space pressure and local outnumber that can paradoxically stimulate the opponent's response to swiftly transfer the center of the game into an area that is behind the pressing zone. At this point, due to the unfinished switch, the team (which is applying IUP) can show decreased compactness and deficit of the correct defense alignment for performing safe and effective defense by applying this pressing tactic. **The risk of the IUP application lies mainly in speeding up the play of the opponent with the ball forward.** The play system of the team, which is trying to apply this type of pressing, should definitely emphasize the anticipation play-tactical behavior, purposeful organization of their alignment, and correct positional configuration of the whole team. The type of the offensive play (short distance between the players) also influences the possibility to apply IUP and vice versa (similarly Turek, 2015).

The space localization of IUP is situationally limited, because it's applied in the area of the current loss of the ball, which has a stochastical character. In spite of this, the IUP is mainly applied on the opponent's half, which represents typical playing area for this type of pressing, and it's connected to several tactical rules. In relation to IUP, Lucchesi (2003) says what we must do if we want to apply this type of pressing:

1. **To put pressure on the player with the ball**

2. **To break as fast as possible all the pass corridors** between the player with the ball and his team player who are likely to receive the pass

3. **To be prepared to cover the supporting players who are positioned in the depth** and to whom a long pass can be directed; not to cover only the players who are directly near the ball but also the players who are further away from the center of the game; the whole team should take the pro-pressing positions. According to Turek (2015) the vertical division of the playing area is dominant for the IUP.

Apart from these tactical aspects, we have to realize the impact of IUP application on the opponent's half. **After regaining the possession of the ball in the area as deep as possible on the opponent's half, the nearness of the opponent's goal is becoming an attractive leitmotiv of this type of defense.** From this fact, it's also obvious that IUP is directly linked to the process of building the offensive after gaining the possession of the ball. In this context, we can talk about so-called double switching (after losing the ball follows an immediate attack on the opponent and after regaining the possession of the ball the players continue attacking).

IUP is positionally demanding due to the fact that the team, which lost the possession of the ball on the opponent's half, must switch to defensive stage, positionally reorganize the players so that they are able to create time-space pressure on the player with the ball and close all direct pass corridors in order to prevent the opponent getting out of the pressing situation.

The ability of the team to activate IUP after losing the ball, as well as successful regaining the possession of the ball, is directly connected to the positive (from defensive to attacking stage) and negative (from attacking to defensive stage) switching of the basic stages of the game. This is a team tactical activity without which the effective application of this form of pressing would be impossible to realize. The processes of switching to defense and attacks are equal due to uniformity of these basic stages and, therefore, we can say that while one team (the one which has lost the ball) switches to defense, the opponent, who has just gained the possession of the ball, switches to attack. **Both processes of switching represent an extremely short periods of the play time at the moment of switching from attack to defense and vice versa, with the emphasis on the continuity of the play.**

However, let's not forget about so-called plan B, which represents an alternative for the play after an unsuccessful IUP. After a standard loss of the possession of the ball, it's also possible to apply IUP in special situations after "an intentional loss of the ball" when the ball is under control of neither of the two teams; neither of the teams is in the possession of the ball. Turek (2015) describes the process of this type of situations through so-called intentionally wrong pass behind the opponent's defense line when neither of the teams has the ball. "This neutral ball" being approached by the players of both teams creates a special situation in which the players got rid of the ball deliberately by performing "a wrong pass," they are trying to regain the possession of the ball and apply IUP in a designated playing area. This sort of situation differs by its intention from the pressing situations of an immediate regain of the ball following a spontaneous loss of the possession.

The practice and improvement of this tactic, which is based on an extreme movement synchronization of the whole team, allows the team to achieve a time-space coordination of correctly aligned players in the APZ (active pressing zone). This isn't possible to achieve without a suitable training method, which should include the improvement starting from the basic playing activities and their applications in the pressing actions as well as their chain on the level of an individual, group, block of players, or the whole team resulting in the team tactic. Ideal forms for the practice and improvement of these pressing tactics are elementary and complex playing forms (playing exercises, preparatory games, and most of all modeling exercises). The basic level of practicing the play-tactical elements used in the pressing tactics is described in the chapter 4.3 in the eight-level model of the pressing practice sequence.

3.3.7 Additional Comments on the Special Theory of Pressing Tactics

For all forms of zonal pressing, the explicit priority also is, apart from gaining the possession of the ball, the control of the game without the ball. The control is based on the intentional transfer of the center of the game to the required location in the playing area by applying the manipulation of the active playing space or active playing zone. It's precisely this attribute by which the principle of the proactive defense is achieved as well as the fundamental characteristic of active defense in the form of pressing defense. The control of the play, also when the team isn't in the possession of the ball, is enabled exactly by applying the principle of defensive proactivity, which creates conditions for the space manipulation and coordination of the course of the game.

When creating a defensive form in a pressing tactic, the main target is to achieve the correct positional alignment of mainly the players in the APZ but also other team players. In order to achieve this aim, the teams use **variable pressing movements** of the players, which focus on the center of the game as well as the area directly near the midfield. The mechanism of the transfer in the playing area is represented by movement of one or more players of the defending team from their team positions, which were allocated by the basic alignment and the game concept, for the purpose of **creating the correct positional defense form alignment for the pressing application.** The defined pressing tasks require a temporary outnumber or at least balance in the APZ and **creation of time-space pressure on the player with the ball by performing an active manipulation in this area.** The mechanism of the transfer in the playing area has variable forms determined exactly by its alterability.

The transfer of the players is a domineering tool for creating the correct defensive form in pressing. The aim of this transfer is the movement of the defending players, who are trying to create this form, out of the standard alignment in order to shorten and narrow the playing area of the opponent with the ball or at least reduce his playing time and create a temporary outnumber in the center of the game and in the area directly near the midfield. Thus the time-space pressure is created during the course of the pressing defense application. When performing the transfer, it's necessary to take into consideration the distance of the transfer, which often significantly limits the speed of the pressing form application. An important role in the optimal transfer performance is also played by the speed the players take time to react to the playing situations, which trigger the whole mechanism of the pressing transfer of the players into their correct positions (quality and speed of the defensive game reading). The application of the defensive transfer is directly related to the position of the defending player toward the ball. The active position of the player is created when the player is located under the ball's line, which allows him to actively enter the process of defense. On the contrary, the passive position means that the position of the defending player is over the ball's line, which limits his ability to assist in the defensive process.

The typology of the movement is directly related to the variability of the playing area, its horizontal-vertical division (width-horizontal transfer, vertical withdraw backward, moving forward) as well as the number of the players (transfer of the formations, blocks, chains, and groups). In connection to this, the typical movements in the pressing technique are movement forward for the purpose of doubling. In the case of defensive chain, the players perform synchronized backward movement, extension of the pressing pump as well as width transfer of the pressing pendulum. The characteristic feature of the pressing movement is the transfer into the "ball's zone," which includes, together with the center of the game, a wider area near the ball.

This zone is part of the tactical thinking of the defending team when forming the correct defensive alignment with a direct impact not only on the ball itself (the center of the game) but also the playing area near the midfield.

This type of perception has direct influence on the correct alignment of the defending players in the pressing tactics from the situational, effective, and time-space point of view.

When evaluating the specific types of zonal pressing, it's necessary to take into account the space zone in which the pressing tactic is applied. The location of this zone limits the character of the playing behavior of the player with the ball and his team players. Each zone has its specific playing dominance, which determines the character of the paying behavior of the opponent with the ball (defense zone-security, midfield zone-variability, and attacking zone-creativity and improvisation) and by which the way of applying the pressing tactic is determined. The opponent with the ball demonstrates different type of behavior in the defense zone, midfield zone, and attacking zone. This affects the character of the pressing tactic applied in these areas.

In the defense zone, the player with the ball is trying to perform a secure play and keep the possession of the ball because any loss of the ball is an immediate threat of the team's goal. The pressure created on individual opponent players in this zone by the team, which is performing pressing, is supposed to prevent a long pass being performed to the pressing team's half. As a consequence of this high position, there's a large area being opened in the pressing team's half for a counterattack of the team that is under pressing.

From this point of view, pressing in the midfield zone is inconvenient; due to the variability dominance and higher pressing resistance of the midfield players the alternatives of escaping from pressing situations are enriched by back passes. Closure of these pressing corridors is problematic; moreover, the area behind the defense line in the midfield zone of the team performing pressing is suitable only for long escape passes behind this line. The principle limit for the pressing application in the midfield zone is the interlude character that is applied by the player with the ball. The higher the dynamization in the center of the game, and the fewer passes are performed by the opponent with the ball when transferring into the attacking zone, the less problematic the pressing tactic application in this area is. On the contrary, long interlude with dominance of width passes is an ideal type of play of the opponent with the ball in order to perform an effective positional preparation for the pressing application in the midfield zone.

Pressing in the defending team's defense, zone is characterized by an increased control of opponent attackers and covering the defense line and free spaces that are an ideal area for defeating the compactness of the pressing team. The dominance of the attacking team is this area is creativity and improvisation, which on the other hand, contribute to maximizing the risk and increasing the team's natural faultiness. These factors also contribute to higher efficiency of pressing in the defense zone, compared to other types of zonal pressing and regaining the possession of the ball is more realistic.

3.4 MENTAL ASPECTS OF PRESSING

Apart from the tactical movement and the technical tactical part, **pressing has its constant and essential mental element related to the psychology of the soccer game itself.**

We accept the pressing application unconditionally, because it is connected with the security and effectiveness of its application. We follow the technology in the practice of the team tactics. This technology enables the whole team to accept it up to the level where the team

feels identified with it. The team building is the basic element for ideal mental adjustment. It's the process upon, which the spirit and the motivation of the team are based. Another level is the individual psychological adjustment for pressing (level of aggression control, space perception, motor and sensory switch, etc.), which helps the player meet the different tasks in the pressing tactical context with efficiency. When pressing is applied, it is necessary to take into consideration the difficulty of the physical and mental condition of the players, which is based on the abilities to engage in the synchronization of movements that is focused on the manipulation of the opponent's space. The motivation and willingness to engage and identify with the tactic model of pressing is directly connected to the team movement. **The way in which the coach implements this model into the tactical resources of the team and the way in which the team engages it is often the decisive factor for a successful team.**

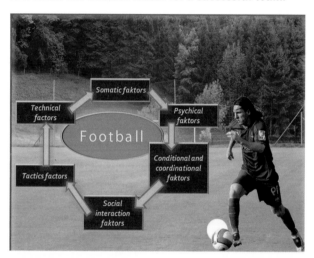

Fig. 3.4-1 Factors of sport performance for soccer

Based on the evaluation of the psychological aspects of pressing, there are two basic points. The first aspect is the **psychological problem of pressing as a tactical instrument.** Concerning the team dynamics, we evaluate not only the mental aspects of its applying but also the method, the way it can be used in the most effective way on the team, resulting in cooperation and not in tactics applied by individual players. The second aspect is **the psychology of individual player** who participates in team pressing and tries to make or emphasize an individual type of playing. Also, the player who tries to reach the complete mental balance that is necessary for the effective application of the pressing tactics. Individual psychological adaptation of this type of player (the level of aggression control, perception of space, sensorimotor switching, level of passion of the player and the team, etc.) helps in the implementation of the different roles into the pressing-tactical framework. On one hand, the self-confident character stimulates the level of passion of the player (gaining control of the ball is an imperative objective). On the other hand, there is a pressure on the player to reduce

the fear of failure because of the multiple repetition in the use of certain tactics, it may imply the loss of sensitivity and perceptiveness (the fear of not to gain the ball disappears and the self-confidence increases). That causes an increment in the active mental space in which the player can perform safely without any anxiety.

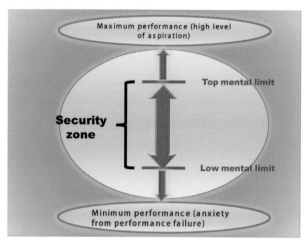

Fig. 3.4-2 Mental limits determining playing adjustment of the player (Erikson, et al. 2001)

The increment of fear to fail in the execution of pressing (ineffective use of pressing or low mental limit) causes a reduction of the zone security, which is often combined with a decrement of the player endeavor (an excellent performance of the opponent player makes it difficult to be attacked by the other players). This results in the so-called **"performance cage,"** which limits the performance during the match. In a situation like this, it is necessary to start by reducing the low level of mental limits (fear to fail) through psychological intervention. It expands the mental disruption in the security zone and eliminates the effect of the performance cage. The ideal training instrument for the mental balance in the above-mentioned situation, which can demand an intensive use of pressing, is the application of the exercise models described in Chapter 4.3 in detail. These exercises introduce authentic situations of a match in a "live" psychological training resulting in the elimination of those negative residues, which limit the performance of the players caused by unsuitable psychological corrections when the proactive defensive tactics are used. The training and practice of pressing then becomes a psychological tool to eliminate the performance blockage with the objective of correcting the use of pressing tactics in the training process.

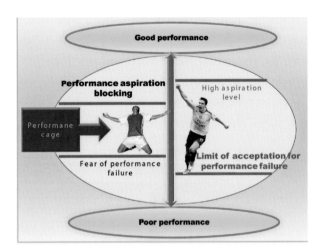

Fig. 3.4-3 Performance cage (Erikson, et al. 2001)

The application of pressing is very difficult and exhausting, not only from the physical point of view but also from the mental point of view. From the point of view of the conditions, the application of pressing tactics is among the most difficult tactical concepts in modern soccer. Excluding the physical requirements, it is necessary to take into consideration the psychological demands and requirements. It is based on the ability of the players to engage in the team maneuvers, which are aimed at gaining control of the opponent's space. The team movement goes hand by hand with team motivation and willingness to engage and identify itself with the model of pressing tactics. The way in which the coach implements this model into the tactical repertory of the team and the way in which the team engages to it is often a determining factor for a successful performance. Very frequently, the question about the right psychological tactics is how the coaches can "sell" their pressing concept to their respective teams and persuade the players that their pressing tactics are advantageous for the team. Apart from the use of suitable persuasive techniques, there are also some occasional psychological tricks that are focused on the stimulation of the player's prestige, self-confidence, and performance motivation.

Concerning the implementation of pressing into the team performance, we recommend making and modeling a challenging situation for the players, which enable them to self-evaluate the issues related to their performance, in other words, enable the movement to a higher level of performance quality. In relation to this, Lucchesi (2003) expected a positive effect when the coach intentionally hurled the doubt concerning the

ability of his players to manage pressing tactics because he believed in himself. A challenging situation arose when the first problems emerged during the process of building a pressing concept for the team; on one hand, this process irritated the self-confidence of the players, and on the other hand, it boosted the role of the coach. The initiation of this proactive defensive concept is one of the important and useful possibilities in the psychological approach of the team.

Based on our experience, we can state that pressing belongs to the group of tactical tools. The use of these tools demands that the players leave the "comfort zone" and move to the "uncomfortable zone," not only because of the physical exertion required but also because of the mental exertion required when utilizing pressing tactics.

Fig. 3.4-4 In applying pressing, the players always run as if they "run uphill" in the "uncomfortable zone."

Because it is a case of team tactics, one of the most relevant aspects of pressing is **team spirit and team synergy,** which outline the psychomotor effect at both the team level and the level of an individual player. The understanding of strategy and tactics assumes the conscious and emotional engagement of the players, who have clear targets that are part of the team objectives. Regarding the application of pressing, and any type of proactive defensive tactics, we can think of the principal objectives of the thoughtful reasoning and performance of the whole team in the sense of a tactical concept.

According to Erikson et al (2001), the assemblage of a soccer team includes the following thematic fields to enable its profiling in order to use the pressing tactics:

1. Vision of the team

2. Clear targets that are emotionally accepted

3. Understanding the strategy and the playing tactics

4. Great inner discipline,

5. Complementary characteristics of the players and their correct/good mix

6. Correct assignment of roles between the players

7. Common benefit preference for personal interests

8. Responsibility of an individual for the whole team.

Through Erikson's eight outlined order of the rules on how to build a good team, we will try to present a detailed examination of pressing and the psychological process of the soccer itself. **In all pressing tactics that are applied by a group or team tactics, the correct assignment of the roles and tasks is relevant.**

Soccer experts and practitioners have been dealing with the optimization of the task allocation and skills since a ball started to roll around the pitch. The basic alignment, which enables the players to use their positions and corresponding playing space, solves this problematic at a structural level. This system is responsible for territorial relations together with the appropriate allocation. The conditions for the teamwork regulations necessary for the typical sequences are based on this system. Not less important part of these, maybe, most difficult issues of strategy and playing tactics (the task allocation, position assignments and competences, privileges and responsibilities of individual players in the space, and the mental relations between the individuals in the team) is to find the solution to potential conflicts arising in the context of space-time. Görgényi (1998,2015) deals with the issue of territory and conflicts within areas as well as the space dynamics of the teams. In this sense, Görgényi specializes in the analysis of the teams and tries to outline the impact of mental processes emerging and taking place also in this environment. These are often considered as the sources of group or team dynamics, which markedly limit performance. In the theory, he elaborated "hunting theory"(regarding the occupation the playing area); Görgényi points to the performance of the soccer team, which depends on the ability of the players to avoid territorial conflicts or the ability to control and correct the process and the effect on the team's performance. The greatest attribute of the effective management of a

soccer team is teamwork, coordinated cooperation, regulated teamwork of the players coming from point zero, which represent the correct assignment of roles and tasks competence and the autonomy of the players. Another subject closely connected to the effectiveness of a soccer team is team dynamics. The team formation has the following stages: team formation, internal fights, stabilization, dynamical balance, disintegration, and breakup. Each of these stages defines the atmosphere and typical team mechanism, which obviously influences team dynamics. The important diagnostic moment for the coach is to distinguish which stage the team is in because this fact limits the effectiveness and successfulness of the tactical concepts and training instruments used. There are some stages where certain tactical solutions are advantageous and vice versa. Similarly, some training programs help to increase scoring success and team cohesion but some of them are less convenient in relation to particular situations of team development. Regarding the necessity to apply pressing tactics, Görgényi (2015) considers "the stage of internal fights" as the optimal stage. In this stage, the players have the tendency to break the arrangement of the tactical rules in order to enforce and confirm their own position in the team. It often involves physical and mental perception. It is also obvious that the impatience during the play the quick increment of interpersonal conflicts and rivalry within the team. This results in the restriction of the ability to cooperate on a higher level, which is based on the mutual interpretation of movements (gestures, nonverbal communication, etc.) and the mutual empathetic perception of the player's cooperation. In this case, the priority of the players is not oriented toward confrontation with the opponent, but to the rivalry within the team hierarchy. Here, according to Görgényi (2015), the tactics match the dynamics of the team. Through the application of pressing tactics or the zonal defense, the players are forced to take individual roles that are directly connected to teamwork and cooperation with the players accepting personal responsibility for the fulfilment of the tasks and, in case of failure, the whole team gets the worst of it. This is how pressing contributes or forces the players to participate in team cooperation, recognizing the targets of the team, keeping tactical discipline, and maintaining full concentration on activity during the whole match. The transfer from the pitch helps to involve these aspects to the off-pitch area, it allows a quick cessation of "internal fighting," and it enables movement to a higher development level (stabilization and dynamic balance). It is a demonstration of the way specific tactics can help by switching the single stages of team dynamics. Apart from these mental aspects of the "Hunting theory" concept, Görgényi also points to territorial aspects and the playing consistency of the space interconnected with pressing tactics that were presented in detail in Chapter 3.1.

Significant psychological factors include the technology of forming mental adjustments and the emotional tuning of the players and the team toward pressing through emotional intelligence.

Erikson et. al. believes: "If the players don't learn to handle the mental energy and strain, they won't be able to effectively use their own performance conditions." Persuasive models should prevail over violent impositions, because they are much more effective and enable more intensive engagement of the team. This is necessary for an adequate mastering of pressing. When the players are conformed correctly, their mental energy should be used for performance acceleration, increment of the enthusiasm and accomplishment of the objectives (improvement of the performance, need for success and victory), the elimination of performance blockage and performance anxiety (fear of failure, loss of team acceptation, error rate of the playing activity). Concerning the relationship between ambitions and performance failure, Erikson et al. (2001) identifies the so-called B-type as a great ambition for performance without the fear of failure in the match. This type of personality uses its own sources. It excels only when it is necessary, it stimulates the ambitions of the soccer player and reduces the fear of performance failure at the same time.

An important requirement for the application of pressing is **to establish a specific team communication model,** which is closely connected to typical pressing situations. It enables all the players to understand these situations; it helps to verbally use the correct tactical reactions, which results in the improvement of cooperation and the increment of the synergy of the players. This communication model makes tactical work a consolidated interpretation and appreciation of the situation for pressing.

It also increases the tactical abilities of individual players who are integrated into the pressing team. Another part of the communication model is also the ability to understand the body language of teammates as well as opponents'. The correct interpretation of body language and their team-mate's movements enables them to read the play faster and more efficiently resulting in a clear understanding of the game plot.

Another pillar of the pressing tapestry of the player and the team is the aggressiveness factor and the intentional handling of this aggressiveness in the both stages of pressing: the warm-up stage and the active stage. The decisive criterion for the application of this aggressiveness is the use and fulfilment of the different roles, in other words, the tactical intentions. In addition to its "battling" use, the misuse of aggressiveness occurs when it is oriented toward internal defense more than to the performance itself. Erikson et al. (2001) considers aggressiveness "fluffy" when the change from a pliable reaction to a fighting one is often the decisive turnover in the psychological work with the team. This aspect is obviously related to the defensive proactivity principle, which is characterized by the structuring of the aggressiveness boundaries. Its expression is game assertiveness, which enforces its own intention in the playing context. A new specific form of control has been put into practice in situations where the team doesn't have control over the ball, and they are trying to regain the ball by using active forms of defense. This type of defensive behavior requires to have the so-called pressing genotype available to the players that, to a considerable extent, have a natural talent to manage the pressing roles. The **pressing genotype** represents the inherent preconditions for a proactive defense and its application into the whole performance in the basic stages of the game as well as in the intermediate stages when switching from defensive to offensive and vice versa. It includes complex movement and mental abilities in order to effectively use pressing tactics in the game context in the repetitive time interval during a match or in many subsequent matches. **The basic preconditions for the pressing genotype include these factors:**

(a) Good natural condition: The ability to achieve high levels of ANP and VO2max during the training process, which ensures the physical readiness to be applied in the pressing activities as long as possible in a length of time and at the highest speed during a match. Deficiencies in this area are the main limiting factors for the repetitive application of pressing, because these deficiencies don't let the players use the necessary movement activity in the required regime, primarily from the point of view of the intensity during the whole match (repeated use of pressing situations, sufficient shifting in the relevant space for pressing as a reaction to changes of midfield area, rearranging the players individually, or changing the pressing situation, etc.).

(b) Aggression control: The ability to regulate the use of aggression up to the point where it doesn't impose a penalty so the work of all the players involved in the pressing activity is not wasted. Pressing is not about fouling. It's about how to maximize the actions intended to regain the ball through the formation of space-time limits to create the disruption of the opponents with the ball (sufficient closeness to gain the ball) and the effective alignment of the players involved in pressing activity. This reduces the possibilities of the player with the ball to a minimum and obstructs implementation of the activities of the opponents with the ball. The types of choleric aggressions where its regulation is subject to internal impulse of the situation and not subject to situation impulse based on the context that enables to play effectively are risky.

The response of the player to stimulus from the external environment is the result of the rational control of natural emotions. Unacceptable aggression is proof of poor selection, insufficient self-control (insufficient intellectual control of the fundamental, emotional response of the player to some stimulus). Any foul blow spoils the whole prepressing situation and movement performance of the whole team and the effort related to the handling of the space is wasted.

(c) Affinity to fight: The game against the resistance (willingness to attack through 1:1) or the active formation of the resistance (willingness to defense through 1:1). Within this typology, we can distinguish the players with inherent defensive proactivity. These players are ideal for defensive pressing forms, it's much worse with defensive reactive types. They need to be taught how to change their defensive reactive behavior to a proactive one.

(d) Immediate game activity after fights: Directed to passes solution of new situations in the attacking sequences, formation, and involvement of new combination elements of postpressing sequence. The repeated failure of the team involved in the defensive activity within the defense context.

(e) Game reading: Understanding the development of playing sequences.

(f) Two-stage for the players: Not only for defense. There isn't an appropriate further application for the one-stage players in the pressing era (except for the players who score). When applying pressing tactics, a remarkable increment of the load on the players, primarily the offensive ones, should also be anticipated. Apart from natural involvement in offensive action after losing the ball, the players need to participate in the proactive defense of the team. They are an equal part of the defensive group, which actively participates in the offensive activity. This is the reason why it is necessary to apply the so-called two-stage player technique where the formation of the team that applies the defensive pressing strategy is preferred. Contradictorily, pressing increases the load of the offensive players considerably, whoever becomes intensively involved in team defense. All players involved in pressing tactics are significantly more loaded mentally, motorically, and positionally.

(g) Space intelligence: Perception of space, the ability to perceive and understand the space in relation to the field.

(h) Switching between playing stages: The immediate execution in intermediate stages of switching from the offensive to the defensive (application of pressing) and vice versa (game management after successful pressing and gaining the ball).

(i) Motivation of the team to defend, mutual cooperation: It is based on the willingness to accept the position in the defensive sequence and to help with the defensive activity to gain the ball, in other words, the planning and preparation of the situations to regain the ball. The principle of cooperation applies also to the egocentrics who believe that they are not suitable for the team, because they aren't able to cooperate, don't want to accept the rules and are less disciplined. In particular, they are not willing to sacrifice themselves for others. Mojzis (2013), presented the results of a very interesting survey. This survey showed, that in certain circumstances, egocentrism (e.g., Ronaldo) that can be the most effective element of team cooperation. The egocentric player who is conscious of the necessities of the team concerning strategies and tactics will be able to cooperate with the teammates and, for this reason, the player will intentionally keep the consistency of the team.

(j) Special typology of the players for pressing is presented by the so-called pressing and postpressing players. For example, Modric and Sneider are typical postpressing players. Their main characteristic is effective performance after successful pressing (game into depth, creative pass in offensive subnumbering, and the ability to retain the possession of the ball even under the direct defensive pressure of the opponent. After a successful pressing, they decisively help to build the counteractions). After successful pressing, the first pass should be directed to these postpressing players. The main characteristic of pressing players (e.g., Vidal, Matuidi, Busquets, Wanyama) is proactive defense, planning, preparation, and the execution of pressing tactics, a sense for the positional formation of the group of players executing pressing, the alignment and the ability to induce the space relations necessary for pressing (shortening, narrowing of the area, selection of the appropriate space for pressing and overnumbering around the midfield area, which is typical for postpressing defensive performance).

The mental peculiarity in pressing is represented by the team factor. It is based on the willingness of the player applying the pressing tactics to share with the team to perform in way that spontaneous excitement won't be directed toward personal benefit but offered to the team, in other words, directed toward coplayers who participate in the defense. Here is the explanation: In the pressing tactics, the player must be willing to work within the team without extending to the point of immediate personal benefits in the game. The player must be satisfied with the team benefits, which are the personal benefits at the same time. It is very difficult to achieve this level without effective team-building and engagement in the team-spirit. In practice it looks like, although the player has done the hard work, the coplayers benefit from it despite the fact that this player is willing to offer it repeatedly within the pressing tactics. The effort that the team can make within pressing can often be transferred to the opponent's players who are outside the direct pressure. However, thanks to this, their performance is of low quality, and it can often result in unforced mistakes and premature tactical solutions. We are talking about the prolonged psychological effect and impact of pressing actions.

In connection to pressing psychology, it is necessary to notice the ontogenetic aspect of development for the players. In relation to the application of pressing tactics, this aspect requires gradual accumulation of tactical skills by young players. This means, to hide the deficiencies, during the careful application of the pressing technical and tactical, of the players aged between fifteen and seventeen (age of their development). Hiding these deficiencies can result in a slowdown in the individual development of players who are too young. The team performance of the pressing tactics can hide the individual imperfections of the players. It can distort the diagnosis of those players who, thanks to the pressing team synergy, seem to be more valuable than they really are. It can have a counterproductive effect, primarily in the above-mentioned sensitive period of ontogenesis of young players. This is the reason why it's necessary to follow the psychological sequence and respect the ontogenesis of the development of soccer players in the junior age.

3.5 BLOCK DEFENSE AND PRESSING TACTICS

The results of the latest analyses of defense forms show that the continuous development of the defensive tactics is heading toward the application of combined defensive forms. In order not to disrupt the integrity of the performance within a defensive stage, there has been a fusion of space compatibility and stress complementary defensive tactics. **The current situation of defensive tactics shows that the combination of block defense and pressing is an effective and reliable fusion.**

The block defense represents an active form of defense. The transition to a proactive position during pressing shows that the block formation in defense can serve as the basis for a preparatory stage for the application of pressing. Blocking is concerned with covering and enlarging the area to minimize the space options for the team who has the control of the ball. The block defense also represents a form of area occupation through which the opponent's offense must pass. But, using an effective alignment, which closes the corridors and minimizes the empty space, the opponent is blocked from passing or following to the ball.

Continuous transition to and from blocking is connected to the change from defensive reactivity to defensive proactivity, i.e., the proactive defense. Switching between block defense and pressing has its advantages; all the space attributes of block defense are ideal for the preparation of pressing (foreshortening and size reduction of the area, the compression of the active area and the complete preparation for the initiation of pressing). The consistency of movement between both forms of defense is evident; this enables mutual influence between, and change from, one form to another (Despite being two different tactical defensive tools). This consistency lies mainly in the ability to control the game without having the ball, i.e., checking and actively influencing the opponent's attacks.

There are three types of defensive blocks. They are primarily defined by the placement of a defensive line on the pitch and by the formation of an effective depth for the zone blocking scheme. These determinant spaces are the basic conditions for the application of the block defense. They are associated with other rules that enable an active compression of the area, the situational blocking of the corridors in depth to influence the opponent's attacking sequence, the placement of players in the center of the pitch and a flexible positional transition according to the ball's position. The team's positional defensive maneuvers look like a "short" alignment, which combines a significant reduction in the opponent's maneuvering abilities toward the goal with the constrained use of the width dimension of the pitch. The decisive result of the block defense is to play on a "small" determined pitch with respect to the ineffectiveness of the opposing team's

offensive; this requires considerably greater proficiency to achieve.

In block defense, the defensive formation moves along the width of the pitch or forward and backward depending on how the opponent drives the ball and how the player moves within the midfield. At this point, the defense waits for the opponent to make a mistake.

The position of the defensive line is the decisive factor for the application of the defensive block. In relation to the offside rule, the position of the defense line is just in front of the center line (1.5 m) on the team's own half. In this way, the defensive line is placed at the beginning of a highly positioned block, which is often connected to the application of offensive pressing on the opponent's half of the pitch.

The large potential space behind the defensive line is a big disadvantage of this **high defensive block position.** This space is almost entirely on the opponent's half of the pitch, and it can be efficiently used by the opponent through a successful penetration of the defensive block, accomplished either by long passes through the block zone or by the unsuccessful linking of the block with offensive pressing. For these reasons, the application of a forward block must be conditioned by a team tactical synergy. This requires synchronized movement of the players, quick defensive reading, an appropriate positional strategy, and a spatial formation of the defending team (figs. 3.5-1 and -2). One of the disadvantages of the high block is the restriction toward the back area. The effort of the goalkeeper or defenders in order to keep the ball can be extremely risky. It's also a significant initial opportunity for the attacking team to apply pressing.

The conditions for applying a **medium defensive block** are the position of the defensive line on the boundary of the middle line and the defensive zone; for this reason, it is very important to maintain the depth. It requires the participation of midfield defenders and a flexible movement of the defensive line toward the opposing goal or toward to their own goal (opening and closing the block). The crucial condition for maintaining the compactness of the medium block is the cooperation of the defense to coordinate the middle defensive line. In relation to the defensive safety position, the medium block can be considered the most unstable form of block defense. Apart from the offensive possibilities behind the defensive line, this type of defense offers auxiliary alternatives to the attacking team for the purpose of retaining the ball in the defensive zone as an escape from the pressure of the midfield block (figs. 3.5-3 and -4).

The basis for setting the depth of **the defensive block** is the extreme movement of the defensive line immediately in front of the team's own penalty area (3–5 m). This type of defense is often connected to defensive pressing. Its successful execution provides an expansive area for the application of fast counteractions into the open area on the opponent's half of the pitch. The disadvantage of the high block is that once it has been broken through, the team's own goal is in immediate danger (figs. 3.5-3 and -6).

The extreme form of the low block is represented by a form called **"parking the bus."** In this form, the defensive line moves either to the boundary line of the penalty area or sometimes inside the penalty area. This type of low block is formed by alignment in front of the penalty area of the defending team, and it is difficult to break through. It enables the disruption of the combined action by the attacking players. Its greatest disadvantage is a complicated transition to an effective offense.

Each of these forms has their advantages and disadvantages. Both pressing and defensive block are defensive team-tactics that implement an inflexible designation of the targeted area. A common characteristic of all forms of block defense is defensive depth (30–35 m), which significantly limits their effectiveness and success. A small active area is easier to defend and therefore the defense can be covered more effectively. Beside the spatial requirements, great emphasis is put on the formation, the shape and the structure of the block, which provides the basis for the retention of its compactness. The ability of the team to keep

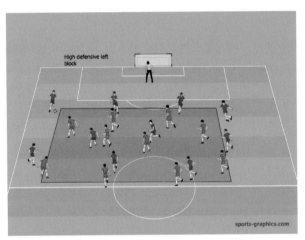

Fig. 3.5-1 High defensive left block

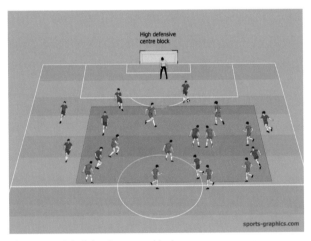

Fig. 3.5-2 High defensive center block

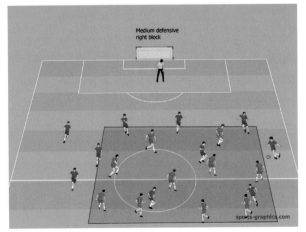

Fig. 3.5-3 Medium defensive right block

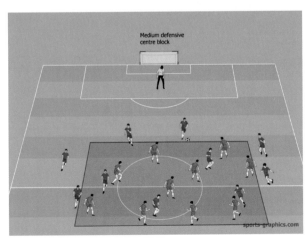

Fig. 3.5-4 Medium defensive center block

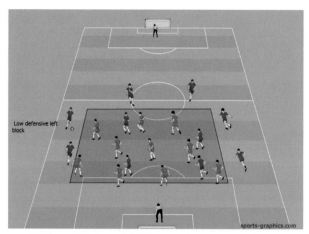

Fig. 3.5-5 Low defensive left block

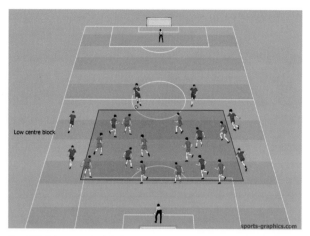

Fig. 3.5-6 Low center block

the defensive block compact, determines the ability of the opponent to break the defensive block. The disruption of the defensive block formation would help the opponent to perform a pass or execute an individual penetration.

The fundamental difference between the defensive block and pressing is that the defensive deals mainly with the alignment during the opponent's offensive sequence resulting in an effective reaction to the offensive players. On the other hand, pressing deals with the proactive performance of the defending team toward the player with the ball. The defending team brings the player under immediate time-space pressure forcing him into actions that result in defensive proactivity. In other words, when the block defense is used, the defending team tries to block the space of the opponent as a reaction to the opponent's offensive movement. When pressing is used, the defending team tries to impose alternatives on the opponent using a proactive attitude that forces the players to make mistakes thus worsening of their performance, i.e., the loss of the ball. The defensive block represents a reactive model of defense while pressing represents a proactive defense. When the defensive block is used, the defenders attempt to gain the ball through the, often unforced, faults of the opponent using an effective manipulation of the active area. There is an active pressure on the opponent during the application of pressing tactics that causes a faulty performance resulting in the recapturing of the ball.

From an organizational point of view, the defensive block is the result of a correct positional alignment of the players and a high level of defensive consistency, which is currently a necessary tactic for any team after losing the ball.

With respect to the organization of the basic formations of a team, an extraordinary difference between the block defense

and pressing is that the pressing alignment is formed mostly as a result of the movement of the players involved in it toward the opponent's goal while the block defense alignment is formed by the movement toward the team's own goal(i.e., away from the pitch center) and also toward the opponent's goal (i.e., toward the pitch center). This happens in the case when the opponent uses a wide pass or a back pass.

In the context of the game, it is possible to create a block defense not only by the movement toward the team's own goal but also toward the opponent's goal depending on the situation and the performance of the opponent.

Pressing conclusion of the block defense forms has its logic, which is based on a spatial and positional preparatory of the players' alignment. This alignment is formed by the principles of the space occupation. However, the difference is that the pressing alignment is clearly focused on the center of the game while the block alignment is oriented according to the center of the game's position. This is determined by the alignment s basic reactive (block) or proactive (pressing) focus. The block defense formations can be easily shifted to pressing alignment. This is possible to achieve by specific movements in the center of the pitch. In similar way, it's possible to form a defense with a block defense and shift the team near their own goal a by positional shift of the players in the game center. Positional shifts enable changing from pressing to block defense or vice versa (according to fig. 3.5-7, 8, 9, 10). If the opponent with the ball is in the zone of the defensive block, it is possible to immediately launch pressing (i.e., move backward to back positions), depending on the tactical intention or playing strategy of the team.

We can see a transition from pressing to block and from block to pressing during the application of pressing.

After switching from pressing to block, it is necessary to respect the rules of the shifting zone, under which the block formation moves at least one zone lower in order to maintain the principles of the defensive reaction after an unsuccessful pressing action. As a part of a special defensive tactics, we can intentionally use pressing elements in order to slow down the progress of the opponent's offense (i.e., its development) to gain time in the formation of a lower zone positional defense block.

This means that after an unsuccessful offensive pressing action, there is the possibility to form a middle or low block because the high block can't ensure an effective defensive reaction where the defensive pressing failed.

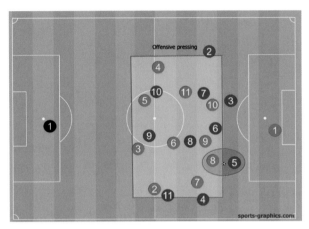

Fig. 3.5-7 Offensive pressing

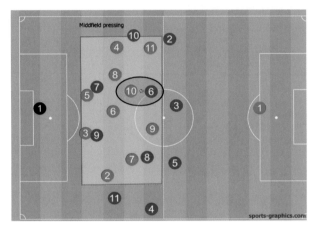

Fig. 3.5-8 Midfield pressing

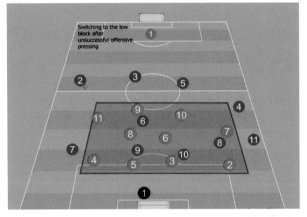

Fig. 3.5-9 Switching to the low block after unsuccessful offensive pressing

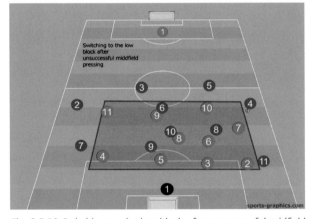

Fig. 3.5-10 Switching to the low block after unsuccessful midfield pressing

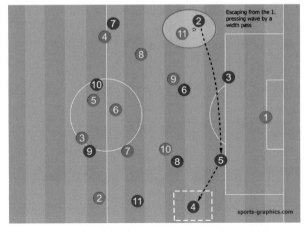

Fig. 3.5-11 Escaping from the one pressing wave by a width pass

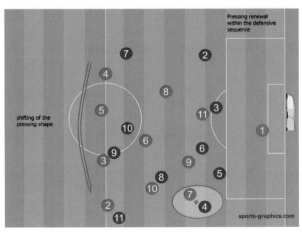

Fig. 3.5-12 Pressing renewal within the defensive sequence

Apart from this fact, the renewal of a second wave of pressing is possible as long as the depth of the midfield is kept under control. However, the repeated failure of this type of defense can bring excessive risks because of the outnumbering in the area behind the pressing line (figs. 3.5-11 and -12).

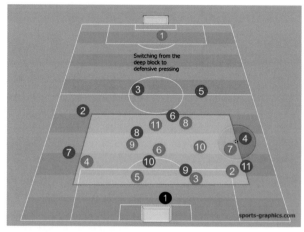

Fig. 3.5-13 Switching from the deep block to defensive pressing

When we talk about a transition from block to pressing, it is possible to perform this transition in the same zone in order to apply pressing in a synchronized manner and to arrange the block formation into a pressing alignment. The violation of the time limit when the alignment is changed from a defensive reactive formation to a defensive proactivity can result in an ineffective defense proactivity, which is essential for successful application of pressing tactics (figs. 3.5-13, -14, and -15).

The solutions proposed here concerning defensive tactics are present in connection to the application of the block defense and pressing in different areas and to the application of various defensive scenarios in modern soccer. The next chapter (3.6) will offer the progressive pressing concept of the pendulum and pump, which is built upon an asymmetric defensive position that requires a different understanding of the space relations during the application of defensive proactivity.

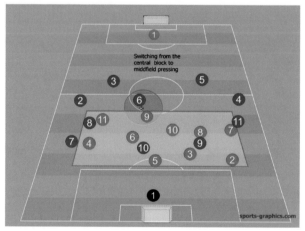

Fig. 3.5-14 Switching from the central block to midfield pressing

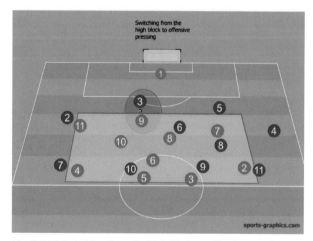

Fig. 3.5-15 Switching from the high block to offensive pressing

3.6 "PENDULUM AND PUMP" PRESSING, OR HOW PRESSING SHOULD BE PLAYED IN THE NEAR FUTURE

As the global tactics in soccer develop, there is an internal process within the application of tactical-play tools that goes hand in hand with changes in play-systems. To be more exact, there are evolutionary changes, within particular tactical-play tools, that are parallel to changes in tactical-play schemes within certain play systems. Of course, the same applies to pressing tactics that are in use. Throughout the history of pressing,

different forms of pressing had a more natural character. Currently, the various applied forms of pressing tactics are more sophisticated and are often combined with compatible forms of defense, such as the block defense. The block defense is constructed from the point of view of the spatial alignment of players and applied maneuvers that are more compatible with pressing tactics.

We shouldn't forget that when revising special defensive-tactical concepts, the coach's creativity, and individual access, which enables reflection on the traditional concept of pressing, as enriched by individual experience and philosophy may become apparent.

Our pressing concept, the "pendulum and pump" model, is our vision for a proactive defense. We have already applied this concept at the club-based and team-based level (Sparta Praha, FC Tatabanya, Ozeta—Dukla Trencfn, U-19 Czech national team). Its addition to the portfolio of many teams' defensive tactics is the question for the near future.

The conceptual plan for pressing focuses on **two primary areas of game principles:**

1. The team's own play-security

2. The effective threat of the opponent

In relation to the many variables that can occur during pressing situations, their appearance is hardly predictable. Playing intelligence enables game awareness and its correct interpretation; this is the decisive factor for optimizing play risk with respect to play-security and game effectiveness.

Active team pressing in the target zone requires the participation of the whole team, the correct defensive alignment of the pressing team and the concentration of the team in the predetermined strategic space. This requirement can be applied across the entire pitch; however, when the opponent is in control of the ball, especially in the area up to 30 m from the opponent's goal, application is justifiable only when required by developments occurring during the match.

Another form, within the typology of defensive proactive tactics, is **immediate ultraoffensive pressing.** This tactic is applied immediately after the team loses possession of the ball anywhere on the pitch (it is best applied on the opponent's half of the pitch after an unsuccessful offensive sequence). Its advantage is that the opponent who gains the ball can orient himself toward defensive action to change the alignment of the offensive formation. Other spatial benefits stemming from successful repossession of the ball can be reached. The transitional phases from offense to defense, and vice versa, are decisive for the application of pressing.

Apart from these two forms, provocative pressing (PP) can also be utilized. Proactive pressing is applicable during the game phase when the opponent has possession of the ball and the defensive team's formation is not well organized. Ideally, it is applied within 30 m of the opponent's goal. Provocative pressing has a strong situational character; spatial limitations in its application do not exist. The basic objective of this tactic is not to regain the ball, but to provoke and discomfort the opponent who has possession of the ball. When applying PP, it is clear that ball possession will not be regained, but the time needed to reorganize the defending team will be gained.

By intentionally controlling the pace of defensive activity, the opponent's activity can be reduced. This allows the realignment of the defending team in order to reach a positional optimum for the particular situation, this is termed "the correct alignment." A couple of examples of correct alignment when performing pressing tactics: fig. 3.6-1a, b, c, d, and e.

Team pressing in the target zone is the result of the defensive cooperation of the whole team with a clearly identifiable choreography of movement: i.e., the coach in the predetermined area. When using team pressing, it is necessary to define the area where pressing will be applied and to adjust the positional alignment of the defensive players to this area. When performing the pressing tactic, the team's alignment must correspond to the actual situation. This consists of the opposing team's alignment, the formation of one's own team, the position of the game center and the configuration of active play-area. The pressing formation blurs the boundaries of any basic alignment. Shifting the players to an effective formation must be coordinated in space and must be situationally appropriate.

Pressing (Upper, Lower) Pendulums and Pump

Pressing is most advantageous when applied on the opponent's half of the pitch, far away from one's own goal. After regaining the ball in this area, through successful pressing tactics, the resulting play-action can be the most effective threat to the opponent. The closer the

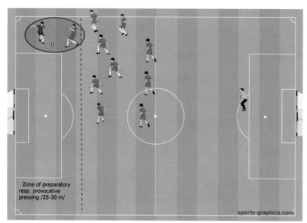

Fig. 3.6-1a Models for correct alignment when performing pressing tactics

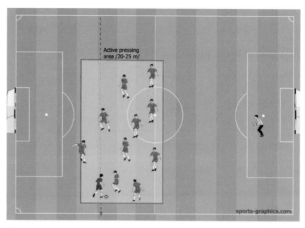

Fig. 3.6-1b Models for correct alignment when performing pressing tactics

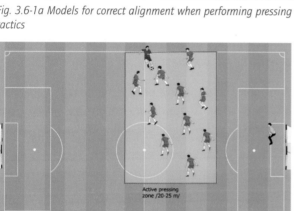

Fig. 3.6-1c Models for correct alignment when performing pressing tactics

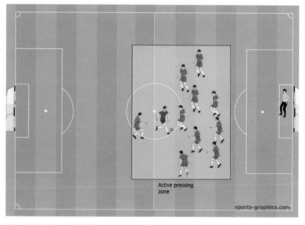

Fig. 3.6-1d Models for correct alignment when performing pressing tactics

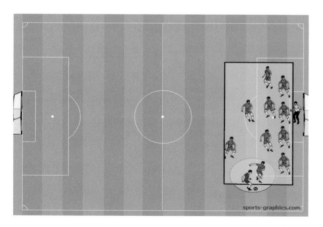

Fig. 3.6-1e Models for correct alignment when performing pressing tactics

ball is to the opponent's goal when repossession occurs, the greater the effective threat is. In modern soccer, the opponent's half of the pitch is the ideal playing area for repossessing the ball and transitioning to the attack. The ideal playing area for the application of team pressing is on the boundary between the offensive and central zones. The disadvantage of regaining the ball on one's own half of the pitch, after applied pressing (defensive midfield/ center field pressing), is that the opponent can react to

this situation by applying its own immediate ultraoffensive pressing. The only benefits to one's own team in this situation are ball repossession and the possibility of offensive action. **This means that the successful use of pressing on one's own half of the pitch is less advantageous.** To avoid the consequences of utilizing classic zone pressing on the team's own half, the area where team pressing on the opponent's half of the pitch should be applied was delimited. For the purpose of using this type

Fig. 3.6-2 Correct alinment for the application of pendulum and pump pressing

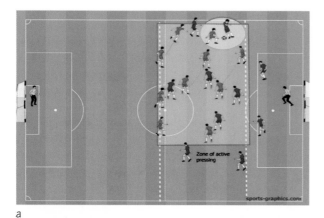

a

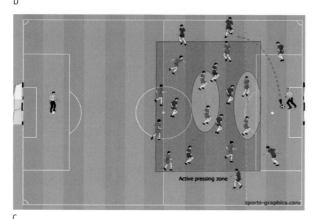

b

c

Fig. 3.6-3a,b,c Dynamic changes in pressing alignment, "pendulum and pump," at the escape way from pressing to the opposing vertical

of pressing tactic, we have defined two basic group maneuvers. They are necessary for the initiation and maintenance of the team's pressing tactics on the opponent's half of the pitch. **The depth of the active pressing zone (APZ)** is an essential factor for the achievement of effective team pressing. Its optimal size ranges from 20 to 25 m. This is related mainly to the fact that a large playing area can't be effectively and, most importantly, proactively covered. Because of this, we have introduced two basic pressing maneuvers that enable the team to resolve the depth dimension of the active pressing zone efficiently: at the level of the attacking line (pressing line) as well as at the level of the defensive line (the alignment depth of the defense formation—pump).

When forming **the active pressing zone (APZ),** the decisive factor in defining the depth dimension of the active operational area for the pressing team is coordinated and situationally conditioned cooperation. For the purpose of managing the active pressing zone (APZ), we use the "upper pendulum" pressing maneuver; this enables the boundary of the attack line to be set and defensive movement through the application of auxiliary back passes toward the goalkeeper; i.e., back-passes toward other players in the defensive formation across the width of the pitch. This covered part of the pitch is also the area where the defensive midfielder moves around. The pendulum pressing maneuver is performed by the attacker who is joined either by a player from the offensive formation or one of the midfielders who corresponds to that area (fig. 3.6-4).

When using the pendulum, the upper-positioned player closes the back pass corridor and lower-positioned player

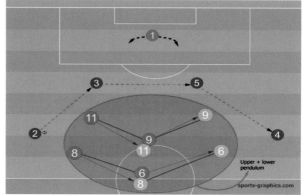

Fig. 3.6-4 Mechanism of upper and lower pendulum

covers the center of the pitch from the width-pass. These areas will be used by the attacker, harried by pressing, as he tries to escape from the pressing situation. The fundamental role of the upper pressing pendulum is to counter the auxiliary back pass by the player with the ball toward the goalkeeper: i.e., to escape from the immediate pressure of the player who is performing the pressing through a width pass toward a team player who is in the formation or to force him to attempt a long forward pass to the area that is covered by other players of the pressing alignment.

The fundamental role of the pendulum maneuver is to force the opponent with the ball to attempt an escape type play-action by blocking the escape alternatives (back pass toward the goalkeeper, width pass toward a team player in the formation through the vertical). This in turn enables the team to withdraw from the pressing situation; in the case of a successful escape from the pressing situation the team can attempt to renew the pressing alignment using minimization; i.e., the effective movement of the players into a pressing alignment. Correct motor and sensory perception, appropriate tactical-play habits, a reasonable level of spatial awareness, and extraordinary physical conditioning are necessary for the optimization of these pressing activities.

Physical conditioning concerns the ability to work repeatedly at the ANP level during the course of the match. At the high-point during pressing, it is necessary to work above the ANP level. When interval work does not exceed the ANP level for 15 s, there is no threat of decreasing motor and sensory perception. Due to this fact, it is important to keep the physical load below the APN level with a break at the correct ratio of 1:6. The intermittent nature of game-play does not often provide the necessary rest interval needed for physical regeneration over the course of the game. The players require an extraordinary level of preparedness when applying this method of defense. Dragun (2015a) believes it is impossible to leave the conditioning coaches out of the game. They are responsible for the functional readiness of the players. Pressing and its successful execution definitely requires some kind of developmental increase in motive abilities, mostly through persistent practice. For Dragun, a decisive factor is the optimal development of aerobic exercise capacity and aerobic exercise output, in addition to their integration into the training process, which can be accomplished using different methods and tools.

The optimal development of aerobic exercise capacity enables a more frequent use of intensive active pressing tactics. In order to develop an aerobic exercise capacity that maximizes oxygen consumption for as long as possible, high intensity exercises have to be applied, at just under the level of the anaerobic limit, to the training process during the preparatory stage. The anaerobic threshold is defined by a lactate level of 3 mmol lasting for several tens of minutes, representing 70 percent training time (Dragun 2015b).

Soccer teams whose training process is at the highest level keep their players occupied with "homework" during the off season. It is common for players to take 10 to 12 km runs at the above mentioned pace during the second half of the off season. These runs are assigned by the conditioning coaches with respect to a heart rate corresponding to a lactate level of 3 mmol (Dragun, 2015b). This type of high intensity exercise continues during the first weeks of preparatory exercises as well. This system is also called HVT (High Volume Training). According to the Italian conditioning specialist Arcelli (1993), this is the period of development of the peripheral aerobic components that enhance the functional abilities of the player to get oxygen to the muscles.

Other high intensity exercises are chosen in order to **enhance aerobic output.** These high intensity exercises, which last for several tens of minutes, effects the heart muscle. It's volume increases and causes left ventricular hypertrophy; heart contraction increases the volume of blood pumped into circulation (Dragun 2015b). When developing aerobic exercise capacity, the HIT (High Intensity Training) system is also used; this system increases maximum oxygen consumption (VO_2 max/kg/min). The relative oxygen uptake value for soccer teams adhering to the European standard is at the level of 65 ml/kg/min. However, this level may not be sufficient for the intensive and systematic application of pressing tactics. The most advanced "pressing" teams should have a relative oxygen uptake value over 70ml/kg/min.

Arcelli (1993) claims that to develop central aerobic components, hill running needs to be included in the training process. Through this activity pressure on the heart muscle increases, this results in an accelerated enhancement of heart beat frequency and larger incremental steps toward strength building in comparison to traditional distance runs. Furthermore, from the biomechanical point of view, the risk of rear upper thigh injury is lower. The "Fascetti effect," which improves the dynamic speed aspects of movement, is applied in connection to hill running and for the purpose of ensuring heightened abilities during pressing.

The globalization of pressing tactics and their application brings specific requirements in the area of the condition and preparation of soccer teams. The modern trends in the condition and preparation are not concerning only to the greatest working ability of the human organism under the most intensive regime but also to the ability to recover from the most intensive exercises performed in the fastest and most effective possible way. In connection to this, we can talk about a progressive principle called Cap-Rec (Capacity × recovery), which is being described more and more clearly in the modern approaches. It might be the only way to reach the totalization of the conditions (volume, intensity) of the human organs, which takes into account the physiological limitations the player. Without testing the individual load connected to the evaluation of the physiological impact on "high intensity" exercises, the effectiveness of the exercises regarding the condition of the players seems to be problematic.

The principle of the pressing pendulum lies in the fact that, in case a defensive player can escape from the high pressure applied by the players participating in the pressing maneuver, shifting along the shortest and most effective routes allows the player to get to a new center point in order to keep the pressing effect reducing the motoric performance and to distribute this effect equally on the both players in the pendulum (economy of the movement volume). Its aim is to maintain the maximum space efficiency in order to cover the new pass in the defensive corridors of the opponent with the ball. As shown in pic 3.6-4, the players change their roles in the pendulum scheme resulting in an effective coverage maintaining the pressing effect in the space. We shouldn't forget about the fact that when a player shifts the pendulum

around the pitch, the other players also shift in a pressing formation to setup the "correct position" (fig. 3.6-5). A specific situation arises when the ball is shifted from one vertical side to another in which the escape from a pressing situation can be performed by the stopper, in other words, the goalkeeper. There is a change in the pressing alignment, which is done by withdrawing the upper pendulum. The lower pendulum is kept active, and the preparation to restore the upper pendulum takes place at the stage when the ball is in the center of the offensive zone (OZ) (Midfield vertical).

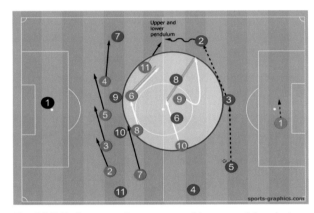

Fig. 3.6-5 Performance of an upper and lower pendulum in team configuration

The advantage of the pendulum maneuver is that it distributes a quota of the movement equally over all the players participating in the activity. It isn't restrained to any basic alignment. The upper pendulum maneuver is performed by two players (mainly the attackers) in the alignment 4-3-3, 4-4-2, and 3-5-2. In case players use the 4-2-3-1 or 4-1-4-1 formation, one of the players positioned in the upper midfield is also involved in this pressing maneuver. Another advantage of the pendulum is that it can be performed from any basic alignment. There are no limits for its effective use (fig. 3.6-6a-e).

The only limit is the two-membered conformation. The pendulum b pressing essentially includes the mechanism of wide shifting, the position changes as well as the role of the players. When shifting the defensive line, there are standard defense zone rules related to the defensive width coverage. Pressing pendulums can be considered as a decisive mechanism that offers defensive asymmetry of the alignment. In connection to this, we find it also important to point out the role of defensive midfielder or number "6" (six) who, in spite of making the game faster (fast shifting, speed of the passes, fast rotation of positions),

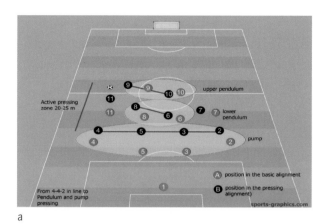

a

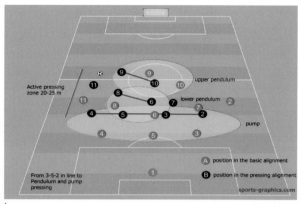

b

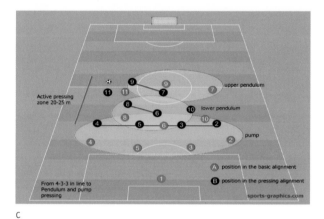

c

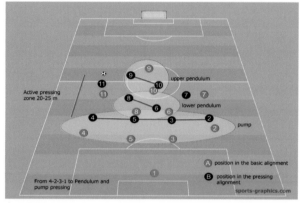

d

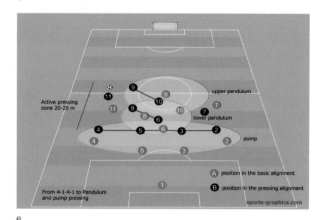

Fig. 3.6-6a,b,c,d,e Switching from different basic alignments to pendulum and pump pressing alignment (red= formation in the basic alignment, black= formation in the pressing alignment)

e

can no longer keep up with the shifting; that is precisely the reason for calling the center defender. Due to the security, calling the center defenders is an extremely risky movement (confrontation of center defenders in situation 1:1). Therefore, we recommend to double this position in the formation in order to make the asymmetric alignment (one is always higher) in relation the midfield area. We consider this solution to be safer and more effective from the defensive point of view, because the player in the upper position can help in the offensive play actively. The positive side of doubling the number "6" position is to cover the space before the center defenders with the so-called defense sandwich forms preventing the opponent to push into this area using deep penetration passes.

Due to the insufficient coverage of the active pressing zone, the principle of defensive security can't be effectively applied with only one pendulum. To ensure the coverage of the pressing area, there is another element of the proactive defensive formation that should be applied, the so-called lower pressing pendulum, which is parallel to the upper pressing pendulum. It is executed by the midfield players. The intention is to cover the most dangerous area in front of the center players and the area where the shield midfielders are. By a synchronized application of both pendulums, we can keep the distance from the opponent with the ball and the players who can execute an alternative escape from the pressing situation. Double parallel pressing pendulums contribute to increase the space-time pressure around the midfield area. It works as a space valve, which closes the getaway corridors and prevents the player with the ball from executing any offensive tactics. We can also say that the upper and lower pendulums are the most important pressing maneuvers. It enables the player to quickly attack the opponent with the ball and to build basic pressure, which mainly contributes to a direct improvement of the situation. It's very difficult to start applying pressing without the above mentioned tactical maneuver because the space-time parameters of the defensive pressure are a consequence of it.

It's not possible to achieve the optimal "reduction" in the defensive process just by shortening the pitch from the "top." The players in the defensive line or defensive formation must also join in the compression of the pressing area through the execution of the pressing maneuver known as "pump." enables the manipulation (shortening or lengthening) of the depth of the area favorable for the application of the pressing tactics. Thanks to the pump, the application of the pressing tactics allows to keep a depth of 20–25 m from the active pressing zone. The movement mechanism of the pump depends on the correct descending formation or on an increase of the active area which, at the same time, depends on the actual performance of the opponent in center, and the time-space distress or distraction caused by the active players around the center (the player attacking the opponent, the players of the upper pendulum). This is noticeable when the opponent under pressure or being attacked, with no possibility to do a long kick forward, chooses to perform a back pass or a wide pass in order to get away from the pressing situation. This is a signal to push the defensive line as high as possible toward the center line in order to bring the depth of the active pressing zone closer to 20–25 m, which is the optimum pressing distance. Moreover, pushing or forcing the defensive line as close as possible to the center or dividing line causes the players attacking the opponents to move out of the area forcing them to leave

the offside alignment. Except from the changes in the direction of the attacker movements, it's possible to achieve the main task by tricking the opponent psychologically preventing them to use any offensive action. Thanks to this, the risk of performing a successful pressing is significantly lower. The pump mechanism is beneficial the pressing team because it shortens the depth of the active area (fig. 3.6-7).

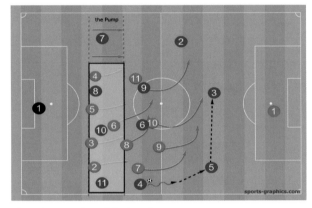

Fig. 3.6-7 Function of the pressing pump

The control of the depth of the active pressing zone is the essential task of the tactical performance when applying the pump, which is focused on a synchronized movement of the whole defensive line toward the center.

When a player executes a long kick behind the defensive line, all the players in the defensive line start to move toward their own goal in order to gain the control the ball being driven by the opponent applying pressing and to adjust the relevant lack of defensive depth. This is compensated using the tactical movements of the defensive line toward their own goal. When the back passes are directed toward the own team's goal, it is a signal to quit the pump toward the opponent's goal.

In connection to the pendulum and pump concept, some typical defensive positions can be outlined. They often occur by applying this tactical tool. It involves four positions for the upper and lower pendulum (upper pendulum: two attackers and lower pendulum: two midfielders), one position for the midfielder (the attacker in the center, one position for the midfielder securing the weak area, and four positions for the players applying pump (players in the defensive formation according to the alignment). The positions within individual pendulums depend on the situation and change according to the strategy. Something similar happens to the position of the attacker and securing player, their positions change depending on the type of pressing situations according the strategy being applied. The positions in the pump are maintained during the whole pressing activity.

The practical application of the Hunting territory theory (Görgényi, 1998, 2015) for zonal defense and pressing was described in details in Chapter 3.1. Based on this description, we can give you a visualization of the territorial aspects of the pendulum and pump pressing and their dynamics, as shown in figs. 3.6-8a,b,c.

Thanks to the area covered during the application of pressing within a zone, we can describe the basic pressing mechanisms used in the zone where pendulum and pump pressing are applied. These mechanisms reinforce the effectiveness and security of pressing during its application. The position of the players avoiding a wide pass during the application of the pendulum pressing also changes. The basic purpose of these pressing maneuvers is to lead the opponent player with the ball to an effective area where it's difficult to escape from, causing obstruction and though impeding the player to finish successfully the application of pressing. It involves the control of the opponent's space through the use of specific pressing maneuvers, which enable the players to direct the opponent to an advantageous area where it's easier to perform pressing effectively. It's evident that, in order to use the correct position in the alignment of the players, it is also necessary to evaluate correctly the relationship between the area and the space. Another necessary element is the ability to understand the mental state of the play, which results in the reading and understanding of the game itself. After an effective use of maneuvers that can force the opponent player with the ball fall into situation where pressing can be applied, there are some escape alternatives:

1. **Auxiliary passes toward the goalkeeper**

2. **Wide pass toward the distant player** in the formation through one or two vertical widths.

3. **Long or medium kick** to a less concentrated pressing alignment in the active pressing zone or behind the defense line of the team who performs the pressing.

For an effective escape from a pressing situation using auxiliary back pass toward the goalkeeper, it's necessary

to handle the play by his leg. It's the only tool that enables the player to overcome the pressing activity of the opponent.

After escaping from the pressing situation, the player performs a wide pass that annuls the effectiveness of the pressing alignment and disrupts the positional rearrangement of the players to a new center position that must take place (pendulum maneuver) using a wide shifting of the defense block following the movement of the ball along the width of the pitch. When planning the pressing tactics, it is important to set the targets. Except for the planning of the main target, which is how to gain the ball, it is possible to reduce those tasks to partial targets such as making the opponent's action slower in order to create an effective defensive formation or to simply gain time in order to reorganize the new alignment. It's often connected to a regulated intensity, which often relates to an economic and optimal momentum resulting from the pressing context. The manipulating maneuvers applied to opponent to make them move into a specific advantageous area belongs to the group of typical strategic pressing tactics that are often related to the quality of the opponent team. We should keep in mind that the application of pressing is only possible when the situation allows it and when the mental and positional situation of the team is favorable for its application.

If the player with the ball is forced to perform a long kick forward, because pressing is being applied to this player, the probabilities of gaining the ball successfully is 70 percent. Statistical analysis clearly shows that the probabilities of performing a successful long kick of a defenders or defensive players is bigger than the probabilities occurring during a confrontation with the attackers. Gaining the ball represents a successful alternative for the pressing team. However, the possibility of the team losing the control of the ball to reciprocate pressing on the opponent who've just stolen the ball after a long kick is very remote. The hidden tactical motivation intentionally inducing the configuration of the tactics can be considered to be the getaway alternative under the opponent's pressing.

Another important aspect of the pressing tactics is the activity of the team who've gained the ball after a successful proactive defense. In the postpressing stage, we may think about the positional advantages offered by a successful pressing defense. Also we may think about specific attacking tactics after a successful recapture of the ball.

a

b

c

Fig. 3.6-8a,b,c Territorial aspects of pendulum and pump pressing

We can say that, after regaining the ball, the correct pressing alignment is the optimal alignment for the upcoming offense as well as to initiate the offensive action (overnumbering for attack). The optimal postpressing scenario is, from this point of view, relatively simple due to the fact that it's built on the so-called **compulsory second pass toward the offensive depth** (constructive, creative). In case the application of pressing to the offensive depth

is not performed on time (not later than the second pass after gaining the ball), the team will lose the most favorable time to "take advantage" of the opponent's offensive alignment. Therefore, losing this opportunity allows the opponents to reorganize themselves and to switch to a defensive formation. We intentionally described the second postpressing attacking pass, because the first postpressing pass is more consistent and more advantageous for the team. If the first pass can be performed right after the application of pressing to the offensive depth, it will offer the team a time reserve for a more comfortable performance of the postpressing attack by trying to prolong the positional instability of the opponent team.

Immediate (Ultraoffensive) Pressing

Many theories of immediate ultraoffensive pressing (Bielsa, Guardiola) apply the six seconds rule. It limits the time interval of its application after losing the ball. After this period of time is finished, the defensive team returns back to the offensive formation within the pressing zone on their half of the pitch (central zone, defensive zone). In our personal pressing theory, we don't consider this rule as most the effective one for all configurations. Sometimes, the most advantageous situation to regain the ball can occur after this time limit. That's why we don't have to consider the six seconds rule of the immediate ultraoffensive (IUO) pressing as a necessary rule. The strict application of this rule can be considered as "formalism." The situation happening immediately after losing the possession of the ball has to be taken into consideration independently from the classical zonal pressing that is significantly organized from the very beginning. This situation is not defined by the space and doesn't have any specific stages. It can be considered as a defensive hit. The specification of its space is defined by the area where the ball was lost, which means that pressing may occur in any area or zone of the field.

Apart from the active zonal pressing, in this type of pressing the opponent controls the ball. The pressing is defined by the time parameter of its application, which is activated immediately after losing the ball on any part of the pitch. Its offensive character corresponds to the aggressiveness and mental balance of the players applying pressing (fig. 3.6-9).

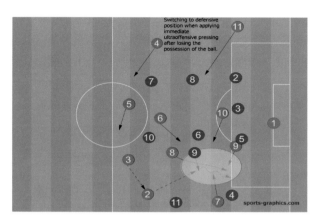

Fig. 3.6-9 Switching to defensive position when applying immediate ultraoffensive pressing after losing the possession of the ball

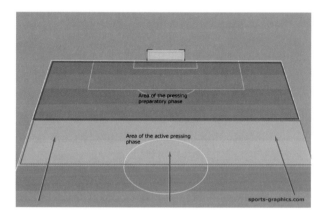

Fig. 3.6-10 Optimal area for pressing activation

Basically, the immediate ultraoffensive (IUO) pressing belongs to the counterpressing tactics, in other words, the gegen-pressing, which has been taken from the Anglo-Saxon or Klopp pressing terminology.

The basic tactical advantage of the immediate ultraoffensive is in the successful implementation of the double hit that can have a great impact on the opponent. The player in the offensive alignment not only loses the ball, but the team becomes disorganized in the outnumbered formation against the pressing block of the attacking players. In this type of pressing, gaining the ball is not the only tactical target. Another target is to slow down the opponent with the ball so the team can get more time to apply pressing successfully. It also enables the team to structure the defensive alignment.

Pressing Attributes

Due to the general tactical rules concerning to space, it is obvious that there is an intentional manipulation of the active area when applying the pressing rules. In principle, when defense is applied, the players make the active area smaller and try to form a "small pitch." On the contrary, when offense is applied, the players make the active area larger and try to form a "large pitch." It's connected to the width alignment at the moment the players have the control of the ball and also to the narrow alignment when the players attempt to regain the ball. Smaller areas are easier to defend (more effectively and safely) and for this reason players close it for defense. After gaining the ball, players make it larger by opening the area for the offense. The optimal space when pressing is applied is shown in fig. 3.6-10.

Many different results may be expected after pressing tactics are applied ranging from successful effects to the unsuccessful ones.

1. Unsuccessful pressing attempt (the opponent keeps the possession of the ball)

2. Reapplying pressing after unsuccessful attempt (use in the same defensive sequence)

3. Escape from pressing by performing back pass (engaging the goalkeeper) or a wide pass (engaging player in the same formation)

4. Exiting a pressing situation and successful reposition of the offense into a weaker area of the active zone or by using the area outside the active zone that is insufficiently covered (weak side, the area behind defense line).

5. Decrease in the activity the player being attacked that leads to a direct loss of the ball.

6. Decrease in the activity the player being attacked that leads to the solutions resulting from the loss of the ball.

7. Consequent defensive effects resulting from the positional movement of the defending player in relation to the player seemingly taking advantage of this defensive activity.

8. Successful pressing (regaining the ball in a direct contact with the opponent).

Failure of pressing brings the overnumbering of the offensive team, which represents one of the most counterproductive elements of the pressing application. On the contrary, a successful pressing brings positive results to the defensive team right at the moment the player gains the ball. The postpressing stage is the most important part of the game. The main point of the defensive effort is to gain the control of the ball after a successful application of pressing. After pressing has been applied successfully, the main responsibility is to keep the continuity of the strategies following this stage, i.e., successful organization of the offense that is made by a defensive tactical action. It's necessary for the team to learn what to do after performing either a successful or unsuccessful pressing.

Despite the fact that the pressing maneuvers don't necessarily lead to an immediate possession and control of the ball, the main task of the pressing movements is focused on closing the alternative pass corridors of the opponents in order to escape a subsequent pressing situation. This task is also focused on the preparation of positional strategies, which is advantageous for the players when reorganizing the pressing formation. This enables the players to take the control of the ball from the opponent with the so-called **positive pressing effect delay.** It isn't necessary to gain the ball through the application of the pressing maneuvers. There are other maneuvers and possibilities that players can apply using the space to help any other player in the team to gain the ball afterward. **In pressing, every player should aim the performance and action to benefit the team.** The need of a defensive team synergy confirms the necessity of cooperation among all the participants in application of defensive proactivity.

Mostly, the whole team is engaged into pressing. However, in the midfield, only a group of four or five players positioned in the correct alignment are engaged directly into the pressing activity. It enables them to build the space-time pressure in the midfield.

Only one or two players directly attack the opponent with the ball, who is the one participating in the configuration one of the alternatives pressing reaction. The whole idea is to take the control of the ball from the opponent. In the event of an unsuccessful pressing, in which the opponent starts to perform an offensive action taking advantage of the situation due to the positional handicaps of the players, is considered to be a fatal failure.

In connection to pressing, it's necessary to take into consider more types of pressure in the playing context. They are related to the time-space dimension of the proactive defense to create disruption to the player with the ball. We can distinguish:

1. **Pressure on the player with the ball:** the leg length position in order to have the possibility of a direct contact with the ball.

2. **Pressure on the area:** the space options where the player can place the ball are restricted by closing the corridors in order to prevent any pass alternatives.

3. **Time pressure:** the time necessary for the adequate activities in a specific situation is shortened (time shortage) and, therefore, the quality of the performance decreases. This situation forces the player to perform movements as fast as possible in order to avoid shifting and moving of the pressing block. This time shortage that limits the time necessary to keep the opponent under the pressure can cause a decrease in the quality of the performance and also tend to accelerate the actions necessary to build favorable conditions to create the resistance as a reaction to this type of defense.

4. **Psychological pressure:** the tension created to disrupt the natural mental stability of the opponent players by the pressing tactics, which often contributes to an easy and unforced loss of the ball. Apart from the technical deficits, the mental effect of the pressure also causes a limitation of adequate choices for different solutions; as a result, this tension can optimally block the player to whom it is applied on. It is often related to the position of the player within the area in different situations.

5. **Pressure on the match development:** injuries that can result from inadequate selection of solutions or low quality in the implementation of the correct solutions. This type of pressure is often connected to psychological dispositions and the typology of the players.

To perceive these pressure results in a specific pressing resistance. In modern soccer, it enables to handle the pressing tactics as one of the requirements for the application of the offensive stage and to hold the ball. The time space pressure, as a necessary precondition for applying the proactive defense, is related to pressing. It represents the critical decrease of the basic time in order to perform the activity that is followed by the restriction of the space in the manipulation of the ball and the use of adequate space to perform the pass as a result of an effective closure of the correct corridors. The result of it is the physical and mental disruption of the players with the ball.

The traditional habits are different in applying the pressing tactics. The basic movement schemes are mainly changed when performing an immediate pressing. The changes of these habits are related to the changes in the way the area is perceived. The visual control before receiving the ball becomes natural and the way in which it is perceived it's necessary for the organization of the precondition. Correct decisions in the performance executed upon the correct perception of the area are relevant for the pressing tactics. In case the visual control is not possible to perform due to distress, the decisive element becomes the implementation of maneuvers based on the practice (experience from the learned from other situations), the perception of the game, and the organization (inherent preconditions).

The correct positional alignment of the players participating in the pressing formation is an important element in the application of the pressing tactics. Nowadays, teams use some defensive conformations such as 3–7 (three players situated between the opponent with the ball and his goal), 2–8 or 1–9 or even 0–10. Apart from the traditional model of 5–5, the development in pressing tends toward the formation of 1–9 where one player situated between the opponent with the ball and goal tries to block back passes. Then other players move around in the blocks, therefore the movement is determined by the position of the midfield pressing. In relation to the application pressing tactics, we need to point out the fact that bad a pressing performance can be dangerous for the team. It's worthy for the team to analyze the application of pressing is not correctly performed.

In connection to pressing, we distinguish following situations: **prepressing** (before pressing is initiated), **pressing** (application of pressing), and **postpressing** (the consequences of successful or unsuccessful pressing). These methodological tools can help to answer elementary questions, such as how, when, and where to apply pressing or what follows the pressing situation from the playing point of view.

The process shown in the performance of the pressing tactics consists of following stages. Their interconnection conform the compactness of the pressing.

1. **Preparation for pressing** (pressing activation): In the structuring of active pressing zone, it's important the creation of a suitable positional configuration of the players involved in pressing positioned in a predefined and a predetermined space through maneuvers based on the cooperation in the area of the pressing zone.

2. **Pressing application** (initiation of the pressing situation) represents the culmination of the pressing tactics. It relies on an effective use of the short time interval in which the offensive maneuver is completed through a direct "body to body" contact or through lengthening of the time-space situational pressure to cause disruption on the opponent player. Thanks to this maneuver, the opponent is forced to apply specific actions in order to exit the pressing situation (escaping solution) or to perform low quality actions resulting in loss of the ball subsequently or immediately after the application of pressing.

As it is in other sport disciplines, the pendulum and pump pressing theory already discussed can have their justification at the moment when the result confirms its application. The fundamental contribution of it was confirmed in the European Championship U-19 in 2011. The national Czech Republic youth representation successfully applied these pressing tactics all along the whole tournament. Thanks to this pressing defensive concept, this team could reach the final match of the European Championship where they were defeated by the Spanish team. The difficulty of these pressing concepts lies in the standard requirements of the physical conditions of the players and the team organization, the correct positional alignment, not only of the players participating in the pressing situation but also the activity of the whole team

PART 2

to maintain the required pressing formation for all modifications performed. Sensory motor activity of movement and space, the understanding of the game and the ability to read the situation in the game belong to other relevant requirements for the players who participate in this concept. The effectiveness of this defensive concept has convinced a lot of top European youth teams (Italy, Croatia, Germany, England, Spain) as well as the youth teams on the club-based level (Lazio Roma, Manchester United, FC Liverpool) and youth team-based level of Sparta Praha. After the match between Czech Republic and Italy, Ariga Sacchi personally praised the admirable endurance of the defensive organization exhibited when the pendulum and pump pressing were used. It was the significant acknowledgment of the use of pressing tactics presented by the Czech team. The team was encouraged to keep their principles in both defense and offense performance. It's important for the players know their own movements, which is very a necessary element for the implementation of a successful cooperation. When pressing is performed correctly, it's possible to apply it all along the whole course of the match as well as in all the matches consecutively played (during the European Championship of U 19 in 2011, there were six matches in eighteen days).

Likewise the traditional zonal pressing, the pressing concept of pendulum and pump previously described is connected to the block type of defense but maintaining an asymmetrical defensive alignment of the pendulum pressing also applied in the block formation. Whereas the actual model of symmetric formation prevails in block alignment, the presented block model is positionally asymmetrical the same as the pressing configuration. Regarding the defensive model performed in the block and pressing tactics, the block alignment is identical to the pressing one. From a positional point of view, it's considered as identical defensive configurations. Their advantage is the elimination of positional failures during the shifting or displacement from block to pressing formation and vice versa. Apart from the symmetric alignment, the asymmetric alignment is more demanding in sense of space perception. Concerning the performance of the same block and pressing formation alignment, its

real advantage is that the alignment of the players in the transition from passive to active or from reactive to proactive defensive arrangement stays the same. Due to this fact, this transition can be used at any given moment. Keeping an analogous basic asymmetric alignment for the block and pressing makes their mutual combination more effective; what's more important, it enables a smooth transition from pressing formation to the block formation and vice versa. Thanks to this, the combination of both defensive tactics significantly increases the parameters of the effectiveness and security of its application, which contribute to the logical interconnection of defensive concepts in most successful teams. For illustrative purposes, we are presenting graphical configurations of the defensive pressing and the block alternatives, which are based on the pendulum and pump principle. In the next chapter, we will offer some typical configuration schemes of basic defensive formation for pressing and block application in defense, which take into consideration the basic positional principles of the pendulum and pump pressing (figs. 3.6-11 to -18).

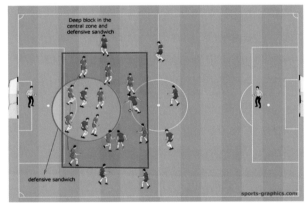

Fig. 3.6-11 Deep block in the central zone and defensive sandwich

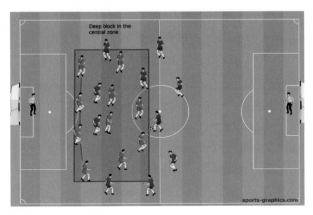

Fig. 3.6-12 Deep block in the central zone

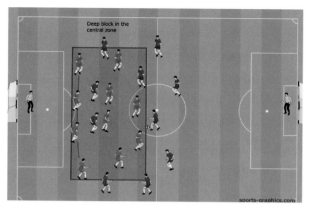

Fig. 3.6-13 Deep block performed by pendulum and pump

Basically, as already proposed, maintaining an identical configuration for the alignment and structure of the basic pressing and block configuration minimizes the risk of an incorrect defensive formation of the players as well as exceeding the time parameters in the transition from active to passive formation of the defense and vice versa. The practical impact of the analogous positional asymmetry for both basic defensive configurations (pressing and block defense) is achieved by maintaining the alignment continuity. It enables a smooth transition from one defensive formation to the other one. It also enables an effective combination and interconnection of the defensive action with a minimum of risk concerning time loss or incorrect positional configuration of the defensive players. Despite more conservative symmetric alignment, this type of positional concept of the block and pressing tactics enables a smooth execution of the transition from defensive reactivity to defensive proactivity. It helps to integrate these elementary defensive principles into a more effective way of playing performance in the defensive stage. This demonstrated type of pressing tactics shows that, in relation to the situational dependency of the optimal shifting of the players to form an effective pressing configuration, it's necessary to practice the pressing techniques using the correct methodology. This is the only way to achieve the integrity of the pressing activities and to teach the players how to perform pressing. Pressing can be started after the correct understanding of the situation and after foreseeing the development of those situations that can be achieved by a permanent cognitive stimulation for the play, which is considered as the necessary fact. In the application of the pressing tactics, the cooperation of the players and the situational conditions

within the area around the ball show that pressing is not about improvisation. It's about the intentional defensive performance, the pressing strategy, and the tactics.

Due to the actual situation of soccer and the prediction of its further development, it's necessary to consider the strategy of a match in the presented description of pressing as a high quality active defensive activity. Based on the philosophy of the coach and available typology of players, each team has the most advantageous style. This style gives a description of the pressing tactics taking into account the analysis of the style of the own team players as well as the opponent performance. It's also necessary to take into consideration a special match strategy to explain the basic tactical conditions in the application of the pressing tactics in order to perform pressing. Depending on the typology of the opponent and their own team, this strategy fundamentally influences its application in the performance of a match. The strategy gives shape to the plan of the effective interaction between the coached team and the opponent considering how, when, and where pressing should be applied as well as the type to be applied. This strategy is based on the analysis of the opponent performance as well as their own team, the correct evaluation of the strength and weak points of both teams, their confrontation in the field and the immediate conditions of the actual match.

The purpose of the match strategy is to reduce the space of the opponent and to create space that can help to apply the strength of the whole team in order to optimize the pressing tactics. A successful performance will depend entirely on the level of strategy of the coaches.

We will use two examples that show the process of the strategic solution of the defensive pressing concept in a specific match. If the opponent has strikers able to play the high ball effectively, then we shouldn't use high pressing. High pressing will force the opponent to do long kick forward, and it will enable them to engage these strikers into the play. The team should allow them to perform their own combinations on their half of the pitch.

Another example is when the defenders of the opponent team move slowly. This is the reason why the team shouldn't attempt to perform offensive pressing. This will intentionally force the opponent to direct the ball into the midfield zone in order to prepare themselves for fast confrontations toward the opponent goal immediately after gaining the ball through pressing and to take advantage of the weak point the opponent's speed.

Whether or not the analysis of the opponent indicates their weak points, it's convenient to direct the strategy toward these weaknesses of the opponent team to create confrontational situations that are very difficult to cope with. Similar situation happens in application of the provocative pressing in which the team uses the playing handicaps of

the opponent. For example, the team wants to take advantage and use the handicap of right defender who has problem to join the game their half of the pitch. In this case, the provocative pressing must be applied in the midfield zone or in the opponent's left vertical part of the defensive zone. Using this action, the team can manipulate the strategy toward their immediate pressing and forced the opponent to perform handicapping movements or to regain the control of the ball using active zonal pressing.

The application of the pressing tactics is adapted to the specific circumstances of the opponent outlined in the strategy plan. **The aim is to achieve the highest possible profit during the match.**

The adjustment of the level of defensive actions (from the passive block to active pressing) is part of the strategy for the pressing tactics application. It often depends on the typology of the players, their presumptive interaction in the confrontation during the match and the quality of the opponent. It also depends on the development of the match.

During the application of the pressing tactics, a strategic thinking of the coaches is decisive for the optimization

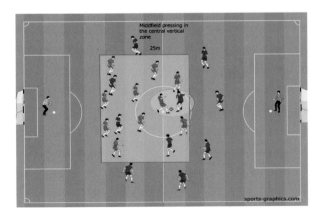

Fig. 3.6-14 Formation from the deep block to pressing

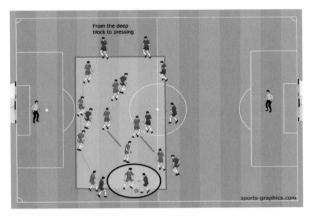

Fig. 3.6-15 Center block

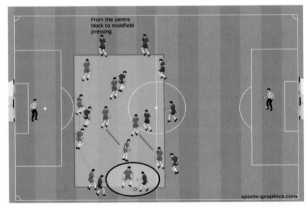

Fig. 3.6-16 Formation from the center block to midfield pressing

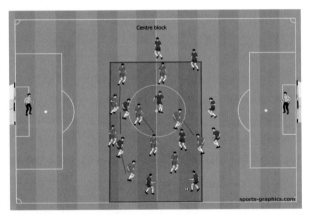

Fig. 3.6-17 Midfield pressing in the central vertical zone

Fig. 3.6-18 Formation from central block to midfield pressing

and secure performance of defensive tactics. Detailed implications are mostly applied in similar performance-related teams (provided there is a comparable team in the same match). The variable theories are integral parts of the pressing tactics strategies, which are not in rigid schemes but are realistic and adapted to the match. These strategies are changed according to the match and their changes depend on the typology of the opponent, the conditions of the match, the player's characteristic features, and the intentions of the team. Bruckner (2013) adds: "The coach must foresee and assume. Of course, you must use your own improvisation in couching!" The questions for strategic thinking of the coaches stay open for every single match. The interaction of all the variables forms above mentioned, and the variability of factors are relevant to the strategy for pressing application in every specific match.

4.0 PRESSING TRAINING THEORY AND PRESSING THERAPY, OR HOW TO HEAL THE GAME BY PRESSING

It seems that most of the top teams have the pressing defensive tactics in their repertoire. It doesn't automatically represent the guarantee of successful results of the team but it's definitely difficult to imagine a contemporary successful team without this form of active defense. Of course, not all the teams use the pressing method on the same level but it's quite hard to imagine a contemporary top team where whatever form of pressing would be absent. We think, taking into account today's playing trends, that the pressing application can help effectively, not only in regaining the possession of the ball but also an important tactical element of decreasing the opponent's offensive effort. It means it's not only a good quality defensive element but also an effective tactical tool for devastation of the opponent's attacking effort.

Apart from defensive features, the variable sophisticated pressing tactics also include offensive elements of the game. Diagnosis of the game emerges from the knowledge of its course, mental perception, and creating an optimal training communication in the game concept. To find metaphors of the game belongs to the geniuses of the coaching work who are connected to the course of the game as an active element. These impulses come from the game, and they return immediately into the game in the form of confronting new trends through coaching magicians who "heal" the game of soccer in its evolutional progress. The immanency of the game's development is this way built on the ability of some of the coaching giants to capture the course of the game into their thoughts, transfer the thoughts into the words and, through the communication about the concept of the game, return them back into their own teams' play where they have their significant purpose.

Based on the facts that are mentioned in the previous chapters, we can conclude the specific requirements for the training process and the use of the specific training elements for the practice and improvement of the individual element of the pressing (e.g., play in a narrowed area, attack on the opponent, movement into the center, approaching the players, movement toward the player, taking over the players, handing the players over, movement after the ball, attacking the player with a ball, doubling, intentional manipulation with the space, intentional coordination of the players performing the pressing on a formation, block or a whole team level, understanding the pressing time-space, and complex elements necessary for the play in a block and a group of players entering the pressing situation). If we want to apply timeless elements in our team's play, we must also transfer them into the training process by applying a timeless method. For the purpose of making the pressing practice more effective, in the practical part of this trilogy, we will deal with algorithmization and sequence of individual steps of the practice and improvement of pressing with the focus on the training elements, which are necessary are the most convenient from the point of view of the training target. **There is a rule, especially in pressing, that the playing performance is a reflection of the training process so the emphasis, which is put on its contextual focus, has a purpose.**

Apart from the mentioned play-tactical features of the pressing, it's also important to mention, in connection with this, the basic possible elements of the playing behavior of the players who are under pressing as well as the playing reactions against the pressing application from the opponent's side. As every type of play has its defense weapon or the most effective fight-back tool, there are effective defense weapons against the pressing application too, which allow to acquire pressing resistance, in other words the playing resistance toward this type of defensive proactivity. One of the most effective antipressing reactions of the players who are under pressing can be:

- In an attacking stage, **quick and safe pass** to a team player, if possible the furthest one, so we can get out of the pressing situation

- **Interlude consisting of a fast circulation of the ball** followed by rich movement offer from the side of the team players in order to prevent the opponent from reaching the pressing situation,

- **Intensive movement** of the team players without a ball on the principle of "showing"

- **Fast transfer from the attacking stage with shortened interlude,** which allows the player to perform a safe transfer through a critical area that is covered by an opponent's pressing alignment, long, and accurate pass into the attacking free area

- **Avoiding the attacking opponent,** running out of the pressing situation and an individual technical self-release from the pressing situation

- **Diagonal play transfer** into the opposite or at least further vertical

- **Enticing and maneuvering movements of the team players,** which the pressing is used against, and they are meant to uncover the area near the game center in order to enable the release from the pressing situation

- The player with a ball is demanding **an annulment of the pressing situation by provoking a foul** (the local outnumber is losing its purpose)

- **Ability to transfer the center of the game in vertical direction** (perpendicular, long passes) movement

of the player behind the defensive line as well as in horizontal direction (wide passes) that forces the opponent, who is applying pressing, reorganize his pressing position

- **Outnumber of the players who are applying pressing causes undernumber in other part of the playing area,** and it's important to teach the players, who are under pressing, to find exactly these areas and try to consciously transfer the play into the zones, which are weakened by this.

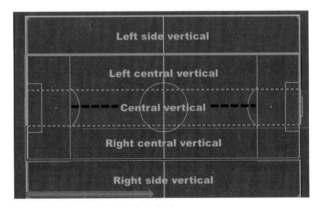

Fig. 4-1a Space division of the playing area

For the needs of better methodical management of the pressing practice in the training process, we divide the playing area horizontally into the defensive, middle, and attacking zone and, from the vertical division point of view, we divide it into the right side vertical, left side vertical, right middle vertical and left middle vertical zone, which includes the area from 16 to 16 along the whole width as shown in the picture 4-1.

The main and fundamental motive when creating the training tools and complex programs for the therapy by pressing is the practice, improvement, and stabilization of the defensive behavior of the team the way it's offered by the game itself. That's space for the coach's creativity, which allows him to prepare the training tools that are close to the game and thanks to this he can achieve conscious coordination of the defending players through the correct position play, manipulation with space, and maintaining all the play-tactical details necessary for an effective application of the pressing tactics. Bruckner (2013) requires fixing the correct action by using the training tools. This has its purpose especially in the pressing therapy management. According to him, almost all the soccer specialists, coaches, officials, journalists, experts, and fans know "what to do" but only a small percentage of them, including the specialists, know "how to do it." We tried to do this, at least for the presented pressing topic, by giving the answers in the diagnosis (what it actually is, how it was created and how it appears in the game) and the therapy (how to manage it, what it takes from the point of view of the method and acquirement and how to deal with it the game), which offer the prognosis (its place in the structure of the game, how it will be included into the game content in the near future and the predicted form of the play in the following years) in the direction of the further evolutional advancement of the defensive tactic in soccer.

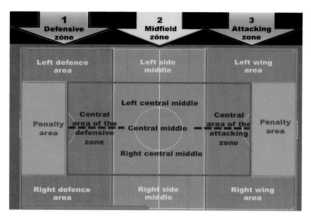

Fig. 4-1b Space division of the playing area

4.1 THE PHILOSOPHICAL ASPECTS OF PRESSING TRAINING

From the point of view of the content and the use of the specific tool, we mustn't forget about the philosophy of the connection between the training process and the match at any moment of creating the training process. The match situations, as well as special match pressure, must be constantly a part of the training process just like the efficiency of the training process, which is determined by the transfer of its content into particular match conditions or individual match situations. A match must be the source of the content of the training process. Although the philosophers often can't answer the question, whether chicken or egg was first, a soccer coach must clearly understand the priority of what is happening in a match and the whole content of the training and the preparation develops from this. From this point of view, the question of a long-term planning of the training process is controversial especially if we look at its specific play as well as overall content. In the philosophy of copying a match, we are trying to reach the form of the training conditions which, on the principal of modeling match situations in the training context, allow significant imitation of match situations not only from the space alignment point of view but also imitation of emotional resonance point of view that is typical for match conditions.

Concerning the content, we are recommending to expressly conclude from a match and to return from the training process back to the match by a transfer. This is actually a double transfer. After the game analysis, we are bringing the analyzed content into the training and consequently we are transferring the intentionally practiced elements back into the match. This philosophy of the content also determines the way of implementing the elements of the play into the training. This is reflected in the sequential algorithm including the features of the process and the situational characteristics of the play elements or the game stages. The principal of the match model survival (configuration and pressure) in the training and acquiring experience with the elements in the training is the condition for reaching the effect of the training process and a guarantee of the transfer into the match without which the advisability of the training work would be significantly questioned or probably even sterile.

For practical completion of this material, we are offering in the Volume 3 the manual of the specific playing exercises, preparatory games and modeling exercises that allow the coach to establish a specific training program easily that is adapted to the needs of the team in the form of sequential algorithm for the practice, development, and improvement of the pressing.

According to the offer of the manual (part 3), it's possible to build a sequential algorithm by assembling the individual exercises in order to have all the levels included or highlight the levels that are the most important for the team from the point of view of acquirement and improvement of the pressing tactic. Some levels might sometimes be overdimensioned in the sequential algorithm of the specific team's pressing practice, for example, by the level 1 (first stages of the practice) and vice-versa, the team that is significantly more advanced in the practice and improvement of the pressing will have an increased rate of higher levels, for example, 6, 7, and 8, included in its sequential algorithm. The advantage of the offered exercise manual for the pressing is the possibility to create variable "custom mate" training programs for the particular team taking into account the real development of the team's playing performance. Some exercises are constructed to allow the parallel practice and improvement of several levels, thus the possibility of the practical use is widened.

We mustn't forget that apart from the play-tactical behavior, the training tools are very effective for the training also due to maintaining and increasing the basic condition (general and special endurance and special speed), which has a great importance in maintaining the level of concentration abilities, increases the potential of the mental performance and enables the player to maintain better promptness in order to perform a good quality pressing game. Considering the frequently repeated explosive entries, the pressing game requires a fast microregeneration that provides the steadiness of the applied pressing or entry into a new pressing sequence. The advantage of the pressing training is that the training tools for its practice often very effectively replace the use of the less special and isolated athletic elements in the training. Moreover, they put the emphasis on a special play-tactical character of movement skills that is not only the intention but it's often also the aim of their construction. We also mustn't forget about the fact that when practicing the pressing, owing to the interactive character of the applied training tolls, we are also at the same time developing the antipressing behavior of the players and increasing their pressing resistance. In relation to this, we think it's important to present the repertoire of antipressing elements of the playing behavior that will allow us to react efficiently to the pressing applied on the defending players. This repertoire consists of the following antipressing elements:

- **Real estimate of the playing risks** in specific pressing situations

- **Ability to play against maximum playing resistance** of the defending opponent

- **Securing the area behind the game center** against eventual loss of the possession of the ball

- **Management of the deep, timed passes of various length**

- **Fast micro-combinations,** avoiding the defending opponent by dynamic-technical elements and a whirling motion of the team players

- **Ability to hold the ball until the last moment of the specific attack**

- **Circulation of a ball** with one or two-touch interlude

- **Make use of the ball's speed**

- **The play transfer** (wide and diagonal passes)

- **Unhurried solution of play situations,** ability to play under time-space pressure while maintaining a qualitative level of play solutions, play-frustrating tolerance toward out number

- **Periphery vision,** ability to perceive out of the center and transfer the play, ability to change the pace of the play

- The sense for an effective **entry into the opposite movement rhythm** toward defending players surprising and courageous individual solution of the pressing situation by tempo-dribbling (carrying the ball away)

- **Hiding the playing intentions** and solutions until the last moment

- **Purposeful change of the game center**

The main and fundamental motive of the pressing training philosophy is the principle you play the way you train. In other words, the play in a match offers direct impulses for creating a meaningful training program with the focus on the whole game but also on the details. We can confirm that, especially for pressing, it's not a methodical phrase at all.

4.2 PROBLEMATIC AREAS IN PRESSING TRAINING AND THE SEQUENTIAL CONCEPT OF PRESSING TRAINING

From the "attacking defense" point of view, we can't expect immediate effect of the training even in the most advanced teams. But according to our experience, it's necessary and maybe sufficient to have the period of two to six months in order to gain the standard pressing skills. It directly depends on the ability of the team to learn and the typology of the team as well as the effect of the training model, which we are using for the practice and the improvement of the pressing tactic. Johann Cruyff considers as the optimal period of time, in professional teams, for acquiring the pressing with its all features (psychomotor and technical-tactical factors) the period of two years (which is impossible today, two months or shorter space of time must be sufficient for handling the pressing tactic even if not perfectly). Before we get to the specific pressing tactic elements, it's necessary to be aware of the most frequent problems and mistakes in the pressing training.

The most common mistakes are

- **Motor deficiency of individual players** from the movement skills point of view

- **Movement asynchronism among the players** when providing the movement into the center of the game and approaching the opponent players who come into consideration for an auxiliary pass

- **The distance between individual formations** that results in creating space holes between the formations and its outcome is insufficient space density

- **Excessive distances between players and formations** and incompatibility of some formation

- **Insufficient narrowing and shortening of the area around the center of the game** that results in early physical exhaustion

- **Offside and foul reduce the effect of the pressing** resulting in inability to create the pressing situation and the necessity to reorganize the position of the defending team

- **Incompatibility of the team players to carry out the mental entries** that can be demonstrated by unequal speed of the playing, thinking, movement asynchronism, and so on

- **Signal value of the play situation isn't perceived the same way by all the players** who are supposed to be involved in the play situation from the pressing point of view (disproportion in the tactical thinking of the players, in individual-tactic as well as group performance of the players, inability to concentrate, and so on)

For the needs of the pressing, it is necessary to count on intensifying the training process in all its levels but mainly in its pace. For maintaining the sequence of this type of play as well as the increase of the effect on the acquirement level, we have tried to create the algorithmization of this process as well as we've tried to maintain the sequence in the practice and improvement of individual steps in order to reach the most effective transfer into the match conditions. For this purpose, we have built multi-level training concept so-called sequential algorithm for the pressing practice, which represents didactical training process technology based on Kacani (1995) concept. In this connection, the sequential algorithm represents individual steps and stages of the practice that are included in the training process as a logical sequence in order to keep the demand increase on the level of an individual's playing activity, coordination of defending players, the play of formations or blocks, and also the concept of the whole team's play while the logic of the course of the play in a match is implicitly reflected in the global scheme of the specific play type or play-tactical element practice. It's a formally contextual scheme that is based on rational and logic sequence of the training processes and steps. This scheme speeds up the process of learning, acquirement, and improvement of the play-tactical content of the tasks, which are related to the playing system. These tasks are also related to the specific way of play that doesn't always have to depend on the playing system, but it can represent only a partial tactical maneuver for the specific time or space stage of the play or a strategic playing element for an individual match.

Algorithmization of the pressing tactic is in progress basically in three lines:

- On the level of an individual's play and interaction of two opposite players.

- On the level of a formation, group and block's play.

- On the level of the whole team's play.

The highest level of the practice, within the modeling, is integrated pressing practice directly into the game and play context that is offered by the game itself, and it's reflected in the construction and the content of the modeling exercises.

4.3 PRESSING PRACTICE LEVELS

For the needs of the pressing practice training, we are introducing the basic playing elements, which are also a useful methodical tool that presents individual steps or the pressing practice levels where every following step represents a higher quality level. The presented sequence includes an increase of the level from the elementary parts (fight 1:1, occupation) up to the complex playing behavior in pressing (modeling of different pressing tactics).

Based on the sequential gradualism of the individual pressing elements, we have formed **the following levels of the pressing practice:**

Level 1—A play in 1:1 situations, avoiding the opponent, attacking the player with a ball, forechecking, resistance increase in fights.

Level 2—Tight occupation and approach to the players, space defense, slowing down the opponent, outnumbering, and under numbering.

Level 3—Flexible switch from attacking to defending stage after the loss of the ball possession and also switch from defending to attacking stage after a successful application of pressing.

Level 4—Focus on a ball, search from a ball, attacking the player with a ball, double attack.

Level 5—Creation of a temporary local outnumber and time-space pressure, movement synchronization, movement to the game center and synchronized movement of the players block, density increase, avoiding the movement toward own goal, vertical movement, horizontal movement.

Level 6—Intentional creation of pressing situations, signal value of playing situations for the pressing application, identification of the pressing triggers, zone feeling, manipulation with space.

Level 7—Promptness to exchange the players' functions temporarily, rotation of the players, effective occupation of the playing area.

Level 8—Wide area modeling of the complex playing behavior for the desired pressing strategy, team coordination.

Every level of the pressing practice includes special playing actions unconditionally necessary for the development of this type of play, which is enriched by their mutual chaining and dimension of the tactic that focuses on coordinated cooperation of an individual formation of a block of players. As a more explicit example, we are presenting the characteristics of individual levels, which allow us to model the complex playing behavior, necessary for effective pressing application, by the use of an exercise manual.

Level 1, "ability to fight 1:1": we prefer the situations 1:1, 2:2, 2:1 in a narrowed area as a concluding step of the pressing practice, because it brings out the emphasis of the game body to body. High frequency of the solutions 1:1 in a narrowed area causes desensitization of the players toward time-space pressure and increases an effect of the solutions in situation of an individual enforcement, and it increases the willingness of the players to enter the physical contact with their opponent. An important moment is also the element of the defense activity, which is primarily focused on a ball. An intensive training work in situations 1:1 has a stimulating effect in a success in fights as well as basic self-esteem of a player. Moreover, the analogy with a match situation on a level of an individual player as well as experiencing the elementary pressure is compatible with the requirements of the trained type of play. An adaptation to the pressure in 1:1 situations and automatization of the moving part of the playing action are the direct effect of the exercises. The decisiveness and the pressure resistance are improving parallel, the need for self-enforcement increases, and the periphery vision improves together with the soft recognition of space relations either from the attack or defense point of view. An intensive training work on this level enables the players to optimize technical-tactical as well as conditional basis of the playing behavior in 1:1 situations.

Level 2, "occupation": focus on group-tactical behavior of the team after the loss of the possession of the ball, overall space closure in order to slow down the opponent's attack as much as possible, gain time, reorganize the team players' space positions, and form a defensive alignment of the team. The emphasis is put on the elements of the zone defense, the movement of the players in the area within the formation, approach to the players coming into the designated area. In addition, various forms of the preparatory games 3:2, 3:3, 4:3, 4:4, 5:4, 5:5 allow the players to play the game in outnumber or fewer number, which is a preparation for defensive play in outnumber in the game center with first signs of doubling, attacking the player with a ball, and space relocation in the direction of a ball.

Level 3, "switching": it represents an element of fast tactical thinking and playing action in which the players learn to perform fast mental and motoric switch from an attacking stage to a defending stage immediately after losing the possession of a ball. Fast switch to the defending stage right after the loss of the ball can take an opponent by surprise and increase an effect of the applied method especially when we apply attacking and immediate ultraoffensive pressing, because the opponent's defense didn't reorganize their attacking alignment in time.

Level 4, "attacking": in the pressing practice, the attacking definitely represents intermediate level of advancement in this type of play where the player with a ball

acquires a significant signal value. Owing to this, he becomes the center of the actively defending opponent's attention. On this level of the pressing tactic, all the action of the game is concentrated around the player with a ball, the players are systematically led to orientation toward the ball and this effort often leads to doubling the attack on the player with a ball in order to make this pressure a significantly disturbing element, which limits the quality of the attacked player's playing activity. The training exercises are an analogical tool on the level 2. However, the methodical-organizational configuration and the basic instructions are oriented toward an active attack on the player with a ball, double attack on him as well as overall orientation toward ball. We activate personal confrontations with the player with a ball in the center of the game. We are systematically leading the players to avoid the movement toward his own goal but to concentrate on gaining the possession of the ball while moving toward the opponent's goal instead. The imperative of gaining the possession of the ball, if possible by constructive gaining, is becoming the main motivation of the playing effort.

Level 5, "outnumber": on this level, we use play-tactical elements acquired by practicing the previous levels where the center of our effort is the focus on the center of the game either in a sense of densifying the area, vertical move, horizontal move, or in a sense of spacious occupation of the game center. We intentionally lead the players to define their physical presence in the area within the ball's distance and thus reach the time-space pressure on the player with a ball. By this, we create the specific groups of players who are in charge of the designated areas. Also we are trying to form blocks of players who spontaneously and situationally react to pressing situations by densifying and occupying the area directly near the center of the game. The success of these maneuvers will prevent outnumbering, and it'll help to maintain the number equality. Apart from this, we put the emphasis on the coordination of the players who are applying the pressing technique.

Level 6, "pressing situations": it's a higher stage of the pressing practice, because at this stage, we are already expecting successful handling of the previous stages and inclusion of tactical-movement maneuvers elements

PART 2

in order to manipulate the opponent intentionally and purposefully into moving to designated areas. The team, which is performing the pressing technique, is in these areas waiting the type of configurations that have a signal value for the team from the pressing release point of view. Besides this, the construction of the playing exercises and preparatory games is formed in such a way that it increases the players' sensitivity to the application of one of the pressing techniques in the predesignated zones and border lines (defensive, midfield, attacking, or immediate ultraoffensive). In this level, we already consider the zone feeling as a space feeling element that is necessary for an effective pressing management. At the training of this level, the players acquire the ability to differentiate the playing area strategically (significant from the course of the game point of view, game stages, and playing situations). They also learn to distinguish the basic zones from the inner point of view such as the perception of the playing area, which is reflected in specific technical- tactical actions of an individual player, block of players, or the whole team.

Level 7, "exchange of the players functions": this level represents situationally determined space transfer out of the designated player's function and promptness of the player to temporarily complete the playing tasks required in the area he is entering, whether it's defensive or offensive character of the task. The most common transfer is within the formation, but the most frequent movement in pressing is a transfer to a higher formation (e.g., from midfielder to attacker, from defender to midfielder) or a transfer by two formations (e.g., defender as temporarily defending attacker in attacking zone). The content of the training elements is the practice of this type of pressing or the promptness to perform it in the principal of new space relations in defensive repositioning of the team that is applying the pressing technique. By this, we don't mean the usual universalization of the players' functions. We mean the space universalization where the player can

handle a scale of the movement patterns and play chains when being transferred by one or two formations in vertical movement as well as in horizontal movement from the side to the center and vice-versa (mutual alternation) in a manipulation with space.

Level 8, "modeling": it's the most important stage of the pressing practice, because it's not only the completion of the whole training work done this way but also a stage that allows the coach to work with the team as a whole, and it enables him to model situations, which form complex playing behavior in specific situations as well as in specific chains of the player's actions. Last but not the least, it helps the coach to coordinate the team on a level of a block of players who are directly practicing the pressing technique or on the level of the team as a whole. The most significant characteristic of the pressing exercises used in this level is the construction of the exercises, which allows us to work with all the relevant elements and typical sequences of this type of play on the principal of modeling. The basic methodical tool used in this level is the simulatives exercises (SiE). Apart from creating a quite authentic playing context, they also stimulate the typical playing emotionality as a part of their construction and an effective coach's training.

It's obvious that taking into consideration the character and the contextual focus of the mentioned pressing levels, the variability of the playing requirements must be reflected into the quality of the construction of used preparatory games and other pressing tools. It's important to mention that in some training sections we will be dealing with an isolated practice of an individual pressing element while in the other sections we will be able to perform an accumulated practice of several elements, chains of playing actions or overall behavior in different forms of pressing. Also in this case, we recommend to keep the practice sequence and to transfer from isolated chains to complex chains that are enriched by match variability and authentic conceptuality of the game.

4.4 METHODICAL COMMENTS ON PRESSING TRAINING

Taking into consideration the presented play-tactical characteristics of pressing and assembled sequential algorithm for its practice, it's clear that the highest form of practice is overall modeling of play behavior in all its forms. This practice level is the completion of training acquisition of pressing tactics in which the skills construction is the domineering element in the principle of modeling the typical course of play behavior. The outcome of play diagnostics and the outcome of own team's analysis should precisely be the fundamental source for creating an effective training plan, which includes the application of the specific model elements for the practice and its proactive defense improvement. The typical methodical-organizational form, which is used when applying "the modeling" principal in training process is the application of simulative exercises (SiE) because they offer situations, which occur only in play context. The most significant requirement for the training process and the training skills is today definitely considered the application of modeling on the principle of an "adequate shielding." This provides maximum similarity of play situations and play sequences in a match and in a training process as well as an effective transition of required play style into the context of the match. Obviously, the match offers the best contextual inspiration for the training process, which is in the form of play structure and plenty of match details and microsituations that should be transmitted into the construction of the training process. Mourinho in the connection with this says: "Details make difference."

Several interesting practical fundamentals for pressing training process are offered by Peter (2010):

1. To develop **"the space feeling"** when practicing pressing.

2. To learn to **defend together.**

3. **Mutual communication** is important.

4. Defensive four-chain requires completely **different movement** than three-chain.

5. In **1:1 situations**, it's necessary to get the ball and the opponent player; it's important to keep practicing these situations.

6. In **doubling**, it's important to use the shortest and logical route.

7. When having a pair of defending players, it's important to keep the same alignment level so the depth alignment of the other defender creates space for the attacker neither too close to him (he would create space for the second attacker) nor too far from him (he wouldn't be able to interfere).

8. **Not to practice four-chain separately from the rest of the team.**

9. When a pair of players on the side is attacking, it's necessary **to close the central area** by the team's own alignment and to block the track of the possible dangerous pass into the central area.

10. **It's important for four-chain what the player does with a ball.**

11. The **function of libero** is partially transferred to a goalkeeper.

12. **By a movement, the defender forces the pass to get into the occupied central area.**

13. The position of **CB** securing **FB** is supposed to be according to the attacker's leg.

14. **To train in a situational and realistic way.**

15. The position of the goalkeeper in training forms should be like **CB** next to a goal not in a goal.

16. **Keeping an eye on details and accuracy,** closing tracks and creating pressure.

17. The point of view is different from zone defense and pressing, it's sharper on play situations and on creating signal situations.

18. **Cooperation between defense and attack** is important and so is common movement and overview of the situation.

19. Important **to coordinate the player's running** with the track of the ball.

Peter (2012) points out that "match writes the best training forms." Vermeulen (2003) in relation to the change of main orientation of the training focus says: "The biggest change was the match training. The training before looked like a working therapy without a specific intention. First, there was a conditional block then followed a technical block and a bit of tactics. The first block wasn't related to the second block and by end of the week you had completed a mixture of everything. That was all. However, the training ought to be done in order to perform better in a match. So a match is an essential guideline for training." High similarity level of authentic match contexts containing training elements is a necessary condition for required transfer from a match into training and vice-versa. Magath (2004) in connection to the content of the training process expressively says: "The players determine by their play what we will be coaching. The players equipped by weaker technical-tactical skills must compensate their playing handicap by an increased amount of running work!"

According to Kacani (2005), in order for the training content to become a model of the match, the practiced playing activities and sequences must be performed the same way as in a match. When the player understands what is expected from him in the play, the learning and transfer are becoming more effective. The transfer from the player's perception is not automatic at all. The players must realize the connection between the training and play situations, which occur in the game. One of the training process tasks is to create the conditions and stimulus in the course of the training, which enables the players to understand the essence of the play situations. Also it helps them to comprehend the course of the play sequences as well as their position in the stages of the game especially when the team isn't in the possession of the ball, and they are trying to gain it back. The modeling exercises have precisely the best supposition for this because they contribute to better understanding of space relations, position of the players in active play area, and the intentional manipulation with space in order to get the ball back into possession.

4.4.1 Basic Characteristics of the Simulative Exercises (SiE)

The simulative exercises (hereafter SiE) are considered to be the most effective methodical-organizational practice form of pressing tactics improvement (as well as attack management) and their algorithmization. SiE is the authentic expression for situational method in soccer. According to Kacani (2002), SiE understands the player's action in the play and his performance, which is influenced by the situation, as a compact element of learning and training in which appear individual motoric, psychical, physical as well as play-contextual factors on a different development level, but they always appear together. They represent a complex play stimulation focused on play performance increase. According to Marziali and Mora (2003), a coach should lay emphasis on play-situational exercises, which contain characteristic soccer elements (ball, team players, opponents, game rules, adaptation to the time, and space of the play, the use of the designated playing area and defensive or attacking action realization in the area in a specific time and so on) generated by the play confrontation, psychical pressure, and emotional involvement in the match context. Technical-tactical memory enables the players to recognize the situation, which they have already experienced in their training and helps them to transfer the situations almost instinctively into the match without any time loss when evaluating them and making tactical decisions. Although SiE are a new methodical-organizational form (for the needs of play preparation and improvement of an individual's performance as well as the whole team's), their importance is a logical impact of methodical trends focused on improvement of the ability "to play matches." They are the coaches' expressions to improve the effect of the training process, which is focused on purposeful influence of the course of the game, playing thinking, and consequently the playing performance within the situational method.

Classical specification of methodical-organizational exercise forms doesn't strictly define SiE, but the training practice "has discovered" them due to the necessity for improvement and stabilization of playing performance in defensive as well as in attacking stage of the team's play (Borbely and coli. 2001).

It's a methodical form of exercise within playing action range with changeable conditions in preparatory game or a team's own game. From the organizational point of view, SiE are very close to playing exercises. However, from the contextual point of view and from the point of view of relating SiE to playing performance in a match, they are closer to the play itself rather that preparatory play. They can be a part of playing training or more precisely, playing practice as well as the whole team's playing preparation. Especially due to "the modeling principal," it's possible to consider SiE as the most adequate reflection of playing and the most effective mean of transfer into the content of the match. The modeling principal in training process tries to imitate the outer features (movement characteristics) and inner features (mental characteristics) of the game context in the similar time-space match. It's related to all sports preparation elements: from physical to technical, play-tactical, and psychological. However, the core is definitely the play-tactical modeling focus and the repetitive replay of play situations and closed play sequences by which we deliberately create play-tactical configuration of the team. Apart from this, the modeling method also allows us to imitate the predicted play's conditions, way of playing as well as the opponent's playing resistance. Thank to this, we can already create in training the expected time-space playing conditions and solution to the type of play-tactical tasks, which the team will most probably encounter in a match with the next opponent. This way we will get the effect of the opponent's play "in advance" with all play-tactical impact. After the analysis of the opponent's play, it's important, in connection with this, to predict and apply such playing elements, which are applied into the course of play sequences in an appropriate time line and with natural variability. Their main advantage is that they develop complex playing skills by replaying the whole play sequence schemes and at the same time they include automatization aspect, improvisation, and creativity as a necessary defense and offense element. They are implicitly an impact and expression of the algorithmization level of the play. In other words, we can include the automatization aspect into SiE in a way that we offer the team players several alternatives (algorithmic processes and schemes and movement maps)

for solving identical play situation or play sequence. The choice of "ideal way" toward reaching the target in solving the play's problem stimulates the creative part of the player's personality. If the complexity of "replaying" the specific play stage is understood this way, the modeling exercises are significantly getting closer to preparatory play although the improvement of the complex playing action can have one-stage or multistage character. In this sense, we can also consider them as one-stage or multistage modeling exercises. SiE are, as a part of a special team's preparation for a play, applied in a play practice as well as in play training. They have a character of a situational playing preparation (similarly Kacani, 2005), and they represent integrated complex training focused on an improvement of the overall playing ability of a player or a team.

Apart from improvement and stabilization of technical and tactical aspect of playing action, SiE also enable formation of a chain and pragmatic combination from these aspects, which increases the performance potential of individual players, formations, and teams, and they offer more effective application of play-systematic intentions. They significantly profile the playing performance, and they fulfil the partial aspect of the game concept. It's important to include into the training similar elements, which create a confrontation similar to a match, and they reproduce emotions and pressure, which are similar to a match (Marziali-Mora, 2003). The inclusion of these training elements also improves (considering the complex playing ability) the players' resistance to a situational pressure similar to a match. In connection with technical aspects of playing performance, it's important to point out the specific possibilities of SiE to increase the level of dynamical as well as integrated technique. It means that by using these methodical-organizational forms, we don't only improve the basic technique, but we obviously improve dynamic-tactical aspect of playing performance too. The most important part of this, from the overall playing performance point of view, SiE stimulate the integrated technique level in a significant way. What does an integrated technique actually represent for the overall playing performance? It's the highest form of technical playing performance, which isn't subject to playing stress. It's exactly the level of automatization that allows the player to concentrate more clearly on understanding and reading the game, situation analysis, optimization of entering the play sequences comprehension of play context thanks to gaining longer time space for playing reaction. By creating so-called playing time comfort, we create conditions for game reading stimulation and better understanding of the game concept as well as preparation effective playing behavior of an individual, block, and the whole team. The automatization factor of performance technical part also enables to set "the player's concentration potential" to so-called contextual elements of playing performance (game reading, perception of relevant signs in situations, game understanding, perception of playing area, and the players' movement in the area, understanding of space relations, creating optimal solutions to play situations, entering play sequences in order to maintain the logic of their course, coordination increase of the block players, formations or whole team, and so on). Distribution of the player's concentration can this way be fully used for the needs of understanding the and the course of playing actions. The whole movement part of the technique is so significantly automatized that it doesn't require (not even in situations under massive playing stress) any special attention, and it helps the player to transfer its crucial part to reading and understanding the play as well as to making relevant play decisions in solving situations and in entering the course of the play sequences. Apart from that, it allows the player to follow the movement of his team players and opponents and it makes his playing thinking more effective, which reflect in increased effect of his playing performance. So it allows more effective entry into the course of the play and better game context (similarly Sivek, 2005) and effective participation in the course of the play. This technique level is related to integration of the game context and immediate connection to the course of the game.

According to Marziali a Mora (1997), SiE should lead the players in the area to being able to behave safely and most effectively in certain play situations. Unconditional didactical aspect is the logical connection of players' movement with tactical concept. By gradual defensive SiE enrichment, by attacking playing elements, keeping the play's continuation and continual change of basic play stages, this methodical-organizational form changes into multistage form, and it gets closer to those in team's own game or more precisely, modeled game.

Deliberate modeling enables individual players, formations, block, and the whole team **to improve the complex playing ability and playing action** with the focus on required defense or offense schemes. Besides that, they help with practicing the basic types of playing systems in individual game stages with the emphasis on specific details within the practice of individual stage, special playing tasks, or a particular playing situation. SiE imitate permanent playing situations to which the player systematically adopts and by required playing actions, he enters them and he learns to predict their development or course. The purpose of SiE is to create model match situations into which are deliberately included elements of team's game concept, anticipation of play configurations as well as play sequences proportionality of movement load adequately stimulates development of player's bioenergetics systems and it's more similar to conditions in a match. The extension of situational variability enables to create highly realistic match conditions and therefore it makes the transfer into the match easier. This way of shaping SiE represents a significant move toward imitating conditions of a match in training process. Based on imitation of play situations and tasks in the construction of training process, either from the point of view of bioenergetics match load or play-tactical complexity of solved tasks or situations in specific game stages together with the details of the whole playing performance of individual players, formations, blocks and the whole team, we classify SiE as one of the most progressive and the most effective methodical forms. Not only from the point of view of transferring the requirements into play-systematic characteristics of a team but also from the point of view of complex playing abilities of animations allowing game algorythmization (standardization—schematization) and creation of typical automatisms (game schemes) in a team's play. They enable to prepare the players for the conditions of situational unexpectedness, to improve and stabilize their playing performance in conditions almost identical to a game. The conditions imitated by SiE create a game context, which is similar to a match also thanks to typical match chaining and connection of play combinations. They also offer authentic logic of dividing the space for the typical game context and emotional stimulation similar to a match. At the same time, the character and individual players, we have methodically divided SiE into two main groups:

1. Preparatory SiE (one-stage) for defensive or attacking stage. They represent the type of methodical-organizational form, which offers the practicing players relatively authentic game context of the specific game stage together with changeable play-tactical tasks. It influences the situational variability in solving play tasks of model situations with an opportunity to work on details and algorythmization of the practiced stage or a part of the stage in connected play sequences. The strength of playing resistance can be set from minimum to maximum depending on the training aim, the practice of a specific stage or a part of the stage as well as the level of ability to practice the particular play scheme.

2. Playing SiE (multistage) with fluent course of the game with natural change of play stages. It's possible to characterize this type similarly to the previous type. However, in these exercises, we move from one-stage practice to continual retention of the course of the game with continual change of individual stages. Although these exercises have eminently playing character they are close to own game due to a continual change of play stages with the emphasis on play management elements, algorythmization, automatization, and the practice of the complex playing ability, which is set into the required play-system frame. In addition, thanks to its multistage preparatory SiE focus on simulation of play situations and creation of play-tactical tasks for a specific play stage playing SiE (as a logical conclusion of shaping the "ability to play") already include continual change of basic play stages (switching) and real features of a game course. According to Riva (Lucchesi and colleagues, 2003), the moments of gaining the possession of the ball or loss of the possession of the ball are one of the most important moments in a match where the way the team react in these situations is considered as crucial because it's related to the changes in playing mentality. SiE, as a methodical-organizational form, offers improvement of playing actions, which are necessary for the specific way of play as well as specific game context. In the context are also created authentic conditions for the development of complex players' playing ability on the level of an individual's playing performance; also, on character, we can very effectively improve

the part of the game where the stage change happens. In connection with this, we can state that the most important moments of the game are definitely related to the changes, which happen at the stages border and during continual transition from one stage to another, which we refer to as defensive or offensive switch (from attack to defense or from defense to attack). It's connected to the change of players' position in the area as well as the overall change of team organization. We mustn't forget about the changes related to mental switch of the players (in connection to a game stage), which are significantly stimulated by SiE. While the coordination level of formations, block as well as whole team. So it's a complex practice method for improvement and stabilization of the ability of the players "to play soccer" or more precisely, to perform in a real game context. SiE are comparable to preparatory play, but they are closer to a match, and they represent a complete fragment of a game with a significant imitation of a game course. Methodical aim of SiE is not to create only outer but also inner conditions for the improvement of complex playing capability. While motoric part of playing performance (skills and efficiency) represents the outer conditions cognitive requirements for the "play" (recognition of signal signs in play situations, their perception and mental processing and reading and comprehension of the play) represent the outer conditions. Training integration and entering the creating model by the application of SiE creates required the player's inner reflection (in the form of creating neutral nets movement maps) thus the brain compatible purpose of the training focus within the range of situational method is.

We can consider SiE as a training parallel of brain-compatible teaching in a specific game context. In the conditions of training preparations, brain-compatible training (hereinafter brain-com training) represents a complex approach to the training process, which concludes from the current knowledge about a player's brain character of the player's behavior. From the training focus point of view, it's therefore important that the training stimulus are coherent with the game's requirements in order to stimulate the creation and strengthening neural nets and movement maps for the play on the level of the players' central nervous system.

What we can consider as the most important thing, from this point of view, is to bring the training process closer to the game context and its content. In connection with this, Turek (2004) says that memory is a process and some type of reconstruction of various information blocks redundantly placed in different areas in a brain. For example, if we are watching a black and white or some other colored ball in a match rolling along the sideline, our brain processes separately, and it also concludes from the way the soccer player's brain stimulates itself and how it learns in natural playing conditions. If we really want to avoid professional folklore in soccer, the coach should have the knowledge of what happens in a player's brain and how it happens during the course of motoric learning and he should also know what is effective for the performance development and how to apply it in a training process. To understand the essence and SiE principal better, let's try to clarify in a short summary the core of brain-compatible training the way we understand it according to innovative trends in didactics (Turek, 2004). This type of training enables neurons to connect and create new neural nets or to strengthen the existing ones thus the playing actions became more effective as well as the the color, shape, movement, and location of the ball in a pitch in four different areas in the brain. These areas are connected in a neural net. If we add to this, the movement of the team players and the opponent players' positions, the neural net is widening and the image of the play situation must be again assembled in the brain into a new image (similarly Sylwester, 1997). However, the memory is not permanent, it falls apart and the brain forgets. For reaching the required sports performance, it is therefore important to slow down the break-down of movement-memory track. It slows down by the repetition of play elements because the necessary synaptic links between particular neurons are created by repeated playing or modeling in the training. The neural net is being formed, which is necessary for successful mental-motoric management of play situations, and their movement support is also being strengthened. The brain gains play experience, which is necessary for keeping the link between neurons. In a remarkable cycle of playing impulses and concluding playing reactions, the brain builds itself through electrochemical processes induced by their perception and experience. This way the neurons and their

synoptic links are activated and organized (similarly Conant, 2003). For the needs of brain-compatible training, we think it's appropriate to specify three basic "passions" of a brain, which are introduced by Cloniger (in Atakent, Akor, 2003):

1. searching for new,

2. searching for excitement, and

3. avoiding danger.

which influence the methodical aspects of a training process in a significant way. So if the passions of brain are supposed to be effectively connected through the training process, the training process should contain the trial of new elements (activity and creativity of the players), imitation of emotional satisfaction (enjoying the training), and creation of an environment without fear, worries threat (development of playing self-esteem). In every case, the emotions play a vital part in moko-training, because they relate to concentration and motivation of the players. Brain-com training prefers in the training process the principal of learning by trial and mistake, which stimulates the development of playing thinking. This is based on the principal of solving the game situations and involvement in solving the play sequences. The requirement to understand the game context based on the ability to analyze and evaluate its specific aspects as well as the ability to apply the desired playing behavior scheme is directly connected to deep learning in the training process, correct timing, feedback as well as linking the correct neurons and their formation into neural nets (similarly Turek, 2004). The principal of training by trial and mistake enables the players to find the correct playing solutions as well as to eliminate the incorrect ones. In addition, if we offer the players in modeling exercises ready playing solutions and desired course of the play, we enrich the element of experiments we minimize the mistakes. By this, the training process becomes significantly more effective, mentally more appropriate, and more effective from motoric point of view. Even if the motoric management is during the training unsuccessful, offered solutions are kept in the motoric map of the player and they can appear in an effective form during the course of the match context due to the successful mental training. For strengthening and confirmation of the training scheme of the desired playing behavior, it is necessary to repeat them continuously, improve them, and apply them in a real match context even if only in training conditions. Turek (2004) introduces the principals of brain-compatible teaching in a summary review from which we will try to conclude a few methodically relevant rules for applying SiE in the training process itself.

1. The brain is a parallel processor that carries out simultaneously more functions and activities depending on how it exchanges information with the environment. Recommendations for the training: The training stimulus should be variable, and they should be enriched by training in an environment with various methods and applications of varied organizational forms.

2. The search for the meaning happens through recognition and generating the pattern schemes. The brain has also tendency to look for pattern schemes. According to Hart (I 983), the pattern scheme is a real entity (activity, the process, system, and situation), which the brain that is looking for information can recognize by the signal points and keys (movement, shape, position, and signal signs of a situation). The more effective the brain is the more complex, softer and more detailed pattern schemes it can identify. The ability to recognize the pattern schemes enables the brain to choose an adequate program by which it manages and reacts to the specific situation. The search for the pattern schemes represents the way by which the brain is continuously trying to understand the meaning of a situation and the brain is able to consequently comprehend the sense of perceived information. Recommendations for the training: The training methods must conclude from a real game context. They should take into consideration the players' experience, they should be equal to the players' skills and ability, and they should be comprehensible from the players' point of view. The transfer into the match context is necessary otherwise the methods lose their essence.

3. Emotions have cardinal importance for the recognition and generating the pattern schemes. Recommendations for the training: The coach should create a favorable social environment, the atmosphere of mutual trust, and positive approach of the players toward the training process.

4. The learning includes conscious and unconscious processes. Recommendations for the training: In training process, we often learn more than we realize and the major part of the training stimulus is in our subconsciousness. That means that the training stimulation is already important when being applied and even unsuccessful solutions in the training have their purpose.

5. The brain understands and remembers best if the skills are stored in the natural space memory. Recommendations for the training: It's recommended to use the methods, which enable the players to create and imitate real play situations and the most authentic game context including modeling natural space relations for the play.

SiE are definitely one of the most progressive forms of imitating the match conditions in the training process, and they are also the most effective method of the play practice. They enable the players to experience the real play situations, improve the ability to solve the specific play tasks of individual players and formations, and they also help the players to shape the play-systematic features of the team's performance. Marziali and Mora (1997) suppose that the methodical training in this sense reproduces conditions, which are changing during a match, stimulates creativity and responsibility of players, supports higher sense of understanding and mutual respect, develops ability to enter the course of the play, analyze it, make a decision and act upon the decision.

The elements of this methodical form are based on transfer of the play requirements from training conditions to match conditions and vice versa. It directly participates in shaping parts of playing performance. SiE take into consideration the coach's philosophy to which the play-tactical context adopts. It's also necessary to take into consideration the play-typological ability of the playing material, which is currently available. The coach's assumption in connection with the playing potential of the team is often crucial because it helps to realize the play-tactical abilities of his own players. Taking into account especially the effect of the modeling exercises in training, they deserve a special place in current situational didactics of the training process and maybe even more detailed additional educational material on training method. Taking into account especially the effect of modeling exercises in play training, we consider "modeling of the training" by SiE as the decisive improvement form of the complex performance for the practice, the improvement, and stabilization of playing performance in the context of pressing tactics. Within the development of complex playing ability, modeling of the training includes all special configurations of impulses, which are essential for an effective play (individual movements, abilities, technical skills, tactical knowledge, psychological game elements-interaction, emotion, playing thinking, specific bio-energetic load, play-tactical complexity of the training impulses, and so on). Moreover, according to Krause (1993), SiE enable the coach to meet the requirement of preparing the particular patterns of thinking and performing for the players in the game context as well as abilities to develop their improvisational skills.

4.4.2 How to Work With SiE in the Training Process

For the needs of the training process, it is necessary to create such a system of SiE (Borbely and coli, 2001), which contains the required elements of the game. SiE enable to create an intentional game context in the training in which the players must use the stated play elements meaningfully. Thus, we will reach the desired level of the game's algorythmization and achievement of the play-systematic requirements of the intended play in individual stages. The systematic repetition of these exercises and work on details enables the players to build a purposeful playing performance of the team, which gradually gets the desired form. The script of the game is significantly becoming visible and gradually it's possible to move to more complex varieties in defense of attack without the tactical intention being slowed down by misunderstanding (tactical) or wrong (technical) performance of tactical tasks.

Apart from the required game context (auxiliary return pass, one-touch interaction, simple direct pass, direct pass to the third player, running into free area, fast relocation of the game center, and so on), it's important to also include into assembled modeling exercises a certain authenticity of the play situation in a specific stage of the play by replaying the whole defensive schemes or offensive sequences, which bring "real" variability of play situations from match. One of the biggest advantages of SiE is the space feeling development of players as an essential

condition of the play 'in space" and "with space." Understanding of the time-space logic, the position of the play in the time-space as well as the character of the physical load in a match creates realistic conditions for the level increase in complex ability to play soccer. Without being able to perform in a time-space manner when applying pressing tactics the defensive trend is difficult to realize in a "live match." For the game rules, which we want to show on the specific play situations, we think it's necessary to apply widespread modeling on the principal of replaying the defensive schemes from the attacking stage all the way to the goalkeeper's performance. In this form of the practice, it's important to take seriously management of the exercise from the space point of view as well as the work with details (movement timing, defensive manipulation with space, movement maneuvers of the players, temporary exchange of the players' positions, defensive coordination, and so on). The paradox of the training process in soccer is that except the players in direct contact with the ball most of the players move around the pitch for ninety minutes without the ball (but running "after the ball"). However, there is shockingly little attention focused on this movement "after the ball." That's precisely why the modeling of the movement without ball has deep importance in the training. SiE have proved to be effective elements in proactive defense practice, as well as attacking, because they increase coordination between participating players, improve space vision of the player himself and his team players, and they allow the play-pragmatic space inclusion in the playing area either in defense or offensive. Although the realization of the modeling situations in training doesn't always have to be successful, the functioning subconsciousness of the player perceives the similar solution varieties from the training, and it spontaneously finds new solutions in the game. The experiences of the players from training are important for the optimal solutions of the play situations because the play situations are often modification of the training model situations. For the needs of the practical use of SiE in the training process, we think it's appropriate to present the decisive signs of this methodical-organizational form.

Modeling exercise offer

- The scheme of the modeling situation, which is included into the construction of the exercise

- Stimulation of the required playing behavior of own team

- Preparation of the playing reaction as a typical advanced preparation for the opponents action

- Interactive-confrontational game context

- Real playing conditions, which we are expecting in a match

- Expected playing behavior alternatives of the opponent and modeling the types of the playing performance pattern schemes of own team

- Various levels of playing resistance when applying specific play conceptual intention

- Players' movement organization (movement around the game center, movement in noncenter areas, players' position, the ball's magnetism and breaking through the magnetism)

- Chance to improve the playing behavior in critical moments of the game immediately after losing or gaining the possession of the ball by improving the players' concentration and playing behavior directly at the moment of stage change

- Coordination of the ball's movement direction

- Comprehension of the time-space logic

- Solution of play tasks in micro-situations and macro-situations

- Emotional load in the game context in order to improve play-emotional intelligence (aggressiveness management and tactical patience)

- Emotional experience as part of the training process

- Breaking down the players' tendency to remain in "the comfort zone"

- Improvement of the players' playing intellect

- Playing conditions in the training process thus more effective transfer into the team's playing performance

The creation of play automatism by SiE must also take into consideration, apart from the basic coach's philosophy, the playing potential of the team and its typological composition. The practiced defensive movement schemes of the players in pressing tactic lead the players to the movement synchronization and tactical coordination when applying pressing. Thus happens pressing automatism and generalized pressing scheme, which provides the correct alignment of the players and their coordinated entry into pressing. The entry is not intentionally prepared but it happens by chance during the course of the game. In this type of pressing, where it's also about proactive defensive improvisation, the habits from intentional pressing are very useful. This is where the influence of the defensive automatisms and the ability of the transfer into coincidentally arisen situations are visible, as it is in spontaneous pressing. When constructing the SiE training process, the rule is: "We conclude from a match and we get back into a match. In training we try to do what we will be expecting the team to do in a match!" For the needs of the practical use of SiE in the training process, we offer the following sequence of the steps and rules, which are applied in pressing schemes playing practice:

1. **"Presentation"**—graphic presentation, computer animation of SiE before training, or visualization as a preparation for modeling.

2. **"Replay step by step"**—slow motion replay of defensive movement schemes of SiE in the middle circle by using the system of "throwing" so all the players of the defending team understand the time-space relation and their place in the active pressing zone.

3. **"Movement practice step by step"**—the beginning of the player's own practice by copying the pressing movement schemes in a real play area in slow motion.

4. **"Replay step by step"**—the pressing schemes replay in individual zones in real alignment and pace for the specific pressing type.

5. **"Play in real"**—the whole pressing sequences replay in real space and time in the conditions close to the game (number equality, authentic course of the game, and real play area).

6. **"Sharpening"**—match replay with the elements the automatization and enrichment by situational im-

provisation elements, work with details and the final drill of the specific pressing scheme.

The tactical training "on dry" or visualization of the play on a tactical board seems to be necessary for the achievement of the desired play-tactical ability of the player by SiE application. When practicing the particular play sequence, which is included into SiE, it's important to apply the form of the modeled game context in which the players authentically feel its situational aspects and they allowed "to experience" in training conditions the expected and the required playing reality of the match. The practice is gradually becoming more complex owing to the movement "realization" of the playing pressure "identical to a match." By gradual increase of the playing confidence when realizing particular ply sequence and after managing the basic movement schemes, it's allowed to let the players interpret the specific play situation as well as the choice of the play solution and the type of the maneuver, which is the most suitable for the particular moment. Apart from handling the movement and play-tactical tasks, this practice offers the players "insight" into the solution of the pressing situation or the course of defensive play sequence. It teaches the players the appropriate pressing behavior and enables them to comprehend the logic of team pressing and an individual participation the process (not only from the movement point of view but mainly from the mental: space relation, timing, intention of the play intention, coordination and so on). Another feature of SiE is that it offers the players specific defensive schemes with models of proactive solution of defensive play situations. In modeled the training, the players must often perform movement, which is suggested from the outside and it doesn't always correspond to their natural movement skills or their neural genotype and many impulses, which enter the game from the outside (defensive course of replaying individual SiE we often stop the play or we correct the course of the action and rewind it back to the section in which our solution wasn't compatible with our expectations or play intentions and consequently we correct the course of the sequence. Repeated replay "as on a video" and often "step by step" (slow motion) allows us to check the corrected solution, at the same time it fixes the required playing performance of the players

and it elaborates the practiced pressing schemes. When applying this form of practice, the coach should dispose of certain level of patience, not go mad at the players because of unsuccessful attempts, and he should trust "his" SiE. The match concentration and the tension forces the players to use some of the modeled solutions learned in the training which echo in his playing subconsciousness and movement map. Thanks to this game concept, game intentions of the team, preferred pressing tactic, and so on). Modeled training allows "to live" these play situations and "to process" the impulses from them in order to transfer them into the match. Precisely the modeling in training gives the player "the scheme for the match." This makes it easier for the player to understand the movement as well as the mental aspects of the game, specific play-tactical nuances of the desired play and also to prepare the neuro-physiological foundation of the playing performance together with complex play inclusion.

By repetitive replay of SiE, we create situational stereotypes in solving play situations and we increase the sensitivity of the players to the outer signs due to which they gain a signal value. During the the player often can instinctively use the solutions acquired in the training. At this moment, we are talking about the match transfer. The quality of the play solution and the situational suitability of scheme "modeled" from the training is the parameter of the contextual and constructional adequacy of the applied SiE. As Roxburgh (in Ames, 2015) says: "You need to teach the players in the training how to isolate the problems from the play and then to develop it; that's art. A well-trained eye is necessary for this." We can work with the defensive stage the way we work with the attacking stage, which is a logical conclusion of successfully handled pressing tactic; however, we must take into consideration its basic principles and "place" them into SiE focusing on attack.

4.4.3 Strong Emphasis on Small Details in Pressing Practice Training

The current training method of play-tactical practice is due to dominance of zone defensive principals and SiE preferences marked by a strong emphasis on work with detail in the training process. When practicing pressing, we are moving from thick features of movement coordination of the team's maneuvers (herd-initial group attack on the opponent representing the instinctive level of movement maneuvers) through coordinated cooperation (pack-formed and planned application of movement actions) to sophisticatedly detailed team synergy in pressing tactics application. The application of the movement maneuvers perceived in detail, which is based on individualization of position tasks in pressing position, requires and what he is meant to do there), which allows them to perform defensive manipulation of the opponent and at the same time secure the team's compactness when applying proactive defense.

In this connection, we can divide the work with details into team level details (movement maneuvers and their correct time-space coordination, topography of the movement in the specific pressing scheme, and position alignment for pressing) and details on a level of a player, who is participating in the pressing activity. Details on this level are represented by playing activity, which are adapted or modified for the needs to achieve the most effective participation in realized pressing defensive action.

The work with the detail of the "right" timing is a part of detailed approach when applying pressing tactics. It's a decisive adequacy precise knowledge of movement algorithm from the coach's side. It allows the coach to include the logic of this proactive defensive tactic into the construction of the training elements in order to enable the players to understand the structure of the movement schemes, their specific tasks in the application during the game and detailed demands on the player's playing activity necessary for the achievement of the conscious coordination in defensive team work. Detailed play-tactical topography of the defending players' movement and specific demands on the quality and the character of the playing activity contribute to their conscious coordination (concluding from the comprehension of the cardinal questions: where the player is supposed to move, when he is supposed to go there factor especially in the pressing

practice and its improvement. The right "timing" means the right moment for the preparation and pressing tactic application. If the pressing switch is applied too early or too late, it mostly influences the playing activity of the tactic in a negative way.

The details become relevant elements of the practice and its improvement, if the emphasis is placed on the playing activity and its correct inclusion into play-tactical context. In connection with this, Bruckner (2015) considers the pressing takeaway of the ball from the opponent as a constructive action, which has, apart from the technical part, the upgraded structure too. The upgraded structure is based on the speed of the playing activity and in the details perfection, which gives the game an extra value of the tactical coordination of the defending players at the right time. According to Bruckner, all playing activities of an individual moved to a higher dimension and together with the mentioned factors they represent the playing upgraded structure of the contemporary soccer. If the soccer upgraded structure is not respected in the training process, it can lead to a soccer mediocrity. Bruckner (2015) considers the work with details in today's modern soccer as the entirely most progressive element of the coach's work.

Strictly applied and followed defensive tactical principals, which were described in detail in the chapter about the theory of pressing (chapter 3), must also be part of the practice, acquirement, and improvement of the pressing tactics. In the part 3 (Practical manual for pressing) of this pressing trilogy, we will try to present the variable offer of the pressing training elements that will enable to create and fix the playing activity correctly. They are connected into a play-tactical chain of actions realized in the right space and mainly at the right time in order to create an effective pressing time-space. Rationally constructed training program for the practice and play improvement (not only in the defensive stage!) allows the players to eliminate playing ballast in the game context, and it increases the game's attraction and authenticity.

4.5 PRESSING PROGNOSIS

Waiting until pressing becomes soccer atavism is in a distant future of tactical horizon. It's difficult to predict which development reactions and play trends it will bring. The basic essence of trends lies in the fact that it should not be about devaluation of the game but its progressive transformation. So what is the direction of soccer development convergences?

1. **Synergization**—strategy and tactics improvement of individual players as well as the whole team enabling the application of conscious coordination of more players in order to multiply their performance.

2. **Conditional totalization**—optimization of physiological response of players when maximizing their physical load in a match.

3. **Game mentalization**—on a team level (team spirit, teambuilding) as well as on an individual player level (game reading and comprehension, play brain creation, mental training) focusing on support of team's and individual's performance.

4. **Global physiology**—focused on regeneration, drinking regime, diet and the application of the supercompensation in load dozing principal. Evolution of the game definitely won't stop, however its direction is influenced by the coaches who bring something new into the game and they move the game into another dimension. Sacchi (in Wilson, 2008) says: "As long as the humanity exists, something new always arises. Otherwise, soccer would die."

If we want to get to the core of soccer evolution, we can apply the generally accepted knowledge that one of the inner from the game directly emerging mechanisms, through which partial and radical changes happen in the game, is continuous confrontation of attackers and defenders, which shows significant signs of algorithmization despite stochastical course of the game. An effort of teams to beat each other is an innovation source of expressive means of playing in the whole range of sport performance in soccer, starting with its anatomical, physiological, and psychological aspects and ending with sociological aspects.

So it is obvious that both game stages, defending and attacking, participate in mutual improvement of the game by which the game of soccer internally ensures its own development. Defending versus attacking is present everywhere in the game, and it's a mechanism, which is naturally involved in the game and which spontaneously influences the game's natural development. We can't say that this development is not managed because coaches, specialists, and experts catalyze it, speed it up, and assist it. However, this mechanism isn't possible to take out or remove from the game, neither it is possible to ignore it because it concludes from the fact that the game is played with one ball and the players (if they want to be successful) must fight for it. Supposition of the game development in its quality level increase trends is to keep the balance between attacking and defending stage of the game or between the attack and the defense, taking into consideration the fact that it's possible to defend in attacking stage and to be offensive in defending stage (proactive defense form). In other words, we know today that the imaginary border between attack and defense doesn't overlap game stages border but in each stage is also the nucleus of the other.

Sketched historical parallels of pressing show that coaches must also develop together with the game. They are the initiators and trendsetters who create game changes. We are not far from the truth if we say that soccer balances its own evolution by pressing tactics application.

Hegemony of pressing in defense stage in present shows us that **the principal of defensive proactivity is becoming one of the play domains of soccer in the moment of losing the ball and fundamental mean for its regaining through defensive aging.** The proactivity principal is natural for attacking game stage even if some concepts use it only for keeping the ball and the motive of its deep direction is overlapped by other play-tactical intentions (e.g., game management). In contrary, proactivity in defense is exceptionally evolutional level involving the play by application of pressing tactics as well as an impulse for management changes, building and in the end, the attack finalization (postpressing stage). **Evolution of the game is clearly showing that, from development point** of view, the defending stage is more likely to react and its changes are an impulse for the change of attacking ways.

Ethos of pressing doesn't represent all consuming principal, which fills the play area by monothematic content, but it represents generalized way of regaining the ball in the most suitable time-space conditions even with the highest possible motoric and mental effort; however, the reward doesn't always have to be "sweet" and can even cause real disorder in their own ranks.

Let's try to sketch out the shortened direction prognosis of the game evolution including pressing. The future of the play direction related to pressing tactics leads to combination of block defense in the midfield zone or near the half-distance line to which the pressing conclusion is connected (middle and offensive pressing). After a successful application of pressing tactics follows postpressing offensive conclusion directly into the area of the biggest play resistance or through vertical area, prefinal conclusion of offensive sequences directed to the center and passes to approaching team players directly into the penalty area.

Active play area depth was changed by changing the basic defense manner and frontal transfer to space defense. Active play area depth was significantly shortened from 50–60 m to 30–40 m and, in near future, it will continue shortening even more toward reaching pressing optima 25–30 m. Implemented way of play will change by this too, because it will demand from players to work intensively in a very small and tight area. Time-space parameters will also change. For breaking down defense blocks, they will require conscious coordination of more players offering multialternative solutions of game situations especially behind the defense line by applying timed start-ups for the defense. It will bring a significant change in habits connected to the change of basic players' movement. There will be increased demands on visual space check, its correct perception relating to tactical pragmatism and realization of fast play decisions. Play reactions to defense pressure will be solved by speed parameters of the game requiring fast withdrawal from the pressure, maximum center dynamization, forceful ground passes, and increased number of players starting-up for the defense. The type of players, who will be employed, will be primarily the fast type of players with necessary

dynamics-technical skills, with the right touch for game situations and time-space parameters of the game. It will be an unconditional requirement for effective and safe breaking down compact and flexible defense blocks, which are able to transfer into more effective pressing than it is today. Recent multiyear pressing development will probably move toward higher improvement. In connection to pressing, there will be greater importance in fast switching, which will enable prompt pressing tactics implement, and it disable the opponent to create an effective defense position in time. We are expecting more significant inclusion of midfield defenders into active offensive together with side defenders even in opponent's penalty area.

It will be more efficient and convenient to run into the area rather that to sustain it the area and wait for the action. Attacking is better if you have the area behind you than if you are already in the area. An important areal rule for the attacking players will also be the willingness to create an area for team players by own movement work. It will be similar if defensive stage too where the player who benefits from the movement work doesn't necessarily have to the player performing the work but the player directly included into pressing activity. We suppose that the important tactical activity will be a conscious space manipulation and application of similar screen mechanisms as in basketball.

Obviously, the changed requirements of the game will inevitably have to be transferred into the timeless methodology with changed aims and into the content focus of training process in order to enable the creation of the required way of playing. The importance of timelessness and updated technology will allow young players to prepare for soccer in the nearest future. We expect there will be a preference in the use of brain-compatible training, which will support correct play reactions in a match and make it more effective. Practical impact should be model exercise orientation, which can help players to develop complex play skills and to transfer these skills more easily into the match.

We can't guarantee the predictive validity of our prognostic theory because the principal of self-development of the game can still influence the direction of the game evolution in a surprising way. Based on the historical parallels, which are presented in the historical part of this volume and on own empiricism we are offering the presented development model. Its validity will be proved or disproved in the next few years of the game development. However, in every case, we believe it will be a positive stimulus to consider and it might also catch attention of those who directly, in their everyday coaching practice, coparticipate in creation of new personal philosophies and concepts while they have no idea that they have become (or will become) part of natural evolution process of the soccer game.

Important factor of the game self-development is the ability of teams to learn to play and react to new trends which stop being progressive at that moment and the teams can be resistant toward them. This is the moment when something new and progressive must appear in the scene. The same applies to pressing which, however, has been developing for longer time than some other progressive elements of the game but it shows that even the best pressing is playable. Thanks to good quality deep analysis of the game and follow-up adjustment of the training process content, teams are finding an effective pressing fighting tool (pressing resistance, ability to play under pressing, play resistance toward pressing). By this, the team's tactical effect is beginning to decrease significantly because the other teams are able to deal with it much more successfully than they were in the beginning. Together with positive aspects of the use of pressing, pressing also might to be abused, which can lead to its development decadency by "killing" the game.

Considering the fact that pressing is only one of the important components of tactical portfolio of current teams we mustn't forget about conditional skills of the players. In current soccer, physical parameters of the players are acquiring the form of modern gladiators enriched by technical skills, which were in the past a distinguishing mark for "technical" players, speed parameters of applied movement regime, and the contextual speed of playing. Playing performance must be compulsorily enriched by tactical potential enabling the player to apply the most effective playing activity set into the game's continuity at the right time and the place in order to provide efficiency and safety of the teams' play.

When presenting pressing in more sport areas, we found out that more of them hide within themselves rules, which

stimulate development of the game process and prevent the game's direction going toward game-tactical regress, which can sometimes threaten the evolutional direction of the game. Maybe the soccer itself could bear some of these play restrictions in the future, however, they would have to be applied with exceptional sensitivity in order not to disrupt the natural essence of the game.

Restriction of a goalkeeper's play is used in futsal, which is relatively closest sport to soccer. The result is the necessity of improving the contra-pressing play skills. However, the skills must be creative and gained on level of technical ability applied in the play under pressure as well as on strategic and tactical level of solution choices for play problems, which players with a ball encounter when their opponent is applying pressing.

Basketball is another sport in which the open confrontation is clearly supported by the rules. Time limit for attack is one of the play restrictions. The rule "over half" means that after the attacking team crosses over to the opponent's half of the court the players can't return the ball into their half. By this, the time and space for passive play is restricted, in other words defending by stretching the time and hiding the ball in a large area from attacking players. It happens often in soccer that technically and tactically advanced team, after scoring a leading goal, is able to hide a ball from the opponent by carrying out uninteresting sequence of passes while using the whole playing area. The rules allow moving the game center backward even 50 m, all the way behind the basic line. Imagine where basketball would be, if the rules allowed this. If we want battles and if we want to support pressing effect, we should consider the playing area restriction or time restriction in authentic offensive as it is in handball. In handball, if you don't make an attempt to score a goal within the time limit, arbiters will take your ball.

Forechecking in hockey is supporting rule about icing. Hockey players, who are pressured by forechecking, can't just simply shoot the puck into the attacking zone, skate across the whole ice-rink and continue fighting in the opponent's defending zone. Who would then apply forechecking, if they knew that it's most common effect is that the whole formation has to lawfully return into their own defending zone after opening forechecking? Another important space restriction, which supports personal battles in hockey in the defending zone, is the rule of offside, which becomes effective after pushing the attacking team out of the zone. This way, the attacking team is forced to go through many battles in the attacking zone without the ability to release themselves from pressing pressure by returning to neutral zone.

Ball games were always an inspiration for pressing in soccer. These days, it doesn't only have to be basketball or hockey but mainly, soccer's younger brother, futsal. Game speeding, open confrontation of pressing, and contra pressing in futsal were achieved by applying the rule, which restricts number of goalkeeper's contacts with a ball passed to him by his own team players within one action. This way, the pressing has green light. An inspiration to consider for soccer could be an idea of further change of the game rules, which would make the game more attractive. However, the natural essence would remain, so it wouldn't become a different game than the one we are used to...

When drawing up the soccer prognosis, we must be aware of the fact that whatever play-tactical schemes, which worked and were progressive at the time don't have to be that effective and progressive as the time goes due to inner condition changes. In other words, what is effective today is strictly based on yesterday and it doesn't have to be valid tomorrow. And precisely this circumstance must be respected by whatever strategic vision of game evolution.

Final Word on Part 2

The trilogy of pressing is conceived thematically in the order of history, theory, and practice on purpose because historical roots of pressing offer content completion of the evolution process as well as understanding its theoretical foundation. Theoretical aspects, also thanks to history, enable the understanding of the key pressing tactics elements and allow their painless implementation into the game concepts of top teams. Theory of pressing, supported by its history, allows effective transfer of this knowledge into applicable form in the training process. It is the form of constructing effective skills and meaningful training programs and also in tactical preparation of the team, by application of the pressing tactics in play concepts based on comprehension of the essence and usage of pressing in team strategies. Something was already indicated in connection with this by Milutinovic (in Vienna, 2007) when he said: "We must respect soccer of the past we must study soccer of today and we should predict the game of the future."

PART 3

HOW TO DO IT—
A PRACTICAL MANUAL FOR PRESSING

FOREWORD TO PART 3

Every first rate sporting event (World Championships, European Championships, the Champions, and European League matches) bring about something new and trendy, which consequently influences any further direction of soccer. No developed soccer nation can afford to ignore soccer trends, they cannot dwell on traditional preparation concepts and not to take into account the evolution of soccer performance.

Team performance is the face of every coach. Playing styles present the philosophy, character, and ambitions of a coach. Everybody wants to win, everybody wants to be successful, but the journey to such success is sometimes illogical, unrepeatable, and in many ways very different from the prescribed steps, rules, and methods.

In the defensive action of top performing teams, the rigorous narrowing and compact defending of space is apparent and clearly visible through coordinated movement of the defensive block in width and depth of the soccer field. Such prerequisite must be met by every team irrespective of the system of play they present.

On the basis of several analysis, one may assert, that the actual result is mostly determined by the transition phases, i.e., the reaction and conduct of team players after winning the ball, their effort to finish adopt defense positions as fast as possible. This ongoing development trend has become an inherent part of the playing concept in most soccer teams on every level and we should not forget that in the actual training process.

Today it is harder to train than it was not so long ago. Players have more merit, better quality, they are by far more capable and versatile. Soccer is being dynamized, the frequency of recurrent short term and highly intensified actions is rising, often even in incomplete convalescence conditions. competition, in the home league, or in Slovakia, naturally had to be displayed in the training process. Their overall number, volume and the actual intensity has decreased. During this time period, an important role in the training units was largely played by preparatory, modeled and guided plays, with the main goal and focus to win the ball in a constructive way, and thus creating conditions for own offensive action. In

preparatory games, 1:1, 2:2, or 3:3 situations prevailed, in which we put stress on well-managed personal duels, dynamic technique, and situation solving under space and time pressure. Players were led to greater concentration, compactness, team play, and mutual coaching.

Michal Hipp during training

From my own experience, I must assert, that practice and improvement of these game phases is not at all so simple, and it requires a quality and responsible preparation, proficiency, and preparedness of the coach. My own coaching experience confirms in me in my conviction, that one of the outstanding assertions to becoming successful in matches is quality training process, and also thanks to such a process we have made it, under the leadership of Vlado Weiss, to a title, up to the group phase of the Champions League. Transition phases in our game strategy play an important role and, therefore, we paid attention to them in our training units quite frequently. As a result, we were in this action, in confrontation with teams such as Celtic Glasgow, in matches with top European teams, predominantly in our center Partizan Beograd, FC Porto, Inter Milan, or Glasgow Rangers, more than an even opponent. Match utilization in the European competition, in the home league, or in Slovakia, naturally had to be displayed in the training process. Their overall number, volume, and the actual intensity has decreased. During this time, an important role in the training units was largely played by preparatory, modeled, and guided plays, with the main goal and focus to win the ball in a constructive way, creating conditions for own offensive action. In preparatory games, 1:1, 2:2, or 3:3 situation prevailed in which we put stress on well-managed personal duels, dynamic technique, and situation solving under space and time pressure. Players were led to greater concentration, compactness, team play, and mutual coaching.

I must mention, that in domestic matches, we often started our pressing situations deep in the opponent's field, and, on the contrary, in matches with top European teams, predominantly in our center zone. It depended on the quality of the opponent and the perception of our goal's safety. As to the actual use of pressing defense, we tried to create conditions for speedy ball winning and, at the same time, to put a space and time pressure on the opponent.

The training process with the representation, in contrast with the work in the club, had different specifications. While on the club level, you had the players available practically twenty-four hours a day, in a national team, it was only in prescribed association terms. Representation players came to meetings from different clubs, different national competitions, with different playing schemes, tactic, or with a different way of play. Therefore, we tried to communicate with them, talk to them, make it a means in order to maximize the training process. One of the advantages was a greater play quality, and the actual play intelligence of the players on such a level. A highly robust and healthy team was put together, which made it all the way to the quarter finals in the World Championships in South Africa in 2010. I think that the team formation stands and falls on good communication at all levels.

For my team, transition phases and the pressing defense system are important means of defense tactic at winning the ball back. Simply stated: we reply to our opponent's attack with an attack of our own. The basic task is to win the ball, and that is without returning to our own goal, while we put emphasis on the defensive forward movement toward the focal point of the game. In switching, or in changing from attack to defense, I try to highlight to the players the fact,

that only by our active play we can force the opponent to making a mistake that can result in the opponent losing the ball. In the actual championship matches, our pressing zone usually begins at the first part of the center zone in attacking position. In this part of the playing field, we try to put pressure on the opponent by pressing toward the sidelines. Toward the back, we must be constantly organized in order to be able to prevent any opponent's surprising contras. Our training process contains different types of preparation drills of passing, with the focus on forcefulness and straightforwardness of the passes and on the passing technique. For increasing the effectivity and success of team play in small space, to the preparation part, I add different types of positional drills in small space with a smaller number of players (3 or 4) + neutral players (2 or 3), who are limited by their number of touches. Within the scope of play training, once or twice in the weekly microcycle, I use the modeled play on three thirds with temporary overnumbering in the particular zones. At the winning of ball, I try to lead the players to a simple, speedy, and most of all a straightforward attack. Here, accuracy is inevitable. With all the training drills, I try to constantly communicate with the players, lead them to thinking about the particulars. I find the actual outcome of methods or training drills very important.

We live in a time, when a flood of new information many times exceeds our time and technical possibilities. Internet is an essential tool of us, coaches. I am thankful for the publication *All About Pressing in Soccer*, that was made complete, after having provided historical roots and pressing theory, by a practical pressing manual, which brings the topic of pressing into the training experience with a wide scale of drills on individual level, groups of two, three, four, formations, and blocks of players, as well as on the level of the entire team.

Fellow coaches, let's not be afraid to "steal" good ideas, know-how and methods! None of us are perfect, we are all constantly learning. Knowledge, understanding, and handling the system of pressing defense is one of the basic prerequisites of success in match conditions. Today's soccer requires all the involved a great deal of effort, functional preparedness, and concentration. The dynamic growth of trends in soccer must legitimately effect the appropriate organization and handling of the training process.

–Michal Hipp
Former coach of the Slovak national representation

5.0 A WORD OF INTRODUCTION TO THE PRACTICAL MANUAL FOR THE PRACTICE AND IMPROVEMENT OF PRESSING

In the practical manual of exercises, we have included several exercises for pressing practice at every level, by which we do not want to limit the creative abilities of users and their attention to the exercises offered. We assume that the exercises offered by us will only serve as the initial introduction and aid to which every user will add their own ideas and creativity in constructing their own training means for pressing practice and improvement. Most exercises presented are practically verified in training experience of trained teams by improvement of the pressing play approach. Unusually large attention, in the scope of detailed description of exercises, we dedicate to their organization, course and nevertheless to the methodical-organizational notes, which enable us with the effective usage, correct application, and nevertheless their correct understanding.

Considering the final motive being the practice and improvement of the pressing tactics, we focused mainly on presenting the higher forms of exercises (pressing training level 5, 6, 7, 8), oriented on the play-motion cooperation of three- and fourchain formations, blocks, and the entire team. However, in the book edition, we devoted ourselves to elementary exercises (pressing training level 1, 2, 3, 4) for the development of pressing tactics for individuals, groups of two, groups of three, and groups of four, that is undoubtedly of great importance for perfect pressing handling.

In completion of exercises, we have not forgot about the present elite stars of pressing, who may offer an interesting and inspiring contribution to crossing one's shadow of knowledge and move to creativity and imaginativeness in creating their own training repertoire for the practicing and improvement of pressing strategies.

5.1 PRESSING ON AN INDIVIDUAL LEVEL

Play Practice and Improvement in 1-on-1 Defense

Play in 1-on-1 situations, attacking a player with the ball, increasing resistance in duels, methodology, and didactics

1-on-1 Play Meaning for Pressing in 1-on-1

1:1 play in constricted space is preferred as the base point to the practice of pressing, because it accentuates contact play. The basis of every defense tactics is 1-on-1 play. Individual tactics has great meaning in soccer and, therefore, it is very important, from a young age, to consistently devote oneself to practice and improvement of conduct in duels.

Practice of conduct in duels should start in juvenile age. In youth soccer coaches like to pay attention to the training of the basic techniques, but the practice of duels is neglected and the 1-on-1 play meaning is undervalued. Integration of duel practice to the training units of children and youth should not cause problems—it depends only on planning, organization, and motivation. Children like to compete and only need time, opportunity, and interesting fun ways and means of training to acquire the principles of successful conduct in duels. Efficient and successful conduct in all player combat is the basis of every play system. System of the game without correct conduct in combat is not effective. Skillful and responsible approach to situation in 1-on-1 is the bottom line of individual and group tactics, as well as the tactics of the entire team. The team that wins most combats usually wins the match.

Features Important for Success in Combat
FITNESS:

Physical endurance, efficiency, and stamina—agility—speed (reactive, athletic, starting), coordination and strength (appropriate muscular body strength, especially of the upper part and midpart of the body, the so-called core and dynamic strength of lower limbs), stability and balance

TECHNICAL:

Movement without ball, running technique (forward, backward, sideways, turns, changes of direction and running speed, moving on the front part of feet, step shortening, legs slightly bent, lower center of gravity, firm body, lateral body position). Jumps and falls and their timing.

TACTICAL:

Copying opponent's movement, space selection, ball watching, rival with ball and own net line movement, not to fall in to rival's cheater moves, "studying" the rival (his weaker and stronger leg, his tricks, and his frequent ways of bypassing and solving combat situations), ability to create pressure on the rival and the ability to lead (influence) rival's movement direction (pressure him "outside" or "inside"), ability to decide when to slow down or stop the rival, when to take over the ball, defensive cheating maneuvers, keeping appropriate distance from rival, ability to synchronize individual tactic with defensive block performance principles and team tactics, switching defense and offense performance (and vice versa).

PSYCHOLOGICAL:

Focus, will, positive aggression, decisiveness, courage and willingness to take risks, confidence, anticipation, a sense of awareness and fair play, comprehension of game situation, good spatial orientation. The goal is to quickly apprehend, take in, and grasp the diversity of combat situations, to know and to handle how to solve them in order to get the ball and switch to offense activities.

Connecting Individual Tactics in the Context of Team Tactics

Team play concept:

- game tactics in defense, ways of ball acquiring

- pressing on team level

- creating (blocks of two to four, even five)

- pressing on group and formation level.

DUELS (1:1) Pressing practice and improvement methodology is focused on increasing quality of basic play elements presenting given pressing levels. The higher the standard of pressing making individual components, the higher the quality of pressing in entity, meaning entire team pressing. Therefore, game analysis is an important part of the training process development, and it should respect the team needs. Practice and improvement methodology should focus on improving the weakest links for building pressing conduct in a particular team. Every level of pressing practice includes special play activities, enhanced in mutual chain building, and a tactical dimension focused on coordinated cooperation in a particular formation or block of players. These enable, with the use of an exercise register, the forming of complex playing performance necessary for effective inducing of pressing in the game.

In light of the character and capacity focus of referred pressing levels, it is clear that the diversity and variability of play requirements must be projected in the quality construction of prep games and other training means used. It must be noted that some training means concern isolated practice of individual pressing units, while others enable accumulated practice of several elements, or more precisely game activity chain practice and overall playing performance in offense or midfielder pressing. In such case, we recommend keeping the practice sequence and going from isolated chains to complex chains enhanced by match diversity and authentic game context.

Practical Means for Pressing Practice and Improvement on an Individual Level

DRILL 1: WINNING THE BALL IN OPEN SPACE

Drill aim and focus: technique and game tactics in 1-on-1 (pressing drill level 1, 4).

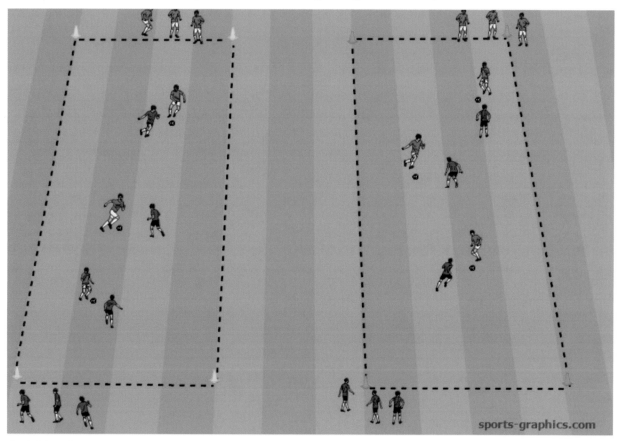

Fig. 5.1-1 Duels 3 × 1-on-1

PRACTICE ORGANIZATION:

- Two rectangles the size of 15 m × 20 m, placed next to each other.

- Create four groups of four to six players.

- Two teams in one rectangle.

- Teams split into two groups, at 4 to 2+2, at five-member groups to 2-3, and at 6 to 3+3.

- Groups take turns at exercising.

- Two to three players from one team form 1-on-1 with two to three players from the other team.

- They exercise in both spaces at the same time.

- They alternate after every action.

DRILL FLOW:

- Every player of one group has a ball.

- Game 1-on-1 starts at coach's signal.

- Players of the defense group attempt to take the ball from their opponents.

- After taking the ball, they immediately switch roles.

- After thirty seconds, at the second coach's signal the drill is over.

- Competition: which team wins more balls.

- Other two to three players from every group step up.

METHODICAL-ORGANIZATIONAL NOTES:

- Charge 30 seconds, rest 30 to 40 seconds, repeat several times (according to the players' capacity).

- We pay attention to the correct technical and tactical duel conduct.

- We can dose charging by repeating several series, and in breaks we correct shortfalls in solving duels.

DRILL 2: CROSSING LINES AND ON SMALL NETS GAME IN A SQUARE

Drill goal and focus: play in 1-on-1 situation, bypassing the opponent, attacking the player with ball, increasing resistance in duels, switching from defense to offense activities, and vice versa (pressing drill level 1, 3, 4)

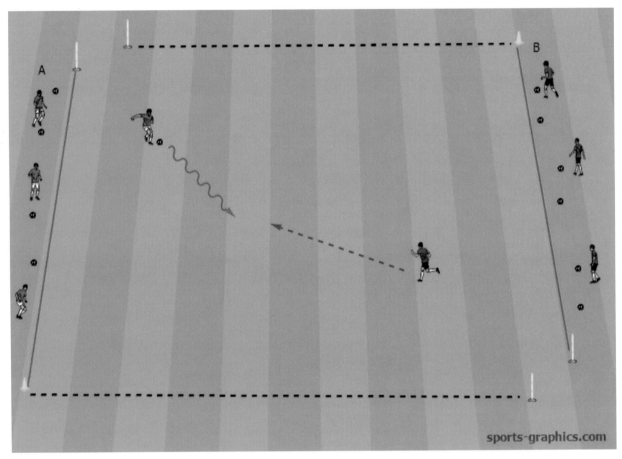

Fig. 5.1-2 Game on small nets and target lines

DRILL ORGANIZATION:

- Square the size of 20 m (15 m), two opposite sides make up target lines.

- Two small nets are placed in the corners of the playing field.

- The coach appoints two equally strong groups "A" and "B" that are positioned against each other behind the target lines.

- Every player in group "A" has a ball.

DRILL FLOW:

- The first player in group "A" dribbles to the square and in a 1-on-1 situation tries to lead the ball over the opposite target line or to achieve a score in the small net (=1 point).

- When player B acquires the ball, his task is to lead the ball over the opponent's target line or to score (1 point).

- The drill lasts 30 seconds. The game continues after achieving a score, or in case of the ball getting out of the square (we use spare balls).

- After 30 seconds, the next pair immediately starts a new action.

- The game is organized as a two-team competition.

NOTES:

- Game 1:1 resembles match conditions, because a player in defense should prevent his opponent to come around him and at the same time not to allow a vertical pass.

DRILL 3: GAME 2 X 1-ON-1

Drill goal and focus: duels in lateral position (pressing drill level 1, 4)

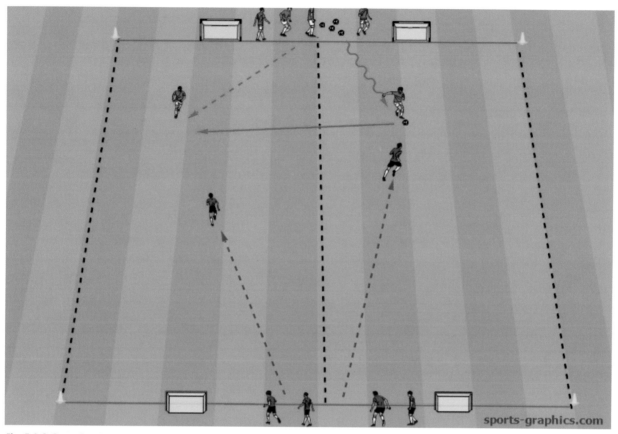

Fig. 5.1-3 Game 2 × 1-on-1

DRILL ORGANIZATION:

- Two playing fields the size of 20 m × 10 m next to each other.

- On the shorter sides in every field, there are small nets opposite to each other.

- In every field, there is one defender against one striker, staying on one-playing surface, they must not cross to the other playing field.

- The other players are outside the playing field.

- Spare balls are prepared next to the field.

DRILL FLOW:

- Offender starts the drill by leading the ball to the playing field (or the coach by passing the ball to the striker).

- Defender runs against the striker with the ball and in a 1-on-1 game. He tries to prevent him from escaping

and scoring in the net, he tries to press him outside the playing field.

- At the same time, a striker and a defender run into another playing field.

- Striker with ball has the opportunity of individual 1-on-1 action or to cooperate with another striker in the neighboring field.

- If he passes the ball to his teammate in the neighboring field, a duel follows in the other playing field.

- After getting the ball, the defenders have the same options to attack the opponent's net individually or in cooperation.

- After two minutes, two new pairs start a new action.

COACHING:

- Defender is off against the striker to keep him as far as possible from his own goal.

- Not to attack the opponent frontally, but placing oneself into the lateral position already 3- 8 m ahead (the distance depends on the opponent's speed).

- Stop moving forward in time and try to catch the speed and direction of opponent.

- Keep distance from ball.

- Move with identical pace and in the same direction as the opponent and attack the opponent in the right moment.

- Defenders in lateral position try to press the striker outside the playing field, to block their way to their own net and at the same time to get the ball.

DRILL 4: 1-ON-1 IN SEVERAL PLAYING FIELDS WITH SHIFTING

Drill goal and focus: play in 1:1 situation, opponent bypassing, attacking player with ball, defending a particular space and line, hints of zone comprehension (drill pressing level 1, 4)

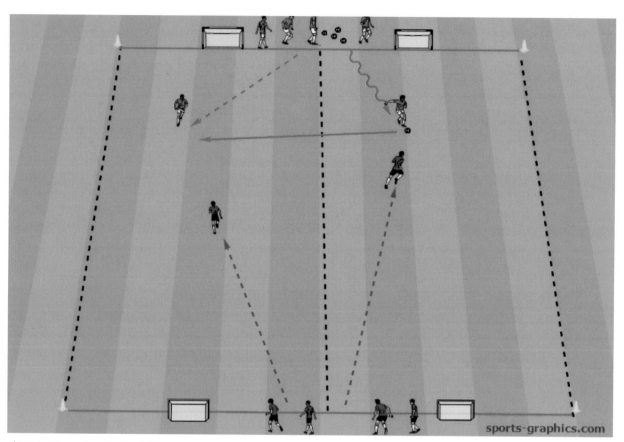

Fig. 5.1-4 Game 1-on-1 with shifting

DRILL ORGANIZATION:

- Space along the halfway line is split into small playing fields with the size of 16 m × 8 m.

- Pairs of equal strength are placed in the fields.

- Prepare enough spare balls to ensure a smooth drill.

DRILL FLOW:

- Player with ball leads the ball to marked space, that is being actively defended by a defender starting from the center line, and tries to prevent the player with ball from taking it across the marked zone.

- If the bypassing is successful, the player with ball continues to another playing field.

- If the defending player gets the ball, he continues with the ball to another playing space, and the player that lost the ball stays as a defending player in that playing space.

- This way the player passes through all the playing spaces.

- Defending players cover first one and subsequently the other half of the marked playing space.

METHODICAL-ORGANIZATIONAL NOTES:

- Defending players need to be reminded, that they have to head out from the halfway line and start attacking the player with ball immediately after his crossing the marked space line and address stealing the ball no later than when the player with ball crosses the center line.

- In the drill, we focus on heading out against the player with ball, on consistent attacking and body on body play, as well as creating zone comprehension in the defense player.

- Attacking opponent with ball, contact with opponent, as well as to perform the actual stealing at full speed and match verve.

- We pay attention to correct duel performance.

- Shifting of players with ball is used to free up the defending players and taking the starting position on the halfway line.

DRILL 5: 1-ON-1 PLAY IN LENGTHWISE SPLIT SIXTEENTH

Drill goal and focus: practice and improvement of duels in frontal and lateral position (pressing drill level 1, 3)

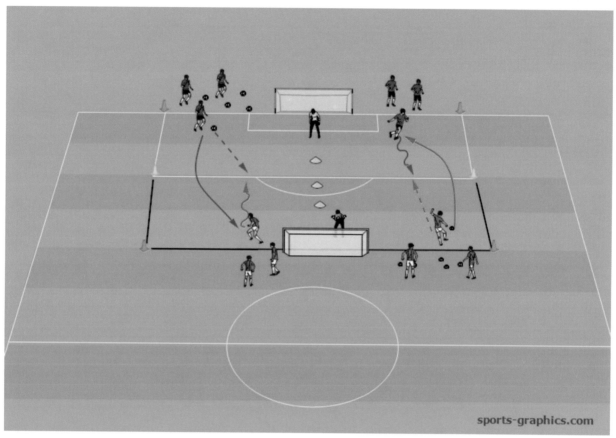

Fig. 5.1-5 Play2 × 1-on-1

DRILL ORGANIZATION:

- Playing field is made of expanded penalty area split lengthwise in two, with two nets with goalies.

- Two teams stand against each other and every team is split in two groups, which are positioned to the right and to the left of tenet.

- Every group of the individual teams on the right side of the net has a ball, the other groups have no ball.

DRILL FLOW:

- First player in group with ball passes the ball to first player of the other team without ball and runs forward as defender.

- Opponent takes ball to movement and tries going around his opponent and score.

- Vice versa, the defender in 1:1 situation tries to prevent his opponent from shooting and tries to get the ball.

- If defender wins the duel, he has a chance to attack.

- When the action is over, a duel begins in the other half of the playing field.

COACHING:

- In no case, discuss drilling individual tactics quickly and superficially, however, patiently and systematically.

- Applying positional play with the goal to slower the pace (attacking) of the opponent.

- Paying attention equally to the opponent and to the ball.

- Keeping appropriate distance from the opponent and watching out for a chance of getting the ball.

- Influencing opponent's movement. Watching his way of ball control

- and adjusting own defense activity to the specific qualities of opponent (fast striker, technically little efficient, his frequent tricks, etc.)

- Deciding for taking the ball at the right moment and in a favorable situation.

- Charging at the ball decisively and aggressively, not charging hastily, not fouling, anticipating situation, and timing the action.

DRILL 6: FAST SWITCH FROM ATTACK TO DEFENSE

Drill goal and focus: switching from attacking to defensive mechanisms (pressing drill level 1, 3)

Fig. 5.1-6 Switching from attacking to defensive mechanisms

DRILL ORGANIZATION:

- The playing field (expanded penalty area) with two nets with goalies, marked into three horizontal zones.

- Players are split into two teams, and every team is split to two groups—on the right and on the left of the nets.

- Prepare sufficient balls.

DRILL FLOW:

- Team B player leads the ball to the attacking third, where he is attacked by "A" player.

- After shooting or losing the ball, player "B" turns around and attacks another team player in the middle third "A" dribbles from the goal line toward the opposite net.

- Player "B" semiactively attacks "A" (during this activity, fast switching from attacking to defending activities is most important).

- After this duel situation in the central zone, continues team "A" player to the attacking zone, where he is attacked by team "B" player. This duel is acted out with full strength.

- After the duel, player "A" turns around and in the middle zone attacks another team "B" player, who dribbles from the goal line toward the other net.

COMMENTS:

- The main job is to immediately switch to defending activity after having finished the attacking.

- Quickly take the position between the ball and own net.

5.2 PRESSING ON A GROUP LEVEL

The meaning of group tactics for a well-working defensive is irrefutable in modern day soccer and should be seen as early as in the training of young players. The quality of defensive is supported mostly by blindfoldedly managed solutions of typical play situations inside the team: all movements, moving off the ball, flinching, transition phases, compact shifting, that portray in every play situation as absolutely thought-through, planned, and overall coordinated.

In world class soccer, this quality can only be reached, when besides every player's excellent individual level, also the basis of group tactics and movement within the team to the smallest details are worked through and functional.

Most importantly, this perfectly worked through group tactic on every position guarantees perfect defensive tactics and forms high effectivity of the play system.

On those grounds also the top players regularly practice group tactical solutions for play situation, in order to achieve stable automatisms. After pressing on individual level, group tactic presents another stepping stone toward the goal of achieving an active defensive mechanism, aggressive pressing being at the base of it.

Systematics of practice and improvement of pressing on group level:

- Pressing in groups of two

- Pressing in groups of three

- Pressing in groups of four

- Pressing on the level of block

- Pressing on the level of groups

Group tactic = defending together

- defending in groups of two

- defending in groups of three

- defending in groups of four

Numerical inferiority/ undernumbering	Numerical equality	Numerical superiority/ overnumbering
2 against 3	2 against 2	2 against 1
3 against 4	3 against 3	3 against 2
4 against 5	4 against 4	4 against 3

5.2.1 Pressing on Groups of Two Level

We speak of tactical group defensive action as early as at intentional cooperation of two players in defensive roles. This basic cooperation is gradually complemented by other players. According to tactical intentions, we simultaneously introduce didactically adequate number of opposing players.

In the training process, we should respect methodical principles and proceed from the simple to the more complex:

numerical superiority - numerical equality - numerical inferiority, undernumbering, numerical disadvantage

Group tactic = defending together

Group of two defense

Numerical superiority	Numerical equality	Numerical inferiority
2 vs. 1	2 vs. 2	2 vs. 3

DRILL 7: SITUATIONAL DOUBLING

Drill goal and focus: practice of situational doubling from the front (pressing training level 1, 2, 3, 4)

Fig. 5.2.1-1 Situational doubling from the front

DRILL ORGANIZATION:

- Playing space is the sideline from the half line to the penalty line.

- We mark a line with cones in between the penalty corner and the sideline.

- There is a portable goal with a goalkeeper on the halfway line in the sideline.

- A striker with balls stands beside the goal, and another one without ball is in the wing-back-area facing his teammate, with back turned to defender. The distance between the strikers is around 15–20 m.

- A fullback takes position about 2–3 m behind the striker's back.

- A right or left midfielder stands in front of the portable goal.

- The other players are outside the play area.

DRILL FLOW:

- The signal of the action's beginning is the attacker's pass, from the halfway line parallel with the sideline, to his teammate one the sideline.

- The attacker's objective, after taking over the ball, is to dribble past the line marked by cones.

- The fullback attacks his opponent and in a 1-on-1 situation tries to slow his opponent down, in order to gain time for his own right or left midfielder.

- The fullback stands in a way in order not just to slow his opponent down, but also to offer him space by the sideline.

- The right or left midfielder runs to doubling from the outer side, hence from the sideline.

- When the attacker dribbles with a lot of energy toward the center, the right/left midfielder starts running toward the ball and attacks the ball.

- When the defenders get the ball, they have a chance to attack in a 2:1 situation on the goal with the goaltender.

- The action can take a maximum of forty-five seconds, and after the given time limit is up, the coach stops the game.

- The drill also takes place in the opposite vertical line.

METHODICAL–ORGANIZATIONAL NOTES:

- The fullback retreats, doesn't attack, in order to gain time for his own left/right midfielder and forces his opponent to lead the ball "outside."

- Because the doubling left/right midfielder runs up from the front and from the outer side, he gets into an advantageous situation.

- Situational doubling is to be drilled on the sideline as well as in the center zone with the right/left midfielder and the right/left forward.

- Drill takes place on the right and on the left sideline.

OPPONENT WITH BALL ON CENTER SIDELINE (DOUBLING PRINCIPLES):

- Defense in numerical superiority means, for the opponent, to coordinate, to attack actively and aggressively, and to take ball as fast as possible.

- Moderate structuring of defenders in depth means advantageous basic position before the start of doubling.

- Defender closer to ball attacks opponent in order to force him to dribble toward his teammate moving behind him.

- That creates an advantageous situation for shared attacking, followed by taking of ball.

- Player, moving farther away from ball, watches out for the situation, when the dribbling opponent moves ball farther away from his leg.

- Then, both defenders attack the ball with the goal to separate the opponent from the ball and win the ball under their control.

MOST COMMON MISTAKES:

- Defenders are passive and only await attacker's activity, defender closer to ball moves very close to opponent and attacks opponent too hastily, uncoordinated, often fouling for this reason.

- Defender closer to ball doesn't force his opponent to dribble toward his teammate.

- Structuring in depth is missing, defenders are on one line.

- Defenders are far from each other and the other defender cannot join in the action in time, and therefore instead of a 2:1 play situation arises a 1:1 situation.

- Defenders do not create pressure on opponent with ball and move far from attacker.

- Both defenders act uncoordinated, their action is isolated, and they do not communicate together.

DOUBLING ON THE CENTER SIDELINE IN THE DEFENSE ZONE, NEAR OWN GOAL:
Center back's task:

- To solve duel 1-on-1 situations behind opponent's back.

- To keep the right distance from opponent (not too close, but also not too far from the opponent), avoid body contact, to play without fouling.

- To attack ball in case of opponent trying to turn toward goal.

DEFENSIVE MIDFIELDER'S TASK:

- To be more active.

- To run toward ball.

- To attack ball.

- Not to attack opponent too hastily or sharply.

DRILL 8: PRACTICING DIFFERENT FORMS OF DOUBLING IN SIDELINE

Drill goal and focus: focused doubling practice in different play situations (pressing training level 1, 2, 3)

Fig. 5.2.1-2 Practice of different doubling forms

DRILL ORGANIZATION:

- Playing area, formed by the sideline starting at penalty box up to the halfway line, marked by cones.

- Portable goals are set up on base lines, with goalkeepers in goals.

- In play area, there is a striker and a right or left fullback, other players are outside the play area.

- A player stands by the goal on the halfway line and another team player is on the center vertical line.

- Defense players are spread out according to their playing positions: inner defenders are close to the penalty box, defense center players stand in between the penalty box, and halfway line in the center vertical line and the left/right midfielders are ready by the goal past the halfway line.

- Prepare enough balls and divide them between goalkeepers and players, in order for all to have several spare balls.

DRILL FLOW:

Drill course will depend on the direction of the pass to striker on sideline:

- (a) from goalkeeper from halfway line

- (b) from team player in center zone

- (c) from team player on halfway line

(A) DRILL FLOW WHEN THE PASS COMES TO STRIKER FROM GOALKEEPER

- Action started by goalkeeper by passing the ball to striker, whose task, after taking ball, is to achieve shooting chance and finish the action by striking goal, which is placed on penalty box level.

- After the pass to the striker, the left/right fullback starts toward the opponent and attacks the opponent with ball in a 1-on-1 situation.

- Defensive midfielder comes to his help from the halfway line in a situation, when left/right fullback has moved into space with ball and is attacking opponent.

- Two defenders try, in a 2-on-1 play situation, prevent dribbling, and take opponent's ball.

- Having taken the ball, defensive players attack the goal with goalkeeper on the halfway line.

- The action can take maximum forty-five seconds and when this time is up, coach stops the game.

(B) DRILL FLOW, WHEN THE PASS TO THE STRIKER COMES FROM TEAM PLAYER IN THE CENTER ZONE

- Attacker starts the action from the center zone with pass to teammate on sideline. Striker on sideline tries to achieve striking situation and finish by striking the goal on the penalty box line.

- Left/right fullback, after pass, attacks player with ball, tries to block opponent from dribbling along sideline and forces him to move toward center of playing field.

- After pass, defensive midfielder starts toward the sideline and stands in a way to help his teammate and at the same time double in a 2-on-1 situation.

- Two defenders try, in a 2-on-1 situation, prevent striker from striking, and subsequently take his ball.

- After having taken ball, defense players attack the goal with goalkeeper on halfway line.

- Drill can take maximum forty-five seconds and when this time is up, coach stops it.

(C) DRILL FLOW, WHEN THE PASS TO STRIKER COMES FROM PLAYER ON HALFWAY LINE

- Signal to start the action is striker's pass from halfway line, parallel on the sideline, to teammate on sideline.

- Striker takes pass coming from back, with his back to goal, his task being, after taking ball and after turning around, dribbling to achieve striking situation and finish the action with a strike on the goal in the penalty box.

- Left/right fullback attacks opponent and in 1-on-1 situation tries to slow opponent down, in order to gain time for his left/right midfielder.

- Left/right fullback stands in a way, not to just slow down opponent, but also to offer him space by sideline.

- Left/right midfielder starts from halfway line and runs to doubling from outer side, thus from the sideline.

- When striker dribbles too energetically toward the center, left/right midfielder runs toward ball and attacks ball.

- When defenders win ball, they have opportunity to attack, in 2-on-1 situation, on goal with goalkeeper, that is on the halfway line.

- The action can take maximum forty-five seconds and when this time is up, coach stops the game.

METHODICAL–ORGANIZATIONAL NOTES:

- The action can take maximum 45 seconds and when this time is up, coach stops the game.

- Coach calls pass direction.

- Position of the defender, who comes as second, is very important, because striker can get to striking situation. Ideal situation is 2-3 m behind left/right fullback-anglewise behind him, closer to goal. He cannot be very close or very far from teammate.

- Exception is situational doubling from the front, because player running to doubling, runs to space from sideline.

- Inevitable condition for successful doubling is also mutual coaching, and the person responsible for that is the player running into doubling, in order to make his teammate aware that he is coming to help.

- Drill takes place in opposite sideline.

FREQUENT MISTAKES:

- Defender coming as second stands on same line with left/right fullback, and therefore in depth structuring is missing; mutual assistance is impossible in this position, and therefore it comes to misunderstanding.

- Player communication is missing.

- Players move slowly, verve is missing.

- Players foul often.

DRILL 9: PLAY ON SMALL GOALS 2:2 AFTER SPRINT INTO PLAYING FIELD

Drill aim and focus: play in 2:2 situation, attacking opponent with ball, defense in group of two, switching from defense to attack (pressing training level 1, 2, 3, 4)

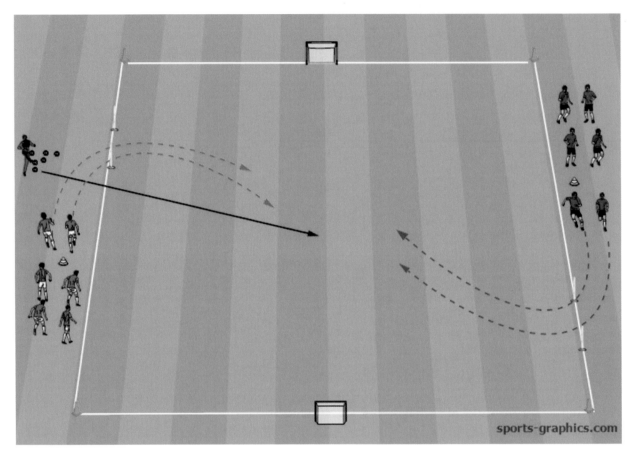

Fig. 5.2.1-3 Play 2-on-2 on small goals alter sprint

DRILL ORGANIZATION:

- Rectangular playing field 30 m × 20 m, with two small goals on shorter opposing sides.

- Coach appoints two equally strong groups that stand against each other diagonally past longer sides of the playing field.

- Players form groups of two.

- 5–8 m in front of both groups, mark with sticks a "gate to playing field," with approx. with of 1 m.

- Coach, standing beside the field, has the soccer balls.

DRILL FLOW:

- Signal to start the action is a pass from coach toward the middle of the playing field.

- After the pass, the first two players from both groups run into the field through the "gate" and try to get to the ball as fast as possible.

- A one-minute 1-on-1 play on small goals follows. The play does not stop after a goal, neither after the ball gets out of bounds, but continues steadily for one minute; when the ball gets out of playing field, coach passes another ball in the game.

- When the game is over, the players stand at the end of the line on the opposite side (change of sides).

- After one minute, duel of other two players follows.

- The game is organized as a two-team competition.

- When all the players take their turn, teams will actually have switched sides.

METHODICAL NOTES:

- Coach always has the option to interrupt or stop the drill, and to intervene, explain in detail and with focus, and repeatedly drill any crucial, key phases of duels.

DRILL 10: GAME 2-ON-2 ACROSS THE CENTER ZONE

Drill aim and focus: drilling space defense focused on ball (pressing training level 1, 2, 3, 4)

Fig. 5.2.1-4 2-on-2 play across the center zone

DRILL ORGANIZATION:

- It is played on two goals with goalkeepers in prolonged penalty area. The length of the playing field is about 40 m.

- It is marked with cones an approximately 7 m long center zone across the whole width in the middle of the playing field.

- Attackers spread on the sides of the portable goal and are split into groups of two. Each group of two has a ball.

- Defenders also form groups of two.

- The group of two defenders currently playing, takes positions in the marked center zone and the other defenders stand ready at the fixed goal.

DRILL FLOW:

- The group of two attackers start the action by dribbling from their base line toward the center zone, where the two defenders stand ready.

- The first task of the attackers is to beat the two defenders by dribbling or by combination and pass through the center zone. They get one point for completing this task.

- When the attackers manage to pass through the center zone, 2:2 game continues in the penalty zone. For completing the action, the attackers get another point.

- Defenders try to stop the attack and win the ball. In case of a successful defense, they attack the portable goal and get one point.

- The game lasts for one minute and when this time limit is up, the coach stops the game, and then another group of two defenders and attackers take their turn.

NOTES:

- The coach counts points and organizes the game as a competition of teams.

- Defenders' task is to slow down or stop the offense action of the opponent as far as possible from their own goal.

- The coach does not interfere during the course of the drill, but corrects the defense play in between actions and in case of any mistakes, he demonstratively goes through the correct solution of the particular situation.

PRACTICAL RESOURCES FOR DRILLING AND IMPROVEMENT OF PRESSING AT THE GROUP TWO LEVEL IN A 2-ON-3 SITUATION

DRILL 11: 2-ON-3 PLAY ON THE SIDELINE ACROSS LINES ON SMALL GOALS

Drill goal and focus: Practice and improvement of play in undernumbering (pressing training level 1, 2, 3, 4)

Fig. 5.2.1-5 2-on-3 play on the sideline across lines on a small goal

DRILL ORGANIZATION:
- The play area is marked by cones as a wider sideline: lengthwise from the sixteenth to the halfway line and the width up to the level of goal zone.

- On one base line, formed by the halfway line, stand a small goal, about 3 m wide, made of sticks.

- On the base line, which is on the other side, and which is the prolonged side of the penalty area, put two small goals, about 3 m wide, made of cones.

- Make with sticks a small, about 3 m wide goal by the center circle.

- Players are split into a team of defenders and a team of attackers.

- Defenders form groups of two according to their positions, left/right fullback, left/right midfielder, defensive midfielder, center midfielder. Defense players play in their positions.

- The other team is made up by offense players, and they form groups of three.

DRILL FLOW:

- The action starts, when one from the group of three attackers dribbles into the playing fields from the base line identical with the halfway line.

- A 3-on-2 play follows.

- The attackers' task is to utilize the overnumbering and lead the ball through one of the small goals, which are on the prolonged sixteenth line.

- Defenders practice defense in undernumbering on the sideline, and after winning the ball, they should pass the ball into one of the small goals (on the base line or by the center circle).

- The play goes on for one minute and after that another group of attackers and defenders takes their turn.

METHODOLOGICAL NOTES:

- Coach addresses the players in breaks in between actions.

- Moving fast toward the opponent and slowing down their attack.

- Pressing the opponent out of the playing field.

- Not to allow a tunnel pass onto the upcoming attacker through the defense.

- Mutual communication of the two defenders is crucial.

DRILL 12: 2 AGAINST 3 PLAY ON CENTER VERTICAL LINE

Drill goal and focus: practice of defense combinations (pressing training level 1, 2,3,4)

Fig. 5.2.1-6 23 play on center vertical line

DRILL ORGANIZATION:

- The play takes place in prolonged penalty area up to the halfway line.

- In the left and right wing areas on the center line, mark by sticks 3 m wide small goals.

- Players are split into two teams, a group of offense players and a group of defense players.

- There is a goalkeeper in the goal.

- There are always three attackers against two defenders and the other players are besides the playing field.

DRILL FLOW:

- Group of three attackers are to score into the original goal with goalkeeper.

- Defenders are, in cooperation with the goalkeeper, to withstand the overnumbering, and after getting the ball, they are to pass the ball into one of the small goals.

- The play starts with one of the attackers dribbling.

- When defenders win the ball, they should pass it into the side vertical line, into one of the two small goals on the center line.

- The play lasts 90 seconds; after the time is up, another group of two defenders and two attackers is on.

VARIATION:

- The game is started by the goalkeeper by throwing the ball to one of the attackers.

NOTES:

- Defenders practice defense combinations: backing each other up, defense against lay off, defense against a tandem, against change of positions, taking over, and handover of players in width as well as in depth and doubling.

- Mutual communication of defenders is critical.

DRILL 13: PLAY 6-ON-4 ON THE NUMBER OF PASSES AND 3-ON-2 ON ONE GOAL

Drill goal and focus: slowing down opponent's attacking action in numerical inferiority (pressing training level 1, 2,3, 4)

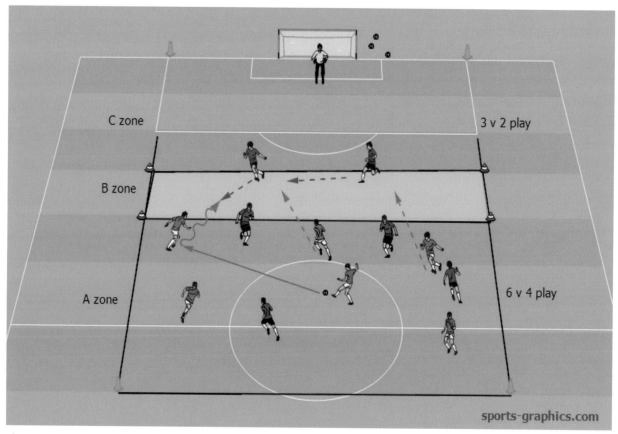

Fig. 5.2.1-7 Play 6-on-4 on number of passes and 3-on-2 on one goal

DRILL ORGANIZATION:

- Play area is a prolonged penalty area up to the second half of the playing field.

- The play area is split into three unequal zones 20 m from the goal line (zone C), center zone B is 10 m long, and zone A is 30 m long.

- There is a goalkeeper playing in the permanent goal.

- Appoint two equally strong groups of six in a way to put all the offense players in zone A, four defense players in zone A, and two defense players in zone B.

DRILL FLOW:

- The game is started by offenders in zone A They play on two touches 6-on-4 on the count of passes.

- The objective of the offenders is to keep the ball (interaction) and play at least six mutual passes without being interrupted.

- After six passes, three players from the team of offenders can go over to zone B.

- Follows a free 3-on-2 play on one goal with goalkeeper in zones B and C. The rule of two touches does not apply here.

- When defenders win the ball, a game on two touches 6-on-6 follows in zones A and B. The game is also played on six passes (= 1 point).

- Alternate defenders in center zone after every play.

- One game is over after a successful action of attackers or after a successful keeping of ball by defenders (six passes).

METHODICAL NOTES:

- Pay attention to correct, synchronized, and effective defense in groups of two.

- Watch the movement of ball and the action of opponent carefully.

- Watch out for the defenders not to play in 2-on-3 against "their own" team player, but that they keep the principles of spatial defense.

- Demand speedy switching from defense to offense activities.

- Demand mutual coaching from players.

5.2.2 Pressing on the Group Three Level

SYSTEMATICS

- Group tactic means to defend together as a team

DEFENSE IN A GROUP OF THREE

Numeric advantage	Equal numbers	Numeric disadvantage
3 against 2	3 against 3	3 against 4

1. Defense in outnumbering (numeral advantage) 3 to 2

2. Defense in group of three in a 3 to 3 situation On numeral equality)

3. Defense in a group of three against outnumbering in a 3 to 4 situations

PRACTICAL TOOLS FOR PRACTICING AND IMPROVING PRESSING AT THE GROUP THREE LEVEL IN 3-ON-2 SITUATIONS

DRILL 14: 3 TO 2 PLAY SITUATION IN WING AREA

Drill goal and focus: practice and improvement of 3 to 2 play on the side vertical line (pressing training level 1, 2, 3)

Fig. 5.2.2-1 Practice to solving 3 to 2 play situation on the side vertical line

DRILL ORGANIZATION:

- Mark the playing field composed by the penalty area and prolonged side vertical line

- Appoint three defense players, who play in their positions (combination of positions: wing fullback, wing midfielder, defensive mid fielder, center midfielder, stopper)

- Also appoint two offense players

- Goalkeeper plays in the goal

- Place a small goal made of poles on the side vertical line

DRILL FLOW:

- The drill is started by an offense player on the side vertical line by dribbling away from the sideline.

- The objective of the offense group of two is to get by dribbling or by cooperation to the penalty area and finish the offense action.

- Defenders' objective is to double the player with ball, along with the third defender trying to disconnect the second attacker from the game.

- After winning the ball, defenders have the possibility to attack on the small goal.

- The drill takes about two to three minutes (the coach lets them finish the offense or defense action), subsequently another group of defenders and attackers follows. The drill can be organized in a way to only swap the offensive group of two, and the defenders only swap after two or three actions.

METHODICAL COMMENTS:

- Two players start against their opponent with the ball, attack him, and try to put him under pressure (doubling).

- In a 2 to 1 situation, they focus on the ball and block the space in the proximity of the ball in order to slow the opponent's dribbling, and prevent him from continuing directly toward the goal, and at the same time they prevent him from passing the ball to his teammate in depth or in width.

- The third defender is checking the other offender and takes up space in order to prevent an in-depth pass.

- Completion of this action is speedy steeling of the ball from the opponent and starting up an attack.

- The coach corrects any mistakes during the break in between two drills.

DRILL 15: PLAY SITUATION 3 TO 2 ON THE CENTER VERTICAL

Drill goal and focus: practice and improvement of 3-on-2 play on the halfway line (pressing training Level 1, 2, 3, 4)

Fig. 5.2.2-2 Drill solving 3-on-2 game situation on the halfway line

DRILL ORGANIZATION:

- Playing area is prolonged penalty area up to the halfway line.

- Place three small goals made of sticks on the halfway line in every vertical area (right, left, and middle).

- Choose three defense players, who play their positions (a combination of left/right fullback, left/right midfielder, defensive midfielder, defensive midfielder).

- Choose two offense players.

- There is a goalkeeper in the goal.

DRILL FLOW:

- The drill is kicked off by dribbling of one of the offense players.

- The aim of the team of the two offenders is to get to scoring by dribbling or by cooperation.

- The aim of the defenders is to double the player with ball, while the third defender tries to disconnect the other offender from the game.

- After winning the ball, the defenders have the option of scoring into one of the three small goals.

- The drill takes two to three minutes (the coach leaves them to finish the defense or offense action) and then another group of defense and offense player starts. The drill can be organized in a way as to swap only the two offenders and the defenders are swapped after two or three actions.

METHODICAL COMMENTS:

- Two players start against their opponent with ball, attack him, and try to put him under pressure (doubling).

- In a 2 to 1 situation they focus on the ball and block the space around the ball in such a manner as to slow the opponent's dribbling, and prevent his direct way toward the goal, and at the same time not to let him pass the ball to his teammate in the depth or into the width.

- The third defender keeps checking the other attacker and fills the space as to prevent a pass in depth.

- Finalization of this action is a speedy stealth of ball from the opponent and starting up an attack.

- The coach corrects any mistakes in breaks in between two drills.

PRACTICAL RESOURCES FOR PRACTICING AND IMPROVING PRESSING AT THE GROUP THREE LEVEL IN 3-ON-3 SITUATIONS

DRILL 16: SPEEDY EXCHANGE IN A 3-ON-3 PLAY

Drill goal and focus: improvement of defense in groups of three (pressing training level 1, 2, 3, 4)

Fig. 5.2.2-3 Game A against B, B against C, C against D, and D against A, and so on

DRILL ORGANIZATION:

-   The playing area is prolonged penalty area marked by cones.

-   Place a portable goal against the permanent goal.

-   Goalies play in the goals.

-   Make up four groups of three.

-   Prepare a sufficient amount of spare balls to ensure a smooth and uninterrupted game.

DRILL FLOW:

-   Two teams A and B play each other and two teams C and D are outside the playing field, near the goals.

-   Team A attacks team B and at the end of the action or after loss of ball, they leave the playing area and move behind the goal.

-   Team B attacking C follows, and after the end of the action C plays against D, subsequently D against A, and so on.

- The team of three, who are outside the playing area, have to quickly move and get organized in order to be ready to fulfill their defense roles.

- The group, who have just been in defense, must quickly switch to play offense.

COACHING:

- The drill requires full concentration, focused defense, and speedy switching.

DRILL 17: ATTACKING WAVES OF THREE GROUPS OF THREE

Drill goal and focus: improvement of defense in groups of three (pressing training level 1, 2, 3, 4)

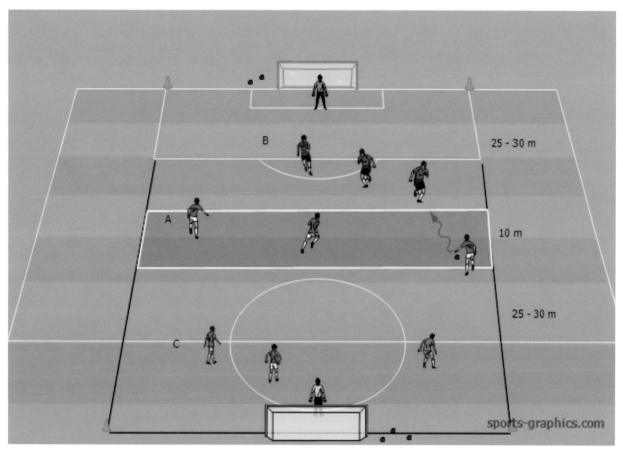

Fig. 5.2.2-4 Attacking waves across the neutral zone

DRILL ORGANIZATION:

- Playing area is the width of the penalty area and the length of 230 ft. split into three zones: 98 ft., 32 ft., 98 ft.

- The center zone is "forbidden zone," where it is not allowed to defend, and only can be passed through by that group of three that is currently playing offense.

- Place a portable goal on the base line opposite the fixed goal.

- There are goalkeepers in the goals.

- Pick three groups of three, if possible of equal strength.

DRILL FLOW:

- Team A attacks team B and the group of team C stands ready at the opposite goal.

- After the action is over, or after winning the ball, the group of team B attacks C and, likewise, afterward, team C plays against the group of three A, and so on.

VARIATIONS:

- The team that is currently attacking, has the option to win the ball back still in the attacking zone after having lost it (they are not allowed to defend in the forbidden zone).

- The group of team in defense, after winning the ball, tries to get out of opponents' pressure and move the game into the center zone.

METHODOLOGICAL COMMENTS:

- Care about active movement, orientation in space, speedy shifting toward the ball.

- Focus on doubling and isolating the player with ball.

- It is also important to switch quickly between defensive and attacking action and the ability to play under pressure.

PRACTICAL RESOURCES FOR PRACTICING AND IMPROVING PRESSING AT THE GROUP THREE LEVEL IN 3 TO 4 SITUATIONS

DRILL 18: SOLVING A GAME SITUATION IN THE SIDE AREA

Drill goal and focus: practice solving a 3 to 4 situation in wing areas (pressing training level 1, 2, 3)

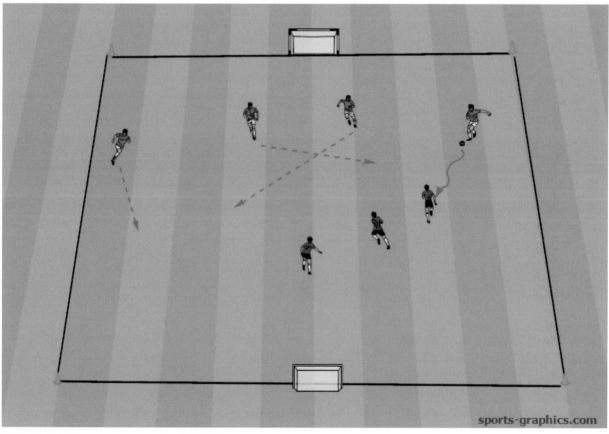

Fig. 5.2.2-5 Solving a 3 to 4 game situation in side areas

DRILL ORGANIZATION:

- Mark a 98 x 98 ft. square.

- Place small goals opposite to each other on base lines.

DRILL FLOW:

- There are three defenders and four attackers playing on small goals in the square.

- The game is always kicked off by the dribbling of a left/right forward.

- Apply the offside rule.

- When the defenders win the ball, they have the option to attack on the opposite small goal.

VARIATIONS:

- Game on four small goals.

COACHING:

- Focus is placed on creating a defensive diagonal and on covering each other.

- Defenders should act in coordination, in order to create a compact block.

- The defender closest to the ball is to move in a way in order to press the opponent with ball toward the sideline.

- The other two players are to cover him and at the same time move in space in order to prevent the opponent to make an in-depth pass.

DRILL 19: SOLVING A GAME SITUATION IN THE CENTER VERTICAL AREA

Drill goal and focus: practice solving defense in center vertical area (pressing training level 1, 2,3)

Fig. 5.2.2-6 Solving a 3 to 4 game situation in the center vertical area

DRILL ORGANIZATION:
- Place small goals opposite to each other on base lines.

DRILL FLOW:
- In the square, there are three defenders and four attackers playing on the small goals.

- The game is started by the dribbling of one of the center strikers.

- Apply the offside rule.

- When the defenders win the ball, they have the option to strike at the opposite small goal.

METHODOLOGICAL COMMENTS:
- The defender in the center attacks the player with ball and the other two players cover him.

- The group of three defense players make up a compact defense triangle and, by their movement, they try to prevent in-depth passes.

- In such an alignment, the defenders move backward all the way to their goal.

DRILL 20: GAME ON TWO PARALLEL PLAYING FIELDS IN OUTNUMBERING

Drill goal and focus: defense against numeral advantage (pressing training level 1, 2, 3)

Fig. 5.2.2-7 A 3-on-3 game on two parallel playing fields against one portable goal and two small goals

DRILL ORGANIZATION:

- Place two portable goals in both corners of the penalty area.

- Place four small goals on the opposite side of the field on the level of the center circle.

- Create two parallel playing areas in between these two goals and lengthwise mark an approximately 16 ft. wide neutral zone.

- In both playing areas, there are three defenders and three offenders, and there are goalkeepers in the portable goals.

DRILL FLOW:

- Offenders play on the portable goals with goalies in them.

- Defenders are not allowed to cross the neutral zone.

- The offense players cooperate with their team players who play in the other playing area—they can pass the ball to each other and one of the offenders can run across to the other side and create a 4 to 3 outnumbering.

- Apply the offside rule.

- After winning the ball, the defenders have a chance to attack the small goals in cooperation with their team players in the other playing area.

COACHING INSTRUCTIONS:

- Close off direct access to the goal.

- Prevent deep passes.

- Block the player with ball.

- Create compact defense configurations (triangle, diagonal).

- Disconnect opponents without ball.

- Apply the offside rule.

DRILL 21: A 3 TO 4 GAME ON TWO GOALS AFTER SWITCHING

Drill goal and focus: speedy switching from offensive to defensive action against outnumbering (pressing training level 1, 2, 3)

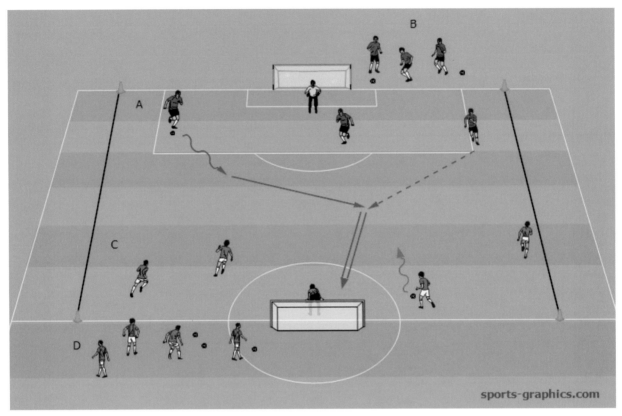

Fig. 5.2.2-8 A 3 to 4 game alter switching

DRILL ORGANIZATION:

- The playing area is the prolonged penalty area from the goal line up to the halfway line.

- Place a portable goal on the halfway line.

- Make up two groups of three defenders according to their positions, and appoint two groups of four attackers.

- Give balls to the defenders (group A and B), the defenders stand on the left and on the right of the fixed goal.

- Offender (C and D) are next to the portable goals.

- There are goalkeepers in goals. Have spare balls ready in the goals.

DRILL FLOW:

- The game is started by three "A" defenders without their opponents, by a short combination, ending against a portable goal with goalkeeper.

- Immediately after ending (regardless whether the defenders scored or not), the goalkeeper passes the ball to one of the "C" offenders and starts a 4 to 3 play.

- After the attack, the defenders immediately switch to defensive action, and after they win the ball, they attack the portable goal.

- The game lasts four minutes, and then "B" defenders start against "D" offenders.

VARIATIONS:

- Defenders attack in 3 to 1.

- Defenders attack in 3 to 2.

- After finishing a defenders' attack, the coach passes a ball in the game from past the sideline.

- Players, who are not currently playing, relax actively (practice their technique, do running drills, play 5 to 2 "five-a-side").

COMMENTS:

- Demand speedy switching from offense to defense action and vice versa.

- Defenders are to move in a compact block and must pay attention to covering each other.

- They are to move backward in a compact block, in order to slow down the opponent's attack and at the same time not to allow an in-depth pass past the defense.

- In a situation, when the right/left forward has the ball, they are to press him toward the sideline, and in a favorable situation, they are to double and isolate him, so that he cannot cooperate with his team players.

DRILL 22: PLAY IN UNDERNUMBERING IN ZONES

Drill goal and focus: practice and improvement of 3 to 4 play (pressing training level 1, 2, 3)

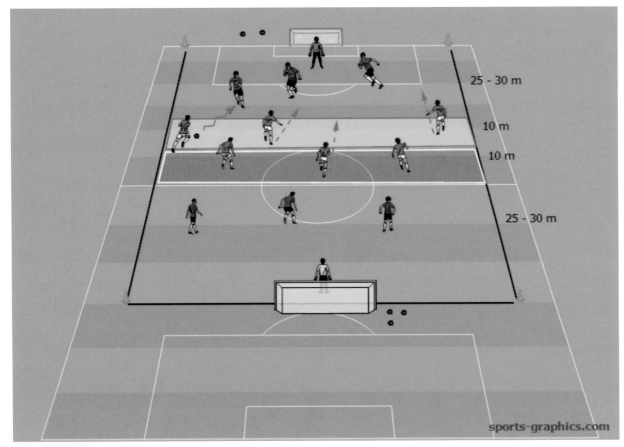

Fig. 5.2.2-9 4 to 3 play on one goal in zones

DRILL ORGANIZATION:

-   The playing area is a rectangle, 131 feet wide and 262 feet long.

-   One of the base lines is formed by the goal line with the permanent goal, and the opposite base line is on the other half of the playing field with a portable goal.

-   The playing area is split in four zones: 98, 33, 33, and 98 ft.

-   There are goalkeepers in the goals.

-   In each of the four zones, there are players positioned in a way, where there are three defenders in front of both goals, and there are three offenders in the center zones.

DRILL FLOW:

-   The game is started by the goalkeeper passing the ball to one of the offenders, followed by a play of three offenders against three defenders on one goal.

-   Defenders play only in their zones and the three offenders cross over from their zone to attack, accompanied by one offender from the other center zone, to create 4:3 outnumbering.

-   After having finished the action, a 4 to 3 attack on the opposite goal follows.

-   If the defenders win the ball, it is their task to make a pass to their team players in front of the opposite goal. If successful, they win a point, and after that a new play is started from the goalkeeper in the opposite direction.

COACHING INSTRUCTIONS:

- The basic task here is ball-oriented space defense.

- The coach demands compact movement of groups of three toward the ball, covering each other and

thorough formation of defense units (defense diagonal, when the focus point of the game is on the side of the playing area, and a defense triangle, when the ball is moving in the center.)

5.3 PRESSING ON A THREE- AND FOUR-DEFENDER CHAIN LEVEL, FORMATIONS, DEFENSE BLOCKS CREATION, AND TRANSFER FROM BLOCKS TO PRESSING

1. Defense in the three-defender chain

2. Pressing on the foursome level, formations, defense blocks creation, and transfer from blocks into pressing

3. Movement of the defending chain backward, withdrawal, and controlled withdrawal

4. Extension of defensive line forward, pushing the opponent out and a pump

5. Switching after losing and gaining the possession of the ball

6. Solution of typical situations in a game of four-defender chain

1. Defense in the Three-Defender Chain

It's not that long time ago when the soccer history had a space defense revolution, which was focused on the ball with a four-defender chain and recent 2014 World Championship presented us with a three-defender chain making this another step in the space defense evolution. As the name also reveals, the defense chain in this case, in contrast with four-defender chain, consist of three players. This type of play is also very effective. A team usually plays with three-defender chain only in cases when they perform space defense. This organization can also be alternatively maintained when the team prefers personal defense; however, it's not common. When performing space defense, the three-defender chain moves back and forth (along the width of the pitch as well as vertically depending on the center of the game); in coordination with other parts of the team, the space is occupied. The back triad actively moves mostly on one level and in one line.

The three-defender chain moves in the direction of the ball in a very closed and tight formation. It positionally covers the midfield area, initiates tactical movements of the defending formation (forward, backward, and to the sides), occupies the opponent's center players on the principle of mutual securing with and without defense reserve. In specific situations, they take over players, double them and according to the situation; they individually either approach or withdraw from the opponent players. When performing a fast counterattack through free center of the pitch, they slow down the opponent's direct movement by retreating. The players of the three-defender chain must be tactically mature and strong in air and ground fights.

Even if a team plays with three defenders in one line, many times it's not really a three-defender chain but five defender chain because the three defenders are also being supported by two-side defenders who are a playing a bit higher. Although the chain mechanism of three defenders is strengthened in side verticals, the chain must be also active in wing areas. Therefore, we can often hear about so-called pendulum chain. The three-defender chain was rediscovered in recent years (2012). Many teams, mainly the teams that focus on real offensive soccer, use the three-defender chain play system.

As an example, we can present FC Barcelona, Bayern Munich (although it also plays with four-defender chain or changes their alignment during the course of the game), some Italian A Series teams, and it was also used in some 2014 World Championship matches in Brazil. The main advantage of the three-defender chain is the fact that, in situations when an opponent team plays only with one attacker (which is quite common), the team can play with one extra midfield player who can also participate in the offensive and defense after losing the possession of the ball, by which he makes the higher pressing extension easier. The three-defender chain's basic alignment (triangle, funnel, and diagonal) is identical to the four-defender chain. The differences are in details. When playing with four-defender chain, both center backs stay in the back when attacking.

They always follow the ball and in attacking stage of the game, they have tasks in opening the play. In interlude, they secure from the back especially when transferring the center of the game. In case of losing the possession of the ball in midfield or attacking zone, they secure the space behind the ball so that the opponent is unable to perform fast attack. When playing with four-defender chain, it's important, after losing the possession of the ball, to have at least one defense midfielder who promptly switches to defensive activities and returns to the area in front of center backs. A play with four-defender chain in defense and centric formation creates suitable possibilities for occupying of the width and depth of space. If the space is divided correctly, the running sections are shortened. This allows teams to achieve a very compact and safe organization in dangerous areas, which makes doubling easier. This way, teams can create an outnumber near the ball in any area. If the area is in equally divided in a defense stage, the team is able to switch efficiently to attacking activities after gaining the possession of the ball. When playing with three-defender chain, all three defenders stay behind the ball. In a situation, when the team loses

the ball, this type of alignment is appropriate because the attacking stage is secured by a compact chain. As the three players can't cover all the width of the pitch in defense, side midfielders must join the chain mechanism. When the opponent attacks through side vertical, side midfielder, who isn't near the ball (he is positioned in the opposite vertical), moves to the defense chain. In case the center of the game is in the side vertical, both side midfielders enter the defense formation by which they create a five-member chain. By connecting three-defender chain with one or two defensive midfielders, we can create a very compact formation in the central dangerous area. A play with a three-member chain allows the team, after gaining the possession of the ball, to achieve a very good wide and deep division, which enables the players to perform more effective transfer from defense to attack mainly by combined play.

THE TYPES OF THE THREE-DEFENDER CHAIN IN SPECIFIC (AND TYPICAL) PLAY SITUATIONS:

The defense triangle

When the ball is moving in the center and center back player is attacking the opponent with the ball, the side players from the three-defender chain move behind the center player in order to create a defense triangle. If the opponent's wing players (or side midfielders) enter the attack, the side players of the triple-chain widen the triangle and, at the same time, the side midfielders move to the triple-chain level in order to occupy the area in the side verticals and created fifth-number chain.

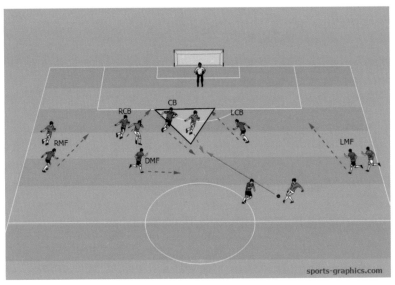

Fig. 5.3-1 The defense triangle

The defense diagonal

If the opponent is attacking through the side vertical in the area in front of the side player of the chain, this defender approaches the player with the ball in order to prevent him from escaping and taking the position in the center in front of the goal. The other two defenders from the three-defender chain are relocating to the center to occupy the area where the opponent is positioned. If the opponent is playing with two attackers in the middle vertical, the side midfielder, who is further away from the ball, moves to the defenders level for the purpose of completing the chain.

Fig. 5.3-2 The defense diagonal

The retreat

An opponent's fast counterattack requires the defenders to retreat to the level up to 20–25 m in front of their goal in order to take the free space behind the defense from the opponent. The defenders are supposed to maintain the depth division even if retreating, they must be checking the player with the ball and occupy the middle vertical in order to prevent the opponent directly approaching the goal. By performing the retreat, the opponent's attack is slowed down and the players gain time for the team players to return. It's important, especially for the defensive midfielders, to return quickly.

Fig. 5.3-3 The retreat

Fig. 5.3-4 Maintaining the pressing height and retreating after the opponent's escape pass

Maintaining the pressing height

For maintaining the compactness, the three-defender chain moves near the midfield players. If the midfielders don't succeed in blocking the opponent with the ball or they attack him too late, the opponent has a chance to perform a pass behind the defense block. In this case, the defenders must retreat in order to occupy the area and prevent the opponent from getting behind the defense block, which can be successfully achieved if executed in a coordinated manner. That's why the opponent can't make the alternative of performing a depth pass and it's usually followed by a width pass, which gives the midfielders a chance to align themselves and move as a compact formation. If the midfield players successfully manage to block the area in the center zone, the three-defender chain extends higher for creating a compact block.

Fig. 5.3-5 Extension to the chain, a pump

Extension of the chain

If the opponent is performing a pass from the back, the whole team extends forward. The opponent, who has received the back pass, is being attacked by the player who is positioned the nearest to the opponent. If the opponent, who is receiving the pass, is completely free, and it's not possible to put him under pressure, the team doesn't extend and stays withdrawn.

Comparison of the four-defender and three-defender chain

Game situation	The four-defender chain	The three-defender chain
Opponent's diagonal passes	The side defender, who is far from the ball, is position far enough to be able to catch a diagonal pass.	The chain covers a more narrow area; therefore, there's a higher danger of diagonal passes.
Midfielders' defense	Midfielders form the second defensive line, and they usually don't retreat to the defensive chain level.	According to the situation, the side midfielders take the roll of full back players so they create a five-defender chain.
Midfield players' alignment I	Mostly consists of four midfield players (4-4-2). What can frequently happen is that the side verticals aren't sufficiently occupied (especially in the play system with the center diamond).	The side midfielders are right wing players who play along the whole length of the side vertically an din 3-4-3 alignmnet; they support the wing attackers' attacking acttions.
Midfield players' alignment II	In certain situations, they are sometimes in a numerical disadvantage compared to the teams playing by the 3-5-2 system.	Under certain circumstances, they are sometimes in a numerical advantage compared to the teams playing 4-4-2.
Defenders' attack	At least one of the side defenders always actively takes part in the attacking actions in the side vertical. Three defenders usually stya in the back to secure the attack.	Three defenders are located in the back during the offensive stage and secure the team players' attacking action. Side midfielders take over the role of side defenders during the attacking stage.

If a team applies a personal defense, the players mostly play in the back with "a free player" (libero) who usually doesn't play against an opponent; he secures the other players. Therefore, this type of play doesn't allow a three-defender chain creation. If a team only performs a personal defense in a defined narrowed area, the application of the three-defender chain is possible. If a player, who performs a personal defense in the side vertical, moves higher toward the side vertical to another opponent player, libero takes over this player's opponent player. In this situation, the second defender, who is further away from the ball, moves to the center to replace libero, and takes over his function. This is precisely the type of play that represents a classical chain mechanism in a nontypical play system. This type of play, when a free player moves in the center and two players on his left and right perform a personal defense on extended attackers (they are in 1-2 alignment or even with a prestopper in 1-3 alignment), is frequently used in many lower competitions. The chain with a free player is sometimes used in top soccer too, and Greece became a European champion with this type of defense organization. The libero's play requires a high tactical level and very flexible action. Depending on the play situation, libero must swiftly change his position and type of defense. He sometimes plays behind defense as a free player and secures the players in front of him and in other situations; he extends to the personal defenders level and plays in one line with the intention to push an opponent to offside position. If necessary, he takes over an occupation of one of the extended attackers. The player, who performs a personal defense, can move forward to the midfield players or to the side vertical in order to double his team player. In this situation, libero then moves to the position of his team player and at the same time, the side defender, who is further away from the ball, moves to the center and takes over libero's function. This organization is referred to as a chain mechanism. The difference between classical chain and flexible personal defense is that this type of defense organization adjusts to the opponent's attack sequences despite the merits of personal defense being used. However, in spite of slight differences, the chain principle is maintained. A play with a personal defense and a free player requires an excellent game-reading and coordinated cooperation of libero with the players who perform a personal defense.

PART 3

Fig. 5.3-6 Movement of the defenders when applying the personal defense.

PRACTICAL TOOLS FOR PRACTICING AND IMPROVING THREE-DEFENDER CHAIN PLAY

DRILL 23: 3V3 PLAY WITH AN END PLAYER

Drill goal and focus: the three-defender chain play with aim to prevent the opponent from performing a depth passes to an extended attacker (level of the pressing drill 1, 2, 3).

Fig. 5.3-7 3v3 play with an end player

DRILL ORGANIZATION:

- The penalty area is extended to the central line by extending the playing area.

- There is a marked 7-m zone for the end player in front of the penalty area. By this, we create three unequally large zones: penalty area central zone for the end player, the zone from the central line to central zone.

- A goalkeeper is in the goal.

- Four attackers are playing against three defenders who are aligned so that 3v3 are in the zone from the central line and the fourth attacker is the central zone.

DRILL FLOW:

- The drill is started by the attackers whose task is first to perform a ground pass to their team player into the central area and then, by 4v3 cooperation, score a goal.

- The offside rule doesn't apply in the central zone.

- If the pass to the attackers in the central zone is executed successfully, the play continues in the central zone and penalty area. The attackers must extend as the end attacker mustn't finish immediately after the depth pass. The goal is valid after at least one of the team players touches the ball.

- Also in case the pass to the extended attacker isn't performed successfully, the play continues and the attackers are trying, either individually or in a combination, get through the central zone in order to finish.

- The aim of the defender chain is to prevent the perpendicular pass to the extended attacker from being carried out by choosing an appropriate place and movement; thus prevent a goal from being scored.

- When the attackers gain the possession of the ball, they try to get from under the pressure. In case of losing the ball in the penalty area, they must remove the ball from the sixteen and get the ball over the central line by performing 3v3 play as the extended attacker can only defend in the penalty area.

- The play lasts three to four minutes and after this time lap, we change players or after one minute, we repeat the drill with the same group but the extended attacker position is taken by another attacker.

VARIATIONS:
- The attackers play by two touches.

- The end attacker can shoot at the goal after taking over the ball.

COMMENT:
- The drill is suitable for practicing attacking and defensive tactics.

- The key task is the defense against opponent's depth passes behind the defense line.

- The essential part is the space defense that is focused on the ball and which reacts flexibly to the ball's movement. The defense reacts to a fast combination play of the opponent who is preparing the place for performing a perpendicular pass to an extended attacker in front of the penalty area.

- The important part of this is mutual communication between the two defenders, mutual securing and coordinated action, which isn't only focused on a correct blockage of space but also creation of outnumber near the ball (doubling).

- The drill is suitable to include in the main part of the training unit focusing on tactics.

DRILL 24: 3V3 PLAY WITH THREE PASSERS

Drill goal and focus: organization of defense against numerical advantage with an effort to prevent the depth pass from being performed (level of the pressing drill 1, 2, 3)

Fig. 5.3-8 3v3 With three passers

DRILL ORGANIZATION:

- The penalty area is extended to the central line by extending the playing area.

- Opposite the goal with a goalkeeper, we place on the central line two small goals.

- We divide the players into three-member groups: attackers, defenders, and passers.

- The passers are aligned so that the two are behind the goalkeeper's line on the right and left of the goal, and the third one is in the playing area.

DRILL FLOW:

- The action is started by the goalkeeper performing a kick off or throwing the ball to the passer in the playing area who immediately passes the ball to one of the attackers.

- It's followed by 4v3 play in which the passes can play only by one touch.

- The attackers are trying, also with the help of the passers, to get into shooting situation and score a goal.

- During the course of the action, the attackers must use the passer at least once.

- The action must be finished by one touch.

- The defenders are trying, by performing flexible pressing, prevent the other player from performing a perpendicular pass to the passers next to the goal and occupy the space so that they are able to prevent the other player from creating shooting situations or getting the ball.

- When the defenders gain the possession of the ball, they have an opportunity to attacks the two small goals on the central line.

- The attacking action is finished by scoring a goal, out or losing the possession of the ball. The players then return to their original alignment and a new action is started again by the goalkeeper.

- The players change their roles after five minutes.

VARIATIONS:

- The attackers play only by two touches.

- The attack must be finished within eight to ten seconds, otherwise the attackers lose the ball and defenders try to start their attack on the small goals.

METHODICAL COMMENTS:

- We are drilling pressing in harder conditions—inferiority in numbers. Even in these conditions, the defenders must make an effort to solve playing situations effectively by correct occupation of the area, in order to prevent the other players from performing the depth passes, by an individual penetration or opponent's combination play.

- The play requires fast decision making, commitment, and concentration.

- The defenders must move in compact block and maintain mutual securing.

- When a side attacker has the ball, the defenders are pushing him to the sideline and, at the suitable moment, they double him and isolate him so that he can't cooperate with his team players.

DRILL 25: 4V3 PLAY OF THREE TEAMS

Drill goal and focus: flexible and compact defense (level of the pressing drill 1, 2, 3)

Fig. 5.3-9 Play A- B-C 4v3

DRILL ORGANIZATION:

- The playing area is an extended penalty area all the way behind the central circle on the other half of the pitch.

- We place a portable goal opposite the fixed goal.

- Goalkeepers and the goals.

- We form three four member teams A, B and C.

- B and C teams, each with three players opposite each other, occupy the area in front of the goals. They are without balls. The fourth players of B and C teams are prepared with a ball next to their goal.

- The four players of A team have a ball and are ready to perform an attack against B team.

DRILL FLOW:

- Four attackers always play against three defenders.

- The fourth player of a team in defense is prepared with a ball next to his goal.

- The four players of A team perform an attack against the three players of B team.

- After finishing the action (goal, finishing, out or loss of the ball), a team leaves the playing area and the four players of B team attack the opposite goal against the three players of C team. The attack of B team is started by the fourth player by dribbling away from his goal into the playing area.

- After finishing the action (goal, finalization, out or loss of the ball), B team leaves the playing area and the four players of C team attack the opposite goal with three players of A team (one player of A team stays with the ball next to his goal). The attack of C team is started by the fourth player by dribbling away from his goal into the playing area.

- After finishing the action (goal, finalization, out or loss of the ball), C team leaves the playing area and the four players of A team attack the opposite goal with the three players of B team (one player of C team stays with the ball next to his goal). The attack of A team is started by the fourth player by dribbling away from his goal into the playing area.

- The teams take fast turns in offense and defense.

METHODICAL-ORGANIZATIONAL COMMENTS:

- The defending team moves in the direction toward the ball. The defender, who is closest to the ball, shifts, and the team players secure the area behind him.

- We maintain the active movement, orientation in space, and fast movement toward the ball.

- Fast switching from defensive to offensive action and the ability to play under pressure are important too.

- If necessary, the defenders can withdraw in a compact block in order to slow down the opponent's attacking action and at the same time prevent the opponent from performing a pass into the depth behind the defense.

DRILL 26: 3 + 1 PLAY AGAINST FIVE WITH ONE GOAL IN TWO PLAYING AREAS

Drill goal and focus: practice and improvement of the chain's transfer (level of the pressing drill 1, 2, 3, 4).

Fig. 5.3-10 The three-defender chain transfer drill

DRILL ORGANIZATION:

- Drill is done on one half of the pitch.

- A goalkeeper is in the goal.

- The playing area from the central line all the way to the penalty area is divided vertically into two equal parts.

- We place two small goals in both parts on the central line.

- Five attackers are divided so that two players play in each of the two parts and the fifth attacker moves around whole playing area.

- Defenders (three-defender chain and defensive midfielder) can play along the whole width.

DRILL FLOW:

- The action is started by the attackers, and their aim is to get through the defenders and finalize the action.

- The two attackers are in both parts, and they mustn't cross from one half into the other; they can only perform passes from one half into the other. The fifth attacker can play anywhere in both parts.

- The defenders and the defensive midfielder are moving around according to the center of the game from one part into the other in order to prevent the attackers from penetrating the defense.

- In case the defenders gain the possession of the ball, they have a chance to perform an attack on one of the small goals on the central line.

VARIATIONS:

- We increase the number of attackers by two so that three attackers play in each half in 7v4 play.

- The defense only consists of three-defender chain without the midfield player.

COMMENTS:

- The defenders must move fast and flexibly along the width of the pitch in order to create numerical

PART 3

balance or even an outnumber and get the attackers under pressure.

- When performing a fast and correct move, the defenders can isolate the opponent from his team players in the other half of the pitch, attack him aggressively, and remove the ball from him.

2. Pressing on Level Four, Formations, Defense Blocks Creation, and Transfer From Blocks Into Pressing

Four-Defender Defense

1. Four defenders, four-defender chain

2. Four midfield players:

(a) in a line (in 4-4-2, 3-4-3, and 4-1-4-1 system)

(b) nonlinear-diamond

Systematic

A group tactics means to defend together

Defense in a Group of Four

Numbers advantage	Equal numbers	Numbers disadvantage
4 against 3	4 against 4	4 against 5

A four-defender chain means much more than just the fact that four players simply stand in the back. Playing with the four-defender chain influences the whole team's play because the team must, for the purpose of providing an effective and successful defense; function as a united entity that is permanently focused on the ball in order to create an outnumber in the area near the ball.

The ball-oriented space defense of the four-defender chain allows the whole team to create an outnumber in different areas of the pitch; thus put pressure on an opponent. The opponent players, who are further away from the ball, are not being directly occupied, but the space is blocked so that more distant and unoccupied players can also be isolated and cannot receive a pass from their team player.

This type of play completes several aims and tasks at the same time:

The opponent player with the ball is under time and space pressure, his action is made harder, and he is more likely to make forced mistakes, which can be used, by coordination of more players, for gaining the possession of the ball and after fast switching, the players can start a dangerous counterstrike.

- The players, who are attacking the opponent, are secured; therefore, their goal isn't in direct danger even in case of failed attempt to gain the possession of the ball.

- The opponent with the ball is deprived of the opportunity to perform a dangerous pass into the depth in the specific time-space pressure while making an effort not to lose the ball. He is forced to use less dangerous passes from the back or into the width, which are more predictable and easier to catch.

- With an appropriate division, the depth and with of the pitch is well covered, and it's easier to solve the situations when the opponent has an opportunity to perform a pass behind the defense.

- The movement and actions of the chain allow the team to achieve an optimal solution of effective defense tasks in outnumber, equal number or inferiority in numbers.

- With an appropriate movement and orientation in space, the four defenders can cover the whole width of the pitch even with shorter running stages.

- Well-coordinated movement through the width and length of the playing area and creation of the defense forms (defense triangle, diagonal, or funnel) make the defense easier and the chance of successful defense is increased too.

- The action of the four-defender chain represents one of the forms of the group tactics (pressing on a group level); however, it must follow the principles of pressing on a team level and respect the rules of the space defense, which focuses on the ball.

- In an organized space defense, every player is responsible for the area assigned to him and the opponent moving in this area.

Creation of blocks and pressing

The way the defense chains moves is the essential automatism for building the pressing on a group and team level. The four-defender chain determinates the height of the block's position; thus determines the pressing height, position, and movement of the whole defense block. In the principle, the defense chain, together with the whole team (including the goalkeeper), adjust their movement according to the movement of the ball; they copy the ball's movement track. The movement of the defense block, which is oriented on the ball, is a preparatory defense activity. This activity can be in the form of movement toward the side verticals, extending forward (pump and pushing the opponent out), or withdrawing backward toward the team's goal in order to have the whole team prepared to apply pressing at the right time and the most suitable place as a peak of the defensive action with the aim to take the ball from the opponent. Untied and coordinated movement of all players ensure the ability of the team to occupy the space so that the opponent's attacking action is made harder or impossible by narrowing and shortening the pitch by which the opponent team's activity to defeat the defense and threaten the goal are decreased.

Compact and flexible movement of the whole defense block toward the ball creates an outnumber in the area of the ball's movement, which creates suitable conditions for gaining the possession of the ball. Positions and alignment of the opponent players without the ball and secondary and if the blocks moves correctly, the players, who are away from the ball, stay unoccupied yet under control because the numerical advantage around the ball isolates them from active participation in the attacking action.

The block creation and the block's movement after the ball are only reactions to playing situations, and they are the only conditions, which inevitably conclude in pressing and maximum activity with the aim to take the ball from the opponent. Transfer from a block to pressing and vice-versa is the fundamental part of highly efficient defense that enables the team to have the opponent actively under control and gain the possession of the ball more easily.

The basic and typical playing situations in the play of the four-defender chain and their solutions,

methodology of the practice and improvement of the four-defender chain play in relation to creation of blocks and pressing application too:

- Every player has his zone. The designated zone varies depending on the movement of the ball.

- If the ball is either in the right or left side vertical, the chain moves and creates a defensive diagonal.

- The chain attacks an opponent in the central vertical by creating a defensive triangle.

- The four-defender chain determines the height of pressing.

- If the opponent has an opportunity to perform a pass behind the defense, the chain withdraws backward, in so-called controlled withdrawal.

- In other situations, when the opponent moves the center of the game back to their half of the pitch, the chain moves forward and pushes the opponent (pump).

- In few cases, the chain can get the opponent into an offside position.

- The chain's activity sequence: movement—creation of blocks—pressing.

- In the space defense, a mutual coaching of players is indispensable.

- A gain or loss of the possession of the ball is followed by switching.

Solution of the typical situations:

1. The four-defender chain's play against playing system with one extended attacker.

2. The four-defender chain's play against playing system with two extended attackers.

3. The four-defender chain's play against fast counterstrike.

4. The four-defender chain's play against diagonal passes.

5. The four-defender chain's play against opponent frequently performing long and high passes to or behind the chain.

Every player has his zone

The four-defender chain, as well as other players, moves in their designated areas in order to block the space between the ball and their goal.

Fig. 5.3-11 Every player has his zone.

The opponent player without the ball, who enters the space of another player, must be occupied in this area and the opponent with the ball must be attacked.

Fig. 5.3-12 Every player has his zone depending on the movement of the ball.

The movement of the opponent player into another zone is followed by handing over and taking over this player. By this, if well-coordinated, we can ensure economical movement of the defenders without unnecessary running periods. Every player in a defense moves in his designated zone and during handing over and taking over the moving opponent the running sections of the players can't cross, because it represents a danger of freeing the space. The running sections can cross only behind the partners back. After taking over the opponent, every player stays in his zone.

The designated zone varies depending on the movement of the ball:

- To the side (left or right, creation of a defense diagonal)—movement to the side verticals

- Attacking the opponent in the central vertical and creation of the defense triangle

- Forward—after the opponent's back pass, pushing out an a pump

- Backward—retreat, controlled withdrawal

TRANSFER—MOVEMENT TO THE RIGHT OR LEFT SIDE VERTICAL

Creation of a defensive diagonal

The side defender moves toward the player with the ball while other team players position themselves diagonally

Fig. 5.3-13 Every player has his zone depending on the movement of the ball: handing over and taking over players.

Fig. 5.3-14 Transfer of the chain to the side vertical and creation of the defensive diagonal

behind him in order to secure each other. This is how the defense diagonal is formed. If the opponent team plays with two attackers, both center backs stay in the midfield zone and cover the extended attackers or the center backs move toward the side vertical and the attackers are covered by full back and center back who are on the more distant side from the ball. The way the chain moves may also depend on the skills of the opponent attackers; if the opponent's got high attackers who are dangerous in a play with head, it's more suitable for the center backs to stay in the central vertical because full backs are usually players who are shorter, fast, and flexible, but they aren't strong head-players.

Methodology principles when defending in the side vertical:

- Fast movement toward the ball.

- Maintaining the distance between the defenders and creation of a compact formation.

- Maintaining the height of attacking.

- Handing over and taking over attackers who move in the in center vertical.

DRILL 27: DEFENSE IN THE SIDE VERTICALS IN 4V7 PLAY IN THREE VERTICAL ZONES

DRILL FLOW AND ORGANIZATION:

The pitch is divided into three vertical zones. Three attackers play in the side verticals and one attacker plays in the central vertical. The attackers cooperate; however, they mustn't leave their designated zone (level of the pressing drill 1, 2, 3, 4, 5).

Fig. 5.3-15 The drill of the defense in the side verticals in 4v7 play in three zones

COACHING:

- The coach guides the players during the breaks between the playing sections.

- Very important aspect is also movement and choice of the place of the full back on the more distant side of the chain.

- The defender on the more distant side must move so that he keeps constant distance from the center back in order to maintain the compactness of the chain and must be prepared to catch diagonal passes from the side vertical.

DRILL 28: CREATION OF THE RIGHT (LEFT) DEFENSIVE BLOCK

Drill goal and focus: practice and improvement of the defensive block's play in the side vertical (level of the pressing drill 1, 2, 3, 4).

Fig. 5.3-16 Creation of the right defensive block and pressing in the right vertical

DRILL ORGANIZATION:

- The play takes place on one half of the pitch from the goal line to the central line in the right vertical, which is widened from the sideline to the level of goal area on the opposite side.

- Five attackers are playing with a fixed goal and a goalkeeper.

- Opposite the fixed goal on the central line, we place a portable goal and a goalkeeper.

- On the central line, from the sideline, we mark with cones a 5–7 m wide small goal.

- Five attackers are play against by six defenders, according to their posts: right full back, two center backs, two defensive midfielders and right side midfielder.

DRILL FLOW:

- The attackers are trying to score a goal into the fixed goal with a goalkeeper.

- The task of the defenders is to create a defensive block in the right vertical and proceed into aggressive pressing application.

- In case of gaining the possession of the ball, the defenders have an opportunity to attack the portable goal or get the ball through the marked line on the central line.

- The play is drilled three to four times lasting 5 or 15 minutes; however, the coach can interrupt the play if necessary due to corrections.

VARIATIONS:

- The play in the left vertical.

- 6v6 play.

- Instead of the portable goal, we place two or three small goals on the central line.

METHODICAL COMMENTS:

- The opponent with the ball, who is near the sideline, is being attacked by the side midfielder that is secured by the full back.

- The whole defensive chain (in this case it's a three-player chain) moves toward the sideline and creates a defensive diagonal behind the side midfielder; thus, the full back is a bit higher in order to secure the side midfielder and catch any passes toward the sideline if necessary.

- One of the defensive midfielders moves toward the sideline in order to close the space and double his team player if the opponent brings the ball inside.

- The other defensive midfielder moves in front of the center backs.

- If the opponent gets behind the side midfielder by performing dribbling or a pass, the opponent is attacked by the full back that is secured by center back that is nearer the ball.

- The out maneuvered side midfielder or defensive midfielder double from the back (situational doubling).

- According to the coaches instructions, the players force the opponent to dribble the ball toward "outside" (to the sideline) or toward "inside" (to the side vertical).

- In case the ball is positioned more inside the pitch, between the side and central vertical or in the central vertical, the center backs together with defensive midfielders form a defensive triangle. The full back and side midfielder move more inside in order to block the area and prevent the opponent from performing passes to the depth.

- The trainer coaches during the drill and after a successful completion of the drill, one of the center back players coaches further improvement.

DRILL 29: THE MOVEMENT OF THE DEFENSIVE BLOCK IN THE BASIC ALIGNMENT

Drill goal and focus: the team's movement according to the movement of the ball (level of the pressing drill 1, 2, 4, 5, 6, 7, 8).

Fig. 5.3-17 Pressing in designated areas

DRILL ORGANIZATION:

- The whole playing area of the pitch is used for the drill.

- Goalkeepers are in goals.

- The defending team is in the basic alignment according to the playing system used in matches.

- On the pitch, we mark three to four playing areas measuring 20 × 20 m, which are occupied by two or three attackers without the ball.

- The attacking team can be undernumbered.

- The balls are prepared in the goal of the attacking team.

DRILL FLOW:

- Every action is started by the goalkeeper performing a pass into the designated areas.

- The attackers are trying to keep the ball under control in the specific area.

- The pass directed into the marked area is a signal for the whole defensive block, which is moving toward the area with the ball and the players, who are nearest the ball, create a pressure intending to take the ball away.

- After gaining the possession of the ball, the team proceeds into a fast counterstrike on the opposite goal.

VARIATIONS:

- After a specific number of passes, the attackers can also perform passes between other playing areas and attack the goal together.

- We place the playing areas differently, according to the area in which we want to practice pressing.

METHODICAL COMMENTS:

- The signal for starting the pressing application is valid for all the players whose interest is to maintain the team's compactness; therefore, they keep a stable distance between each other.

- It's important that the players focus on the area where the pass is directed and move toward the ball.

- Necessary element is to put an energetic pressure on the ball and try to take the ball away in a constructive manner.

- After gaining the possession of the ball, the players switch to attacking actions.

Definition of the height of the block and pressing by the four-defender chain

Very important task of the four-defender chain is to control the flow of the whole team's pressing. The chain flexibly reacts to changing playing situations and, at the same time, the full back players coach the movement and actions of the other players.

The most significant task is to define the height of pressing. The players from the back decide when to maintain the height of pressing, which means when to be extended and "play high" and not to retreat, and on the other hand, when to withdraw and move backward all the way to the team's defense zone. The chain-players' ability to read the game allows the whole team to react flexibly to an opposite move of the whole defensive block; to recognize when

to extend from a withdrawn position and push opponent players from their defense zone into the central zone of the playing area.

Definition of the height of the block and pressing by the four-defender chain:

- Maintaining the height of the extension

- Controlled withdrawal

- Extension, pushing the opponent and pump

- Getting the opponent into the offside position. Maintaining the height of the extension

The four-defender chain is always supposed to be making an effort to maintain the extension height for as long as possible and not to withdraw, the withdrawal is allowed only in case of emergency. This type of behavior makes it easier for the team to keep the team's compactness, because the distance between the defensive chain and the midfield players is shorter. If the opponent passes the ball into the area between the defenders and midfielders, it's easy to create a pressing situation, the distance from the opponent isn't big, and the players are able to attack the opponent effectively. Maintaining the height of the extension is also the essential part of ultraoffensive pressing, which allows the players put pressure on the opponent and ball in a compact formation immediately after losing the possession of the ball. Maintaining the height by the four-defender chain must be connected with active movement of other players who must be consistently closing the areas on the opponent's half of the pitch. In this case, it's important for the whole team to create constant pressure on the ball. By doing this, the players prevent the opponent from performing long passes into the depth as the players create a free area on their half of the pitch by extending the whole team. Therefore, the goalkeeper must also cooperate and take over the function of libero. By putting pressure on the ball, the team can regain the possession of the ball fast and create dangerous shooting situations after switching quickly to offensive stage.

The situations in which there's no danger of high pass behind the defense and the four-defender chain can be extended if:

- The opponent player with the ball is under pressure.

- The team is compact and well-organized, the players keep correct division into the depth and width, and the team has enough players between the ball and the team's goal.

- The opponent plays statically.

- The opponent player doesn't receive a pass while moving.

- The opponent with the ball is turned with his back to the direction of the attack.

- After an inaccurate opponent's pass when the opponent is further away from the ball and must run after it.

DRILL 30: MAINTAINING THE HEIGHT OF THE EXTENSION

Drill goal and focus: practice and improvement of maintaining the extension height (level of the pressing drill 1, 2, 4, 5, 8).

Fig. 5.3-18 Maintaining the height when the opponent, who is taking over the ball, is turned with his back to the direction of the attack.

DRILL ORGANIZATION:
- The drill takes place in the area of about 5 m behind the central line until the area between the central and attack zone, from the defending team's point of view.

- Seven players in defensive positions in their positions, four defenders forming a four-defender chain, two defensive midfielders in front of the chain, and one withdrawn center forward (man in the hole) or attacker (in 4-2-3-1 playing system).

- Seven players, who are imitating the opponent, are also in their positions: two center backs, three midfielders (right, middle, and left), and two attackers, or one withdrawn center forward (man in the hole) and one extended attacker.

- The goalkeeper plays with the team, which is exercising the extension height maintenance.

DRILL FLOW:
- The coach determines the course of the attacking action so that the attacking team creates special playing situations, which are necessary for practicing the extension height maintenance (pass to the midfielder who is turned with his back to the direction of the attack, pass from the center back to the side vertical to a static player or inaccurate pass).

- The defensive players repeatedly practice blocking and transfer of the area in the specified situations.

- The successful completion of this exercise is followed by 7v7 play with one goal and goalkeeper in which the attacking players mustn't perform long or deep passes behind the defense.

VARIATIONS:

- 9v7 play (if the 4-2-3-1 system is preferred—four defenders, two defensive midfielders, and three midfielders) or in an exercise that concludes from 4-1-4-1 system (four defenders, one defensive midfielder, and four midfielders).

- 8v7 play (four defenders and four midfielders in 4-4-2 system).

- The play of the whole team in an outnumber 11v7, 11v8, 11v9, or in an equal number 11v11.

Fig. 5.3-19 Maintaining the height in a situation when the opponent is playing statically and doesn't receive the pass while moving.

Fig. 5.3-20 Maintaining the height after an inaccurate pass from an opponent who is forced to run after the ball.

METHODICAL, ORGANIZATIONAL COMMENTS:

-   First, the coach practices the drill with the players in simple conditions without heavy load and effort to take the ball from each other. Instead, he focuses on recognition of the playing situation, space relation, coordinated activity of the defenders and coaching.

-   In this part, the coach is more concentrated on space relations and formation of blocks.

-   After a successful completion of the first stage of the drill, the players practice the drill in a match pace intending to take the ball from each other.

-   The practice in constant conditions is followed by the playing form with changeable playing situations.

-   In this form of practice and improvement, when the formation of blocks has been automatized, the players concentrate on transfer from the block into highly active pressing.

In the training process, we mustn't forget about the close relation between the block defense and pressing application. The block creation is only a preparation of which the peak is aggressive pressing with the aim to take the ball from the opponent. The most effective and complex is highly developed pressing, which concludes from a high defensive block.

An extended defensive block is the essential condition for ultraoffensive pressing, which is the most effective pressing while for the opponent it's the most unpleasant way of active defense. This type of defense is very demanding from the point of view of the players' technical-tactical and condition skills. There are also high demands on the players' mental abilities: switching, review, and game reading.

3. Backward Movement, Withdrawal, and Controlled Withdrawal of the Defensive Chain

If the four-defender chain is high, it creates a lot of free space behind the defense. When an opponent with the ball releases himself from the pressure or the players aren't able to put him under pressure, he has a suitable opportunity to pass the ball behind the defensive chain. If the four-defender chain is under numbered (mostly after loss of the ball in midfield zone), and the game situation for the chain is adverse, it's suitable, for the purpose of narrowing the area or removal of the area from the opponent, to withdraw toward the team's goal. By withdrawal of the four-defender chain, we achieve a slower pace of the opponent's attack and, at the same time, we gain time for the defensive midfielder or other midfield players to return. By narrowing the area, the team makes it impossible or at least harder for the opponent to play into the depth and perform passes behind the defense. The withdrawal must also be controlled and organized; therefore, it must be drilled in the team's training process. During the withdrawal, it's important to maintain the positions and formations in order not to disrupt the organization of the defense and compactness of the team. The withdrawal must be carried out in a block; the players perform the withdrawal from a high to middle block and from the middle to deep block.

In case of losing the possession of the ball, when the team is offensively reorganized and the defensive organization is disrupted, the team must reorganize during the withdrawal into a compact defensive formation as soon as possible. The important part is to maintain the division into the depth and mainly the width in the attacking stage too; thus to secure the team's actions during the defensive stage of the game. Correct alignment of the team during the attacking stage makes fast formation into a block easier even in case of losing the ball.

During the movement of the four-defender chain and the whole defensive block toward the team's goal, it's necessary to follow the principles of the space defense, which focuses on the ball; as it's also important to create defensive formations during the process of withdrawal.

If the ball is positioned in the side vertical, the four-defender chain forms into a defensive diagonal. If the center of the game is in the side vertical, the chain forms into a defensive triangle. The four-defender chain withdraws to the distance of 20 to 25 m from the team's goal. The rule is, the closer the chain is to the team's goal, the smaller the distances between the defenders are and the tighter the chain and consequently the whole block is. It's essential for the whole defensive formation to become narrow and withdraw at the same time and close the direct access to the goal on order to secure the safe center of the defense.

The result of this action is formation of a defensive block in the shape of a defensive funnel, which creates suitable conditions for repeated application of active pressing.

Situations in which the four-defender team cannot be extended any more due to a threat of a pass behind the defense; therefore, the chain must withdraw:

- The opponent center back with the ball isn't under pressure (he is insufficiently occupied or he released himself from the pressure), there's no chance to put pressure on the ball, and he has an opportunity to perform a long pass into the free area behind the defensive chain. If the center back passes the ball in front of him, we can expect a long pass being performed.

- The opponent midfielder with the ball isn't under pressure (he is insufficiently occupied or he released himself from the pressure), and the distance from the chain isn't big. In this case, there's a threat of the depth pass behind the chain.

- The opponent quickly relocates the play into an unoccupied side vertical area. The opponent player has an opportunity to get behind the defense block by performing fast dribbling, or he has a chance to perform a pass behind the defensive chain after gaining the possession of the ball.

- The team loses the possession of the ball during the opening of the game or interlude in the central zone (fig. 5.3-21).

Fig. 5.3-21 The opponent center back with the ball has an opportunity to perform a long pass behind the defensive chain.

DRILL 31: THE FOUR-DEFENDER CHAIN'S WITHDRAWAL WHEN AN OPPONENT CENTER BACK PERFORMS A LONG PASS BEHIND THE CHAIN

Drill goal and focus: practicing the withdrawal of the four-defender chain after a long pass (level of the pressing drill 1, 2, 4).

Fig. 5.3-22 The practice of the four-defender chains' withdrawal after a long pass into the central vertical area and formation of a defensive triangle

DRILL ORGANIZATION:

- The drill takes place on approximately two-thirds of the pitch.

- The participating players are four defenders against four attacking players.

- The four-defender chain is in a high position right behind the central line on the team's half of the pitch.

- A goalkeeper also participates in the drill.

DRILL FLOW:

- The exercise is started by the attacking player performing a long and high pass from his half of the pitch behind the four-defender chain into the central or side vertical.

- The long pass is a signal for the attacking players to take positions behind the defensive chain and for the defenders it's a signal to move toward their goal.

- The task of the attackers is to gain the possession of the ball, and the defenders' task is to perform an organized withdrawal and create defensive formations (triangle in the central vertical and diagonal in the side vertical).

- The pass is followed by 4v4 play with one goal.

- If the defenders get the ball, they are trying to keep it (with the goalkeeper's assistance) and perform a pass to the other half of the pitch.

- The play lasts two to three minutes.

VARIATIONS:

- Four defenders and two attackers in 3v4 drill.

- After gaining the possession of the ball, the defenders perform passes into two or three small goals, which are placed behind the central line.

Fig. 5.3-23 The practice of the four-defender chain's withdrawal after a long pass into the side vertical and formation a defensive diagonal

INSTRUCTIONS FOR THE COACH:

- The coach demands from the defenders fast movement toward their goal.

- The defenders start the withdrawal process right before the long pass is performed.

- The controlled withdrawal must maintain the organization and mutual securing: in the side vertical, the center back player, who is nearer the ball, takes the direction toward the ball and the other center back together with the full back secure him by which they create a defensive triangle. The other full back, who is further away from the ball, occupies the area next to the defensive triangle.

- If the ball is directed to the side vertical, the chain transfers into a defensive diagonal.

- The goalkeeper is extended from the goal and secures the defenders even after gaining the possession of the ball and cooperates with the defenders.

- The emphasis is put on the correct occupation of the area, gaining the possession of the ball as well as on gaining the rebounded balls.

- The mutual communication and coaching is practiced too.

DRILL 32: WITHDRAWAL OF THE WHOLE TEAM WHEN THERE'S A THREAT OF A PASS BEHIND THE DEFENSE AND FORMATION OF THE DEFENSIVE FUNNEL

Drill goal and focus: practice of the whole team's withdrawal when the opponent's free player has an opportunity to pass the ball behind the defense (level of the pressing drill 1, 2, 3, 4, 5, 8).

Fig. 5.3-24 Formation of a tunnel during the withdrawal and narrowing the area

DRILL ORGANIZATION:
- The drill takes place all over the pitch.

- Two teams are practicing the drill against each other—the defending team with full number of the players and the attacking team can be under numbered.

- Goalkeepers are positioned in their goals.

- The defending team starts the drill in a high or middle block.

DRILL FLOW:
- The drill always started by one of the attacking team's free player performing dribbling on his half of the pitch.

- The dribbling performed by the free opponent is a signal for an organized withdrawal of the whole defending team.

- The defending team withdraws so that the four-defender chain gets to the distance of 20 to 25 m from their goal.

- This is followed by a free play with two goals.

METHODICAL COMMENTS:
- If the team is in an extended position and the opponent player with the ball isn't under pressure, which causes a threat of a pass behind the defense into the free area, the whole team must withdraw by which the players take the free space from the opponent team.

- It's important for the players, who make decisions, to learn to predict the situations when the opponent intends to play long balls behind the defense (the opponent defender is preparing the ball before performing a pass; as well as the way the opponent player runs toward the ball reveals his intention to play a long ball) orto recognize the situations when the opponent player has an opportunity to pass the ball behind the defense (the player with the ball isn't under pressure).

- First, the defenders must disconnect from the attackers and move backward by 2 to 3 m, at the same time, they must observe and analyze the game situation whether the opponent player is really going to perform a long pass or not. In case the long pass behind the defense is performed, the defenders withdraw deeper; however, the withdrawal must stop in the distance of maximum of 20 to 25 m from the goal.

- During the withdrawal, the players don't only move toward their goal but they also move to the middle. By doing this, they create a funnel, which makes it harder for the opponent to perform a counterstrike. The funnel also blocks the area so the opponent is unable to pass the ball behind the defense. Slowing the opponent's attack down allows the midfielders to return and create an outnumber in the area near the ball.

- The withdrawal must be controlled and well organized. The withdrawal must also respect the principles of mutual securing and in the area near the ball it must result in formation of defensive shapes (in the side vertical it's a defensive diagonal and in the central vertical it's a defensive triangle). The mutual defenders' securing is also supposed to eliminate the opponent's chances to extend a long pass behind the defense because the opponent, who disposes of a fast attacker, can create a situation of a direct threat of the team's goal and, at the same time, increases the chance of gaining the possession of the ball.

- A well-organized withdrawal also increases chances to gain rebounded balls. The team is able to accomplish this important task if all the midfield players return into the withdrawn block and mainly if the defensive midfielders move to the center of the game.

- The distance between two players during the backward movement as well, depending on the ball, must be constant and maximum 10 m.

- The withdrawal is ideally carried out in a block: from high to middle block and from middle to deep block.

- For the formation, it's important to remain compact; as well as it's essential the players win personal fights after transfer from a block to pressing.

- Just as important part is a flexible reaction of the four-defender chain and the whole defensive block to changeable situations. If the defense performs a withdrawal due to which the opponent team loses the space for performing a long pass behind the defence line and the opponent player performs a short pass instead a long one, the defensive block is extended and by the signal given by the four-defender chain, the players push the opponent players out of their half of the pitch in the direction of the ball and create pressure on the ball (pump).

A withdrawal in the situation when the opponent midfielder with the ball isn't under pressure (he is insufficiently occupied or he released himself from the pressure) and the distance from the chain isn't big.

In this situation, when the opponent midfielder is unoccupied, there's a threat of the depth pass behind the chain being performed either to the extended attacker or the side midfielder.

When the play is transferred into the central zone of the playing area, the four-defender chain moves between the defensive and central zone and in this area creates, together with other players, a compact central defensive block, which allows the players to apply central pressing. Pressing in the central zone requires a high level of adaptability and flexibility when copying the ball's movement and creating time-space pressure on the ball, because the opponent players have more space for getting out of the pressing situation behind and in front of the defensive block. The play in the central zone demands from the four-defender chain, which determines the height and width of the defensive block, a flexible, and fast reaction to changeable play situations. High demands are also on fast extension or withdrawal of the chain as well as on the width movement depending on the ball's movement.

Fig. 5.3-25 The Withdrawal when the opponent midfielder has an opportunity to perform a pass behind the tour-defender chain

Defending in the central zone requires from the chain to perform an excellent coordination with other players. An important task of the midfielders is to block the space by fast transfer so that they create pressure on the player with the ball and makes the opponent player unable to perform the depth passes behind the defense, use wall pass, or run out of the tandem. Instead, the midfielders force the opponent player to pass the ball from the back or into the width. The four-defender chain can also play right in front of the penalty area, about 25 m from their goal, either because the opponent team has a play advantage or they have performed a controlled withdrawal in order to take the space from the opponent and make the opponent players unable to perform a fast counterstrike. They may also play right in front of the penalty area due to their coach's instructions that requires them to transfer into a fast counterstrike from the withdrawn positions. In these situations, the whole team creates a deep defensive block.

DRILL 33: THE PRACTICE OF THE WITHDRAWAL WHEN THE OPPONENT MIDFIELDER ISN'T UNDER PRESSURE AND FORMATION OF BLOCKS

Drill goal and focus: withdrawal when the opponent has an opportunity to perform a pass from the central zone behind the defense (level of the pressing drill 1, 2, 3, 4)

Fig. 5.3-26 Withdrawal in 6v6 play.

DRILL ORGANIZATION:

- The drill takes place approximately on two-thirds of the pitch.

- The participating players are four defenders and two defending midfielders against six attacking players.

- The four-defender chain is in a high position right behind the central line on their half of the pitch and the two defending midfielders are in front of the chain.

- The goalkeeper also plays with the defenders.

- The attacking players are divided into two extended attackers and four midfield players.

DRILL FLOW:

- The exercise is always started by one of the attacking team's side midfielders performing dribbling.

- The side midfielder performs a pass from the side vertical to a free

- player in the central vertical (we leave one of the attacking players in the central vertical free in the first stage of the drill).

- The player in the central vertical takes over the ball and moves it toward the four-defender chain.

- The task of the defending players is to perform a perpendicular pass behind the defense and create a shooting situation.

- The defending players and the goalkeeper are trying to take the space from the opponent by withdrawing and gain the possession of the ball.

- After gaining the possession of the ball, the defenders pass the ball to the opponent's half of the playing area.

VARIATIONS:

- Six (defenders) to eight (attackers) play.

- After gaining the possession of the ball, the defenders have an opportunity to perform a pass to one of the three small goals on the opponent's half of the playing area (there's one small goal in each vertical).

- 8v8 play on two thirds of the pitch with two goals and goalkeepers.

- 11v11 play on the whole pitch—withdrawal from high to middle block and from middle to deep block.

Fig. 5.3-27 Withdrawal of the defensive block in 11v11 play

COACHING:

- The coach requires fast movement from the defenders toward their goal.

- The defenders must quickly recognize the situation in which there's a threat of a pass being performed behind the defensive chain (game reading).

- The controlled withdrawal must maintain the organization and mutual securing.

- The crucial parts of the withdrawal are the movement activities and coaching, which conclude from the four-defender team. They are followed by the midfielders and the whole defensive block's actions while the compactness of the whole team must be maintained.

- We first practice the situations only with the four-defender chain. After that, we practice the cooperation of the defensive chain with the midfielders during the withdrawal process and after a successful completion of these parts of the drill, we practice the withdrawal of the whole defensive block. In this case, it's actually a transfer of the central defensive block to a place in front of the penalty area and formation of a deep block.

- After following the principles of the space relations, we practice a transfer from a block defense to active pressing in order to maintain the compactness during the withdrawal too.

- The aim is always to gain the possession of the ball.

- The goalkeeper is extended from the goal and secures the defenders even after gaining the possession of the ball and cooperates with them.

- We practice mutual communication and coaching.

Withdrawal in the situation when the opponent player quickly transfers the center of the game into an unoccupied side vertical area

The opponent player has an opportunity to get behind the defensive block by performing fast dribbling, as well as he has a chance, after taking over the ball, to pass the ball behind the defensive chain. This type of withdrawal is very specific because the players also have to transfer to the depth during the withdrawal process and at the same time, orientate to the opposite defensive diagonal.

DRILL 34: WITHDRAWAL IN THE SITUATION WHEN THE OPPONENT QUICKLY TRANSFERS THE CENTER OF THE GAME INTO AN UNOCCUPIED SIDE VERTICAL AREA

Drill and goal focus: practice and improvement of the withdrawal after transfer of the center of the game by the opponent (level of the pressing drill 1, 2, 3, 4, 5).

Fig. 5.3-28 Withdrawal in 6v6 situation when the opponent quickly transfers the center of the game into an unoccupied side vertical area

DRILL ORGANIZATION:

- The drill takes place approximately on two-thirds of the pitch.

- The participating players are four defenders and two defending midfield players against six attacking players.

- The four-defender chain is in a high position right behind the central line on their half of the pitch and the two defending midfielders are in front of the chain.

- The goalkeeper also plays with the defenders.

- The attacking players are divided into six extended attackers and four midfield players.

DRILL FLOW:

- The exercise is always started by one of the attacking team's center midfielders performing a pass to his team player into a free side vertical or first performing a pass from an occupied side vertical to the center midfielder, which followed by a transfer of the game center into the free side vertical.

- After transferring the center of the game, all the defending players withdraw and at the same time they move to the opposite vertical.

- The task of the defending players is to get behind the defense and create a shooting situation.

- By withdrawal and transfer, the defending players and the goalkeeper try to take the space from the opponent and gain the possession of the ball.

- After gaining the possession of the ball, the defenders pass the ball to the opponent's half of the pitch.

VARIATIONS:

- Six (defending players) to eight (attackers).

- After gaining the possession of the ball, the attackers have an opportunity to pass the ball to one of the three small goals that are placed on the opponent's half of the pitch (one small goal is places in each vertical).

- 8v8 play on two thirds of the pitch with two goals and goal keepers.

- 11v11 play on the whole pitch—withdrawal from middle to deep block.

Fig. 5.3-29 Withdrawal of the defensive block in a situation when the opponent quickly transfers the center of the game into an unoccupied side vertical

METHODICAL, ORGANIZATIONAL COMMENTS:

- This type of withdrawal is very specific because during the withdrawal process, the team also has to transfer to the width and the opposite defensive diagonal.

- The withdrawal process is connected to the change of the right defensive block to the left one or vice versa. In spite of the reorganization during the withdrawal process, the players must maintain the compactness, good organization, and mutual securing.

- Fast movement of the defensive four-defender chain is important in order to create compactness of the whole defensive block.

- The full back, who is more distant from the ball, transfers fast to the opposite vertical toward the ball.

- The center back players follow the full back's movement diagonally in order to secure him if necessary.

- The full back, who is nearer the ball, withdraws into the position behind the center backs players in order to create a defensive diagonal (a withdrawal in the side vertical forms into a defensive diagonal).

- The midfielders and attackers transfer the same way depending on the preferred play system.

- The task of the defending team is to take the free space from the opponent by performing a fast withdrawal and transfer by which the opponent is unable to escape to the wing area or perform a pass behind the defensive chain.

- The distance between two players while moving backward and to the width at the same time must be constant and maximum 10 m.

- The withdrawal process is carried out ideally in a block: from middle to deep block.

- It's important for the formation to always remain compact and for the players to win personal fights after the transfer from a block to pressing.

- The crucial part of the withdrawal process is the movement activity and coaching of the four-defending chain followed by the activity of the midfielders and the whole defensive block while maintaining the whole team's compactness.

- This is the reason why we first practice the situations only with the four-defender chain and after that we practice the cooperation of the four defender team with the midfielders during the withdrawal process; after a successful completion of this part of the drill, we practice the withdrawal of the whole team; in this case it's actually the transfer of the central defensive block, which is oriented in one side vertical in front of the penalty area, and creation of a deep block, which is located in the opposite side vertical.

- After following the principle of the space relation, for the purpose of maintaining the compactness during the withdrawal, the players perform a transfer from a block defense to active pressing.

- The aim is always to gain the possession of the ball start a counter-attack.

- The goalkeeper is extended from the goal, he secures the defenders after gaining the possession of the ball and cooperates with them.

- The players also practice mutual communication and coaching.

4. Extension of the Defensive Line Forward, Pushing the Opponent Out and the Pump

One of the purposes of the extension is the security against a long pass behind the defense from the opponent. The extension and following pressing on the ball are effective only if the opponent player with the ball is under pressure due to an outnumber in the area around the ball; therefore, the opponent can't opt for a pass forward behind the defense. In case the ball gets to a free opponent player and he has an opportunity to perform a long pass behind the defense, the four-defender chain and the whole team must be prepared to carry out controlled withdrawal in order to maintain the team compact.

The play situations, which are suitable for an extension of the whole defense for the purpose of the pump application:

- The opponent's back pass

- The opponent's inaccurate pass when starting the game or during an interlude

- When the opponent takes over the ball on his half of the pitch with his back turned to the goal

- Long kickoffs from the defensive to the central or attacking zone of the team, which was under pressure

- The goalkeeper's long kick offs performed after receiving a return pass form the defender

- After the four-defender chain's controlled withdrawal when a long pass is expected but a short pass is performed

Pushing the opponent out after a return pass

In a situation when the opponent can't find any other solution but a return pass while being under pressure and he performs the pass to the back, the whole team extends in a compact defensive shape toward the ball. The purpose of this is to push the opponent out and move the offside line as far as possible from the team's goal, decrease the threat for the goal, increase and keep the pressure on the opponent, who performed the back pass, and contract the area by which the players prevent the opponent from renewing the attacking action. The process of pushing the opponent out is led by the four-defender chain and must be coordinated with the other team players in the central and attacking formation. The beginning of the pushing is started by a signal that comes from the back from the four-defender chain. An important condition for extension of the defense is the game reading, mainly from the four-defender chain's point of view. For security reasons, it's unsuitable to run out after each back pass.

DRILL 35: THE PRACTICE OF PUSHING THE OPPONENT AFTER A RETURN PASS IN THE SIDE VERTICAL

Drill goal and focus: the practice of the four-defender chain's extension (level of the pressing drill 2, 4)

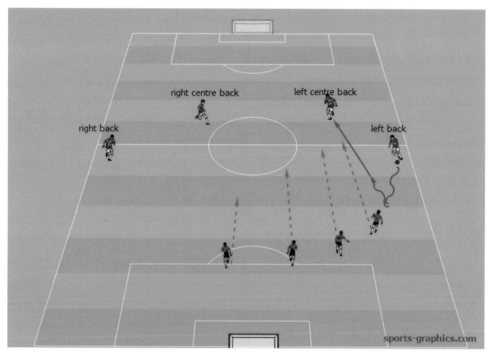

Fig. 5.3-30 The pump: pushing the opponent out (e.g., the opponent's full back passes the ball from the back to the center back)

DRILL ORGANIZATION:

- Four players who imitate their opponent in an attacking stage; they are positioned in the central zone on their half of the pitch are they also play a role of defenders who play on their posts in the four-defender chain.

- The four defender chain, which practices the extension, is positioned opposite on the other half of the pitch between the defensive and central zone.

DRILL FLOW:

- The drill is always started by the attacking team's full back player performing dribbling in the side vertical.

- The four-defender chain transfers to the side vertical in order to block and attack the attacking full back and creates a defensive diagonal.

- In this situation, the player, who is dribbling, stops the ball, and performs a return pass to the center back who was securing him in the side vertical.

- After the back pass, the four-defender chain extends toward the ball by sprinting.

- The practice can be carried out with two four-defender chains, which exchange their defensive and offensive tasks after each action.

- The drill is practiced alternatively in both vertical.

METHODICAL, ORGANIZATIONAL COMMENTS:

- The four-defender chain concludes from the basic alignment between the defensive and central zone on the team's half of the pitch. The chain moves from this alignment to the side vertical and creates a defensive diagonal and extends after the back pass. It's vital to maintain the compactness of the chain during this movement.

- The player, who is the closest to the ball, runs to the ball and the other players move according to him.

- The coach defines the means of communication between the players during the drill. Mutual coaching is indispensable in the space defense. The signal comes from the center back players and this action must be automatized too.

- The perfect load can be achieved when we have an opportunity to practice with two four-defender chains, which take turns after each drill practice—one group works as a chain in attacking stage and the other group practices defense. By this, we can change the load intensity in the defense with less intensive offense.

- The coach makes sure the distances between the defenders are maintained and the movement of the chain during the transfer is fast and compact.

- The coach guides the drill and corrects the mistakes while the exchange takes place or he interrupts the drill and immediately corrects the incorrect alignment or action of the defenders.

- The practice of the four-defender chain's extension is the core of pressing on the whole team level as it doesn't appear isolated; therefore, the defender chain's practice must be immediately followed by the practice with the whole team.

VARIATIONS:

The practice of pushing the opponent by in the side vertical using a block defense (level of the pressing drill 1, 2, 3, 4, 5, 8).

DRILL ORGANIZATION AND METHODICAL COMMENTS:

- The basic alignment practices the push in a preparatory play, preferably in 11v11 play or in an outnumber (according to the number of players, which the coach disposes of).

- The preparatory play takes place all over the pitch.

- The practice is always started by the attacking team's full back player performing dribbling in the side vertical.

- In this situation, the dribbling player stops the ball and performs a return pass to the center back who was securing him in the side vertical.

- After the back pass, the whole team extends compactly toward the ball by sprinting.

- Every interruption of the play is followed by the full back's dribbling and a consequent pack pass; the players play without standard situations.

- The drill takes place in both verticals.

- Mutual communication between the players and coaching are important parts of the drill. The whole team moves jointly according to prearranged signals. These signals define which players attack the ball, block the space, and secure the attacking players.

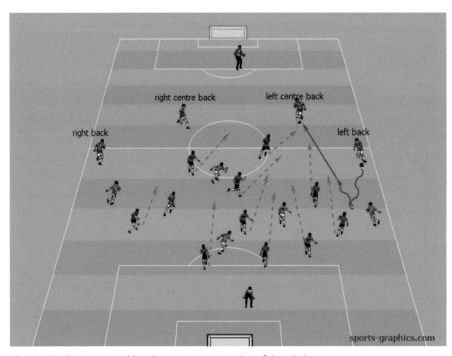

Fig. 5.3-31 The pump—pushing the opponent, extension of the whole team

DRILL 36: PUSHING THE OPPONENT AFTER A RETURN PASS IN THE CENTRAL VERTICAL

Drill goal and focus: the practice of the four-defender chain's extension (level of the pressing drill 1, 2, 3, 4, 5, 6, 7, 8)

Fig. 5.3-32 The pump—pushing the opponent (e.g., the opponent's central midfielder passes the ball from the back to the center back)

DRILL ORGANIZATION:

- The basic alignment practices the push in a preparatory play, preferably in 11v11 play or in an out number (according to the number of layers the coach disposes of), e.g., 11v9 or 11v8.

- The preparatory play takes place all over the pitch.

- The defending team comes out of a deep or middle block.

DRILL FLOW:

- The drill is always started by the defending midfielder or the attacking team's withdrawn center forward attacker (man in the hole) performing dribbling in the central vertical.

- In this situation, the dribbling player stops the ball and passes the ball back to the center back player who was securing him in the central vertical.

- After the back pass, the whole team extends toward the ball by sprinting.

- Every interruption of the play is followed by the midfielder or withdrawn center forward player's dribbling in the central vertical and a consequent back pass; the players play without standard situations.

METHODICAL, ORGANIZATIONAL COMMENTS:

- We are practicing from a deep block (the four-defender chain is in front of the penalty area) or from a middle block (from the basic alignment between the defensive or central zone on the team's half of the pitch).

- The player, who is the nearest the ball (in this case it's the extended attacker or withdrawn center forward (man in the hole), runs to the ball, and the other players move according to his movement in order to close the area and create pressure on the player with the ball.

- The coach is always supposed to demand compactness and fast movement of the whole block.

- The team's aim is push the opponent, move the offside border as far as possible from the team's goal, decrease the threat for the team's goal, and maintain the pressure on the opponent; by doing this, the team makes it harder or impossible for the opponent to renew the attacking action.

- The process of pushing is led by the four-defender chain and must be coordinated with the other team players in the central and attacking formation.

- The aim is always to gain the possession of the ball.

- The goalkeeper is extended from the goal and secures the defenders.

- The players' mutual communication is an important part of the drill. The coach must play an appropriate attention to this part of his team's cooperation.

- The drill lasts fifteen minutes including breaks during which the coach comments and corrects the team's action. During the drill, we connect the play situations after a return pass in the right and left side vertical.

- The coach guides the players between two actions or interrupts the play in order to correct mistakes.

Similar situations to an opponent's return pass happen in situations when the team kicks the ball out of the defense zone to the central or attacking zone; this mostly happens when a team is under pressure. Also, if a defensive player is under pressure, he chooses to perform a return pass to the goalkeeper who consequently kicks the ball to the central or even attacking zone; this creates suitable situations for pushing the opponent. Method of the drill and improvement of pushing the opponent in these situations is the same or similar to a return pass performed by an opponent.

Pushing the opponent after long kicks from the defensive to the central or attacking zone performed by the team, which is under pressure.

Fig. 5.3-33 The pump alters the kick from the team's defensive zone.

Pushing the opponent after the goalkeeper's long kicks after a return pass from a defender

Fig. 5.3-34 The pump after the goalkeeper's long kick

Pushing the opponent after an inaccurate pass during the opponent's interlude or during the start of the play

The push should be the following action of the team even when the opponent team has problems with opening an attacking stage or during an interlude on the team's half of the pitch and the pass is directed to the player, who is in an unsuitable position, or the pass is inaccurate; therefore the receiving player has problems with taking over and control of the ball. In this situation, the four-defender chain gives a signal to the whole team to extend in a compact formation toward the ball and "chase" the player who has problems with taking over the ball. This situation also creates a suitable condition for an application of the pump after an inaccurate pass, which the opponent player has to catch up with.

DRILL 37: PUSHING THE OPPONENT AFTER AN INACCURATE PASS DURING THE OPPONENT INTERLUDE

Drill goal and focus: practice of the four-defender chain's extension (level of the pressing drill 1, 2, 3, 4, 5, 6, 7, 8)

Fig. 5.3-35 The pump after the opponent's inaccurate pass from the central to side vertical

DRILL ORGANIZATION:

- Six players, who imitate the opponent in the attacking stage, are aligned in the central zone. Two players are on the team's half of the pitch in the side vertical in the positions of the center back players. Other two players are in the side verticals; they are little extended to the opponent's half of the pitch. The remaining two players either take positions of attackers or one player is an extended attacker and the other has a post of a defensive midfielder.

- Opposite, on the other side of the pitch between the defensive and central zone, is the four-defender chain that practices the extension.

- The two defensive midfielders are in front of the four-defender chain.

DRILL FLOW:

- The drill starts by the attacking team's player passing the ball between each other.

- The four-defender chain and the two defending midfielders move according to the ball's movement.

- After a few passes, the attacking team's players perform an inaccurate pass from the central to the side vertical.

- After the inaccurate pass, the four-defender chain extends toward the ball by sprinting.

- We practice the exercise alternatively in both verticals.

VARIATIONS:

- The inaccurate pass is directed from the side to the central vertical.

- The four-defender chain practices together with all the midfielders 8v6 (in 4-4-2 play system) or 9v6 (4-2-3-1 or 4-1-4-1 play system).

- The drill is practiced by the whole team (11v6, 11v8, or 11v11).

- The practice of an application of the pump after an inaccurate pass, which the player must catch up with while running toward his goal.

- Pushing the opponent when the opponent player, who is on his half of the pitch or in the central zone, takes over the ball in a position with his back toward his opponent players.

- After a controlled withdrawal of the four-defender chain when the players expect a long pass behind the defense to be performed but a short one is performed instead.

Fig. 5.3-36 The pump after an inaccurate opponent's pass from the side vertical to the central vertical

Fig. 5.3-37 The pump after an inaccurate opponent's pass during the opening of the play

Suitable conditions are also created after an inaccurate pass, which the opponent player must catch up with while running toward his goal.

If the opponent performs a perpendicular pass from his half of the pitch to his team player, who is turned with his back toward the defending players, it's suitable to extend toward the ball and apply pressing.

Fig. 5.3-38 The pump after an inaccurate pass, which the opponent player is catching up with while running toward his goal

Fig. 5.3-39 The pump after a pass from the back when the opponent player receives the ball with his back turned toward his team players

METHODICAL, ORGANIZATIONAL COMMENTS:

- The four-defender chain and the defending midfield players emerge from the basic alignment between the defensive and central zone on the team's half of the pitch. This six-member compact block moves from these positions according to the ball's movement. The block actually copies the ball's movement track. It's important to maintain the compactness of the block even during this movement.

- After an inaccurate pass to the side vertical, the full back, who is the nearest the ball, runs out toward the ball, and other defenders follow his movement so that they form a defensive diagonal.

- One of the defensive midfielders moves to the side vertical toward the ball.

- After an inaccurate pass to the central vertical, the defensive midfielder, who is nearer the ball, runs to the ball. Other players secure him so that they form a defensive triangle.

- After gaining the possession of the ball, the defenders try to keep the ball in the central zone (e.g., play by number of passes).

- The coach determines the way of communication of the players during the drill. Mutual coaching is indispensable in space defense. The signal comes from the center back players and this action must be automatized too.

- The coach makes sure the distances between the defenders are maintained and the movement of the chain during transfer and extension is fast and compact.

- The coach guides the drill and corrects mistakes while the exchange takes place or he interrupts the drill and immediately corrects the incorrect alignment or action of the defenders.

- The practice of the four-defender extension is the core of pressing on the whole team level as it doesn't appear isolated; therefore, the defender chain's practice must be immediately followed by the practice with the whole team.

Extension of the four-defender chain and defensive block after a controlled withdrawal when a long pass behind the defense was expected but a short pass was performed.

Defensive movement maneuvers depend on the ball's movement; therefore, they must be flexibly changed depending on the changing play situations. For example, when a team is in an extended position, and a free opponent player with the ball (mostly the center back) has an opportunity to perform a long pass behind the defense, the defenders already start withdrawing right before the long pass is performed. First, the defenders must disconnect from the attackers and move back 2 to 3 m and at the same time, they must observe and analyze the game situation whether the opponent is really going to perform a long pass. If the defenders take the space necessary for performing long pass behind the defense from the opponent by performing a withdrawal and the opponent performs a short pass instead a long one, the four-defender chain gives a signal to the defensive block to extend toward the ball, push the opponent out of their half of the pitch and create a pressure on the ball (pump).

It's important for the crucial players (the defensive chain) to learn to predict the situations when the opponent intends to perform long passes behind the defense and take the space from the opponent by withdrawing; by which the players prevent the opponent from performing a long pass. An opponent usually reacts to a change of the situation by performing a long pass, which brings a new and suitable situation for an application of a pump. As a result, the height of the defensive block changes during this situation too. First, the team transfers from high to middle block and then back from middle to high block resulting in offensive pressing (alternatively, according to the situation, transfer from middle to deep block and back from deep to middle block). The consequent effect of this type of defensive players' active play is creation of an outnumber near the ball and pressure on the player with the ball. The key condition for a success during withdrawal and extension is the maintenance of the compactness and constant distances to the width and depth, which allow players to block the space and create suitable conditions for application of pressing.

DRILL 38: PUSHING THE OPPONENT AFTER A WITHDRAWAL

Drill goal and focus: practice of the four-defender chain's extension after a withdrawal (level of the pressing drill 1, 2, 3, 4, 5, 6, 7, 8)

Fig. 5.3-40 The pump after a controlled withdrawal

DRILL ORGANIZATION:

- The drill takes place all over the pitch.

- Goalkeepers are positioned in the goals.

- The team is complete and aligned according to the preferred play system.

- The number of players is 11v11 or the attacking team can be under numbered.

DRILL FLOW:

- The drill is started by the attacking team's free center back performing dribbling from his half of the pitch and consequently he passes the ball to the other center back or one of the full back players.

- The defending team creates a central defensive block and withdraws in this block while the opponent is dribbling.

- After the center back passes the ball to his team player, the defending team switches and extends in a compact block toward the ball and applies pressing.

- After gaining the possession of the ball, the play continues until the attacking action is finished.

VARIATION:

- The attacking team starts the drill from their defensive zone.

METHODICAL, ORGANIZATIONAL COMMENTS:

- The impulse for the whole team comes from the four-defender chain and most of the time the signal comes from the center back players who determine the height of the whole defensive block's extension.

- The player with the position closest to the opponent, who is taking over the ball, runs toward the ball with the intention to put pressure on the ball.

The player, who is attacking the opponent with the ball, mustn't stay by himself; he must be supported by the whole team in order not to have behind him a free area, which would allow the opponent to start a new attacking action. Therefore, the whole team must extend toward the ball and during the extension process the team must maintain compactness and division to the width as well as depth.

- In the first stage, the coach guides the action of the whole team, corrects the players' movement maneuvers, space orientation, positional alignment, and space relations in order to maintain the compactness of the blocks and transfer to effective pressing.

- This is the reason why the coach frequently interrupts the drill, corrects the mistakes, and demonstrates the correct action. This type of approach speeds up the process of the players' acquirement of the comprehension of the play, orientation in space, and game reading as necessary elements for effective defensive action.

- In the following stage of the drill, the center back players lead the action.

PUTTING THE OPPONENT IN THE OFFSIDE POSITION

"The offside tactic" isn't used as a frequent tool for elimination of the opponent's attacking actions and it's rarely seen in soccer with the defensive chain. Although the tactic of putting the opponent in the offside position is only used rarely and only in specific situations, the offside rule can be perceived as a significant help when applying effective pressing; therefore, it must be taken into consideration in the play as well as in the drill.

The offside border is defined by the defensive chain's type of play as it's focused on blocking the space, "contracting" the area, narrowing the area (transfer, withdrawal and extension), cocreation of blocks and pressing application. As the defensive block extends in exactly defined situations and the four-defender chain moves toward the central line, the opponent's attackers are put in the offside positions; therefore, the attackers must move back toward their goal in order to participate in the attacking sequence again. This way, the offside rule helps to increase the pressing efficiency. The offside rule is also important for maintaining the height of pressing and taking advantage of ultraoffensive pressing's benefits.

The offside rule allows the players to take an advantage of the situation when the opponent player is moving in the offside area or is entering it and, therefore, it's suitable to leave the opponent player in this position unoccupied and isolated from the possibility to actively participate in the solution of the play situation.

"The offside trap" or an intentional placement of the opponent in the offside position requires perfect cooperation and flawless coordination of the players who participate in the defense.

But be careful: the four-defender chain must also be prepared for the situation when the extended attacker runs from the central position to the side vertical from behind the back of one of the full back players. One of the center backs must take over him and occupy him because the opponent player would be completely free after the opponent midfielder's depth pass behind the defense without breaking the offside rule.

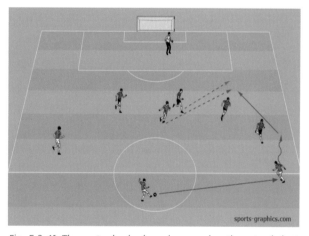

Fig. 5.3-41 The center back player is occupying the extended attacker who is running to the side vertical.

COACHING

The ball-oriented space defense, creation of blocks, pressing, the pump, and pendulum require very good coordination of groups, formations, and the whole team. Therefore, the mutual communication and coaching are indispensable parts of the game. The four-defender chain's got the most significant task in leading the whole team because the signal for the unified and compact coordination must come from the back and in the best of the cases, from the center of the defense, which means from the center back players. The players from the back positions have the best perspective of the course of the opponent's attacking actions and intentions and they have their team players in front of them. The positions of the center back players are usually taken by experienced and tactically more mature players so the probability of the correct evaluation of the space relations, mentalization, comprehension, and game reading is very high. Although the whole team participate in pressing, the outnumber and time-space pressure on the ball is created by a group of only four to five players. Also in this group of players, who are crucial for the efficiency of the whole team, the most important players for the coaching are the back players (or only one player), because they lead the action of the whole group and they decide who attacks, doubles, and secures; thus they decide about the success of the resulting action.

5. Switching After Loss or Gain of the Ball

The stages of switching form a significant part of the team's performance, and they often determine whether the team succeeds or fails. Fast switching from defensive to attacking stage can create suitable prefinal or final situations when opponent players haven't adapted to the situation and reorganized their alignment from offensive to defensive one yet. Of course, the opposite applies too; if the team, after losing the ball, switches to defensive action faster than the opponent team switches to offensive stage, the team has a big chance to regain the possession of the ball and consequently threaten the goal of the badly organized opponent.

SWITCHING FROM OFFENSE TO DEFENSE

The switching represents the element of fast tactical thinking and play behavior in which the players acquire skills necessary for fast mental and motoric switching from attacking to defensive stage immediately after losing the possession of the ball. Especially, when applying attacking pressing, fast switching to defensive stage, after losing the ball, can surprise the opponent and increase the effect of the applied tool as the opponent's defense hasn't got enough time to reorganize their alignment and adapt to the situation. The options for switching from attacking to defensive action are completely different after

losing the possession of the ball. The game situation at the moment of losing the ball determines the option, which is the most reasonable to apply. The rule, which applies immediately after losing the ball, says the players either must get the ball back as soon as possible or at least ruin any effort of the opponent to attack dangerously. In all types of switching, it's important for the team to act jointly on the principle of a common play philosophy. The option of switching is determined by the alignment of the players near the ball as well as the depth and width division of the other defensive players. The switching is also influenced by the coach's decisions, which depend on his coaching philosophy, commonly used play system, the opponent's play system, technical-tactical, and conditional level of the players.

When practicing and improving the switching, it's necessary to create a compilation of prearranged signals used in an effective coaching in order to secure compactness of the formations and the whole team.

The most effective form of switching is connected to ultraoffensive pressing: players attack their opponent immediately after losing the possession of the ball. This type of switching can be used in every zone of the playing area; however, the strongest effect is achieved on the opponent's half of the pitch in the attacking area because it's related to direct threat of the opponent's goal. The essential condition for successful regain of the ball is to have enough players near the ball, this may also depend on the way the attacking action, in which the team lost the ball, is lead.

Another type of switching from offensive to defensive stage is linked to the maintenance of the height of the block and pressing, and it can be used when ultraoffensive pressing fails due to lack of a sufficient number of the defending team's players near the ball or the opponent managed to get out of pressing pressure. If the team is aligned to the width and depth efficiently and correctly, the players can maintain the tension and time-space pressure on the opponent even after losing the possession of the ball. In any case, the height of the block and subsequently applied pressing complicates or prevents the opponent from creating a dangerous attacking action.

If the team hasn't got enough players near the ball after losing the possession and the division for creating a high block isn't appropriate, the players must withdraw to a middle or deep block and form the defensive alignment of a defensive funnel in order to protect the team's goal. The team has to withdraw similarly when losing the ball near the defensive chain (e.g., losing the possession of the ball after dribbling or an inaccurate pass of the defensive midfielder) because this is the only way the players can prevent the opponent from performing a dangerous deep pass.

SWITCHING FROM DEFENSE TO OFFENSE

The alignment of the team, which gained the ball by applying pressing, is right after gaining the ball in an advantageous position because it has a sufficient number of players in the center of the game. After gaining the possession of the ball, the team's aim is to get in a shooting situation as soon as possible as the players have a chance to take an advantage of the moment because the opponent hasn't had a chance to adopt to defensive tasks yet. The situation immediately after gaining the ball doesn't necessarily allow the players to perform a deep pass because the postpressing area is still over dense (of course, if the situation is appropriate, it's more suitable and dangerous to perform a deep pass right away). Therefore, the first task, right after taking over the ball, is to secure the ball by performing an accurate pass to a free player (usually it's a short pass as the center of the game is outnumbered by the team players). The next action allows the players to play the game to the depth (the second or third pass) and threaten the opponent's goal. If the team follows the principle of preparing for offensive stage already during the defensive stage and vice-versa, the players have the correct division to the depth and width and good perspective for carrying out a fast switch with a dangerous play to the depth. Also in case the opponent's alignment doesn't allow the players to perform a pass to the depth or an offensive deep pass isn't performed in time, a sufficient number of players in the postpressing area enable the team to prepare an attacking action by a gradual attack, which seems to be successful.

DRILL 39: 9V9 PLAY WITH A PRESSING ZONE

Drill goal and focus: orientation in a dense area, fast switching, a play to the depth, aggressive pressing in a defined central pressing zone on the opponent's half of the pitch, practice, and improvement depending on the play system (level of the pressing drill 1, 2, 3, 4, 5, 6)

Fig. 5.3-42 Fast switching and pressing in the central zone

DRILL ORGANIZATION:
- The players perform the drill from one penalty area to the penalty area on the other half of the pitch.

- We place portable goals on the penalty area lines.

- Goalkeepers are in the goals.

- In the middle, we define 20-m long pressing zone—10 m from the central line on both sides of the pitch.

DRILL FLOW:
- 9v9 players with goalkeepers in the portable goals.

- The alignment can be 4-4-1 or 4-3-2 according to the play system, which the team is supposed to practice or it can be changed during the drill.

- The defending team starts performing aggressive pressing in the defined pressing zone on the opponent's half of the pitch.

- After gaining the possession of the ball, the team quickly switches from defense to attacking stage intending to perform a fast play to the depth and get to the final phase as soon as possible.

METHODICAL, ORGANIZATIONAL COMMENTS:
- During this drill, the team moves in the basic and compact alignment to the central zone where it transfers to aggressive pressing.

- The important part is flexible switching from defensive to attacking stage with an effort to perform a vertical play.

- The rules of the play can be adjusted so that the second (third) pass must be performed to the depth, otherwise the team loses the possession of the ball, and the play is started by the opponent's goalkeeper.

- The play lasts fifteen to twenty minutes including the correction breaks made by coach.

6. Solutions to the Typical Situations in the Four-Defender Chain Play

1. Against play systems with one extended attacker.

2. Against play systems with two extended attackers.

3. Against a fast counterattack.

4. Against diagonal passes.

5. Against an opponent who frequently plays with long and high passes on or behind the chain.

1. FOUR-DEFENDER CHAIN PLAY AGAINST PLAY SYSTEMS WITH ONE ATTACKER

From the basic alignment, it's obvious there's an outnumber in the central vertical. It's also possible to create an outnumber in the side vertical by energetic transfer.

Typical situations and their solutions:

(a) The ball is in the central vertical or between the central and side vertical:

- The full back players are in the side verticals; they don't have to move too much to the center to the center backs.

- The central vertical is occupied by four players: two center backs and two defending center midfielders.

- Defending midfielders aren't in one line; they are positioned in the depth and they secure each other.

- The opponent's attacking midfielder (withdrawn attacker or withdrawn center forward (man in the hole)) is occupied by the defending midfielder who is more distant from the ball.

- If the extended attacker releases himself by moving toward the ball, one of the center back players occupies him and the other center back secures him.

(b) The center of the game is in the side vertical:

- The four-defender chain transfers and creates a defensive diagonal.

- The center back player doubles the full back who is nearer the ball and always moves deeper than the full back.

- According to the coach's instructions, the players force the opponent to dribble "out" toward the sideline or "in" toward the central vertical.

(c) Long passes behind the defensive chain:

- It's important for the defenders to recognize in time the opponent's intention to perform long and high pass to the extended attacker.

- The center back players withdraw 2 to 3 m from the attacker and then move toward the ball.

- The emphasis is put on success of the center back players in air fights.

- The success of the defense is determined by the defending center midfielders' movement toward the defending chain with the aim to catch rebounded balls.

- Mutual communication and coaching is vital.

DRILL 40: 6V5 PLAY IN 4 + 2 AGAINST 4 + 1 ALIGNMENT IN THE DEFENSIVE ZONE

Drill goal and focus: practice of defensive chaining, space transfer, and transfer of the game center (level of the pressing drill 1, 2, 3, 4)

Fig. 5.3-43 The play against one attacker in 6v5 or 6v6 situation

DRILL ORGANIZATION:

- The playing area is defined by the goal and the line, which is located about 40 m in front of the goal. On the line, we mark two approx. 10 m wide goals.

- The two teams playing against each other in this area are the defending team consisting of the four defender chain and two defending spare men and the attacking team consisting of two wing spare men, two center midfielders and one extended attacker.

DRILL FLOW:

- The five attacking players move toward the goal so that, after a short interlude between the wing and midfield spare men, they transfer the play and continue the attacking action in the side vertical area.

- The attacking team scores goals after a successful completion of the players' attacking actions.

- The defense practices the play against one attacker and four midfielders.

- The defending team scores, if the players gain the possession of the ball by fast removal of the ball and starting a counterattack into two defined areas.

VARIATIONS:

- In 6v6 play, we add a center back player to the attacking players; the center back player always starts a new action by performing a long high pass from the back from the central circle to the extended attacker.

- After an interlude with the extended attacker, the team tries to break the defensive chain by prearranged way (short timed perpendicular pass behind the line, wall pass, running out of the tandem, and so on).The players play to the depth in the central vertical.

METHODICAL, ORGANIZATIONAL COMMENTS:

- The number of players in the teams isn't strictly defined; however, it's possible to alternate the number in order to create the expected match situations in the most authentic way.

- We consistently maintain the alignment of the players according to the preferred play system.

- The defending players are expected to consistently maintain the defensive movement chaining while the goalkeeper must cooperate with the defending formation as an auxiliary libero.

- We thoroughly keep checking the transfer of the defending chain after the ball according to the center of the game (the side or central vertical and high balls to the attacker) when the play is being transferred by the attacking team.

- We also practice the movement and cooperation of the defending players between themselves and the chain so that they block the space correctly and are prepared to catch rebounded balls.

- The full load time can range from six to twelve minutes depending on the pace and level of load in fights.

2. FOUR-DEFENDER CHAIN PLAY AGAINST THE PLAY SYSTEMS WITH TWO EXTENDED ATTACKERS

Two center back players play in the central vertical against two opponent extended attackers. The opponent can also play with one or two withdrawn center forward players (men in the hole). The defending midfielders are responsible for these players. All the players create 4v3 or 4v4 situation. The play situations demand good cooperation between the center back players and defending midfielders. Cooperation between the full back players and side midfielders is also important in order to create a secure occupation of the space.

Typical situations and their solutions:

(a) The ball is in the side vertical or between the central and side vertical:

- The opponent team's midfielder with the ball is blocked by the defending midfielder who is nearer the ball and forces him to dribble the ball out. The other defending midfielder follows the movement of the center of the game, secures his team player; thus, they both together occupy the important center in front of the four-defender chain. The center back players maintain the height and don't withdraw. The full back players move closer to the central vertical.

- The attacker, who runs into "the path" toward the ball and takes over the ball, is doubled by the center back and the defending midfielder who is nearer the ball. The midfielder is more active and attacks the player with the ball, and the center back comes into the area with the ball as second because he mustn't let himself be lured out of the chain by the approaching player in order to occupy the space. The other defending midfielder also moves closer to the area where the ball is located. The area around the ball must be blocked so that the attacker with the ball can't turn around and perform a depth pass to the other attacker who can run into the free area behind the extended center back. The full back players move closer to the central vertical.

- If the ball is directed toward the attacker, who is further away from the ball, the four-defender chain players create the defensive triangle; the player with the ball is attacked by the center back player, who is nearer the ball and the other center back and side midfielder secure him. Both defending midfielders move toward the four-defender chain in order to dense the area around the ball or catch all rebounded balls.

- If the opponent midfielder with the ball is free and isn't under pressure, as he was able to get around the opponent player, there's a danger of a pass behind the defensive chain being performed. Therefore, the four-defender chain must withdraw and the defending midfielders must also return fast in front of the withdrawing chain. The side midfielders move closer to the central vertical.

(b) The attacker releases himself while moving toward the side vertical behind the back of the defending midfielder:

- The attacker is occupied by the center back. The other center back and the side midfielder (nearer the ball) withdraw in order to be able to secure and double their team player, in case of a pass being performed.

- The full back player, who is in the further side vertical, moves toward the central vertical.

- One of the defending midfielders moves back toward the approaching attacker in order to catch the pass or double the center back.

- The other defending midfielder also withdraws and occupies the area in the central vertical at the same time.

(c) The center of the game is in the side vertical:

- The whole four-defender chain transfers toward the side vertical. The center back players withdraw, and they both remain in the central vertical in order to cover the extended attackers. This game situation can also be solved in another way; the center back player, who is nearer the ball, secures the full back. The other center back and side midfielder, who is more distant from the ball, cover the attackers.

- The full back, who is nearer the ball, moves toward it, focuses on the ball and blocks the area in the side vertical so that he is as close as possible to the opponent with the ball (by being more distant from the opponent he offers the opponent space for fast dribbling). He attacks the opponent and tries to push him to the sideline. He attacks the ball, slows the opponent's movement down by which heal lows his team player to perform situational doubling (most frequently it's the side midfielder). In this 1 to 1 situation, good quality fighting manners are vital.

- The side midfielder runs from the outer area toward the ball in order to situationally double the full back.

- Also if the full back doesn't succeed in pushing the opponent to the sideline and the opponent dribbles the ball inside (toward the central vertical), the full back attacks the ball.

- When the opponent winger passes the ball to the extended attacker, even if he is being doubled by the center back and defending midfielder, the full back must immediately after the pass withdraw toward the goal in order to make the extended attacker unable to perform wall pass to his team player in the side vertical.

- Both defending midfielders withdraw in order to be closer to the chain and be prepared to catch a pass or to be able to double the attacker immediately after the pass from the wing.

- The prevention tool against possible passes from the side vertical behind the defensive chain is withdrawal of center back players and defending midfielders, when wing player has the ball under control or he has managed to escape.

(d) Tandem of the full back with side midfielder:

- This represents a specific situation in the side vertical, which requires special solution because if the opponent's full back enters the area and the defenders are not correctly aligned, there may be an outnumber in

Fig. 5.3-44 Defense against tandem in the side vertical

the side vertical and the opponent can break through the defense.

- The simplest solution is when the side midfielder runs with the approaching opponent's full back, occupies him from the inside so that he makes the side midfielder unable to perform a pass or he catches the pass.

- If the side midfielder doesn't manage to form a tandem with the approaching opponent player, the full back must detach from the opponent with the ball, who he was attacking at that time, and occupy the approaching defender.

- The player with the ball is taken over by the center back player who is nearer the ball and is doubled by one of the defending midfielders. The other defending midfielder remains in the central vertical and the whole defensive chain toward the side vertical so that both opponent's extended attackers are occupied by the second center back and side midfielder who is more distant from the ball.

- This type of situation requires good coordination between the defenders and midfielders as this situation involves posts and functions exchange. Therefore, we must focus on this coordination in the training process in detail.

DRILL 41: 4V4 PLAY IN AN EXTENDED PENALTY AREA

Drill goal and focus: cooperation of the center back players and defending midfielders (level of the pressing drill 1, 2, 3, 4)

Fig. 5.3-45 4v4 play in an extended penalty area

DRILL ORGANIZATION:

- We mark the playing area that we extend to the central circle by extending the penalty area.

- On the line opposite the fixed goal, we place two small 3-m wide goals.

- A goalkeeper is in the goal.

- The four players, two center backs and two defending midfielders, play with the goalkeeper.

- The attacking team consists of two extended attackers and two midfielders.

DRILL FLOW:

- The players perform 4v4 play with the big goal and the goalkeeper, and the task is to score a goal. In case of losing the possession of the ball, the players don't draw back; they immediately attack the opponent.

- The four defending players play on their positions and cooperate with the goalkeeper in order to make the opponent unable to form attacking actions.

- In case of gaining the possession of the ball, the defending team has an opportunity to attack the two small goals.

VARIATION:

- We create two groups that perform 4v4 play and take turns.

METHODICAL, ORGANIZATIONAL COMMENTS:

- The center back players practice defensive cooperation with the defending midfielders in the play against two attackers and two midfielders.

- We emphasis close cooperation inner defenders and defensive midfielders

- The opponent player with the ball is blocked by the defending midfielder while the other defending midfielder secures his team player.

- The center back players maintain the height, don't draw back and cover the attackers.

- The attacker, who successfully receives the pass from his team player, is attacked by the midfielder and doubled by the center back player who is nearer the ball. The midfielder is more active. The area around the ball must be blocked so that he attacker with the ball can't turn around and perform a pass to the depth to the other attacker.

- The other defending midfielder also moves closer to the area where the ball is located.

- If the opponent's midfielder with the ball is able to get around the opponent player and consequently is free, the center back players must draw back and at the same time, the defending midfielders must return fast in front of the center backs.

- We also practice fighting behavior.

- The play lasts three to four minutes with one to one and half-minute break. The play is repeated three to four times. In the play, where two groups take turns, the load interval is three minutes and rest three minutes.

- The coach corrects mistakes during the breaks between the drills and during the groups' exchange.

3. FOUR-DEFENDER CHAIN PLAY AGAINST A FAST COUNTERATTACK

Fast counterattack has become an important form of breaking an opponent's defense in modern soccer. Therefore, the reaction to fast counterattack is a significant part of a defensive play. It's necessary to include in the training process all the forms of eliminating opponent's counterattack.

The play situations in which an opponent can start fast counterattack:

a. The loss of the ball during an interlude or while opening the play in the defensive zone.

b. The team switches from offensive to defense slower than the opponent switches from defense to offensive stage.

c. The four-defender chain maintains the height even when it's supposed to be drawing back: the opponent's center back with the ball isn't under pressure, the opponent's midfielder with the ball is insufficiently occupied or released himself from under pressure or the opponent team quickly transfers the

play from the central zone to an unoccupied side vertical.

The precautions and actions aimed to defend against fast counterattack:

- Controlled offensive, maintenance of compactness also during attacking stage, correct division to the width and depth, securing the team player with the ball, defensive shield behind one of the midfielders.

- Fast switching from offensive to defensive stage and fast formation of blocks.

- Pressing on the ball (preferably immediately after losing the ball). The area around the ball as well as the space between the ball and the team's goal must be narrowed. If possible, the players shouldn't give the opponent an opportunity to perform a pass to the depth.

- Apply the pump and push the opponent.

- The players drawback, if they don't succeed in applying immediate pressing because the opponent player released himself from under pressure by performing a pass or dribbling or after losing the possession of the ball in the central zone or the team's half of the pitch. The players slow the opponent's progress by drawing back and they gain time for the return of the extended players. The four defender chain draws back fast and forms a defensive funnel. The returning players move spatially and situationally. Very fast return of the defending midfielders is important too.

- Focus on the ball as well as occupation of the players without ball; this means to catch the movement of the opponent with the ball and the approaching players too.

- Tactical foul.

- Putting the opponent to offside position.

- Cooperation with the extended goalkeeper. The goalkeeper works as libero.

- Anticipation of the opponent's action and being prepared to perform fast counterattack.

- Orientation in a large area in 2v2, 3v3, and 4v4 situations.

DRILL 42: PLAY IN 8 (9) TO 10 INFERIORITY IN NUMBERS

Drill goal and focus: practice of the play against fast counterattack (level of the pressing drill 1, 2, 3, 4, 5, 6, 7, 8).

Fig. 5.3-46 8v10 practice of defense against fast counterattack

DRILL ORGANIZATION:

- The drill is practiced between a goal line and the penalty area on the opposite half of the pitch.

- We place two small 3-m wide goals in the two side verticals on the opponent's half of the pitch penalty area.

- We mark the central line of the playing area, which is located between the defensive and central zone on the practicing team's half of the pitch. The marked line is the starting place of the play.

- The team, which is practicing defense against fast counterattack, plays with a goalkeeper in inferiority in numbers eight (4-4 alignment) or nine (4-2-3 alignment) against ten opponent players.

DRILL FLOW:

- The play is always started by the team, which is practicing defense against fast counterattack, and its task

is to attack the two small goals. The drill begins from the marked line so the four-defender chain can be highly extended and the opponent has enough space to perform fast counterattack.

- In 8v10 or 9v10 play, the opponent first defends the small goals and after gaining the possession of the ball, the opponent players' task is to switch to fast counterattack and attack the fixed goal with the goalkeeper.

- The players play without standard situations and each play starts from the line in the central zone.

- The play lasts 15 to 25 minutes including breaks, which the coach uses for corrections. The play is also interrupted after finishing an attacking action or when the ball gets out of the playing area.

VARIATIONS:

- We stretch the playing area, the players play eight (nine) to ten all over the pitch with two goals and goalkeepers and the central line is the starting place of the drill (the opponent has a larger area for performing fast counterattack).

- In 7v10 or 6v10 play, it's easier for the opponent to gain the possession of the ball.

- The play is also suitable for practicing ultraoffensive pressing.

METHODICAL, ORGANIZATIONAL COMMENTS:

- The play offers space for the opponent to perform fast counterattack; thus, there are many opportunities to practice and improve defense against fast counterattack.

- The coach expects the players to remain compact even during attacking stage in order to maintain the distance between the players and continuity of securing the team player with the ball as well as forming a defensive shield.

- The players practice fast switching from offensive to defensive stage and fast formation of a defensive shield.

- Immediate pressing after losing the ball is also important so the players also practice ultraoffensive pressing.

- The drill enables the players to recognize the situations when opponent can be attacked and when to draw back.

- The players practice fast withdrawal of the four-defender chain and formation of a defensive funnel. Fast and controlled return of defending midfielders is essential.

- Vital part is also practice of cooperation between defensive block and goalkeeper.

- It's important to practice the option of putting opponent to an offside position.

4. FOUR-DEFENDER CHAIN PLAY AND DEFENSIVE BLOCK AGAINST DIAGONAL PASSES BEHIND DEFENSIVE BLOCK

When the center of the game is located in the side vertical (or between the side and central vertical), the four-defender chain creates a defensive diagonal and the whole defensive block moves toward the ball in order to narrow the area and create pressure on the ball ("strong side"). This type of situation, when the defensive block moves to one side, inevitably results in freeing the opposite vertical ("weak side"). One of the ways by which opponent can be freed from pressing in the side vertical is an escape pass. This means the opponent transfers the center of the game to the central or opposite vertical or performs a return pass to the center back or a goalkeeper. The most effective form of an escape pass is a cross-field pass to the opposite vertical to the four-defender chain's level or even behind the defense. This type of pass doesn't only represent a release from opponent's pressure but also it represents a danger for the goal and goalkeeper as the opponent can quickly get behind the defense block and create a shooting situation.

Solution of the play situation:

a. The players must focus on the opponent with the ball in the side vertical. By performing a tighter attack and aggressive pressure, the defensive block tries to make the opponent unable to perform a cross-field pass and force the opponent player to pass the ball from the back or play with short passes.

b. In case the defensive block is transferred to one side but the playing situation doesn't allow the players to block the area in the side vertical and create pressure on the player with the ball, the defensive chain must expect the cross-field pass in time. While the cross-field pass is being performed, the four-defender chain detaches from the attackers, draws back, and moves to the side toward the ball.

c. Prompt reaction of the whole defensive block to the change of the game center, correct timing, and maintenance of compactness during the change of the game center are crucial.

DRILL 43: PLAY IN THE VERTICAL ZONES

Drill goal and focus: practice of the play against diagonal passes and practice of withdrawal and transfer of the defensive block (level of the pressing drill 1, 2, 3, 4, 5, 6).

Fig. 5.3-47 Play in the vertical zones and practice of defense against diagonal passes

DRILL ORGANIZATION:
- The drill is performed on two thirds of the pitch with one fixed and one portable goal.

- We divide the playing area into five vertical zones: two side verticals reaching from the sideline of the pitch to the level of the penalty area's sideline, one side vertical with the width of the goal area and two verticals between the middle and side verticals.

- Goalkeepers are in the goals.

- We designate two eight-member teams so that the defending team plays in 4-4 alignment and the attacking team plays in 2-4-2 alignment.

- The team, which practices defense, plays with the goalkeeper who is in the fixed goal.

DRILL FLOW:
- The play is always started by the goalkeeper in the portable goal passing the ball to his team player in the side vertical.

- The goalkeeper's pass is a signal for extension and transfer of the defensive block to the side vertical so that the defensive block must occupy three neighboring verticals and two vertical on the opposite side stay unoccupied.

- The task of the defending team is to transfer the center of the game to the opposite vertical by performing a cross-field pass to a free team player and get to the final phase.

- The defending team practices counteractions against the diagonal pass. In case the players gain the possession of the ball, they have an opportunity to attack the portable goal.

- The players play without standard situations. After each interruption of the play, the players start again by a goalkeeper's pass.

VARIATIONS:

- We stretch the playing area from the fixed goal to the opposite penalty area. Or the drill can take place all over the pitch with two goals and goalkeepers.

- We increase the number of players: 9v9 play, the defending team plays in 4-2-3 alignment and the opponent players in 4-4-1 or 4-2-3 alignment.

- The drill is performed by two complete teams 11v11.

METHODICAL, ORGANIZATIONAL COMMENTS:

- The coach demands the players to remain compact also when the center of the game changes. The full back player, who is closer to the ball, runs to the ball first and at the same time, he moves the whole defensive block toward the ball.

- The point of the drill is to correctly occupy "the strong side" and keep "the weak side" under control as well.

- An important methodical requirement is to demand fast movement of the whole defensive block from one side vertical to the opposite one.

- The play lasts fifteen to twenty minutes, and the coach uses every interruption for correcting the player's mistakes.

5. FOUR-DEFENDER CHAIN PLAY AGAINST AN OPPONENT WHO FREQUENTLY PLAYS WITH LONG AND HIGH PASSES TO AN EXTENDED ATTACKER OR BEHIND THE DEFENSIVE CHAIN

- It's important that the defenders realize the opponent's intention to perform a long and high pass to an extended attacker in time.

- In the central vertical, the center back player, who is nearer the ball, runs toward the ball and the other center back with the full back secure him and create a defensive triangle. The other full back player, who is more distant from the ball, occupies the area next to the defensive triangle.

- If the ball is directed into the side vertical, the chain takes the form of a defensive diagonal.

- The players of the defensive chain must focus mainly on successful solution of air fights.

- The defending midfielders move toward the defending chain in order to be prepared to double and catch the rebounded balls.

- Mutual defenders' securing is at the same time supposed to eliminate the opponent's opportunity to extend a long pass behind the defense.

- The goalkeeper is supposed to cooperate too; he must extend from the goal and take over the function of libero.

- Maintaining the compactness of the defensive block means that the players must keep the distances between themselves and formations even during transfer.

- Mutual communication and coaching is practiced as well.

DRILL 44: 6V6 PLAY AFTER A LONG AND HIGH PASS

Drill goal and focus: practice of the play against long and high passes and practice of withdrawal and transfer of the defensive block (level of the pressing drill 1, 2, 3, 4, 5, 6)

Fig. 5.3-48 6v6 play after a long pass into the central vertical

DRILL ORGANIZATION:

- The drill takes place on half of the pitch with one fixed and two small goals, which we place on the central line to the side verticals.

- We mark the area for passes on the other half of the pitch behind the central circle where we also prepare balls for the drill.

- We designate two six-member teams so that the team, which is practicing defense, consists of a four-defender chain and two defending midfielders. The defensive block is positioned between the defensive and central zone.

- The attacking team consists of two attackers and four midfielders one of which is located in the area designated for passes.

- The goalkeeper is positioned in the goal.

DRILL FLOW:

- The 6v6 play is always started by the attacking team's player performing dribbling from the designated area

followed by a long and high pass directed into the central vertical behind the defensive chain.

- After the pass, the player runs from the area to the attacking half of the pitch and participates in the attacking actions.

- The six-member defensive block draws back already during the opponent's dribbling and prepares for the long pass.

- While the pass is being performed, the defensive chain transfers to the place of the ball's impact, prepares for an air fight with the opponent's attackers and forms into a defensive triangle.

- The defending midfielders also draw back by which they maintain the compactness of the defensive block and are prepared to catch the rebounded balls.

- The attacking team's task is to score a goal into the big goal with the goalkeeper. The team, which is practicing defense, has an opportunity to score a goal into two small goals after gaining the possession of the ball.

VARIATIONS:

- We stretch the playing area from the fixed goal to two-thirds of the pitch.

- In the 8v8 play, the defending team consists of a four-defender chain and four midfielders depending on the preferred system of the play.

- After short dribbling, the player from the area designated for passes, passes the ball into the side vertical. The defensive chain forms into a defensive diagonal while drawing back.

METHODICAL, ORGANIZATIONAL COMMENTS:

- The defensive block already draws back before the long pass is performed because the players are expecting the pass behind the defensive chain.

- The drill imitates the pressing situations in which the players expect a long pass behind the defense block; opponent's center back player or midfielder isn't under pressure, has the ball under control or passes the ball in front of him.

- Correctly applied central pressing also provokes opponent into performing long passes.

- The main task is to take the free space from opponent.

- The coach demands the players to remain in a compact block also when the game center changes.

- The defending players form a defensive triangle in the central vertical; the center back player, who is nearer the ball, focuses on air fight and is secured by the other center back and full back player who is closer to the ball.

- If the opponent performs a long pass into the side vertical, the defenders form a defensive diagonal; the full back player, who is nearer the ball, focuses on the ball and air fight and the other defenders gradually secure him.

- In both situations, the defending midfielders also move into the fighting area in order to catch the rebounded balls and to be prepared to double the defender in case the opponent's attacker wins the fight.

Fig. 5.3-49 6v6 play after a long pass to the side vertical

5.4 PRESSING ON A TEAM LEVEL

Team pressing represents the highest form and level of proactive defense application. **All previous pressing levels should culminate precisely at this point in order to be integrated in a high-quality performance of a team as a whole. Not only is the quality of previous pressing levels a decisive factor at a group level, but also the quality of their connection, affinity, and integration as a team to complement each other and participate harmoniously in an effective, active, and successful form of team defense.** That's the reason why pressing represents the most important stage of the practice. It determines the proportion of success regarding defense. The precise and consistent cooperation of players in time and space, the use of the basic elements of individual and group defense, ensures the pressing effectiveness of the entire team. Relations between levels can also be applied in a reciprocal way: Fundamental concept of the proactive defense elements of the entire team must be also inevitably reflected on different levels of pressing that can be a single player, two players, three players, or a group of players as well on the practice methodology and improvement on these levels.

From the performance requirements of the team, we can also deduce the necessary characteristics and abilities of players, the activities players must master for a successful performance of the team. Effective and the right methodology monitor aforesaid requirements. **The result is that the training process, which is focused on individual and group practice, ensures the individual player or team activity so as to fit the whole concept of pressing and enable the players to respect the way group pressing is applied.** Therefore, the practice and improvement of pressing on group level comes from the previous algorithm and automatisms of lower pressing levels. Using model drills and preparatory matches, these practice and improvements achieve harmonious, consistent, compact, and homogenous teamwork enabling the team reach its top level.

As entirety has an influence on the part, also the way of group pressing must be reflected in the practice and improvement of lower pressing levels. That's why the most important aspect is the application of pressing immediately after losing the ball: in which zone and how pressing is performed on group level. Here we are thinking about a situation where either team prefer immediate pressing after losing the ball of midfield pressing or the team to withdraw and start defensive pressing. The proactive methodology at all levels must respect the types of pressing (situational, directed, or pressing victim) as well as the way in which pressing is directed to the opponent with the ball (toward the "outside" of the side vertical line or toward "inside" of the center vertical line). **The methodology uses modeling exercises and game preparation in order to simulate the conditions of a match, which are to be used in real matches.**

It's important to multiply the algorithm to solve playing situations, which are later used in the matches or against specific opponents in order to achieve necessary automatisms. They make the solution of complicated situations easier and faster. **In the training process, we use formation exercises and performance preparation as the fundamental methodical-organizational forms to secure the principle of "adequate coverage." It means we create situations in the training process that simulate match conditions.** This provides a successful transfer and effective enforcement of routines into situations that may appear in real matches. If we respect the principle that a match is a fundamental part of planning formation and construction of the training process, we create a reflection of the match in the training content, and the training style is directly reflected in matches. Frequent use of formation exercises, and play preparation is beneficial not only from the point of view of the transfer to the match, it also develops all the necessary features and abilities of the players in a complete way: fitness, technical, tactical, and psychological. Moreover, it includes the aspect of automatisms, improvisation, and creativity. This enable awareness of space, space orientation, coordinated cooperation of players, as well as mutual communication. It also improves technique integration, playing judgment, the performance and provides an effective preparation for forthcoming confrontations. In these formation exercises, teams can build pressing strategies using the typology of players according to the coach's philosophy.

The practice and improvement on group level, as part of the training process, includes forms and instruments in simplified conditions to achieve the correct conceptions that enable to solution of new situations: outnumber of players and slower practice pace (walk or trot). Only after completing this first, initial phase, we can start using methodical-organizational forms, which are closer to the match conditions and pace.

Systematic:

Defense of the entire team

Defensive pressing	Midfield pressing	Offensive pressing
Immediate ultraoffensive pressing		

Spaital positioning and pressing direction

(a) Sector pressiong	(b) Personal pressing	(c) Total pressing
(d) Pressing-oriented forward		(e) Pressing-oriented backward

Types of pressing

Guided pressing	Pressing victim	Situational pressing

Team organization

Playing systems	Playing systems	Playing systems
With four-defender chain	With three-defender chain	With five-member chain

DRILL 45: 4 + 4 PLAY AGAINST FOUR PLAYERS FOR KEEPING THE BALL

Drill goal and focus: the cooperation of the four players covering the marked space, the pressure on the ball, and the chain transfer. The goal of the offensive players is to keep the ball, coordination, and play into the depth (pressing drill level 1, 2, 5, 6).

Fig. 5.4-1 4 + 4 play against four

DRILL ORGANIZATION:

- The drill takes place in a rectangle of 40 m × 15 m in size, which is divided into three zones: the center zone, which measures 10 m, and the two side zones, which are 15 m each. The width of each zone is 15 m.

- There are four players positioned in each zone. The players cannot leave their zone.

- The coach located in the center zone of the drill area is prepared for the exercise with several balls at his disposal.

DRILL FLOW:

- The drill is started by the coach passing the ball to one of the side zones.

- Four players in the side zone try to build a situation using fast passes and transferring the center area of their own zone in order to perform a pass through the center zone to the opposite side.

- Each player has max. two touches and, in the frame of one zone, the group is allowed to perform a max. of five passes. The next sixth pass must be directed to the opposite side zone.

- The players in the center zone try to close the space by synchronized and compact movement in order to prevent the passes between two side zones.

- If the ball gets out of the playing area or the group in the center zone catches the pass performed from the side zone, the teams exchange so that the team, of which the player caused the loss of the ball, transfers to the central zone, and exchanges the position with the group from the central zone.

- During the team shifting, the coach passes another ball to the opposite side zone and the game continuous in the opposite zone.

DRILL 46: 4 TO 1 PLAY IN THE SIDE ZONES

Fig. 5.4.2-4 Switching from midfield pressing to fast counterattack

- The organization and the drill flow is the same as in the previous drill, but one player from the center zone moves to the side zone after performing a pass to this zone. The 4 to 1 play takes place having in mind the pass after five passes to the opposite zone.

- In the center zone, there are three players trying to cover the center zone area to prevent the pass to the opposite zone.

- There is always a different player running from the center zone to the side zone.

DRILL 47: 4 TO 2 PLAY IN THE SIDE ZONES

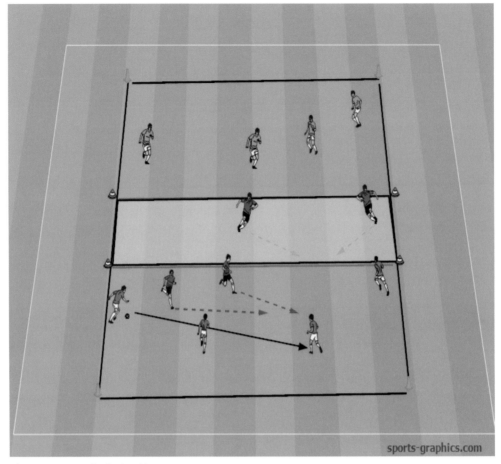

Fig. 5.4-3 4 to 2 play in the side zones

- The organization and the drill flow are the same as in the previous drill, but two players from the center zone move to the side zone after the pass. The four to two play takes place having mind the pass after five passes to the opposite zone.

- In the center zone, there are two players trying to cover the area of the center zone to prevent the pass to the opposite zone.

- There is always a different pair of players running from the center zone to the side zone.

VARIATION:
- The extension of the width from 15 to 30 m.

METHODICAL COMMENTS:
- The coach constantly tries to keep the continuity of group shifting.

- It's important for the group in the center zone to constantly keep the distance from each other and to move depending on the type of drill: four-member, tree-member, or two-member block.

- In drill the players practice doubling.

DRILL 48: PREPARATORY PLAY 4:3 + 3

Drill goal and focus: The practice of undernumbering pressing, the emphasis on performing under pressure using free players and the space orientation (pressing drill level 1, 2, 3, 4, 5, 6)

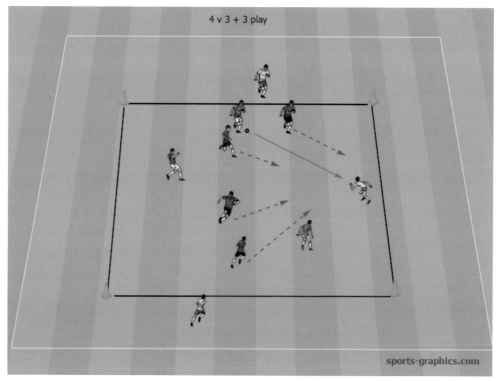

Fig. 5.4-4 Preparatory play 4: 3 + 3

DRILL ORGANIZATION:

- The drill takes place on a square of 20 m × 20 m in size.

- Players are divided into three groups, four players applying pressing, three players holding the ball, and three players are neutral.

DRILL FLOW:

- 4:3 + 3 players (two players outside the square on the opposite sides + one player inside)

- in case of gaining the control of the ball, four defensive, as well as offensive, players have unrestricted number of touches. Auxiliary players have restricted number of touches (1 or 2).

- They play on the number of passes (6:4 play).

- The interval of physical load lasts three minute and interval to rest is one minute. The physical load is repeated four or five times.

VARIATIONS:

- 4 to 4 play+ 2 neutral players perform a number of passes. The group of four players having the control of the ball play in outnumbering six to four, and the play is performed in two touches.

METHODICAL COMMENTS:

- The group of four players without the ball tries, even in undernumbering but in compact formation, to narrow the area using intensive and coordinated movements to keep the opponent under constant pressure.

- In this way, the players can achieve outnumbering around the ball being defended and push the opponents away from the ball.

- The play requires game-reading, prediction of solutions, spatial coordination, cooperation with all the team players, and understanding of gesture and facial communication.

5.4.1 Pressing in Defensive Zone (PDZ, Defensive Pressing)

Defensive pressing is applied in the zone between the central line and the line located 20 m away from the goal post. Although all the defending team players move toward their own half of the field, the task of the whole team is to occupy this area forming a compact block in order to switch to active defensive pressing and to force the opponent to move away from the ball. All players, including the ones playing in offensive positions, have to be involved in this defensive tactic. The current team system (players' alignment) is important for the defensive tactics. The alignment of players depends on their potential, the coach's philosophy as well as the team system. The opponent's style also plays a very important role.

Defensive pressing is the "most effective" form of pressing. It's used against strong opponents to protect the most dangerous areas in front of the team goal post; it also makes the opponent's penetration very difficult because of the reduced area for combined or individual actions.

This type of pressing only makes sense in combination with a fast counterattack, which is most effective in the middle vertical after taking control of the ball. This area is where the most dangerous and fastest direct counterattacks can be performed.

Defensive pressing represents the basic type of pressing, and it is the principle upon which midfield and offensive pressing are practiced.

Advantages of defensive pressing:

- The whole team forms a very compact, consistent, and strong defensive block.

- Occupation of the space in front of the penalty area on the team's half of the pitch prevents the opponent from performing passes behind the defense and makes the deep movements more difficult.

- Defensive pressing makes the narrowing of the area easier; it provides numerical advantage in the area around the ball and creates pressure on the opponent with the ball.

- Because the team retreat to their half of the pitch, it teases the opponent to move in wide separation allowing the player to create sufficient space to perform a fast counterattack.

Disadvantages of defensive pressing:

- Players can often open opportunities when they just wait for the opponent to make any mistake and play in passive block defense instead of applying aggressive pressing.

- After losing the control of the ball during an attack or in the midfield zone, the players must cover larger distances to the return to their

- basic position.

- Losing fights or rebound balls can disrupt the structure of the defense in favor of the opponent.

- The opponent has the opportunity to perform long, high or dangerous passes into the shooting area. Losing the fight or a rebounded ball in this area is an imminent and dangerous threat to score a goal.

Guided pressing is a type of pressing in which some specific areas of the field are intentionally occupied while, at the same time, others are released using synchronized movements of the whole team to force the opponent to perform a pass or to dribble the ball toward the released area.

This type of pressing has two forms: **"toward the outside,"** which means to guide the opponent toward the sideline and **"toward the inside,"** which means to force the opponent to move toward the center vertical line.

Guided pressing toward the side vertical directly to the sideline is advantageous because it offers additional help to narrow the area and to build pressure on the opponent with the ball. After successful taking control of the ball in the side vertical, the most important thing is to keep the ball performing one or two short passes. The number and the alignment of the players in this area don't allow them to perform a depth pass immediately after gaining the control of the ball. Once the team safely have control of the ball, the attacking phase can be executed. This attacking phase can be performed using a fast counterattack in depth. The most effective way to start a fast counterattack is performing a long diagonal pass to the opposite side vertical, because this area is almost unoccupied. The possibility of a fast running and movement toward the opposite vertical will allow the player to use more efficiently the side vertical on the opposite side of the pitch.

Guided pressing "toward inside" has its advantages. It allows the players to double and attack the opponent from different angles. Also, the players will have a better chance to direct an immediate formation and perform a fast counterattack. If the players attack using a deep guided pressing after executing the first pass, they will have favorable and better chances to position themselves and perform a fast counterattack successfully.

The way guided pressing is used depends on the coach's philosophy, the structure of the team and the opponent's style.

Pressing victim is similar to guided pressing, but it's focused on a specific opponent. The principle of this type of pressing is based on space selection, space occupation, and targeting players. It's used to induce the opponent to perform a pass to a weaker or possibly the weakest teammate, who is intentionally left free. The pass to a preselected player is the sign to apply pressing in order to quickly gain the control of the ball.

Another type of pressing is **situational pressing**. It's based on the proactive defense activation related to a specific situational configuration. Situational pressing can occur, for example:

- After high, long passes on a four-defender chain.

- After rebounded balls.

- After high or perpendicular passes toward the extended attacker.

- After doubling in the side vertical, when the doubling player is coming from behind.

- After doubling in the side vertical, when the doubling player is coming from the front.

- After the opponent shifts the center of the game by performing the diagonal pass.

- After a fast pass from the center vertical to the side vertical by the opponent, when it is impossible to catch the opponent's pass or it's impossible to prevent the pass.

- In coordinated space occupation after successful pass by the opponent. This new situation is focused on the ball and must be solved shifting and doubling the players.

- After unsuccessful pressing and consequent position reorganization.

- After an unsuccessful guided pressing or a pressing victim.

DRILL 49: SHIFTING FROM DEFENSIVE BLOCK TO DEFENSIVE PRESSING

Drill goal and focus: the formation of elemental behavior for team work; space orientation; cooperation for coordinated, cohesive defense; to keep the team compactness during the shifting; and movement toward the ball (pressing drill level 2, 4, 5, 6, 7)

Fig. 5.4.1-1 Transfer practice in 10v10 plays without the goals and goalkeepers

DRILL ORGANIZATION:

- The area covers the part of the pitch from the penalty zone to the center zone, right behind the central line on the opposite half of the pitch.

- Two teams, ten players each, play against each other. The players of one the teams are structured in basic formation or alignment.

DRILL FLOW:

- The drill is always started by the attacking team moving from the central line.

- The attacking team main task is to go to the penalty area keeping the ball under control as long as possible.

- In the first stage of the drill, the offensive team must execute a two-touch play. It means that the player with the ball has to touch the ball at least two times.

- The defending team forms a defensive block and occupy the space between the central line and the penalty area. The players track the movement of the ball and go to the center of the pitch. At this point of the drill, the teamwork is easier because the players have enough time to perform this movement.

- The defending players are assigned to their positions according to the most appropriate system selection.

- In the first stage, the whole team practice coordinated movements toward the ball without taking it over.

- After a successful completion of the coordinated movements, there is another stage similar to the previous one but this time taking the ball over.

- The defending team practice applying defensive pressing and, after having the ball under control, the task is to take it beyond the central line.

- The attacking team perform a free play, which means the number of touches in not specified.

- The exercise lasts for twenty to thirty minutes. The coach can interrupt the exercise as many times as necessary, usually for correction purposes.

VARIATIONS:

- We can organize the drill as a play on two goals.

- We can use the drill to practice midfield and offensive pressing.

- The organization the exercise is suitable for practicing the upper and lower pendulum, the pump, and drawbacks.

- Ten to eight practice of pressing in outnumbering.

- The alignment can be changed as well as the system, for example, the system with three-defender chain level.

- Some players can be changed within the team-practicing pressing.

- The offensive team simulates the movement of the nearest opponent.

METHODICAL, ORGANIZATIONAL COMMENT:

- The task of the drill is to practice defensive pressing and improving the cooperation of the whole team, narrowing, and shortening the pitch, form spatial relations, movement synchronization, and timing.

- The defensive team practice creating of very compact, coordinated, and strong defensive block.

- The task is to practice the shifting from defensive block to active and aggressive pressing in order to copy the movement of the ball, narrow the space around the ball, which helps to create numeral advantage in the area around the ball.

- The important part of the practice is mutual communication.

- The drill is used to simulate combat situations; however, the coach can interrupt it due to corrections and forming the correct behavior/conduct.

- The coach can stop the game and to correct any play situation. He points out incorrect position, performance of player or team formations. In these cases, after explaining and giving instructions to correct the situation, he makes the players repeat the drill in order to create dynamic stereotypes and transform the situations into signals to make the players automatize the solutions.

- Repetition of the situation and subsequent corrections are done in a slow pace and then faster to give the coach the opportunity to correct and specify the players' behavior and performance to solve the issues successfully.

- The repetition of the exercises must be done as many times as necessary and should be according to the match tempo in order to automatize the movement patterns, cooperation, and timing.

- The coach monitors and corrects the pressing quality on lower levels as well as duels, doubling, pressing on group level, and formations.

- This drill is also suitable for the practice and improvement of other types of pressing, such as: guided pressing, pressing victim, situational pressing.

- In the preparatory period, the practice of this drill for training units (as well as in youth teams) can be done many times in a week.

- In the main period, the practice of this drill should be integrated into the content of the training unit prematch.

DRILL 50: 8V8 FORMATION, COOPERATION BETWEEN OFFENSIVE PLAYERS, AND MIDFIELDERS IN DEFENSIVE PRESSING

Drill goal and focus: cooperation between the attackers and midfielders in defensive pressing. Practice of upper and lower pendulum (pressing drill level 1, 2, 3,4, 5, 6)

Fig. 5.4.1-2 8v8 play focused on practicing the cooperation between the attackers and midfielders in defensive pressing

DRILL ORGANIZATION:

- The area covered is from one goal post all the way to the penalty area on the opposite half of the pitch.

- Each vertical line (right, left, and central) up to the penalty area on the opposite half of the pitch is marked with cones.

- One goalkeeper is in a fixed goal.

- We form two eight-member teams.

- The players of both teams play in basic formation. The formation is divided into two defenders, four midfielders, and two attackers.

DRILL FLOW:

- 8v8 formation with one fixed goal post with a goalkeeper and three small cones; the team practicing pressing defends three small cones and attacks the goal with the goalkeeper.

- The defensive team is retreated to their half of the pitch. Two attackers move around the central line and try to disrupt the opponent in the central zone with assistance of two extended attackers and midfielders.

- The extended midfielders form upper pendulum and two midfielders form lower pendulum.

- The offensive team is extended; the high defenders and side midfielders are in the central zone. The other players are on the opponent's half of the pitch.

- The drill is always started by the goalkeeper performing a pass toward the player in the central zone.

- The offensive team try to score a goal into the three small cones.

- Once the defensive team have the control of the ball, they switch to fast counterattack and try to finish the action by scoring a goal toward the fixed goal post.

VARIATIONS:

- A portable goal post is placed in the penalty area instead of the three small cones. There is a goalkeeper playing 8v8 on two goals.

- The defending team is aligned in 4v4 formation. The practice is focused on the coordination of the defense chain level and the midfielders. Practice of lower pendulum is suitable as well.

METHODICAL-ORGANIZATIONAL COMMENT:

- After the goalkeeper performs the pass to the player positioned in the inside defender, the attacker closer to the ball runs to it and the second attacker or withdrawn center forward (man in the hole) moves behind the first attacker to protect him—upper pendulum.

- Two defensive midfielders move in a similar way, the player closer to the ball extends behind the player withdrawn center forward (man in the hole) behind the protected attacker. The other defensive midfielder moves deeper and closer to the defenders-lower pendulum.

- The striker attacking the opponent with the ball depends on the playing concept, the system, and the coach's instructions because the attacker's movement toward the ball is different in each type of pressing (guided "outside" or "inside," pressing victim, or situational pressing).

- The other players keep constant distance and secure the compactness of the team.

- We use this drill to practice switching from defensive to offensive actions as well as to practice counterattack.

- The coach can interrupt the play due to movement corrections, choice of the place, players cooperation, and timing. It's suitable to repeat this situation several times and slow.

DRILL 51: GUIDED DEFENSIVE PRESSING TOWARD "OUTSIDE," PLAY ON THREE SMALL GOALS AND ONE GOAL WITH A GOALKEEPER

Drill goal and focus: practice and improvement of guided pressing focused on pushing the opponent out to the sidelines (pressing drill level 1, 2, 3, 4, 5, 6, 7, 8)

Fig. 5.4.1-3 Practice of guided defensive pressing toward "outside" in 11v10 plays (basic play situation: Inside defender is starting the attracting action of the opponent)

DRILL ORGANIZATION:
- The practice of the drill takes place on two thirds of the pitch.

- Three small goals are placed parallel to the goal line opposite the fixed goal with a goalkeeper.

- The team practicing pressing play in full formation with the goalkeeper against 10 opponents. All the players play in their respective positions.

DRILL FLOW:
- The preparatory play is started by the team attacking the fixed goal.

- The team in defense move in a compact block in order to give the opportunity to the opponent to perform a pass to the side vertical.

- After the pass to the side vertical, the team move toward the ball to close the space around it as well as the corridors for possible passes.

- The movement must be quick and by surprise and, as a result, the team get the control of the ball.

- After gaining the control of the ball, the team try to keep the ball and attack one of the three small goals.

VARIATIONS:
- A portable goal with a goalkeeper can be placed instead of the small goals to practice defensive pressing on two goals play.

- The drill is suitable for practicing and improving other types of pressing, such as pressing victim and situational pressing.

METHODICAL, ORGANIZATIONAL COMMENTS:
- Strategic spatial philosophy of pressing is the intentional manipulation of the opponent into specific areas, in this case, the side vertical.

- The main advantage of the side vertical is that the sideline offers additional help narrowing the area and creating pressure on the opponent with the ball.

- The extended attacker running toward the opponent's center forward with the ball, must perform the movement in a way that the opponent doesn't get the chance to pass the ball to the other center forward, which forces the opponent to pass the ball to the side vertical. The attacker starts running from the center back player, making a gentle curve. The performance of the center forward in guided pressing is very important, because it gives the initial impulse to the other team players. His movement allows the opponent to have an opportunity, which is favorable for his own team.

- The movement of players and the space selection allows the opponent to perform a pass to the side vertical and vice versa, also to make difficult to perform a deep pass as well as to transfer the center of the play.

The other/second extended attacker or withdrawn center forward (man in the hole) moves behind the team player attacking the opponent with the ball, occupying the area behind him. That's why the opponent doesn't have the alternative to execute a deep pass; the second attacker forms an upper pendulum together with the other extended attacker **(players 9 and 10)**.

The defensive midfielders move to the central vertical where the opponent's center midfielders are in order to prevent the opponent to perform a perpendicular pass. Those defensive midfielders don't play in one line; instead, they keep a deep structure to form a lower pendulum **(players 6 and 8)**.

The side midfielder closest to the ball playing against the opponent's full back, performs his movement not only to leave the opponent free but also to have him under control. It means, the side midfielder can't block the opponent too closely because it wouldn't give him the opportunity to performance a pass to the side vertical; the full backs positioned in side verticals move closer to the center backs; the center backs move to the central vertical to control the opponent's attackers; the center forward further away from the ball moves to the line between the side and central vertical.

Fig. 5.4.1-4 Practice of guided defensive pressing toward "outside" in 11v10 play (play situation after the pass do the side vertical)

After performing a pass to the side vertical:

Extended player remains in the midfield zone; however, he draws back to the position of the withdrawn center forward.

The withdrawn center forward is shifting toward the ball from the central vertical to side vertical.

The defensive midfielder, who is the closest to the ball, plays a very important role. By performing a quick movement, he has to get closer to the ball to the side vertical all the way to the sideline.

The defensive midfielder, who is farther away from the ball, remains in the side vertical where he occupies the area in front of the center backs.

The center forward, who is the closest to the ball, attacks the opponent with the ball.

The full back, who is the closest to the ball, is moving toward the ball together with the four-defender chain.

The center backs are shifting so that the center back, who is the closest to the ball, is in the side vertical and secures the full back.

The other center back is moving in the central vertical. Both center backs must cover and control the opponent attackers at the same time.

The full back, who is farther away from the ball, is moving so that he maintains his constant distance from the center back in order to keep the compactness of the four-defender chain; therefore, he gets from the side to central vertical.

The full back, who is farther away from the ball, has two options for the choice of the area, which depend on the play conception and the coach's instructions:

a. He occupies the side vertical on the outlying side and draws back to the level of the four-defender chain;

b. He doesn't withdraw deeper; he is extending toward the central vertical leaving the side vertical free and by his movement, he helps to make the area more dense in order to close the corridors for the possible passes.

The pass, which performed by the opponent to the side vertical, is followed by fast shifting of the players with the ball, narrowing the area around the ball and attacking the opponent. The task of this maneuver is to gain the possession of the ball and switch to counterattack.

Fig. 5.4.1-5 Practice to defensive pressing, which is directed toward "the outside" in 11v10 play (play situation after a pass performed to the side vertical)

- After successfully gaining the control of the ball in the side vertical, it is very important to keep it under control with the help of one or two short passes because the amount of players, and their alignment will not allow the player to perform a deep pass immediately after the ball have been taken.

- The attacking action can be made after keeping safely the ball. The attacking action can be performed to the depth as a fast counterattack. The most effective way to start the fast counterattack is performing a long pass to the opposite side vertical. This space is the least occupied and, in case of a fast running toward the opposite vertical, the opposite side vertical of the pitch can be used more effectively.

- The drill is suitable for practicing and improving other types of pressing: pressing victim and situational pressing.

DRILL 52: GUIDED DEFENSIVE PRESSING TOWARD "INSIDE," 11V10 PLAY ON TWO SMALL GOALS AND ONE FIXED GOAL WITH A GOALKEEPER

Drill goal and focus: practice and improvement of guided pressing focused on forcing the opponent to move from the center of the pitch to the central vertical (pressing drill level 1, 2, 3, 4, 5, 6, 7, 8)

Fig. 5.4.1-6 Practice of guided defensive pressing toward "inside" in 11v10 plays

DRILL ORGANIZATION:

- The practice of the drill takes place on two thirds of the pitch.

- Opposite the fixed goal with a goalkeeper, we place two small goals to the side verticals, parallel to the goal line, 2 m from the sideline.

- The team practicing pressing is in full formation with the goalkeeper against 10 opponents. All the players are on their respective positions.

- Once the team have the control of the ball, they proceed to attack toward one of the two small goals or to execute a pass to the small goals.

VARIATIONS:

- A portable goal with a goalkeeper is placed instead of the small goals to practice defensive pressing on two goals.

DRILL FLOW:

- The preparatory stage is started by the team attacking the fixed goal.

- The defending team move in a compact block to give the opponent the opportunity to perform a perpendicular pass in the central vertical or to force the opponent to perform a pass from the side vertical to the central vertical.

- After the pass to the side vertical, the team move toward the ball to close the space around it as well as the corridors for possible passes.

- The movement must be fast and surprising in order to take the control of the ball as a result.

METHODICAL, ORGANIZATIONAL COMMENTS:

- In a situation where a player performs a pass to the side vertical, the side midfielder attacks the opponent with the ball and blocks any movement toward the sideline. This will give the opponent the opportunity to dribble the ball and perform a pass to the central vertical.

- The other players: two defensive midfielders and the withdrawn center forward (man in the whole) leave the opponent's midfielder free so his team player can pass the ball to him. This will allow the team players situated in the central vertical to perform pressing in this area.

- The pass from the side vertical to the central vertical is the sign for the defensive midfielders and the withdrawn center forward (man in the hole) to apply pressing surrounding and attacking the opponent with the ball.

- The task of the pressing players is to capture the ball as quick as possible. Once the ball is under control, the players can initiate a fast counterattack performing a perpendicular pass. It's essential to direct the first pass to the deep offense because it also gives the players more time to comfortably perform a postpressing attack. This ideal situation is not always possible, because the first pass is rather stabilizing and the fast counterattack is often formed by the second or the third pass.

- The drill is suitable for practicing and improving other types of pressing: pressing victim and situational pressing.

- The coach can interrupt the drill to correct movements, place selection and/or players' cooperation and timing. It's recommended to repeat this situation several times in a slow pace.

DRILL 53: DEFENSIVE PRESSING AND SWITCHING

Drill goal and focus: cooperation of defenders and midfielders in defensive pressing, switching to fast counterattack (pressing drill level 1, 2, 3, 4, 5, 6, 7, 8)

Fig. 5.4.4-7 Cooperation of the midfielders and attackers in immediate ultraoffensive pressing

DRILL ORGANIZATION:

- The whole pitch is used for the drill, and it is divided into three zones: defensive zone (30–35 m from the fixed goal), central zone (45–50 m long), finishing zone (20 m from the opposite fixed goal, which has a cone shape. The corners of the pitch are not the part of the drill area).

- 11v11 formation; defensive zone is 7v7 formation; central zone is 3v3 formation.

- The defending team play in 3-4-3 or 4-3-3 formation.

- All the players are located on their respective positions.

DRILL FLOW:

- The drill takes place in the defensive zone. The drill is started by the defensive team in 7v7 formation moving toward one goal.

- Once the ball is under control, the defending team take it across the line that marks the defensive zone and switch to fast counterattack outnumbering in 5v3 formation or 4v3 formation because the opponents can't leave the defensive zone.

- The movement from defensive to central zone must be done within six seconds; otherwise, the team will lose the ball and must return to defensive pressing.

- If the defending team manage to shift to the central zone within the time limit, the action must be finished within the next eight seconds.

- If the team lose the ball or if the ball goes outside of the practice area, the drill always restarts from the defensive zone by attacking the offensive team toward one goal.

- The drill takes fifteen to twenty-five minutes.

VARIATIONS:

- 8v8 formation in the defensive zone and 2v2 formation in the central zone.

- One of the opponent players in the 7v7 formation can return to defense form 4v4 or 5v4 situation in the central zone.

- 7v7 or 8v8 formation in the defensive zone. Once the ball is under control, the whole team switch into fast counterattack. The opponent is not limited while shifting to defense.

- Shifting to fast counterattack starts performing a pass to the opponent in the central zone, which is followed by additional back pass from the players behind.

METHODICAL, ORGANIZATIONAL COMMENTS:

- Defensive pressing is more important during the first stage. The task of the whole team in the compact block is to occupy and defend possible dangerous areas in front of their goal in order to shift to active defensive pressing and take the ball from the opponent.

- All players must be involved in defense (seven players in this play). The actual system of the team is important for defensive tactics purposes. In case of seven players, the options are 4-3 or 3-4 alignment. The main elements are the coach philosophy, the playing system, and the methodology of the opponents in future matches.

- The task of the second stage is to switch immediately into attacking action and to shift to fast counterattack. Immediately after taking the ball from the opponent, the players must be free to perform a pass. After a successful pass to the free player, a fast vertical combination can be applied and this action must be completed as soon as possible.

- Very close attention must be paid to this part of the training process because the defensive pressing only makes sense in combination with a fast counterattack.

- The coach can interrupt the drill due to movement corrections, place selection, cooperation, and timing of players. It's recommended to repeat this situation several times and slowly.

- The main purpose of these drills is to simulate the conditions and the tempo of a real match. This practice will ensure the correct application of the "adequate covering" principle. It allows the maximum replication of play situations and sequences in a match as well as the training process itself. It's an effective to transfer of required conduct into solving of play situation in the match.

- The repetition of the drill and their effective solution creates situations and the necessary automatism, which make the action and cooperation of the players and the whole team easier and faster. Thanks to this automatism, the process of the match improves, due to the fact that the players can instinctively use the solutions learnt in drills and training process.

5.4.2 Pressing in the Central Zone (PCZ, Midfield Pressing)

Midfield pressing is a form of pressing that is often used by the team to gain the control of the ball. It can be used as a base point to pressing tactic (the team mainly play midfield pressing, which sometimes can be switched to other types of pressing). Also it can be used as a transitional pressing because the team can't play defensive, offensive, or immediate ultraoffensive pressing during the whole match. Because defensive pressing is usually used against an opponent player tactically strong, the team must apply midfield pressing in order to be successful.

The central zone is the active area for midfield pressing. It is approximately 15 m on the opponent's half of the pitch and 15 m on team's half. This area can be changed in a way that the pressing activation line moves forward or backward. The "15-15" rule changes into "10-20" or to "20-10." The height of the pressing activation line depends on the coach's philosophy, the opponent's preparation, alignment, and performance as well as the development of the match.

In order to maintain the compactness of the team, the players must keep at all times the size of the active area in defense, their respective positions, and a tight distances between the formations. It's important that all the players return to their positions behind the pressing line after losing the control of the ball and immediately form a midfield defensive block, which is the precondition for a successful application of aggressive midfield pressing. Midfield pressing activation, switching from central block to active pressing, starts when the opponent passes or dribbles the ball to a predetermined active area (pressing signal). During the application of a successful midfield pressing, the opponent is forced to move from behind or to perform a long pass to the running attackers. That's the reason why the defensive block must be prepared for frequent retreats. Retreats are often connected with keeping the active pressing zone, which is followed by the application of pump. The effectiveness of midfield pressing can increase using the advantage of pendulum and pump. Retreating pump and pendulums increase the intensity and safety of midfield pressing. It makes the space manipulation easier and maintains the compactness of the team. All of the above-mentioned facts must be taken into consideration in the application of practice methodology and midfield pressing improvement.

Midfield pressing requires great physical and psychical readiness of all the players, because it is connected to a high and fast concentration and intensity. In this type of pressing, each player has to do lots of sprints to keep a tight distance in order to maintain the compactness of the team. Also, after gaining the control of the ball, the players must be prepared to switch to attacking actions and to perform a fast counterattack.

Advantages of midfield pressing:

- Not big distance from the team's goal.

- Possibility of good cooperation with the team's goal-keeper in long and high passes performed by the opponent behind the defensive chain level.

- Shorter distance from the opponent's goal, followed by ideal preconditions for fast switch from defensive to offensive actions.

- Good conditions for fast counterattacks, which main characteristic is waiting for counter situations from the active defense in the center of the field.

- Keeping the opponent in a safe distance from the team's goal.

- Pushing the opponent out to controlled areas.

- Space manipulation to perform pressing and to build pressing situations.

- Prevention of rectilinear movement so that the play is forced to be performed from behind.

- Correct and fast shifting to the ball and active attack to the player with the ball, which make the completion of pressing easier.

Disadvantages of midfield pressing:

- When applying pressing in the central zone, the attacking zone is completely left out because there isn't any activity supporting the attacks to the opponent.

- A lot of open spaces in the team's half of the pitch offers the opponent suitable opportunities to do counterattacks.

- When midfield pressing is performed efficiently, it can seduce the opponent to execute a long pass behind the defensive chain level. Then the team is forced to retreat frequently to push the opponent out.

DRILL 54: MIDFIELD PRESSING IN 2V2 PLAY AND 2V2 + 1

Drill goal and focus: practice and improvement midfield pressing in the specified area (pressing drill level 1, 2, 3, 4, 5)

Fig. 5.4.2-1 Midfield pressing in 2:v2 + 1 drill

DRILL ORGANIZATION:

- In the center of the pitch, we mark the central zone. The central zone is 20–25 m wide. The central zone is divided into three equal parts: two outside and one in the middle.

- The drill uses the middle part and one outer part.

- The players are divided according to their positions into two equal teams. The players are aligned in the side verticals positions and play in the outer part of the marked zone. The players in central vertical position play in the middle part of the marked zone.

- The players of both teams stand opposite to each other outside the marked area.

- One player from the defensive team moves to the opposite side where the attacking team players are ready for the action.

- Prepare sufficient balls to ensure smooth drill.

DRILL FLOW:

- There is a 2v2 + 1 drill "through lines" on both marked areas. The task of the group of two in control of the ball is to lead the ball to the opposite side of the rectangle.

- The drill starts when two defensive and two offensive players run to the marked area. Then, one player from the attacking team, located outside of the rectangle, performs a pass to a team player.

- The pass is a signal to launch the play and for the third defender in the opposite side of area.

- In a 3v2 situation, the group of two, with the assistance of the third defender, attempt to get the control of the ball and lead it to the opposite side.

- The drill is organized as a competition between the teams. The team score one point for leading the ball to the basic line.

- The drill finishes when the ball goes outside the playing area and four other players run to the pitch.

- The drill takes place on both areas at the same time.

- The teams change their roles after five drills.

VARIATIONS:

- The team undernumbered can apply an auxiliary pass outside the area.

- After losing the ball, the number of players in attacking team can increased by one more player. Then the drill continues in a 3v3 situations.

- Two portable goals with goalkeepers are placed on the line of both penalty areas. Once the ball has been taken successfully to the marked area, the drill continues with a fixed goal with goalkeeper.

METHODICAL, ORGANIZATIONAL COMMENTS:

- The group of two learns how to guide the opponent to the team player in order to form numerical advantage in the area around the ball.

- The player running to the playing area must attack quickly the opponent with the ball.

- After the defenders take the control of the ball, a fast switch to attacking actions must be performed in order to immediately execute the pressing forward and to lead the ball to the basic line of the opponent.

- Mutual coaching of all players is required.

- The coach stops the game and corrects the course of the situation.

- The drill supports elementary habits and midfield pressing automatism because it takes place in the space where midfield pressing mostly occurs. All the team play in their respective positions and cooperate in the different pressing situations.

DRILL 55: MIDFIELD PRESSING IN 10V8 PLAY IN SPECIFIED AREAS OF THE CENTRAL ZONE

Drill goal and focus: practice and improvement of midfield pressing (pressing drill level 1, 2, 3, 4, 5, 6, 8).

Fig. 5.4.2-2 Midfield pressing in specified areas

DRILL ORGANIZATION:

-   The central zone is marked in the center of the pitch. The central zone is 20–25 m wide. The central zone is divided in three equal parts: two outer parts and one in the middle.

-   The marked areas are numbered from left to right no. 1 and 3 represent the outer parts; no. 2 is the middle part.

-   The drill takes place between the penalty areas. The portable goals with goalkeepers are placed at the border line of sixteenth.

-   Two teams are built with specific positions for each player, 10v8 drill. The alignment of the team performing midfield pressing is with four midfielders: 4-2-2 or 3-4-3. The other team plays in 3-4-1 alignment.

-   The defenders of both teams move between their sixteenth and the central zone. The midfielders take their respective positions in the central zone to keep one midfielder system in the outer part and two midfielders in middle part. The attackers are on the opponent's half of the pitch.

DRILL FLOW:

-   The defenders start the drill in undernumbering. They pass the ball to the area specified by the coach.

-   The pressing team move to this specified area. The team form out numbering and create pressure on the opponent with the ball.

-   The movement is performed by the whole team. Depending on the system, the coach determines which positions will be pressured on individual areas of the central zone.

-   The attacking team try to keep the ball helping each other but they can't leave the space that has already been determined by the coach.

-   After taking control of the ball, the team attacks the opponent's goal.

-   The drill takes 15 to 25 minutes.

VARIATIONS:

-   The defender who passed the ball to the specified area runs to the ball in a 2v3 situation in the outer and middle part of the area. The attackers try to cross the central zone to finish the action.

- In a free 10v8 drill, the movement of the attackers must be performed through the central zone. After every interruption, the drill continues by the attacking team's goalkeeper passing the ball to a team player. If a player scores a goal after taking the ball in the central zone, it is a double point. Attackers get one point when they keep the ball in the central zone for 10 seconds.

- In a 9v9 drill with a 3-4-2 alignment performed in the central zone, the rules are the same as in the previous drill: If a player scores a goal after midfield pressing is applied, it is a double point. The players get one point for keeping the ball in the central zone for 10 seconds.

- 11v11 drill performed using the whole pitch. The central zone is marked in three areas. The previous rules are also applied: if a player scores a goal in the central zone, it is a double. The attackers get one point for keeping the ball in the central zone for 10 seconds.

METHODICAL, ORGANIZATIONAL COMMENTS:

- The whole team must move in compact block. Attention must be paid to maintaining the distance between players and formations.

- The drill allows practicing outnumbering in the area around the ball.

- The task is to close the corridors for possible passes.

- The whole four-defender chain level practices taking over as well as handing over of the released opponent's attacker.

- The analysis of the teams and opponents in the previous matches can also be used for the drill as well as a preparation for pressing application against future opponents.

DRILL 56: "INSIDE" GUIDED MIDFIELD PRESSING IN 11V11 PLAY IN THREE VERTICALS

Drill goal and focus: practice and improvement of midfield pressing focused on guiding the opponent to the central vertical (pressing drill level 1, 2, 3, 4, 5, 6, 7, 8).

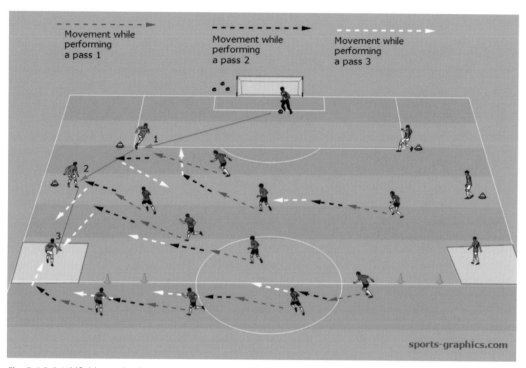

Fig. 5.4.2-3 Midfield pressing in 11v11 play in three verticals

DRILL ORGANIZATION:

- The drill takes place on 2/3 of the pitch

- A portable goal is placed opposite to the fixed goal approximately 20 m behind the central line.

- The central zone is marked so that the goal line forms one border with the portable goal. The other border is formed by the fixed goal placed on half of the pitch approximately 15 m parallel to the central line.

- Also the verticals are marked in the central zone. Small goals are placed along the side verticals at the level of the portable goal.

- Two teams are formed using basic formations against each other.

DRILL FLOW:

- 11v11 drill performed on 2/3 of the pitch. The attackers move toward the portable goal and the two small goals placed along the side verticals.

- A goal scored into the small goals is a double point.

- The task of the team applying midfield pressing, when the ball is in the side vertical, is to push the opponent out of the central vertical. Here is where the pressure on the opponent with the ball is applied.

- After taking the ball as a result of the pressing action, the team can attack toward the fixed goal.

- A goal scored after taking the ball in the central vertical is a double point.

DRILL 57: FAST COUNTERATTACK FROM THE MIDFIELD PRESSING IN 10V10 PLAY

Drill goal and focus: practice and improvement of midfield pressing and switching from defensive to offensive actions (pressing drill level 1, 2, 3)

Fig. 5.4.2-4 Switching from midfield pressing to fast counterattack

DRILL ORGANIZATION:

- The drill takes place on 2/3 of the pitch. In the central zone, around the central circle, we mark a square 20–30 m in size.

- The playing area is marked with a basic 15–20 m line parallel to the central one.

- Two teams are formed. The team practicing the switching is in complete formation (without the goalkeeper).

- The opponents play with a goalkeeper, three-defender chain level, four midfielders, and two attackers.

- Four players, selected from each team, play on the marked central square. In the first team (four players) performing pressing with switching, there are two defensive midfielders and two center backs. In the other team (four players), there are two attackers and two side midfielders.

- The rest of the players from both teams just occupy their positions.

DRILL FLOW:

- Four players (two attackers and two side midfielders) play against the four ones applying pressing in the central square executing number of passes.

- The players with the ball get one point for ten passes executed without interruption.

- In case the players practicing pressing take the ball, they perform a fast counterattack executing a perpendicular pass from the square to free attacker or withdrawn center forward.

- The player passing the ball joins the attacking action in a 7v5 situation. The other players stay in the central square.

VARIATIONS:

- The square can be enlarged for a 6v6 play or be out numbered for a 6v4 play.

- The opponent plays with four-defender chain level.

- The first pass after taking control of the ball is guided to the side vertical.

- Two players from the square can also join the attacking action.

- All defensive and offensive players switch or involve in the action either as attackers or defenders.

METHODICAL, ORGANIZATIONAL COMMENTS:

- It's important to perform the action technically accurate and at full speed.

- The sequences are repeated in case of inconsistencies.

- Attention must be paid to the attacking actions continuity.

- Use outnumbering and avoid 1-to-1 situations.

- The width and depth of the pitch is used for the action. The main task is to look for the shortest and fastest way to build shooting situations.

5.4.3 Pressing in the Attacking Zone (POZ, Offensive Pressing)

In offensive pressing (forechecking), the team performs defense in compact formation far from their goal to push the opponent in front of their penalty area to force the player to lose the ball. The advantage, which offers good possibilities to form shooting actions, is to take the ball near to the opponent's goal. The **basic principle** of this way of defense is that the team, in order to secure their own goal, don't withdraw after losing the ball on the opponent's half of the pitch or within the attacking zone. The team stay extended, switch from attacking to defensive actions and create numerical advantage in the area after losing the ball. This defensive tactics is very effective, and it's bound to combinations with short passes, which secures sufficient number of players immediately when the team lose the ball. An aggressive offensive pressing, in connection with short passes, demands good technical and physical readiness of the players.

On one hand, pressing has many advantages but, on the other hand, it requires fitness above-average and mental preconditions. Players must be identified with this type of pressing and must be motivated as well. Besides stamina, strength and speed, players burn a lot of energy when switching from attacking to defensive actions; they need high concentration and attention, aggression control, extraordinary ability to sacrifice themselves for the sake of the team. Soccer requires knowledge, foreseeing, peripheral vision, intelligence, and the ability to quickly make decisions. A positive approach to offensive pressing is connected to a healthy self-confidence and the sense of responsibility.

Coordinated actions require patience, determination, systematic drills, and improvements to develop reflex so that every player knows how to move in each situation without wasting time but reacting quickly in the match. For a successful completion of pressing, it's important the communication between each player during its execution. The initial verbal instruction should be carried out by a skilled player (defensive midfielder or center back) from behind who can foresee opportunities for pressing application. Even if the communication between players is directly from backward to forward, the impulse for offensive pressing is started by an extended attacker or a center midfielder who determines the action of the other players in the center of the playground. Through this movement the course of the whole defensive sequence is decided. As a result, the defense can use the advantages of guided and situational pressing, pressing victim, and upper and lower pendulum. The drill for a coordinated, compact, synchronized, and effective movement of the whole team takes long time. The result of it is a systematic and purposeful training process that uses the advantages of the drills.

Offensive pressing represents a very intensive way of defense, and this is reason why it can't be applied during the whole match but only in specific stages and situations. We could say that the better the technical condition of the players are, the better the coordination of the team is; and, offensive pressing can be applied in the matches for longer time. It can be effectively used as an element of surprise at the beginning of the match or at the beginning of the half-time in situations where the team loses the match. It can also be used when the opponents kick the ball from the outside of their half of the pitch or in the matches against the weaker opponent.

DRILL 58: 4V3 PLAY IN THE SIDE VERTICAL

Drill goal and focus: practice of offensive pressing in the side vertical (level of the pressing drill 1, 2, 3, 4, 5, 6, 7)

sports-graphics.com

Fig. 5.4.3-1 4v3 drill in the side verticals

DRILL ORGANIZATION:

- The drill takes place on both side verticals, which are extended to the goal area. The length of the areas is measured from goal line to central line.

- The central line and the side verticals are marked with cones placed in two small goals.

- The players are aligned according to their positions in both side verticals. The team practicing offensive pressing is formed by four players: one attacker, one side midfielder, one fullback, and one defensive midfielder. The defensive team play with three players: one center back, one midfielder, and one full back.

- One goalkeeper is placed in the fixed goal.

DRILL FLOW:

- The drill is performed alternating both verticals.

- The goalkeeper starts every action performing a pass to the center back.

- After the pass, the 4v3 drill starts within the marked area.

- The task of the undernumbering team is to score a goal kicking the ball to one of the two small goals on the central line.

- The task of the pressing team is to take the ball using guided pressing toward the "outside" and to attack the fixed goal. The goalkeeper can leave the marked area.

VARIATIONS:

- Guided pressing toward the "inside."

- All the players practice at the same time in both verticals. This is followed by 8v6 play toward the fixed goal and four small goals on the central line.

- 4v4 situation in the side verticals.

METHODICAL, ORGANIZATIONAL COMMENTS:

- At first, the players practice the pressing maneuvers in slow pace. After this part of drill is completed, the team practice 4v3 situation.

- The first pass is the sign to start pressing. The attacker runs in a smooth curve from the inner side toward the center back to perform the next pass, which is directed only to the fullback.

- After the pass to the full back is done, the attacker moves between the full back and the center back to prevent a back pass.

- At the same time, the other players of the defensive team move toward the ball: a side midfielder attacks the opponent's full back with the ball; a defensive midfielder also moves toward the ball and doubles the side midfielder. Together, they form a 2v1 situation. The full back protects the players and occupies the area behind them or occupies the third opponent position.

- The coach makes corrections to any mistakes after the action is completed either scoring a goal or after any interruption of the defense performance. After its completion, the same practice is done in the opposite vertical.

DRILL 59: OFFENSIVE PRESSING IN 4V4 PLAY ON THE HALF OF THE PITCH

Drill goal and focus: practice and improvement of offensive pressing to the opponent's penalty area (level of the pressing drill 1, 2, 3, 6)

Fig. 5.4.3-2 Offensive pressing in 4v4 play

DRILL ORGANIZATION:
- The drill takes place on half of the pitch.

- Small goals are placed on the central line on both left and right side vertical.

- A marking line is made parallel to the central line, in a distance of 15 m, along the whole width of the pitch. This marking line serves as starting point for the players practicing pressing. Also, it's the line that the players are supposed to lead the ball to.

- Two teams are formed. Each team has four players. The pressing team formed by two attackers and two midfielders. The defending team play with four-defender chain.

- A goalkeeper is placed in the fixed goal.

DRILL FLOW:
- The goalkeeper starts the drill performing a pass to a team player from the four-defensive chain.

- The 4v4 play starts.

- The task of the four-defender chain is to escape from the pressing pressure using fast combinations to lead the ball over the marking line and to score a goal to one of the small goals.

- The pass executed by the goalkeeper is the sign for the player to start the maneuver behind the penalty area line and to perform aggressive pressing to the defenders. Their task is to take the control of the ball and to perform a fast attack the fixed goal.

VARIATIONS:
- 6v5 situation when the pressing team is formed by four midfielders and two attackers. A four-defender chain and one defensive midfielder play against them.

- The size of the playing area is reduced for a 3v3 situation.

- Both teams play on two touches.

METHODICAL, ORGANIZATIONAL COMMENTS:

-   The attacking players must be strong and aggressive when confronting one-to-one situations. The task is to take the ball from the opponent and to switch to a fast counterattack in order to finish the play.

-   This drill can also be used to practice defender chain as part of counterpressing resistance strategy.

-   Players are encouraged to be cooperative to use loud communication.

-   The drill is physically very demanding due to its intensity. This is the reason why careful attention must be paid to ensure players get enough relaxation. The Intervals of physical load can take two to three minutes. It's recommended to perform this drill in two groups taking turns after two to three minutes.

-   The coach makes corrections during the team shifting.

DRILL 60: "HIGH" AND GUIDED PRESSING

Drill goal and focus: practice offensive pressing focused on guiding the opponent toward the sideline (level of the pressing drill 1, 2, 3, 4, 5, 6, 7).

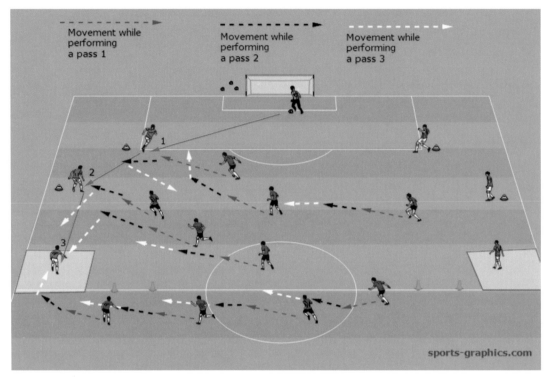

Fig. 5.4.3-3 Practice of offensive and guided pressing

DRILL ORGANIZATION:

- The drill takes place on half of the pitch.

- Two small goals are placed on the central line from the cones, right on the line between the side and central vertical.

- On the side verticals in the central zone, we mark a small "pass" square of 5 × 5 m in size. This square will be occupied by a side midfielder, and it is an attacking space for the pressing team.

- We mark two positions with the cones (center back and full back) in both verticals. These positions are occupied by the players whose task is to copy the opponent.

- The opponent team has six players: three players on the right vertical and three on the left vertical. The positions are center back, full back, and side midfielder. A goalkeeper is in the fixed goal.

- The pressing team occupies all ten positions on the playing area.

DRILL FLOW:

- In the first part of the drill, the opponents perform passes in one side vertical in given numerical order. At first, they practice slowly and then the speed increases. The order of the passes is as follow: goalkeeper, center back, full back, and side midfielder.

- Then the drill is performed in a faster pace and the players copying the opponent are on the small goals.

- The team applying offensive pressing also practice slow. After the movement are correctly synchronized, the drill is performed faster.

- The task of the team is to form numerical advantage in the area around the ball, to take the ball and to attack the fixed goal with the goalkeeper.

VARIATIONS:

- We move the attacking space higher up to the opponent's full back position.

- The practice is "inside" guided pressing.

METHODICAL, ORGANIZATIONAL COMMENTS:

- The main purpose of this drill is to force the opponent to move toward the sidelines, near their penalty area. There intensive pressure on the ball is applied to take the ball from the opponent and to start a fast counterattack.

- In the first part of the drill, the team select the direction and the attacking method; the correct formation and the distance between the players as well the compactness during the movements. The whole team keep short distances between players.

- After the goalkeeper has executed the pass to the center back, the attacker moves in a smooth curve to the center back with the ball to force the center back to pass the ball to the full back. After the pass, the attacker moves further between the center back and the full back to prevent from a back pass.

- The center attacking midfielder or "man in the hole" moves behind the extended attacker to occupy this area to prevent the opponent to perform a deep pass.

- After the pass, the side midfielder moves toward the opponent's full back in order to attack him.

- The defensive midfielder closer to the ball moves to the side vertical toward it and protect the side midfielder.

- The defensive midfielder further from the ball moves behind the first defensive midfielder in order to secure the division into the depth.

- The side midfielder further from the ball moves toward the central vertical.

- The full back closer to the ball moves behind the opponent's side midfielder to occupy his position.

- The whole defensive chain moves behind the full back.

- The next pass is from the opponent's full back to the marked square where the side midfielder is located.

- In this square, where the full back is closer to the ball, the defensive midfielder and the side midfielder move into it to create outnumbering around the ball to take it from the opponent.

- This drill can be practiced also in the opposite vertical.

- The coach explains the movements and selects the place for individual positions; these movements are practiced in slow pace. After the transferring, the players move to their initial formation. After a successful practice of slow movements, the players practice the same movements faster until reaching the real match pace.

- The next stage is the practice of a 10v6 situation with two small goals and one fixed goal.

DRILL 61: OFFENSIVE PRESSING DIRECTED AGAINST INTO THE DEPTH PASSES OF THE OPPONENT

Drill goal and focus: practice of offensive pressing with emphasis on the division into the depth, midfielders and attackers' cooperation, prevention of opponent perpendicular passes, direction of the attacking actions of the opponent toward the "outside" and practice of upper and lower pendulum (level of the pressing drill 1, 2, 3, 4, 5, 6, 7)

Fig. 5.4.3-4 Pressing directed against into the depth passes of the opponent.

DRILL ORGANIZATION:

- The drill takes place on an extended half of the pitch

- Approximately 10 m from the central line to the fixed goal, we place cones to mark two small goals on the intersection between the side and central vertical.

- On the other half of the pitch, behind the central line, we mark a rectangle of 5 m × 20 m in size. The opponent's attacker moves inside the rectangular.

- In a 10v11 situation, the pressing team play without a goalkeeper and the opponent team play with a complete formation.

DRILL FLOW:

- The goalkeeper starts the drill performing a pass to the center back.

- The drill is done without any standard situations. After every interruption, the drill is restarted by the goalkeeper performing the pass to the center back.

- The opponent team have two options to score a point: either performing a perpendicular pass to a team player over the marked goals or performing a pass in the marked area to an extended attacker, who has to finalize the score.

- The opponents are not allowed to do high and long passes.

- The task of the pressing team is, with collaboration of the attackers and midfielders, to prevent perpendicular passes and, at the same time, to force the opponent to move toward the side verticals. Having the opponent positioned in the side vertical makes scoring more difficult.

- After a successful pressing, the team can attack the opponent's goal. If a fast counterattack is performed, the team is only allowed to perform five passes. Otherwise, it loses the ball and a new drill is restarted.

VARIATIONS:

- 8v10 situation.

- Two touches play.

- Instead of the marked area for the opponent's attacker, the drill can be practiced on three small goals.

- Fast counterattack after taking the ball must be finished within six seconds.

METHODICAL-ORGANIZATIONAL COMMENTS:

- Since the small goals are moved deeper into the playing area, and the defensive chain takes place between the small goals and central line, the midfielders, in cooperation with the attackers, must prevent the opponent from passing the ball over the small goals.

- We use the advantages of upper and lower pendulum.

- The main tasks of the drill is to synchronize the movements of all the players in the application of offensive pressing, which forces the opponent to move toward the side verticals.

- The players must maintain small distances and move in compact block.

5.4.4 Immediate Ultraoffensive Pressing (IUP—Pressing Immediately After Losing the Ball)

This special type of pressing tactics is applied immediately after losing the ball. It was gradually configured improving the action on the ball oriented to the defense zone. At the same time, it is a logical consequence of the development and improvement of practice and defense methodology. The development of soccer gradually revealed the sense of movements necessary to play effectively and successfully. The fundamental element of the immediate ultraoffensive pressing is a functional mechanism of a fast strategy to take the control of the ball immediately after a player losses it. A fast recovery of the ball has its advantages when the opponent is directed to build a new attack sequence and is not ready to apply any defensive action at the moment. The use of this strategy is precisely the core of immediate ultraoffensive pressing.

In immediate ultraoffensive pressing, the opponent is neither allowed to hold the ball for long time nor to prepare

a good position for opening an interlude. Moreover, despite the extended position, the player is not allowed to apply effectively a fast counterattacks but, all the opposite, the team have the advantage of controlling the ball as well as the advantage to attack against a disrupted opponent. A team with a clear knowledge on how to successfully switch from attacking to defense actions and vice versa should be also prepared to consider any possibility of failure during these attacking actions. The team create outnumber situations over the opponent usually having much better chances to win the match. Perfect switching is the essential element of immediate ultraoffensive pressing, and it's also the key to success. In individual situations, the basic element of outnumbering is to have enough number of team players supporting the situation. These actions are synchronized performing drills in the center of the field and the same also applies for the transitional parts of the play. This is the way teams can achieve outnumbering after losing the ball and to taking it back very quickly right in the place where the ball was lost. After recovering the ball, the team have enough players around the ball as well as many possibilities to retain it and to switch the action to a fast counterattack. Only the team well positioned and orientated over the area, focused mainly on the ball, can create outnumber in every stage of the match. When a team plays against an opponent, who is applying the same zonal pressing, the switching stage is a crucial factor, which determines the team's efficiency and its result. Due to the quality of the performance and its successful result, the most important aspect, in a match with an equal or stronger opponent, is the decisions made during the switching stages that are beneficial to the team. A successful switching from attacking to defensive actions and vice versa depends on a quick analysis of real situations, foreseeing the process of the sequence and how fast those decisions are made. Analysis and anticipation of playing sequences, quick decisions, correction, and improvement performing situations are all part of the drill process.

Immediate ultraoffensive pressing is a very demanding technique that puts a heavy load on both players and practice methodology. The important achievement is that players learn how to move and react at the moment of losing and recovering the control of the ball. As a result, when players know their defense and offense tasks leant in switching practice and drills, they don't waste time thinking or making decisions. Their reactions and reflex are a response according to the various situations in matches. Success is not achieved only by an individual's abilities but also by coordination of the whole team. However, the main requirement for gaining success is an exceptional cooperation of all the team players in the time and space. This results in heavy demands on methodology and the quality of the training process. The method of exercising and improving immediate ultraoffensive pressing can be brought into practice by performing various preparatory plays as the presence of an opponent the exercises is an essential part of this method and it can be achieved only in the context of the play. However, it's possible to find different flexible didactical and methodological ways of learning this difficult way of play in simplified or difficult training situations. Following exercises should help coaches in this uneasy task and add other impulses for creative formation of their training process in order to improve immediate ultraoffensive pressing.

DRILL 62: IMMEDIATE ULTRAOFFENSIVE PRESSING IN THE SIDE VERTICAL

Drill goal and focus: practice and improvement of immediate ultraoffensive pressing in the side vertical (level of the pressing drill 1, 2, 3, 4, 5, 6, 7)

Fig. 5.4.4-1 Immediate ultraoffensive pressing directed toward "the inside"

DRILL ORGANIZATION:

- The play takes place in the side vertical from the penalty area to the central line.

- We place a small goal on the central line near the sideline.

- The goalkeeper is positioned in the goal.

- 4v3 play on the playing area: the team, which is practicing pressing, consists of full back, side midfielder, defensive midfielder, attacker, or withdrawn center forward "man in the hole." The opponent team consists of full back and center back and side midfielder.

DRILL FLOW:

- The players of both teams are in their positions.

- The action is started by the coach performing a pass directed to the opponent player.

- The pass is followed by 4-to-3 play. The group of three players is playing with a small goal. After gaining the possession of the ball, the team, that is practicing pressing, can attack the fixed goal with a goalkeeper.

VARIATIONS:

- We place the small goal behind the inner sideline of the playing area to the central vertical. This action is an additional aid for the players in practicing directed pressing toward "the outside."

- The opponent team's task is to perform a pass to the attacker in the central circle.

- We place two small goals on the central line.

- 4v4 play. Defensive midfielder joins the opponent's team.

- 5v4 play. Center back joins the team, which is practicing pressing.

METHODICAL, ORGANIZATIONAL COMMENTS:

- In the first stage, the coach practices the movement maneuvers of the pressing team in a slow pace.

- After a successful completion of the first stage of the drill, the players practice the drill in a faster pace.

- In the intensive movement, the task of the players is to create pressure on the opponent by doubling.

Fig. 5.4.4-2 Variation

- The players must maintain distances, form defensive triangles, and keep compactness throughout the play.

- It is also very important to perform a constructive withdrawal of the ball from the opponent and switch to attacking actions fast.

- After the players gain the possession of the ball, they switch to fast counterattack. The first pass must be fixed; consequently, the attacking action is directed perpendicularly toward the opponent's goal.

- After a successful completion of this action, we practice the drill in the opposite vertical.

- The coach corrects all the mistakes while the players exchange the sides.

DRILL 63: 6V6 PLAY FOCUSES ON VERY FAST SWITCHING FROM ATTACKING TO DEFENSIVE ACTIONS AND VICE VERSA

Drill goal and focus: practice and improvement of immediate ultraoffensive pressing and practice of fast switching (level of the pressing drill 1, 2, 3,4, 5, 6, 7)

Fig. 5.4.4-3 6 to 6 play with switching

DRILL ORGANIZATION:
- The playing area is an extended and widened penalty area all the way behind the central circle on the other half of the pitch.

- On the basic line on the other half of the pitch, we place a portable goal opposite the fixed goal.

- There are two teams of six players in each team and two goalkeepers.

- The coach is standing behind the sideline of the playing area, and he has balls at his disposal.

DRILL FLOW:
- Each action is started by the coach performing a pass toward the playing area. It's followed by 6v6 play with two goals.

- The coach gives acoustic signal in irregular intervals and, at the same time, independently from the play situation, he passes another ball into the playing area either into the open space or toward the player who is defending at that time.

- While the signal and coach's pass is being performed, the players can't play with the previous ball. They must quickly adapt to the new play situation.

- Breach of this rule is followed by a penalty kick against the team whose player broke the rule.

- The play is performed without any standard situations. Each breach is followed by the coach's pass into the playing area independently from the fact whose team broke the rule.

VARIATIONS:

- 7v7 play.

- The pitch can be widened all the way to the sidelines, which would be 8v8 play.

- Play performed on two touches.

METHODICAL, ORGANIZATIONAL COMMENTS:

- The play requires full concentration and very fast switching. Due to this fact, the coach mustn't interrupt the play very often and he should allow the players to perform the play freely. Three interruptions in each set are optimal.

- The emphasis is put on the intensity of the play and speed of switching.

- The play lasts four minutes. Interval for rest is sixty to ninety seconds. The whole drill is repeated three to four times.

- The coach corrects the players' action during the breaks between the plays.

DRILL 64: IMMEDIATE ULTRAOFFENSIVE PRESSING WITH PROVOCATIVE RULE

Drill goal and focus: practice and improvement of immediate ultraoffensive pressing (level of the pressing drill 1, 2, 3, 4, 5, 6, 7).

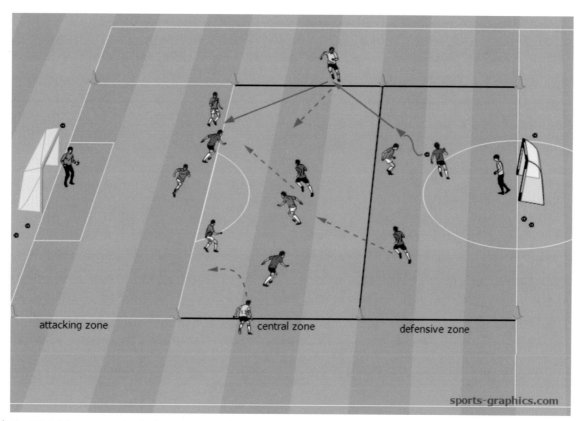

Fig. 5.4.4-4 Preparatory play in three zones 5v5 play with two neutral players

DRILL ORGANIZATION:

- The drill takes place from the extended penalty area all the way to the center line.

- We place a portable goal on the center line.

- We divide the playing area into three equal horizontal zones.

- The team practice the 5v5 situation with two goalkeepers and two neutral players located next to the playing area at the level of the center zone.

DRILL FLOW:

- The team practice a free 5v5 situation on the marked area.

- The neutral players, who play on one touch, assist the offensive team.

- When the offensive team loses the ball in the center or attacking zone, the neutral players run into the playing area to assist the defense team that lost ball to recover it as soon as possible.

- When the team lose the ball in their own defensive zone at the beginning of the action, they are not allowed to switch to defensive stage but must let the opponent finish the attack.

VARIATIONS:

- The number of players and the playing area can be increased.

- The drill is performed on two touches.

METHODICAL, ORGANIZATIONAL COMMENTS:

- The rules of this drill induce immediate ultraoffensive pressing because they force the players to switch from defensive to center or attacking zone as quick as possible.

- It is very disadvantageous to lose the ball in the defensive zone.

- Even the loss of the ball outside the defensive zone can prevent a potential threat because the outnumbering team can recover the ball very quickly.

- There is the possibility to execute some passes intentionally incorrect to the back followed by an outnumbering pressing.

DRILL 65: 5V5 SITUATION ON TWO FIXED GOALS AND FOUR SMALL GOALS PLACED NEXT TO THE PLAYING AREA

Drill goal and focus: practice and improvement of immediate ultraoffensive pressing (level of the pressing drill 1, 2, 3, 4, 5, 6, 7).

Fig. 5.4.4-5 5v5 play on two fixed goals and four small goals placed next to the playing area

DRILL ORGANIZATION:

- The playing area is extended to the penalty area.

- We place a portable goal on the line opposite the fixed goal.

- The goalkeepers are in the fixed goals.

- We place four small goals next to the central line outside the playing area. These goals (two on the right side and two on the left) are facing sideward toward the place where the attacking action is performed.

DRILL FLOW:

- Two teams (with five players each) play against each other. Each team attack two small goals and one fixed goal.

- The drill is performed without any standard situations. After every interruption, the play continues by the goalkeeper of the team, which didn't break the rules.

VARIATIONS:

- Scoring a goal in the small goals is only allowed after the goalkeeper starts the drill. Because of this, it's advantageous for the defensive team to extend to the opponent's half.

- The offensive team can only score in the small goals after some specific time (five, eight, and ten seconds), which makes the conditions of the pressing team much easier.

METHODICAL, ORGANIZATIONAL COMMENTS:

- The rules of this drill induce the defensive team to apply an extended immediate ultraoffensive pressing, because there is no possibility to prevent scoring in the small goals and the chance to take the control of the ball increases.

- Since the small goals are placed next to the playing area, the defensive players must cover the goals from the sideline and force the opponent to move toward the inside (the rule of the drill is a provocative guided pressing).

DRILL 66: 5V5 SITUATION FOCUSED ON IMMEDIATE ULTRAOFFENSIVE PRESSING AND FAST COUNTERATTACK

Drill goal and focus: practice and improvement of immediate ultraoffensive pressing, switching, and quickly finishing the attacking action (level of the pressing drill 1, 2, 3, 4, 5, 6, 7)

Fig. 5.4.4-6 5v5 play+ two focused on immediate ultraoffensive pressing and switching

DRILL ORGANIZATION:
- The drill takes place on an extended and widened area in front of the penalty area.

- We place three small goals on the central line opposite to the fixed goal.

- Five players practice pressing against the defenders performing two passers toward the fixed goal with a goalkeeper.

- The passers are on the left and right side of the playing area at the level of the penalty area.

- A goalkeeper is in the fixed goal.

DRILL FLOW:
- After every interruption, the action is started by the goalkeeper (the play is performed without standard situations).

- The goalkeeper's pass toward his team player is the signal for application of immediate ultraoffensive pressing.

- The passers and the players who exercise the pressing situation are performing the play with fixed goal and a goalkeeper after gaining the possession of the ball.

- The opponent players are playing with three small goals, and they mustn't to pass the ball to the goalkeeper or the passers.

- The play lasts four × four minutes with a rest interval that lasts one minute.

VARIATIONS:
- The playing area can be extended all the way to the sidelines in a 6v6 situation.

- The opponent players can't pass the ball to the goalkeeper or to the passers.

METHODICAL, ORGANIZATIONAL COMMENTS:
- The drill offers additional aid to the players practicing switching from defensive to attacking actions and makes the transfer to fast counterattack easier.

- In order to gain successful enforcement of immediate ultraoffensive pressing, it's important for the players to run immediately and create a pressure on the player with the ball after the goalkeeper performs a pass. Successful attacking actions are made easier by following the rules that don't allow back passes being performed toward the goalkeeper. At the same time, the players who drill pressing, have to occupy the area and the opponent players in order to make it harder for the opponent team to close the passing corridors.

- In transfers, the players have to maintain close distances in order to move through the width and length of the playing area in coordinated manner.

- The players should take an advantage of the possibility to double in order to constructively withdraw the ball.

- The task of the players is to concentrate on performing the first action immediately after gaining the possession of the ball: dribbling to the free area or pass the ball toward the passer or the free team player.

- The players have to look for the fastest and shortest way to finish the attacking action.

DRILL 67: IMMEDIATE ULTRAOFFENSIVE PRESSING OF MIDFIELDERS IN COOPERATION WITH ATTACKERS

Drill goal and focus: practice and improvement of the midfielders and attackers' cooperation, defensive structure in depth, switching to attacking actions, and finishing attacking actions (level of the pressing drill 1, 2, 3, 4, 5, 6, 7)

Fig. 5.4.4-7 Cooperation of the midfielders and attackers in immediate ultraoffensive pressing

DRILL ORGANIZATION:

- The drill takes place on the half of the pitch with different zones.

- In both side, verticals we create zones with sides 5 m × 10 m long, which are occupied by the opponent team's full back players.

- There are two zones in the center vertical. One zone with sides 10 m × 35 m long is for the opponent team's side midfielders. It's marked in the area of the central line. Mother zone, with sides 15 m × 35 m long, is for three opponent players and four players who drill pressing. The alignment of the players is according to the positions of the preferred play system.

- The opponent players can't leave their zones in attacking actions.

- The play can be performed only by ground passes.

In 6v9 play, the team, which is practicing pressing has four midfielders, attacker, and withdrawn center forward "man in the hole." The attacker of the team, which is practicing pressing, can choose between two possible positions, on the right or left half of the central vertical. We mark these two positions with cones. The opponent has four defenders, four midfielders, and one attacker at the disposal.

DRILL FLOW:

- The goalkeeper is opening the play by performing a pass to the center back. The pass is always directed to the opposite side where the position of the team's attacker is.

- The opponent players have got two tasks by which they can score a point: performing a pass to one of the zones where the full backs are positioned and perform a pass to the zone in the center vertical where the two side midfielders are located. By doing this, the team can score two points in one play.

- The side midfielder attacks the opponent's center back after the goalkeeper performs a pass. The task of that player is to prevent the pass being performed toward the zone where the full back player is positioned.

- The action is followed by 6v9 play. The group of six players, who are practicing pressing, must quickly transfer and create pressure on the player with the ball, even in outnumber, as the opponent players are restricted to play in the specified zones.

- After gaining the possession of the ball, the team executes a fast counterattack. The players have got max. of five passes at their disposal to finish the action.

- Immediate ultraoffensive pressing is an intensive action. Therefore, the play takes only five minutes with 60 to 90 seconds rest. The set of exercises is repeated three to five times.

VARIATIONS:

- We remove the zones in the side verticals. The opponent team's full back players are allowed to perform a free play.

- We remove the extended zone in the side vertical. Side midfielders are allowed to move around freely.

METHODICAL-ORGANIZATIONAL COMMENTS:

- The essential purpose of this drill is to practice aggressive pressing with fast movement of the compact block while maintaining short distances in order to prevent the opponent team from performing passes toward the marked areas.

- The coach requires consistent doubling in each zone and involvement of the attacker and withdrawn center forward "man in the hole."

- The drill also requires fast switch from defense to offense and fast combined depth play until the attacking action is finished.

5.5 MODEL DRILL FOR PENDULUM AND PUMP PRESSING

For the purpose of making the drill easier and improving some specific forms of upper and lower pendulum and pump pressing tactics, we offer you some modeling drills to acquire mental, motoric, and tactical knowledge. They are a special theoretical and practical contribution to this trilogy.

In order to make the drill more effective, the traditional training process is enriched by some organizational specific features. We showed some sequences from the matches to the players, where they could see the required play-tactical elements. In slow motion and in repeated play of relevant sequences, we showed the players what to do, how and where to use the specified element. We explained them the flow of the drill. Due to this process, we improved their comprehension and made the process of learning and achieving the efficiency of drill for required tactics faster.

DRILL 68: MOVEMENT COORDINATION OF PRESSING PENDULUMS

Drill goal and focus: practice of mutual movement (distances and angles of transferring defending players (in upper and lower pendulum according to the center of the game and the ball position) (level of the pressing drill 1, 2, 4, 5, 6, 7)

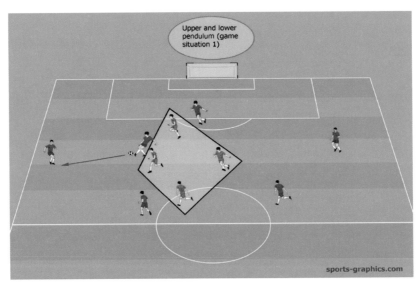

Fig. 5.5-1a Function of upper and lower pendulum in pressing

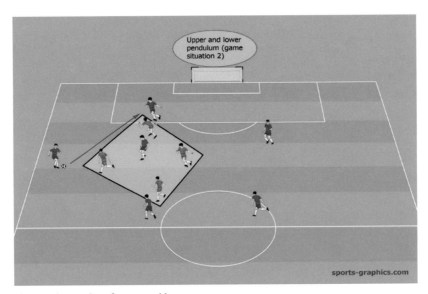

Fig. 5.5-1b Function of upper and lower

Fig. 5.5-1c Function of upper and lower pendulum in pressing

Fig. 5.5-1d Function of upper and lower pendulum in pressing

DRILL ORGANIZATION:

The drill is carried out on the attacking half of the pitch, according to the position of attacking players (players who move in upper and lower pendulum). Six players from the opponent's team (red shirts) are aligned in constructive positions: four defenders, one center midfielder, and one attacker. (Ii is suitable to deploy the members of management team so the other players, who don't take part in this drill, can comprehend the purpose of the drill.)

DRILL FLOW:

The players in red shirts are transferring the play from one side to the other. The players in pendulums are moving to their correct defensive positions according the situation. When players move in pendulums, it is important to occupy the central midfielder in order to prevent him from taking part in the game construction. It is also important to occupy the midfield attacker by performing a "sandwich" technique in order to prevent him from receiving a pass.

VARIATIONS:

- We transfer the play to the center or defensive zone.

- We gradually replace the players (management team) by the players of the team.

DRILL 69: COORDINATION OF PRESSING PENDULUMS AND PUMPS

Drill goal and focus: practice of correct distances and angles of transferring players in upper and lower pendulum and fourdefender chain including the pump movement drill (level of the pressing drill 1, 2, 4, 5).

Fig. 5.5-2a Synergism of pressing pendulums and pumps 8v6 (game situation 1)

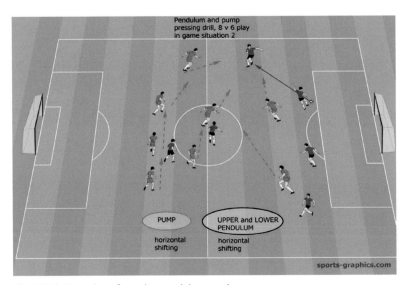

Fig. 5.5-2b Synergism of pressing pendulums and pumps

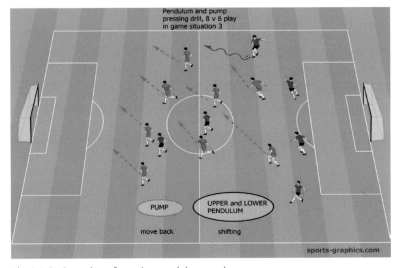

Fig. 5.5-2c Synergism of pressing pendulums and pumps

Fig. 5.5-2d Synergism of pressing pendulums and pumps

DRILL ORGANIZATION:

The drill is carried out on the attacking half of the pitch according to the position of the defending players (players in the pendulums and in four-defender chain). We designate six players (management team) who pretend to be four defenders, central midfielder, and midfield attacker of opponent team. The opponent player is transferring the ball from one side of the pitch to the other, and he's trying to pass the ball in the direction to the extended attacker. Two players are performing the play in the position of the upper pendulum (4-4-2 formation) or withdrawn center forward "man in the hole" and striker (4-2-3-1 formation). Two central midfielders together with the four-defender chain are performing the play in the position of the lower pendulum.

DRILL FLOW:

The team, which has the ball, is transferring the center of the game. The players in upper and lower pendulum are transferring in the correct distance and angle. When the right full back is ready to kick the ball behind defense, the four-defender chain players are moving backward to their own goal. If the right full back doesn't kick the ball, and he returns it back to the center back, four-defender chain players are starting to move forward. The team is pushing the attacker out toward his own goal and push the active playing area. The same happens when the left full back gains the possession of the ball. The players of the defensive formation learn when to move backward and forward according the actions of the opponent.

VARIATIONS:

- Instead of the management team members, we gradually use the players of the team.

- The drill is performed gradually in all zones of the playing area.

DRILL 70: DEFENSE IN PRESSING FORMATION OF PENDULUM AND PUMP

Drill goal and focus: involvement of all the players in order to practice the correct movement tracks of pendulums (distances and angles) and defensive pump in basic pressing formation 4-2-2 (level of the pressing drill 1, 2, 4, 5, 6, 7, 8)

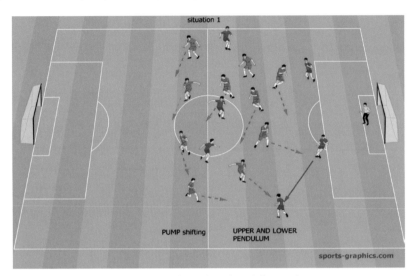

Fig. 5.5-3a Team defense in pressing formation of pendulum and pump

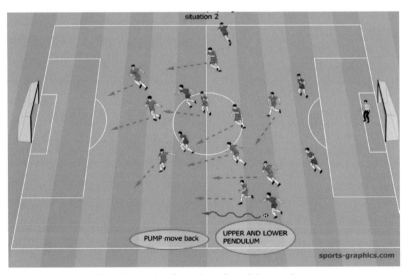

Fig. 5.5-3b Team defense in pressing formation of pendulum and pump

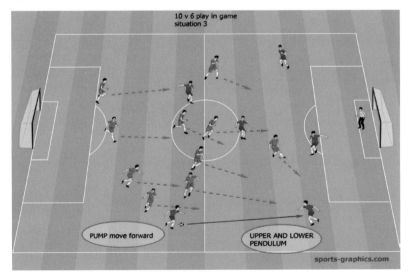

Fig. 5.5-3c Team defense in pressing formation of pendulum and pump

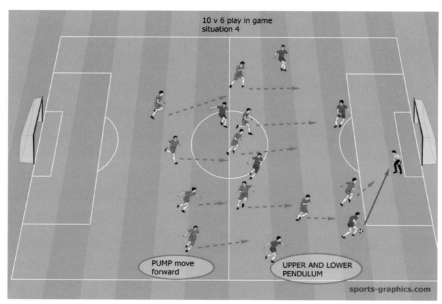

Fig. 5.5-3d Team defense in pressing formation of pendulum and pump

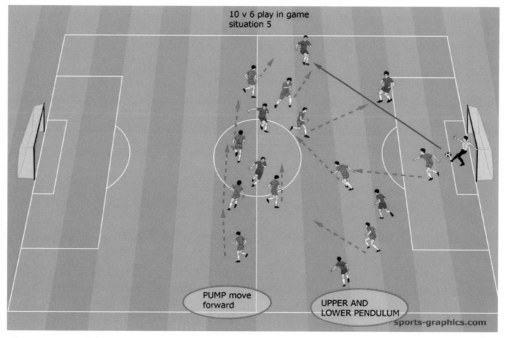

Fig. 5.5-3e Team defense in pressing formation of pendulum and pump

DRILL ORGANIZATION:

- Six members of the management team, who pretend to be the opponent players, form a four-defender chain, and take the positions of center midfielder and midfield attacker. The opponent team's players pass the ball to each other, and the defending players are moving around the pitch according the position of the game center.

- The defending team is in 4-4-2 formation in which four players form upper and lower pendulum, and the other four players form a four-defender chain, which

applies the pump technique. The situational pressing is performed in side vertical.

- The whole pressing formation of the team is moving in synchronized manner according to the position of the game center. According to the number of players, some positions are doubled and synchronized movement of two players is performed simultaneously.

VARIATION:

- The play is performed on the whole pitch with both goalkeepers in the goals.

5.6 PRESSING OF GIANTS (GUARDIOLA, VAN GAAL, KLOPP, SIMEONE, CONTE, BIELSA)

In this part of the manual, we offer authentic tools for pressing tactics drills and practice, which are used by coaches who significantly influenced their teams' play behavior. These coaches offered more effective method of defensive actions. The integral compact training plan, which is often connected to the previous drill, consists of many drills. This leads to achieving natural continuity. In relation to the presentation of this subchapter, we have selected only those

drill, which are the top drills of model play. In a real training process, these exercises are proceeded by the drills, which prepare the team for solving the partial playing tasks. These drills also prepare the team for performing the specific actions and their gradual integration during the course of the training process. By this, the team's performance is becoming more identical to the real match sequences.

DRILL 71: 7V7 PRESSING PLAY AND PRESSING "TRIGGERS" (GUARDIOLA, IN DAVIES, 2013)

Drill goal and focus: focus on familiarization with pressing "trigger" (level of the pressing drill 1, 2, 3, 4, 5, 6, 7, 8)

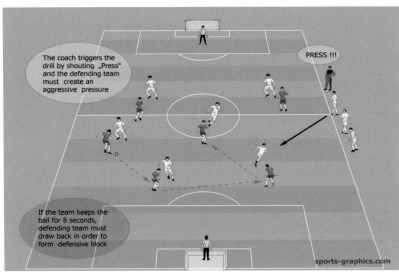

Fig. 5.6-1 7v7 pressing play and pressing "triggers"

DRILL ORGANIZATION:
- There are two teams of six players playing against each other 6v6 play (7v7 play if the goalkeepers are involved in the play). If the goalkeepers are not involved in the play, there are 3–4 m goal lines marked on both sides until the "trigger" sounds. This allows the defending team to perform pressing aggressively and to regain the possession of the ball.

DRILL FLOW:
- The task of the attacking team is to keep the possession of the ball for eight seconds. Defending team is switching from defensive block to aggressive pressing.

After the time limit, the defending team draws back to defensive block. According to the coach's instruction, the other three defending players, who are remaining on the sideline, can be involved in the play. After pressing was activated, these players help the team in defense. The group of three players can switch in order to maintain high intensity of the drill.

COACH'S COMMENT:
- The coach gradually demonstrates the pressing "triggers" and keeps instructing the players until they are comprehended.

DRILL 72: 7V7 PRESSING PLAY AND "SIX-SECOND" PRESSING RULE (GUARDIOLA, IN DAVIES, 2013)

Drill goal and focus: small play, which enables the players to understand the pressing rules and pressing "triggers" through the conditions created by the coach (level of the pressing drill 1, 2, 3, 4, 6, 7, 8)

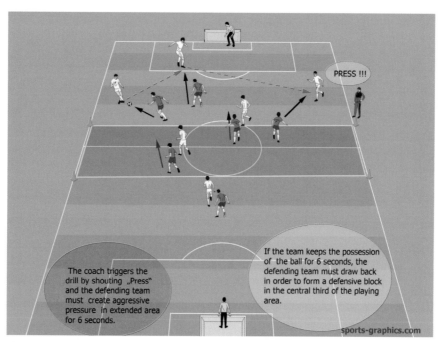

PRESS !!!

The coach triggers the drill by shouting „Press" and the defending team must create aggressive pressure in extended area for 6 seconds.

If the team keeps the possession of the ball for 6 seconds, the defending team must draw back in order to form a defensive block in the central third of the playing area.

sports-graphics.com

Fig. 5.6-2 7v7 pressing play and "six second" pressing rule

DRILL ORGANIZATION:

- 7v7 pressing play with marked center zone, as in fig. 5.5-2. The players respond to the coach's instruction "Press!" and start performing an extended aggressive pressing, which lasts six seconds.

DRILL FLOW:

- If the attacking team holds the possession of the ball during the interval of six seconds, the defending team draws back in an organized manner in order to form a defensive block in the marked center zone. If the team, which owns the possession of the ball, applies the attacking sequence successfully, and reaches the marked center zone with the ball, the defending team draws back and responds either by forming a defensive block or performing aggressive pressing.

COACH'S COMMENT:

- This form of drill enables the players to practice their movement forward from the defensive block to pressing.

- The drill also helps the players to practice different types of block defense.

- The coach is supposed to focus on supporting the players when forming an organized defensive block. This play form is recommended to the defenders who are aware of the importance of the team organization.

DRILL 73: PRESSING PLAY IN ATTACKING ZONE (GUARDIOLA, IN DAVIES, 2013)

Drill goal and focus: maintaining the control of the play without having the possession of the ball through team organization (level of the pressing drill 1, 2, 3, 4, 5, 6, 7, 8)

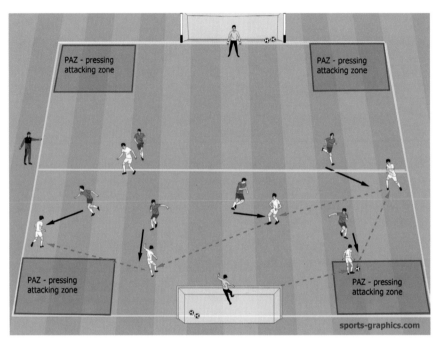

Fig. 5.6-3 Pressing play in attacking zone

DRILL ORGANIZATION:

- 7v7 pressing play takes place on a reduced pitch with four zones in the corners of the playing area.

DRILL FLOW:

- The task of the defending players is to guide the opponent with the ball to the pressing attacking zone, where they can attack him. The possession of the ball can be gained either by throwing the ball to the player or after the ball is kicked by the opponent parallel with the sideline. The opponent's goalkeeper starts the action by performing the pass toward the pressing attacking zone. This pass is the signal for the defending team to start pressing. If we want to make the play more difficult for the team, which has possession of the ball, we apply the a rule, according to which the team can't perform the back pass to the goalkeeper. The team that is applying pressing in attacking zone has more advantage when performing this type of play.

COACH'S COMMENTS:

- The coach is supposed to focus on position of the defending team and on recognizing the pressing "triggers" and aggressive pressing in attacking zone.

- Attacking team must perform at least five passes before they transfer through the central line so the defending team has an opportunity to form and control the opponent with the ball.

DRILL 74: TEAM DEFENSE IN 8V7 PLAY (VAN GAAL, 2014)

Drill goal and focus: development of correct defensive block's decision making about the methodology of defense (reverse movement or creation of pressure on the ball) (level of the pressing drill 1, 2, 4, 5, 6, 8).

Fig. 5.6-4 Team defense in 8v7 play

DRILL ORGANIZATION:

- The play is performed on the area of two-thirds of the pitch without a goalkeeper and with eight defenders and seven attackers.

DRILL FLOW:

- The task of the attacking players in red shirts is to attack the empty goal. Players in blue shirts defend the goal in a compact block. In case the defensive team gains the possession of the ball, the team transfers to the fast counterattack in order to guide the ball to the other side of the pitch.

COACH'S COMMENTS:

- Luis van Gaal: "As a club coach I often used 8v7 drills on the fixed goal without goalkeeper. You have to sense the right time for application of team pressure instead of defending an empty goal. It's a drill, which I liked using as a club coach."

- This drill is focused on the right timing of pressing when defending the opponent's combined play.

DRILL 75: MIDFIELD PRESSING AND MAINTAINING THE COMPACTNESS OF THE 8V9 PLAY (KLOPP, IN TERZIS, 2015)

Drill goal and focus: application of immediate pressure on the opponent's midfielder and preventing the opponent from turning round (level of the pressing drill 1, 2, 3, 4, 5, 6, 7, 8)

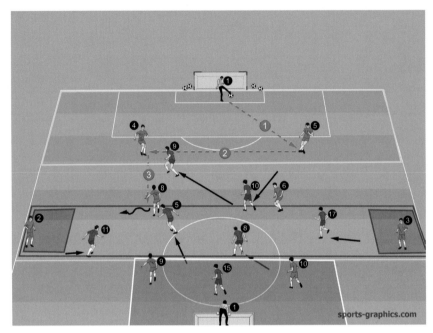

Fig. 5.6-5 Midfield pressing and compactness

DRILL ORGANIZATION:
- The teams are performing 8v9 play on the 2/3 area of the pitch, which is divided in playing zones, as in fig. 5.6-5.

DRILL FLOW:
- The goalkeeper of the red team starts the action by performing a pass toward one of the defenders. The team in red shirts is trying to find the way of how to perform a pass toward the attackers (9, 10) inside the small white zone. The pass can be performed either from the midfielders, who are in the light blue zone, or from the full backs who are in one of the two dark blue zones. If the pass toward the attacking zone is performed successfully, it results in advantageous situation of 2v1, and there is a chance of scoring a goal. The task of the blue team is to prevent the opponent from performing a pass to the white zone and

gain possession of the ball by using midfield pressing. Consequently, the team should be able to finish the counterattack within 8 to 10 seconds.

COACH'S COMMENTS:
- The players, who are performing pressing, are permanently trying to maintain the compactness of the formation.

- The progress of the whole drill is supposed be in high pace.

- The players must react fast and gain advantage in the switching.

- Communication between the players is important in order to maintain shorter distances and team response to change of situations.

DRILL 76: ATTACKING PRESSING, DIRECTING THE BALL TOWARD THE CENTER, AND BLOCKING THE POTENTIAL PASSES IN THE DYNAMICS OF 8V8 ZONE PLAY (KLOPP, IN TERZIS 205)

Drill and goal focus: application of attacking pressing, directing the opponent's initial action toward the inside (level of the pressing drill 1, 2, 3, 4, 5, 6, 7, 8)

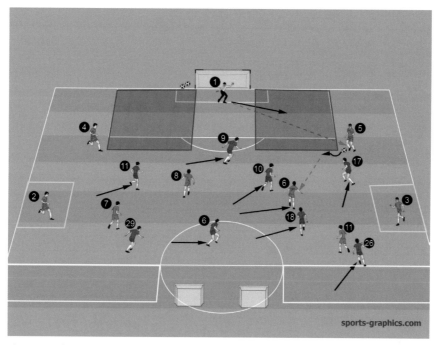

Fig. 5.6-6 Directed attacking pressing

DRILL ORGANIZATION:

- The multipurpose drill takes place on the extended half of the pitch. Two teams are performing 8v8 play (+1 goalkeeper) in formation as in fig. 5.6-6. On the right and left side of the goal, we mark two dark-blue zones. In the side verticals, we mark two yellow zones where we also position the opponent's full backs. In the side verticals on the opposite side of the pitch, we mark two white zones. We place two small goals on the center vertical between the white zones.

DRILL FLOW:

- The task of red players is to pass the ball toward the full back, who can move only inside the yellow zone (1 point). After the successful completion of this task, attacking players must transfer the ball through the center line or receive the pass in the white zone (3 points). The task of the midfielders is to score a goal into the small goals (3 points). The players are not allowed to perform

a pass to the opposite side. If the opponent chooses to perform a back pass toward the goalkeeper to the dark blue zone, the midfielder has to attack the goalkeeper and force him to perform a quick pass. If the goalkeeper transfers the play, his team scores a point. The task of the blue players is to prevent the red players from achieving this intention. This can be done by blocking the corridors for passes, creating a pressure on the player with the ball, and using the correct formation. After gaining the possession of the ball, the blue players must finish their counterattack within 8 to 10 seconds. There isn't any specific limit for the blue players .

COACH'S COMMENTS:

- The players must use good cohesion and communication in order to bock the corridors from passes.

- The players, who are applying pressing, direct the opponent to one of the zones using the correct alignment and movement.

DRILL 77: SWITCHING FROM PASSIVE DEFENSE TO PRESSING AND CREATING A STRONG LINE IN A SMALL PLAY OF 2-STAGE DYNAMIC (KLOPP, IN TERZIS 2015)

Drill goal and focus: switching from defense to pressing (level of the pressing drill 1, 2, 4, 5, 6, 7, 8)

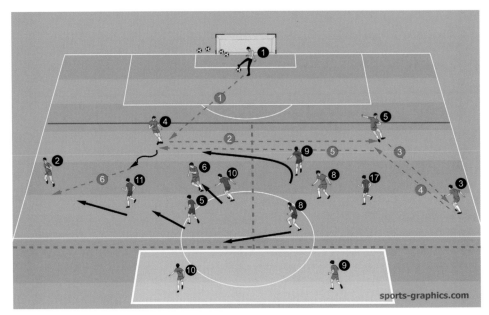

Fig. 5.6-7 Switching from block to defense

DRILL ORGANIZATION:

- The drill takes place in two stages on two thirds of the pitch, which is divided into zones. Approx. 5 m in front of the penalty area, parallel to its line, we mark the whole width with a blue line for the opening play. Approx. 5 m parallel behind the central line, we mark the whole width with a red line. It restricts the playing area. Behind this area, we have a white zone measuring 20–25 m × 10 m. The area between the blue and red line is divided into right and left half by the vertical line. The team of six players, applying pressing, is consists of four midfielders and two attackers, or one attacker and one withdrawn center forward. The opponent's team consists of a goalkeeper, four-defender chain, two midfielders, and two attackers in the white zone.

DRILL FLOW:

- The 6v6 play is performed between the blue and red line. The three opponent's players are on the right half of the pitch, and the other three players are on

the left half of the pitch. They mustn't leave these zones. Two attackers from the red team can't leave the white zone. During the first stage, the red players pass the ball along the blue line. Their task is to perform a pass toward their attackers in the white zone. The players applying pressing are moving in the passive block in order to prevent the opponent from performing a pass to the white zone. By performing their movement, they provoke the pass to the side vertical toward the full back.

- The second stage starts after the opponent's player performs a pass to the side vertical, which also works as a pressing "trigger." The team, which is applying pressing (the blue players), is transferring their play to aggressive pressing. They are not limited by the zones, so they can move freely around the playing area. The rules of this play offer good conditions for outnumbering the opponent in each half of the playing area. The opponent scores a point for every pass that is performed toward the team's attackers or when the players transfer the ball through the red line. The task of the pressing team is to prevent the opponent from performing a pass toward the attackers and dribbling the ball over the red line. The pressing team tries to withdraw the ball and attack the fixed goal with a goalkeeper. The counterattack must be completed within 8 to 10 seconds. Otherwise, the pressing team loses possession of the ball.

VARIATION:

- We remove the red vertical line, so the opponent players can move freely around the playing area.

COACH'S COMMENTS:

- Neither of the teams can perform long passes.

DRILL 78: PRESSING IN THE WING AREA FUNCTIONAL DRILL (CONTE, IN TERZIS 2016)

Drill goal and focus: application of pressing by using the front block against four-defender chain (level of the pressing drill 1, 2, 4, 5, 6, 8)

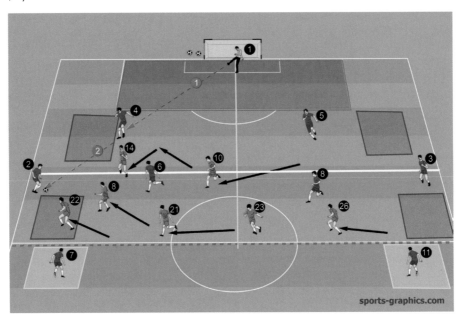

Fig. 5.6-8a Pressing in a wing area with extended position of the opponent's winger

DRILL ORGANIZATION:

- The drill takes place in two stages on extended half of the pitch, where we mark four horizontal sections: penalty area, zone between the penalty area, and the central line (it is divided into two horizontal parts marked with white line) and the fourth part is on the other half of the pitch right behind the central line. The playing area is divided vertically into the right and left half by a yellow line. Apart from the penalty area, we mark each part of these areas: four blue areas measuring 6 m × 6 m (two on the right part and two on the left part), two yellow parts measuring 3 m × 3 m (behind the central line, one on the right vertical, and one on the left vertical). There are two teams: the team applying pressing (red) is performing the play in 4-2 alignment (relating to 4-4-2 formation or 4-2-3-1 formation). If the central midfielder is involved in the play, the players form 4-1-2 alignment (according the system 4-3-3 or 4-3-1-2). The blue players are playing in 4-4 alignment.

DRILL FLOW:

- If the blue winger (seven) stays in the yellow area, red full back (twenty-two) can extend forward and reach the players with the ball (fig. 5.6-8a). In this situation, the red defending midfielder isn't supposed to extend forward.

- If the blue winger (seven) enters the blue area, red full back (twenty-two) occupies him and doesn't extend forward so that he creates pressure on the player no. 2 (fig. 5.6-8b). Red attacking midfielder (eight) is supposed to read the situation and move nearer the player no. 2. In this case, the left full back (twenty-two) is in a deep position so the defensive midfielder (twenty-one) moves within his defensive chain higher (but not too high), and he occupies the blue player (six).

COACH'S COMMENTS:

- The drill focuses on pressing instead of on transferring the play. If the red team loses the possession of the ball when trying to score, the play starts from the beginning (by the goalkeeper) and the players return back to their original positions.

- The red team must use aggressive occupation of potential players, who might receive the pass and they must try to double when gaining the possession of the ball.

- The red team must maintain the compactness of their formation by keeping small distances and synchronized movement. This enables the team to occupy the opponent players more easily.

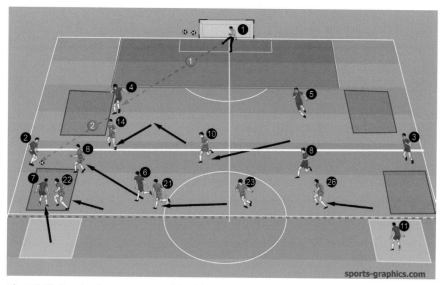

Fig. 5.6-8b Pressing in a wing area with withdraw position of the opponent's winger

DRILL 79: COMPACTNESS IN DEFENSE ACHIEVED FROM THE 7V7 PLAY (SIMEONE, IN DAVIES 2014)

Drill goal and focus: practice of team coordination in the correct area and in the correct alignment, which improves compactness of the defending team (level of the pressing drill 1, 2, 4, 5, 6, 7, 8)

Fig. 5.6-9a Practice of vertical compactness of defensive players

Fig. 5.6-9b Practice of vertical compactness of defensive players in side vertical

Fig. 5.6-9c Practice of horizontal compactness of defensive players

Fig. 5.6-9d Practice of horizontal compactness of defensive players in the central vertical

Fig. 5.6-9e Practice of horizontal compactness of defensive players in side vertical

DRILL ORGANIZATION:

- The playing area measuring 40 m × 40 m is divided into four horizontal and four vertical zones. The width of each zone is 10 m. We place portable goals with the goalkeepers on the basic lines.

DRILL FLOW:

- 6v6 play. The task of the defending team, which is in compact block, is to occupy the area around the ball. The team occupies two horizontal and two vertical zones in relation to the center of the game. Defensive players are applying pressing in the zone where the ball is located, and they are also occupying another vertical and horizontal zone at the same time. The player of defending team, who is the nearest the ball, is attacking the opponent with the ball. Another two players are creating a secure occupation of that player. They are narrowing and shortening the area directly around the center of the game and covering the corridors for passes at the same time. Another three players of the defending team are approaching the attacking players (optimal distance) in order to cover the opponent's players. Their task is also to close the corridors for escape pass and maintain vertical or horizontal compactness of the defensive formation.

COACH'S COMMENTS:

- Pay attention to correct approach of the first wave of attacking players into the center of the game. The same applies to the second wave of the attacking players around the center of the game in order to cover the vertical or horizontal zone around the ball and other spatial zone on the side of their own goal.

- The players of the active defending formation must follow the effective distances between themselves in order to maintain the vertical and horizontal compactness of the team.

DRILL 80: THREE-PLAYER PRESSING PENDULUM (BIELSA, 2014)

Drill goal and focus: practice of dynamic occupation of the area and the opponent in undernumber 3v4 play, practice of synchronized movement (level of the pressing drill 2, 5, 6, 7)

Fig. 5.6-10a The player "C" attacks the position 1, A and B players secure the player C in the defense triangle and cover the positions 3 and 4.

Fig. 5.6-10b Player C secures the position 1 in order to prevent the 1v3 play. Player B is moving to the position 2, and the player A is moving to the position 4. The players form a defense tunnel.

PART 3

Fig. 5.6-10c Player A is transferring to the position 3: the tree position 4 is occupied by the player B and the player C is moving to the position 2. The players form a defense triangle.

Fig. 5.6-10d The player C is securing the position 2 in order to block the link of the positions 2 and 4; the player A is attacking the position 1, and the player B is attacking the free position 3. The defense funnel is formed.

DRILL ORGANIZATION:

- We mark four positions with the poles: two center backs and two defensive midfielders.

- Three players, who are applying pressing pendulum, are occupying the positions of the extended attacker, withdrawn center forward and defending midfielder in order to form a defense triangle.

- The drill is performed in the central vertical without balls.

DRILL FLOW:

- Defense triangle is the basic formation. It is placed in the middle of the square, which is formed by poles. Poles represent the opponent's positions.

- The players are moving dynamically in order to occupy the free positions and cover the possible depth link on the fourth free position.

- According to the situation, defense triangle transforms into a defense funnel in relation to the center of the game and the position of the pressing players.

- If the funnel is created, the extended players cover the area and the center of the game in order to

disrupt the deep linking to the position, which is nearer the center of the game. The position, which is further away from the center of the game is occupied by the third player.

- This composition needs to be repeated several times.

VARIATION:

- The drill of the spatial and opponent's occupation in 3v6 undernumbering, practice of the synchronized movement according to the center of the game (level of the pressing drill 2, 5, 6, 7).

- We mark positions with the poles: four-defender chain and two defensive midfielders.

- The three players, who are practicing the three-player pressing pendulum, occupy the positions of the extended attacker and withdrawn center forward in order to form defense triangle.

METHODICAL, ORGANIZATIONAL COMMENTS:

- The drill is performed without balls and the opponent players focus on acquiring automatism in coordinated activity of three players. Therefore, the movement structures must be repeated several times.

Fig. 5.6-11a The player C is extending to the position 1, the players A and B cover the space in order to secure their team player in the defense triangle and block the possibility of a deep link with the positions 5 and 6.

Fig. 5.6-11b When the center of the game is changed, the player B, who is nearer the center, extends. The player A occupies the free position 6, and the player C occupies the free position 5 in order to make the deep linking in the defense triangle impossible.

Fig. 5.6-11c The same applies to this situation. When the center of the game is changed, the player, who is nearer the center, starts running. In this case, the players A, B and C cover the deep positions and make the deep linking impossible.

- In the first part, changes of the positions are drilled in a slow pace. Later, it is drilled faster. After presenting the correct forms, the drill is practiced faster up to the maximum speed.

- The coach determines the positions, which must be attacked by the players.

- The drill is intensive. The maximum load performance and rest last max. one minute. The whole drill is repeated four to six times.

- During the rest, the coach corrects mistakes.

- By performing an intensive movement, the players form a defense triangle or defense funnel. Despite creating an undernumber, the players keep the correct division into the depth and width. Dynamic movement is focused on creating pressure in the center of the game and mutual securing and occupying the space.

- It follows the principle in which the player, who is the nearest the designated position, extends and attacks the position, which is marked by poles. Other two players are transferring so that they secure the space and make the creation of depth link between the positions impossible.

- If the player from the back position, which is nearer the center of the play, extends, the pendulum principle follows: extended player draws back and occupies the space and released position.

- If there is a change in the center of the game, the rule by which the nearest player attacks, is presented by each player's position change as these positions change due to maintaining the compactness and mutual securing.

- When the movement is performed synchronously, the three-player pressing pendulum allows steady load distribution. It also allows the players to control the activity of the opponent in undernumber, maintain space-time pressure, slow down the opponent's actions in order to gain extra time for the team players to adjust to disrupted defense organization immediately after losing the possession of the ball, ruin the opponent's in depth play and transfer to fast counterattack. This results in improving the efficiency and safety of the play.

FINAL WORD ON PART 3

Resulting from pressing defense analysis, the most leading teams prefer using this form of defensive tactics. These teams can provide the best performance quality not only from the movement point of view but also from the mental potential as the game intelligence and spatial perception of the players are the necessary requirements for successful management of proactive defense. Moreover, in application of pressing tactics, horizontal, and vertical movement connections of the players, blocks, formations come more into focus. Nowadays, it represents defensive top-concept of which efficiency is confirmed by the top teams of contemporary soccer scene.

It seems, that reliable management of pressing defense is not so simple. Successful movement and mental management of pressing defense through special methodology contribute to safe play of the team as well as it enables the team to threaten the opponent effectively.

Unreliable application of pressing defense arises frequent punishment in form of fatal mistakes, which can often influence the match result and during training effort of other players, management team and the whole club. In European leagues, we can often see the character of defensive mistakes changes by application of proactive defense. When applying this form of defense, the mental level of the players in pressing tactics is often the decisive factor of successfulness. We can say, that the lack of mental adjustment, can become unbeatable handicap for efficient application of pressing defense. In case of constitutional deficits in the mental area, the forecast of successfulness in application of this type of defense is limited. Responsibility for application of this defensive method of the play on the pitch lies in the legs and heads of defensive players. However, the responsibility for the players' readiness is in the competence of the coach's and his pressing methodology, his ability to accurately assess the players' abilities and skills.

The decisive factors in performance are movement and mental requirements. They form sufficient foundation for play-tactical repertoire and its flexibility in pressing defense. Mental potential is connected to the wide broad tactical repertoire, which is necessary for effective management of defensive situations and sequences based on the principles of proactive defense.

In this part of the trilogy, we tried to present tactical tools for pressing drills and its improvement by using proven methodology. This methodology is based on the sequence of pressing elements, which are included in all individual pressing drill levels. In these drills, the players can practice defensive schemes of the players' alignment. The tactics of the drills conclude from multiple experience of play situation, which result in a gradual automatization of the solutions. Apart from motoric learning, the advantage of this drill is also, the improvement of thinking, tactical aspects of defensive behavior, the speed of the action, and coordination of the players in defensive stage. We bring the players to the "roots," in order to form and develop the algorithm in the training process, which is formed by the match itself and must be responded to by the players. When defining the focus of the training process and forming the training tools, we conclude from the course of the match in order to provide a higher quality performance in a match on a higher play-tactical level. This level is based on the training microcycle content occurring between the two following matches and modeling exercises, which have specific methodical-organizational form. We assume that the detailed theoretical explication of elementary rules and principles of pressing defense make the implementation of the play systems easier so that they significantly influence the performance of the team in the defense stage. The presented training programs describe play-defensive "know-how," an opportunity to divert from the knowledge-based mainstream in the basic methodology. Through the creative approach, they enable a team to execute an efficient drill and detailed tactical improvement of pressing defensive tactics of a particular team.

EPILOGUE TO *ALL ABOUT PRESSING IN SOCCER*

When outlining the pressing trilogy, *All About Pressing in Soccer*, the main ambition was to focus on current trends in defense and organization and management of teams' defensive activity oriented toward pressing tactics application. We also wanted to provide practical "cookbook," which focuses on how to achieve the practical mastering of defensive proactivity and include it into the playing performance of the team in the fastest and most effective manner through the training process and specific training programs.

Apart from highlighting the historical roots of pressing and the theoretical foundations of defense, which have been improved by the evolution, we have also tried to provide the training "know-how" in order to acquire and master pressing situations. The organization of our book wasn't randomly chosen. We have tried to achieve better comprehension, accurate analysis, and including the pressing tactics implementation to the portfolio of training teams. We don't suppose that dealing with the presented issues on the interpretative axis can automatically guarantee the success. It's only one of the play-tactical fragments of wide broad mosaic in soccer. Also, we aren't claiming the exclusivity and uniqueness of the proposed method. We only have outlined one of many ways beyond the horizon of the progressive defensive modernism, which we have offered to the players during our coaching practice so far. We don't suppose, that this is the only method how to master defensive proactivity; however, it's certainly one of the contemporary ways of how to make defensive activity of the team progressive. It's not the only method, but it's one of the possible ways. It's up to every coach whether he marks direction of his team by his own "ego" or not. Our main target was to bring the players to the "source" of pressing that is focused on defensive activity through the specific training content.

If we have succeeded in inspiring you to search for your own ways and formation of your own training tools and programs, we believe that we have also opened the doors to your own coaching creativity and successfulness, which is only a step away from the achieving the charisma of a successful and competent coach. The way of our perception, which is presented in this book, could be the methodological guideline in outlining the proactive defensive concept of the play based on an efficient utilization of pressing tactics. We shouldn't forget about the fact that without the elementary quality of the players, the effect of even the most progressive concept is significantly illusive. In this case, our contribution remains on the level of a sterile theory. The fundamental task of a coach is to form a team, provide the team with his own face, and made to measure playing concept with clear features of the coach's handwriting, which can cover his team instead of uncovering it.

REVIEW

The publication *All About Pressing in Soccer* by the authors team Laco Borbely, Jaroslav Hreblk, Peter Ganczner, and Andi Singer deals with the issue of soccer pressing in a wider scope.

From the very beginning, its task is to provide an encyclopedic view of this issue in its historical context, to present its general and practical aspects rationally. Last but not the least, it offers some examples of how to perform this practical aspects.

Beside the author's overture and the introduction, the structure of this publication is divided into three main parts. The first part: "How it all began—Historical roots of pressing" deals with the historical development of pressing. The second part: "What pressing is, why, how, and when to apply it—Pressing theory" approaches pressing from the point of view of the theory of the soccer play. The third part: "How to do it—Practical manual for pressing" is focused on the transfer of pressing to its training and practice. The prologue states that the greatest revolution in the development of soccer trends happened in the fifties through the interpretation of great players in the soccer world—F. Puskas—the national Hungarian team at that time. This statement, which sounds very explicit, could cause surprise to a certain degree. It's neither about the nostalgic reminiscence nor the personal adoration of the above mentioned team or its contribution to the soccer world in general and especially the following historical development of pressing. The analysis of the national Hungarian team performance that was shown in documentaries at that time, confirms that the authors precisely applied, captured, and described facts, which the three factors (teamwork, movement, attacking) were based upon. These factors formed the conceptual roots of the next systems, including pressing. In the forthcoming trend development of the soccer world, pressing became an extraordinary symbol of the game up to the present form. In this respect, the above-mentioned statement about the contribution of the Hungarian players legitimates the treasure of the soccer world.

The first part: "How it all began—Historical roots of pressing," which deals with the historical origin of pressing is very important for its final conclusion from the point of view of its total structure. The overall conception is not only about the historical description, it also explains the aforementioned origin that maintains the systematic approach where the analytical and synthetic evaluation of this development is based upon. The basis of this evaluation, the author and his colleagues have proved that pressing is an instrument to limit the offensive that has been transferred from its original reactive form to proactive form in the way as it is presented now.

The author and his colleagues base their theory on the fact that pressing is an integral part of soccer evolution (as it is deduced from the general principle of evolution by Charles Darwin). Thanks to their personal intellect and high professionalism in soccer, they got the essence of the conscious evolution theory. As a result, pressing hasn't only reached a contemporary level but also qualitatively contributed to conception of their performance, as it is presented in the highest professional competitions. The authors, didn't forget to insinuate that the development of pressing, as a specific tool of soccer systems, wasn't always linear and continual. There were some quick movements in this evolution, decelerations, accelerations, and so on, as it was mentioned in the example of Dutch soccer, which skipped the phase of WM system in its individual development. This fact helped to launch faster the principles of total soccer.

The first chapter is also a significant and valuable introduction to the schematic media. It monitors the development of H. Chapman up to the pressing metamorphosis of the contemporary soccer globalization, which makes the topic more transparent, comprehensive, and understandable. In this regard, Hungarian soccer reminds itself in the fifties. As a national team, it applied the phenomenon "we need to help each other during the play." This phenomenon, which the Hungarian players didn't realize, belonged to the concept and principle of pressing. In this sense, we need mention that a similar ideological concept can be seen in other teams such as in Juventus Turin. The players around G. Boniperti, Hansen and so on, preferred the concept of the so-called "playing solidarity" that was relatively close to the Hungarian concept. It's necessary to point out that the Italian presentation of the play wasn't so effective, spectacular, or penetrative as the Hungarian one. In this part of the publication, the outlined historical pressing development shows that pressing, in soccer globalization, gradually developed from a proactive tool to the strategical element, whereas its development is still open.

Another important conclusion comes from the outlined pressing development, which was implicitly expressed by the authors: "pressing was always historically developed in relation to the tactic, specifically as a part of the whole unit. The implementation of both, in reality, always depended on the invention of individual performance, on one hand, and the team performance on the other." We must also mention another strong point of this publication. Due to its complexity and great importance, this separate book surpasses the foreign ones that monitor historical development of pressing. These are the conclusions that declare the extraordinary qualification of the author's team.

In the conclusion of the evaluation of the first part, it's possible to claim, that the whole historical pressing development exposition, which is mentioned above, creates suitable conditions for the following volumes of this publication. As these volumes are related to one another, coaches are able to derive necessary information. The second part of the specialized publication *All About Pressing in Soccer*, from Laco Borbely and his colleagues, which is conceptually and continually connected to the content of the previous first part, offers theoretical solutions, approaches, and conclusions to this specific topic. This part is divided into three chapter, which are logically and systematically sequenced and connected in order to form an individual block of the publication mentioned above.

The second chapter of this theoretical part is dedicated to pressing in team games, the third chapter deals with the phenomenon of pressing theory while the fourth chapter talks about theory of pressing training (the conclusion is dedicated to pressing terminology). Right at the beginning of this review, it's important to point out that in a wide range of publications of this type, which offer theoretical and practical solution to the specific topic, we can see in many cases two extreme views at the theory. That

is either the theory explained by a simple description that lacks the depth and width, which the theory deserves or, on the other hand, it contains an excessive nonsystematic compilation where the essence of the theory is lost. In both cases, it leads even to declarative nominalism, which results in the fact that the theory of the topic is in a passive position toward putting it into the practice.

Assuming that each theory should generalize the knowledge gained from the practice and, therefore, it should offer the practice predictions and prognosis for its further genesis, we can come to the conclusion that the theory should dispose of its own evincible dimension, which offers further possibility for reflection in the practice of the topic. Therefore, we can state that the mutual connection between the theory and the practice should contain both-sided dynamics and both parts should be in an equal position so both of them can contribute to the successful solution of the problem solved.

When analyzing and evaluating the theoretical part of the mentioned publication, written by author's team, it is obvious that this publication has avoided the extremes mentioned above, and it offers the necessary dynamical continuation to the following practice.

Moreover, it supports one's own originality when working out a suitable connection of theory with practice and vice versa. The proof of this is specially the fourth part of this block where the authors focus on the pressing theory in detail, they point out the critical parts when practicing pressing, and they offer sequential concept of pressing practice. However, it doesn't finish by these aspects, the authors also offer valuable methodical suggestions for the pressing practice, they specify pressing practice levels and, using their specialist's intellect, they also offer prognosis for pressing's further development, which is very typical for the authors.

What deserves attention is also the chapter about pressing terminology, which contributes not only to the overall understanding of the specific topic but also contains the author's additional comments, which generally enrich this publication.

We assume that the previous chapters of the second part volume follow, in relation to general focus of the publication, one of the essential intentions. That is to continue in authors' ambition to create a basis for climax of the whole trilogy, which is the concluding part, and it will be entirely dedicated to the choice of practical exercises for training process.

From this point of view, it is therefore possible to understand the whole content and architecture of the second part as an intention to give it an appropriate expressivity, which would contribute to the statement mentioned above even if the final part of the publication is still in the "in status vitae" mode.

If the strategic aim of the presented project of pressing trilogy was fulfilled as intended, and that is to contribute to the pressing practice in a sense of building up good quality individual and team play performances, the specialized publication of author's team would contribute to reaching this target more than it is common in this area. The third part of the publication written by the author

team of Laco Borbely, Jaroslav HrebiK, Peter Ganczner, and Andi Singer is a conclusion of a remarkable effort, which the authors dedicate to the phenomenon of current theory and practice of the game and pressing in modern soccer. The main focus of this part (third part: "How to do it—Practical manual for pressing") is already presented in the introduction where it's stated that it's a practical manual, which deals with the topic of pressing from the point of view the authors' experience and practice and inclusion of pressing in training drills. This is an exceptional part of the publication, which proves that from the very beginning, the authors adjusted their basic strategy to this, and they were taking into consideration the fact that this book would be incomplete without the practical part; without the practical part it would remain to be only a theoretical manual or in better case an academic study, which would influence soccer practice in a limited way.

–PhDr. Mgr. Zdenek Sivek, MBA Vice-president AEFCA

PRESSING TERMINOLOGY

In historical, theoretical, and practical interpretation of pressing tactics, we encountered several occurrences that are typical exactly for the mentioned way of proactive defensive, and they bring a new approach in their analysis, interpretation as well as in their denomination. It's mainly related to the change of the game content, tactical context, and application of play-tactical means, which are introduced especially by the modern pressing defensive. The expressions used in the book are naming the elements of the game, which haven't been explained sufficiently until now, neither have they been defined exactly, and in this context of the game, they require terminological and contextual enhancement. We are also introducing interpretation of some professional terms related to typical way of offensive reaction to proactive defensive as a logical consequence of the basic game stages biunity concept. For more precise comprehension of the professional terminology used in the book, we are offering the following terminology for pressing.

Active play area

Part of play area in which the team develop their play activities.

Alternative defensive

Represents the defensive activity focused on getting the ball in which the defending team is ready to attack immediately. It could also be called "defense for attack".

Alternative attack

The solution of the offensive game tasks which, however, allow them to keep the ball but it's not focused on direct threat of the opponent's goal. It represents the form of passive attack "for defense."

Authentic defensive

Defensive activity in which is preferred the type of game tasks solution which doesn't allow the opponent to threaten the goal directly and finalize the attacking sequence by scoring a goal. It minimizes the goal threat of the defending team and involves the lowest level of offensive.

Authentic attack

The solutions of the game tasks which allow direct-line movement of the attacking play sequence to the opponent's goal or penalty area. The game risks resulting from

natural concentration of opponent's resistance towards their own goal are not taken into consideration. It involves the highest level of offensive in the attacking stage of the game activity.

Defensive block

Defensive players' alignment in different formations which lowers the offensive permeability of the defended area and increases the defensive compatibility of the defending team.

Defense

This represents the natural tendency of the player determined by the play genotype to solve the game tasks, to enter the playing sequence and to participate in the game process in such way that the player prevents the opponent from attacking, eliminates the attacking activity and disrupts collaboration of the attacking players. The player participates in the game process using the type of playing activities, defensive game action and defensive collaboration with the players, by which he creates effective play resistance against the attacking team.

Defensive depth

Vertical distance between two players directly participating in the process of a particular defensive action in which one player is positioned directly in the center and the other in the defensive line level.

Defensive width

Distance between two side players on the defensive line or right next to the defensive line directly participating in the defensive action at a particular moment.

Proactive Defense

This is focused on creating defensive pressure on the opponent with the ball, which results in inefficiency of his attacking actions or in the attacking opponent being forced to make a mistake. In a proactive defense the player and the team create through their activity such time and space restrictions for the opponent with ball and the team players, directly participating in attacking action, that the opponent is brought into the state of emergency and by this, the team and players directly influence, restrict, and decrease the quality of the opponent's offensive playing activity.

Defensive reaction

Game behavior in the defense stage of the game in which the course is determined by the opponent with ball and the defending player reacts to the offensive game activity through the defensive actions.

Defensive triangle

Alignment of the defending players in which the player attacking directly is secured by the team players on both sides, creating a triangular formation.

Dynamism of the game center

Fast movement of the game center by quick monitoring of passes.

Soccer

Modern intellectual and strategic-situation ball game based on interactive-confrontational principal.

Game assertiveness

The player's ability to enforce his own play intention in the context of the game by adequate confidence and active adjustment to the game.

Game activity

Movement demonstration, soccer-specific motor skills. It is performed with ball, without ball and in personal combat. Game activities of an individual Basic game individual means which players use when solving game tasks. By using them, players purposefully enter the game context.

Game dominance

Predominant way of players' behavior in the basic game stages.

Game concept

Detailed concept of the game for a specific match. It's based on choice and application of a specific game system supplemented by specific tactical game aims for the specific match, taking into consideration the character of the game performance of the team as well as the opponent's team.

Playing potential of the player

The level of complex ability which the player can use during the match.

Playing performance

The result of the player and the team behavior reflecting game-tactical intentions, complex play ability and level of opponent's resistance.

Playing process

Current process of the confrontation between rival teams restricted by the rules of the game.

Playing reaction

Adjustment of the psychomotor activity of a player by the changeable parameters of the situation or game sequence.

Playing action

Continuous purposeful psychomotor activity of a player during the game. The individual player's activity meaningfully connected to form a continuous play action. By this, the player reacts to impulses from the game and enters into the context of the game.

Playing thinking

Latent intellectual activity of the central nervous system, characterized by purposeful continuation of interlocked specific operations in which the content is focused on the improvement of game action operative management.

Playing-tactical pragmatism

Game-tactical purpose.

Playing configuration

Position, repositioning and reordering of the players during the game, not only in the pitch but also in time.

Play area

Part of the playing surface in which the game center is located which is defined by two horizontal (depth) and two vertical (width) lines and formed by the configurations of both team players.

Play situation

Static order of changeable parameters of the game (players, ball and area) extracted from the dynamics process.

Play sequence

Logical continuation of playing situations in the game connected into a dynamic context (players, ball, area, time).

Player's invention

Player's ability to make the most of its own motor skills, cognitive and psychical potential to solve motional, technical and tactics problems in an unusual and unpredictable way(Marziali-Mora,2003).

Compactness

Alignment of the team players in the central and post-central area which enables them to participate and influence defensive or attacking action currently in process. It's a position alignment which enables direct participation in the action currently in process as well as its direct play influence.

Complex playing ability

Readiness of players to effectively solve tasks during the game. It's determined by the genotype and level of the abilities achieved and the skills of individual players.

Compression

The intended reduction of the depth dimension of the playing area in order to create so called shortened soccer pitch.

Concept of the game

Model of the game that determines the way the game will be played in order to achieve the intention required.

"Leg length" contact

Approach to the attacked player in order to have the possibility of a direct contact with ball.

Ball line

The line intersecting the ball parallel to basic line. Small game reading Prediction of the process of the direct opponent during the game sequence.

Small defensive game reading

Ability of the defending player to predict direct action of the player with a ball.

Small offensive game reading

Ability of the attacking player to predict defensive action of the direct opponent.

Factor of the player's mental activity

The level of player's inherent disposition as well as empiric experience.

Non-specific transfer

Use of the procedures acquired in problematic situations.

Defensive line

Imaginary line connecting defensive players in a way that behind them there is only an empty space and their own goal.

Offensive depth

Vertical distance between the players with a ball. And the furthest team player in the attacking line who is not in offside position.

Offensive compactness

The type of mutual position of the attacking players that allows the highest possible number of players to join the attacking action directly in the best possible way or to outnumber the opponent in the center area.

Offensive empty space

The sector of play area between defending team's defending formation and midfield formation where the attacking player can be temporarily left unattended. The empty space is also created when the defensive chain is broken by deliberate maneuver of the offensive players in the attacking line.

Offensive depth

Distance between two attacking side players, positioned on the attack line or directly near it.

Offensive triangle

Game alignment of three attacking players in which they create some form of a triangle, taking into consideration the offensive depth of their own team as well as the direction of attacking action.

Opening of game space

Movement maneuvers allowing the preparation of the active area for game center positioning. Movement assertiveness Ability of the players to assert themselves in the game by adequate confidence, active and mutually interconnected movement accepting the logic of the game.

Movement maneuvers

Movement schemes allowing the preparation of the active game area and the alignment of the players for specific game-tactical intention. Significant tactical element of space manipulation.

Post-center area

Part of playing area into which the center of the game is consequently moved during the playing sequence. Movement by zone / zone movement Temporary step-out or step-down by a zone representing the player's vertical movement and game schemes. It's focused on changes and transfer of power ratio in individual formations and space zones of the playing space.

Before-final pass

Interlude resulting in a pass, which allows the receiver to finish the playing situation by a final shot or to engage the "last" player into this solution.

Before-center area

Part of the game area from which the ball gets into the play center. Changeable parameters, impulses from the game - players, ball, area, time.

Game transfer

Transfer of the play center in order to place it into an area occupied by fewer defensive players in which the opponent is not able to apply concentrated play resistance of more players.

Pressing line

Defined line in the playing area where the application of pressing begins.

Pressing situation

Specific situation of defensive contraction and narrowing of the playing area, directly near the player with a ball, in conjunction with local outnumbering of defending players. Its formation allows the application of pressing tactics.

Pressing zone part of the playing area in which the application of pressing begins and ends.

Game dominance principle

Acceptance of game security dominances, variability, creativity, and improvisation in relation to current area positioning of the actual game stage.

Compactness principle

Remaining distance of the aligned attacking or defending players that can not only participate actively leading the attacking or defending action, but also to offer direct support and influence the actual offensive or defense of the team.

Offensive triangulation principle

Alignment of the attacking players in a form of a triangle, which is the foundation of any offensive collaboration between the players.

Offensive outnumber principle

creating temporary outnumber of players in order to lead the attacking action by the means of purposeful movement maneuvers of the attacking players or by successful handling of 1:1 situation in crucial areas for attacking sequence leadership.

Attack principles

Generally valid rules for offensive which limit its course and allow achieving the characteristics of the offensive playing action.

Defense principles

Generally valid rules for defense which limit the course of the defensive in a determining way and contribute to the achievement of the defensive game action effectiveness.

Attack width principle

Movement of the player towards the side lines in which they enlarge the horizontal dimension of the real and active playing area during the attack.

Rotation of players' positions

Temporary change of the positions of players in certain direction concerning a closed group of players who can participate in actual playing sequence.

Shortening of playing area

The reduction of the depth (vertical) and width (horizontal) dimension of an active and real playing area.

Hiding the ball

The way of playing (in midfield zone as well as in other parts of playing surface) in which the movement of the play center is executed in the area with a minimum resistance from the opponent players.

"Weak" or "blind" side of playing area

An area which is temporarily cleared by the defending team due to a movement of players in midfield formation or defending formation towards play center. Its definition starts behind the furthest player of the formation moving towards the play center or towards the opponent player with the ball. Regarding the level of the playing resistance applied, the defending team in this area is significantly weakened.

Strategy

The method which is used by the team players in order to achieve their aim.

System of the game

Model of the basic player's alignment.

System configuration

Predominantly symmetrical structure of the basic alignment of players in the area. It's a solid and rigid formation to which the players adjust their range of positional changes (playing configurations) during the game.

Width movement

Chain of players' movement formation towards the playing center in side verticals.

Specific transfer

Use of procedures acquired in typical situations.

Tactics

Coordinated action of one, two or more players in order to achieve a predetermined playing plan.

Game center area

Part of playing area directly near the ball.

Pressure on the ball

Direct physical approach to the player with the ball, which limits his playing performance and results into lowering the playing activity.

Triangulation

Alignment of players in which the players form a triangular net on the playing surface.

Big game reading

Prediction of development logic in a specific playing sequence.

Player's performance

Describes the level of the player potential which is currently being used in a particular match.

Result pragmatism

Submission to the result in all the play-tactical aspects of the match without taking its visual attractiveness into consideration.

Game visualization

Creating visual form of the game which relates to its aspect of viewable quality.

Play area closing

Maneuvers allowing the alignment of the players positions in the area that significantly limits or even disables the positioning of the playing center into this area.

Rhythm change

Purposeful and pragmatic change of speed and the way of leading the attack.

Zone

Part of playing surface defined by horizontal segmentation of playing area.

Attributes of the play situation

Players, ball, space.

Narrowing of play area

Intended reduction of width dimension of playing area play area and creating so called narrow pitch.

ABOUT THE AUTHORS

PhDr. Laco Borbely

He was born on May 14, 1955, Trenčín. He studied psychology at FFUK in Bratislava and soccer coaching at F1VS UK, which is also in Bratislava. During his student times, he played for juniors and reserves in Slovan Bratislava and, after finishing his study, he was wearing soccer shirts of Czechoslovak first league teams Dukla Banska Bystrica, Sparta Praha, and ZTS Kosice.

After finishing his active playing career, he was coaching various first-league and second-league teams in Slovakia and Hungary (Agro Hurbanovo, MFK Nove Zamky, FC Vrable, Ozeta Dukla TrenCfn, Kohucsi Gabcfkovo, Duslo Sal'a, Koba Senec, FC Balaton Siófok, and FC Tatabanya).

For a few years (2005–2010), he was the president of UFTS (Football Coaches Union of Slovakia) and the chairman of technical committee of SFA (Slovak Football Association) in 2011–2014. He completed various internship programs of UEFA Study Group and international conferences of AEFCA and ITK. In the years 2007–11, he worked as a lecturer of EuroPro License of Czech Football Association.

He is a coauthor of different specialized publications focusing on tactics in soccer (defensive modernism in soccer 1998, offensive modernism in soccer 2001, and the whole team attack I and II 2006), and he is a regular contributor to specialized soccer magazines. Since 2002, he has been working for R1VS (Radio and Television of Slovakia) as a copresenter and tactical analyst of the highest category soccer matches (Champions League, European League, World Championship, and European Championship).

He has a degree in psychology, holds UEFA EuroPro License and since 2013 has been a member of ExCo AEFCA (Alliance of European Football Coaches Associations). In December 2015, he was reelected for a president of UFTS for four-year period 2016–2019 and in October 2016, he was reelected as a member of ExCo AEFCA for the next four-year period 2016–2020.

Jaroslav Hrebfk

Jaroslav Hrebfk was born on December 16, 1948, in Benesov u Prahy. He studied at university CVUT Engineering Faculty in Prague. During his study, he played soccer for six years in Viktoai Zizkov. He took part in academic World Championship in France. After his study, he played first-league soccer in Dukla Praha. After his two-year military service, he played for two years in Pizer and then for five years in Vlasim and, after that, four years in Benesov, where he started his coaching career. He is a professional coaching license lecturer, vice-president of Coaches Union, and is a member of editorial board of a magazine *Football and Coaching*. He belongs to the most progressive Czech coaches.

With his team Benesov, he was promoted to the first league. Then he was coaching Pizer\Viktora Zizkov, Hradec Kralove, Slava Praha, Jablonec, 2x Sparta Praha, and

Dynamo Moscow. He has never been relegated with his team to a lower division.

In Champions League, he was leading a team, which defeated Feyendorf 2x, Porto 2x, Spartak Moscow, drew with Bayern and Ajax. In the highest quality Czech match, he was leading Sparta team against Real Madrid. In European Cup, he beat Schalke 0:4 with Slavia. His team was ranked by European experts as the best European team of the month September 2001. For four years, he was leading representation teams U 19 and won with them Jezkuv Memorial, Slovakia cup, and, in 2010, his team got a silver medal in European Championship where they were defeated after extra time by Spanish team 2:3. Apart from Champions League titles and Cups victories, he considered his biggest success the first place among the Czech coaches in Champions League.

Mgr. Peter Ganczner

He was born in Nove Zamky into a family of soccer traditions (father Ladislav was a long-term active player in SK Zilina; later he was a soccer coach). In years 1975–79, he studied at FTVS UK single-subject study of soccer coaching specialization. He played soccer for Elektrosvit Nove Zamky and, during his study, he was a guest player in Slovan CHZJD Bratislava.

His coaching career was started by one-year practice in Vzlet Brno, in years 1990–95, he run his own soccer school, which he established in Nove Zamky. He gained rich futsal experience by working in as an extra-league team coach Tupperware Nove Zamky. The following years, he was working in the area of performance soccer in Slovakia. His publishing activity is connected to magazines *Football Coach* and *Pro Football* where he contributed

regularly. He is a coauthor of publication "The whole team attack or how the attacking is done today, I and II," which was published in 2006.

Mgr. Andi Singer

Andi Singer was born on June 16, 1946, in Roznava. He has lived in Kosice since 1964.

In 1969, he completed his study at Natural Science Faculty in Kosice and, in 1982, Faculty of Physical Education and Sport in Bratislava. He worked as a high school professor and later as a soccer coach. Since 1994 he's been working in Austria as a professional coach. He received his UEFA PRO License in Prague in 2007.

He worked for a long time in Slovakia in VSS club in Kosice (earlier called zts and later 1.FC). He brought up several talented representatives of Czechoslovakia, more precisely Slovakia, and in 1986 the team of youth soccer players won Slovakia and Czechoslovakia Champion title. While working in the club, he also worked as an assistant coach with Slovak U17 representation. Since 1994 until today, he's been working as a professional coach in Austria where he was coaching several clubs with which he achieved a significant success.

His greatest success is the Austrian Champion with Austria Wien U19 in 2004. Seven of his players from Academy Austria Wien became Austria's representatives. This way he significantly contributed to winning bronze medals in European Championships by U17 and U19 teams.

Apart from coaching, he also works in publishing and lecturing in Austria swell as in Slovakia. In year 2006, he was a coauthor of the book "The whole team attack or how the attacking is done today I. and II."

BIBLIOGRAPHY TO PART 1

Cruyff, Johan, Futbol—Mi Filosofia (S.A. EDIQONES B, 2012),176, s.ISBN 9788466652094.

Davies, C. J., ed., "Coaching the Tiki-Taka Style of Play" (2013), 220, Soccer Tutor.com, s.ISBN 9780957670549.

Maldini, Paolo, 11 Calcio (Sperling and Kupfer edition, 1996), 92, s.ISBN 9788820018610.

Michels, Rinus, Teambuilding—the Road to Success (Reedswain Publishing, 2001), 297, s.ISBN 9781890946739.

Michler, Terry, Dutch "Total Football" (TerrLeawood, Wlrid Class Coaching, 2008).182, s.ISBN 9780978893699.

Willson, Jonathan, Inverting the Pyramid: A History of Football Tactics (London: Orion Books, 2008), 374, s.ISBN 9781568587387.

Winner, David, Brilliant Orange, The Neurotic Genius of Dutch Soccer (The Overlook Press, 2008), 288, s.ISBN 9781590200551.

Zauli, Allesandro. Soccer Modern Tactics (Reedswain Publishing, 2002), 125, s.ISBN 2940012895141.

Websites

Barcelona: the Key Elements of Defense

IHolding Midfield, www.holdingmidfield.com/?p=257, Accessed March 29, 2011.

Cruyff: From Ajax, to Barca

IFootball Espana, www.football-espana.neV36293/cruyff-ajax-barca, Accessed September 18, 2013, Mina Rzouki.

200+ Johan Cruyff Quotes

IFour DimensionalFootball, www.4dfoot.com/2014/06/.../200-johan-cruyff-quot, Accessed June 7, 2014.

btalFootball, TotalAttack—Matthew Flax on Hub Pages, darryk.hubpages.com, Football (Soccer), , Accessed March 15, 2014.

li'ibute to a Master: Don Arrigo-AC Milan Forums , www.milanmania.com, Accessed January 5, 2005, www. spielverlagerung/spielanalyze/Retroanalyze, England-Ungarn, 3: 6, 1953, in-depth, von RM am, October 16, 2012.

BIBLIOGRAPHY TO PART 2

Arias, Miguel Alvarez, El Pressing en elfutbol, www.tacticalperiodization4winners.com, Accessed May 30, 2013.

Ames, Nick, Taking the initiative-interview with Andy Roxburgh on how football tactics are changing. The Blizzard Issue 9, 3.March 2015.

Borb Ly, Laco, Defensive Modernism in Current Football: Space Defense-Defensive Chaining-Pressing (Bratislava: Strateg, 1998), 227, p.ISBN 8096791915.

Borb Ly, Laco, Bubenko Jozef, Griga Stanislav, Moravec Milan, Radolsky Dusan. Offensive Modernism in Current Football: I The Practice and Improvement of Attacking Game (Nove Zamky: Litera, 2001), 234, p. ISBN 8096788566.

Borb Ly, Laco, Ganczner Peter, Paldan Robert, Singer Ondrej. The whole team attack or how the attacking is done today.1.volume:General and special attack theory..Trencfn:AZ Print, 2006.247 p.ISBN 8096950681.

Borb LY, Laco, Ganczner Peter, Paldan Robert, Singer Ondrej. The Whole Team Attack or How the Attacking is Done Today. 2 volume: Practical Manual to Offensive Practice (Trencfn: AZ Print, 2006), 134, p.ISBN 809695069X.

Bruckner, Karei. Personal Interview about Pressing (Olomouc), Accessed December 8, 2015.

Ceccomori, Marco, Prestigiacomo Luca, Riva Andrea, Viviani Mauro. Soccer's 4-4-2 System (Reedswain Publishing, 2003), 218 p.ISBN 59164-065-2.

Drago, Anton. Basic Conditional Manual for Football Players.Notebook 2015/3 (Nove Zamky: UFTS, AZ Print, 2015), 62 p.

Eriksson, Sven, Giiran Rallo, Willi Matson Hakan. On Soccer (Carlton Books Limited, 2001), 153, p.ISBN 1-890946-66-4.

Ganczner, Peter, Borb Ly Laco. "Space parameters and the system of the game." In Profutbal (2/1. SFZ and UFTS, October 2004).

Gorg Nyi, Istvan. The Hunting Territory or the Structure of Team life, Sports

Coach, Summer, Autumn editions (Australian Sports Commission, 1998).

Gorg Nyi, Istvan. Interviews about the concept of hunting territory, its application in sport and application for pressing, Pressing and HT Modszer Megkiizelfteseben, Ladislav Borbelynak, November 4, 2015.

Gorg Nyi, Istvan. A Csapatsportok Territorialis Elmelete-kiinyvfejezet, October 17, 2015.

Hartman, Pavel. Top level football has developed into a new dimension (an interview with K.Bruckner). In Football and Training. ISSN 1212-3390,2013, special edition, 56 p.

Hitzfeld, Ottmar. Die Offensivste Form der Verteidigung. Fussball Training 10, no. 10 (1992): 3–8.

Kacani, Ladislav. On didactical technology of play systems in football. Acta Facultatis Educationis Physicae Universitatis Comenianae 37, (1995): 57–66.

Kacani, Ladislav. Football, Theory and the Practice of Play Preparation (Bratislava: SPN, 2002), 143, p.ISBN 8008031646.

Kacani, Ladislav. Football—Theory and the Practice, Play Preparation. 2nd edition (Bratislava: Krakora Design, 2005), 227, p.ISBN 80-969091-3-4.

Lucches, I Massimo. Pressing (Spring City: Reedswain Publishing, 2003), 105, p. ISBN 1-59164-052-0.

Marziali, Floriano, Mora Vincenzo. Spiel im Raum.Online (Verlag Bfp Versand, 1997), 214, p.ISBN 3937049002.

Marziali, Floriano, Mora Vincenzo. The Zone: Advantages, Disadvantages, Counter measures (Spring City: Reedswain Publishing, 2003), 210, p.ISBN 159164058X.

Mazzalli, Simone. Die Raumdeckung im Fussball.Technik-Taktik-Kreativitat (Verlag Bfp Versand, 2001), 222, p.ISBN 3937049193.

Mojzis, Martin. Two Humps of a Camel (Bratislava: W press pic., 2013), 221, p.ISBN 9788097119638.

Pereni, Angelo, Di Cesare Michele. Zone Play (Spring City: Reedswain Publishing, 1998), 266, p.ISBN 890946184.

Ralf, Peter, Pressing im Fussball. Online Buch, 2012.

Ralf, Peter, Barez Arne, Verteidigenmit System (Philippka Sportverlag,

Munster, 2012), 287, p.ISBN 978-3-89417-218-3.

Ruttensteiner, Willy, Von den Besten Lernenl Spiel, Trainings philosophie fur Futball trainer linnen (OFBbsterr. FuBbaii-Bund, 2010), 199, p. ISBN 3200017600.

Schaare, Uwe, Pressing im Unteren und Mittleren Amateuren Bereich

Unmtigllch? In Futbal- training (Philippka Sportverlag, 1993/4), 29–38.

Sun-Tzu, The Art of War (Brno: B4U Publishing ltd., 2008), 200, p.ISBN 978-80-903850-6-1.

Turek, Ivan, Innovation in Tactics (Bratislava: Methodical-Pedagogical Centre, 2004), 358, p. ISBN 80-8052-188-3.

Turek, Steven, Mit Gegen Pressing Zum Dominanten (Spiel: eBookAktueile Taktik Trends Tell 4, Insitut fUr Jugend fussball, 2015),68 p.

Vermeulen, Herman, Zone Soccer: A Game of Time and Space (Spring City: Reedswain Publishing, 2003), 256, p.ISBN 1591640679.

Wein, Horst, Developing Youth Football Players (Leeds: Human Kinetics Europe, 2007), 253, p.ISBN 0-7360-6948-8.

Zeeb, Gerhard, Fussball training (Wiesbaden: Limpert Verlag GmbH,1996), 280, p. ISBN 3785315503.

BIBLIOGRAPHY TO PART 3

Bielsa, M, Treningova jednotka Athletic Bilbao na stadi6ne Sparty Praha. Videozaznam J.Hi'ebfka, October 3, 2012.

Borbely, L. Defenzfvna moderna v sucasnom futbale (Bratislava: Strateg, s.r.o, 1998), 224, s.ISBN 80-967-91915.

Buzek, M, Prochazka L, Modern (obrana.Praha:Sdruzenf MAC, 2003), 110, s.ISBN 80-86783-00-6.

Davies, J, Pressing & Compacting Play (Atletico: Madrid Tactical Analysis and Coaching Sessions), You Tube, March 18, 2014.

Daniel, J, Schott, U, et al. DFB-Talent ftirder programm: Info-Abende fur Verelnstrainer. 712006.s.16 a 20. Philippka-Sportverlag, Postfach150105, 48061

Munster Daniel, J, Schott, U, et al, DFB-Talentftirderprogramm: Info-Abende fur Vereinstrainer.

DFB-INFO-ABEND • MARZ 2007/ s. 5. Philippka-Sportverlag, Postfach, 150105,48061, Munster.

Formanek, J, Prasad' se 1:1 v ki'fdle a nacentruj (1.cast). http://www. trenlnk.com/index.php/herni-trenink/ prupravne-hry/2420-prosad-se-1-1-v-kridle-a nacentruj-1-cast, March 6, 2012.

Formanek, J, Prupravna hra:6:6 plus 2x 1:1 v prostoru pi'ed brankou. http://www.trenink.comlindex.phplherni-treninklprupravne-hry/209-prupravna-hra-6-6- plus-2x-1-1- v-prostoru-pred-brankou, August 11, 2014.

Gradi, D, Defensive Progressions/Crewe Alexandra/.Elite Soccer: The Collectors' Series, Volume 2, str. 66, http:// lagalaxysd.com/docs/coaches/36_practices_ vol_2.pdf, February 27, 2013.

Hasenpflug, M, Turbo-LernfuBball. Eine Innovative Trainingsmethode fur den Jugend fuBball. 2013. ISBN-13:978-3-8423-6369-4.

Havranek, J, Hernf trenink: Zdvojovanf v z6nove obrane (2. cast), http://www.trenlnk.com/index.phplherni-treninklherni-trenink/1923-hernl-trenink-zdvojovani v-zo- nove-obran-2ast, January 18, 2010.

Havranek, J, Vzdelavanr treneru: FC Barcelona:Presink ti'f hnlcu (4.cast). http://www.trenink.com/index.phplvzdelavani-treneru/uvahy-publicistika-205/1750-fc-barcelona-presink-ti-hra-4ast, March 23, 2009.

Hipp, M, Prakticke prostriedky pre nacvik a zdokonaľovanie pressing, 2015.

Hrubesch, H, 10 gegen 10, Schlusstell, 8- und A-Junioren. http://Www.dfb.de/fileadmin!_dfbdam/17627-200_ba_st1_01.pdf, March 3, 2009.

Hrubesch, H, Mlttelfeldpressing I, Schlusstell, 8- undA-Junioren. http://www.dfb.de/fileadminl_dfbdam/17625-200_ba_ha1_01.pdf, March 3, 2009.

Hrubesch, H, Mlttelfeldpressing II, Schiussteil, 8- und A-Junioren. http://www.dfb.de/flleadmln/_dfbdam/17626-200_ba_ha2_01.pdf, March 3, 2009.

Hutchings, CH, Defending against Wingers I Ipswich Town/.Elite Soccer: The Collec-tors' Series, Volume 2, str. 68–69. http://lagalaxysd.com/docs/ coaches/36_practices_vol_2.pdf, February 27, 2013.

Janeschitz, T, UEFA -8 -lizenz Spezieile Trainingslehre

OFB.Bundessportakademle-BSPA bsterrelch, Wien.2011.

Jones, D, Penalty box battles I cardiff City/. Elite Soccer:The Collectors' Series, Volume 1, 56. www.eiltesoccercoaching.net, February 27, 2013.

Knetter, A, Choose Your Concepts Wisely. Success in Soccer, September 2008, s. 28. http://www.slideilsoccer.org/documents/1302204078.pdf.

Metzelder, CH, Trainingselnhelt. http://www.dfb.de/trainer/a-juniorinltraining-online/trainingseinheiten-detail/07102014-463, October 7, 2014.

Nister, D, Der Ort des Ballgewinns bestimmt den Kanter! Fussballtraining, Die Trainerzeit-schrift des Deutschen Fussbaii-Bundes, 33/2015/ Heftnr.10, s. 29.

Peter, R, ModernesVerteidigen.Fussball von Morgen, Band 4 (Philippka-Sportverlag, 2003), 204 s. ISBN 978-3-89417-160-5.

Peter, R, Semlnarreihe-Abwehrenim Raum, http://Www.sportakademle24.de/category/oniine-seminare/ Peter, R, Seminar.Dortmund-Kamen. 2010.

Peter, R, Pressing Kompakt –(Buch, 2012), http://www.sportakademle24.de/fus-sball-online-buch-pressing-kompakt/

Prazak, v, PrUpravna hra:3:3 se sti'fdanrm Utocnycha obrannych cinnostl.

http:/!www. trenink.com/index.php/herni-trenink/prupravne-hry/1883-prpravna-hra-33-se-stidanim-utonych-a-obrannych-innosti, November 03, 2009.

Schromm, C, Taktische Varianten des Abwehrsverhaltens nach Ballveriustsi-tuationen (BDFL-Bund deutscher Fussbaii-Lehrer, ITK, 2012), https://www. youtube.com/ watch?v=RPUOMMZ1b7U

Stober, B, Konsequenzen aus derWM -Analyze. Comeback der 3/5-er Kette. AEFCA-Symposium, PDF, s.12, Zagreb, December 11, 2014.

Terzis, A, FC Barcelona Training- Session. Alex Fitzgerald SoccerTutor.com, 2013.s. 211–217. ISBN 378-0-9576705-9-4

Terzis, A, JurgenKlopp Defending Tactics.SoccerTutor.com, 2015. ISBN 978-1-910491-03-4

Turek, S, Gegenpressing mit Provokationsregeln perfekt trainierenl Aktuelle Taktik Trends.
Tell 4: Mit Gegenpressing zum dominanten Spiel. http://Www.fupa. net!berichte/
gegenpresslng-mit- provokationsregeln-perfelkt-trainieren-369711.

Htrnl, October 21, 2015.

van Gaal, L, Coaching Philosophy and Practices. SoccerTutor.com, 2014. ISBN 978-1-910491-01-0.

Vieth, N, Zusammenspiei-PDF.FuBballtraining, praxisplaner 09/2007, s.18

Vieth, N, Noch nie war Trainingsplanung so elnfach! Ft.fiball training, 5+6/2007, ft-praxis- planer Sande 1 bis 3-
Uberblick, Trainingsformen-Katalog 8- und

A-Junioren, unterer und mittlerer Amateurberelch, s. 52.

Warnock, N, Defensive Team Shape. Elite Soccer: The Collectors' Series, Volume 1, str. 59. www.elitesoccercoaching.
net, February 27, 2013.

Wolbitsch, M. 2013. Vom 1vs1 Bis Zur 4er Kette Gruppen Taktik, Zu Dritt Verteidigen - 4er-Kette.http://www.vfv.at'vf
vresource/626180095537349611_935343781966275772_T4pykp-S.pdf, September .25, 2013.

Websites

www.uefa.com

http://www.sportakademie24.de/fussball-online-buch-pressing-kompakt!

http://www.abwehrkette.de/dreierkette/

www.fussballtraining.com, Online-Beitrag, VfB Stuttgart, Abonenten/online-beitrage/pdfs/, Accessed November 6,
2007.

http://training-service.fussball.de/trainer/a-juniorin/training-online/trainingseinheiten-de
tail/08052012-329/#!/

http://www.fussball-training.org/taktikldefensivtaktik!fussball-dreierkette.html http:// www.fussballtraining.de/
montagseinheit!gruppentaktik-positionsspiel-trainingsuebungen

http://training-service.fussball.de/trainer/a-juniorin/training-online/trainingseinheiten-de
tail/08052012-329/#!/

CREDITS

Design & Layout

Cover and interior design: Annika Naas

Layout: Amnet Services

Photos & Illustrations

Cover photo: © AdobeStock

Part photos: © AdobeStock

Interior photos: © Laco Borbely, Jaroslav Hrebfk, Peter Ganczner, Andi Singer, unless otherwise noted

Illustrations: © sports-graphics.com

Editorial

Managing Editor: Elizabeth Evans

Copyediting: Amnet Services